INSURANCE AND PUBLIC POLICY

INSURANCE AND PUBLIC POLICY

A Study in the Legal Implementation

of Social and Economic

Public Policy, Based on Wisconsin Records

1835–1959

SPENCER L. KIMBALL

1960 • **The University of Wisconsin Press** • *Madison*

Published by
The University of Wisconsin Press
430 Sterling Court, Madison 6, Wisconsin

Copyright © 1960 by the
Regents of the University of Wisconsin

Printed in the United States of America by
Wisconsin Cuneo Press, Milwaukee, Wisconsin

Library of Congress Catalog Card Number 60–5659

PREFACE

This study tells part of the story of American insurance law. The available data is so vast, and so little of it has been examined, that no one could even hope, as yet, to tell it all. The best that can now be done is to deal fully with the development of insurance law in one state, leaving wider generalizations for the future. From some points of view, either Massachusetts or New York might provide the best base for such a study, because those states were often in the lead in insurance developments. But for a first look, Wisconsin seemed a better choice. Wisconsin, less often a leading state, would probably be more nearly typical of American development; its story would be the story of insurance law for the largest part of America.

Nothing in my researches gives me any reason to suppose that the Wisconsin story is greatly different from that of insurance law in the United States generally, at least in the main lines of development. There is, on the contrary, considerable reason to believe that Wisconsin's experience with the evolving insurance enterprise is typical and can throw much light on the complete story of American insurance law.

The research for this study was done under a grant from the Rockefeller Foundation, as one of a number of similar inquiries into "legal history" in Wisconsin. As interpreted in the larger program of which this is a part, legal history is not a narrowly conceived study of the antiquities of technical legal doctrine, but is an investigation into the interplay of law and society—into the legal implementation of social and economic public policy.

As a study of the history of insurance law, this book focuses on the relationships between the evolving technical law and (1) the rapidly growing insurance business that it implements, and (2) the attitudes and purposes of society at large. In its conception and writing I have deliberately avoided the traditional textbook pattern. I have attempted, rather, to interpret, in the light of the needs of the insurance business and the goals of society, the great mass of legal data respecting insurance. I have organized the available data on the framework of a functional analysis of insurance law. In constructing this framework I have tried to work out a meaningful analysis which would contribute insights into the significant relationships between insurance

v

law and the society of which it is but a part. This functional structure owes much to the writing of others who have preceded me in the field, and most obviously to the pioneering studies of Professor Edwin W. Patterson. However, since my analysis is in large measure original, and is not drawn from identifiable sources but rather from a wide range of instrumental and functional writings about law in general, and insurance law in particular, I have made no special effort to identify the lines of thought from which my ideas have both derived and departed, except where I have knowingly borrowed an idea in rather explicit form.

On the framework of this functional analysis, I have sought to give a reasonably complete picture of the law's implementation of social policy in the field of insurance, for a single American state, Wisconsin. Within the confines of this one state, I have tried to exhaust the primary legal sources, with but one exception. Limitations on time and patience, and on my donor's funds, have led to the exclusion of the voluminous files of the Insurance Commissioner's office as a source of information. This would be a substantial project in itself, and probably a worthwhile one, but it must await another occasion. I have included much information about the Commissioners' activities, however, derived from the statutes, the Commissioners' annual reports, the memoranda and other special reports and data that have found their way into the extensive collection of the Wisconsin Legislative Reference Library or other library collections.

This book seeks to interpret all other primary legal source material, so far as it could be found. I have tried to look at all of the statutes having any bearing on insurance law; at all of the insurance bills introduced, but not enacted, in the Wisconsin legislature; at all of the legislative journal references to insurance law, including the Governors' messages; at all of the legislative committee reports; at all of the insurance cases decided either by the Wisconsin Supreme Court or by the federal court system when based on Wisconsin litigation; at all of the Attorney Generals' opinions on insurance questions; and at all of the material on insurance accumulated by the Wisconsin Legislative Reference Library. This material is voluminous. There were nearly 1,500 reported cases, for example, and approximately an equal number of enacted statutes and a comparable number of unenacted bills. The Legislative Reference Library collection has been growing for half a century, and among other things contains an enormous clipping file for the entire twentieth century, from which I was able to derive a great deal of information about the pull and haul of forces in the legislature and elsewhere, which had effect on the development of insurance law. A substantial number of the references to newspaper clippings and much other miscellaneous material may be traced most easily in that library.

As a guide to a major part of these primary materials, I have had not only the indices provided by the books themselves, which are often inadequate, but also I had the good fortune to have access to the private index of Professor Willard Hurst of the University of Wisconsin. This indefatigable researcher has examined, page by page, substantially all of the primary legal sources in Wisconsin, and has indexed them for his own purposes. Fortunately one of the classifications of his index was "insurance," and thus I quickly obtained access to a large number of statutes, bills, journal references, etc., that otherwise would have been almost inaccessible. Though undoubtedly some of this primary source material has escaped me, it must be relatively little. In any case, the mass of source material discovered and examined was very large, posing serious problems of selection and digestion.

In addition to the primary sources on which the study largely rests, I have looked at a large quantity of secondary material in the form of published and unpublished articles, books, memoranda, etc., both on insurance law and economics and on more general aspects of American and Wisconsin history. My researches in this material were not exhaustive, but they were extensive enough to provide innumerable helpful insights for interpretation of the raw data of Wisconsin insurance law. I have made reference to much of this secondary source material in the footnotes, which appear in both editions of this book, and in the notes which appear only in the fully documented edition. No useful purpose would be served by a complete list of the sources examined, except as they have been specifically used in this study. Hence the documentation is intended only to substantiate the statements made in the text; I believe it does that fully.

Grateful acknowledgement is made to the Rockefeller Foundation for their grant, which gave me a completely free year to accumulate the data for this study and to write the first draft. The Foundation, however, is not responsible for any views I have expressed. My thanks also go to Dean Daniel J. Dykstra and the University of Utah College of Law for freeing my time from teaching and other duties at that institution while this research was done and the book written.

Especial thanks are due to Professor Willard Hurst, not only for providing the opportunity to engage in this study of legal history but also for his constant encouragement and help. He read all of the manuscript, much of it at two different stages, and made innumerable helpful suggestions on both its content and style. Equally important to me were his private indices, described above, to the primary legal materials of Wisconsin. Thanks are also due to my wife, Kathryn, for unfailing encouragement and infinite long-suffering and patience, and to Mr. M. G. Toepel, Mrs. Hazel Kuehn, and Miss Kathleen Kepner of the Wisconsin Legislative Reference Library, for their help throughout the preparation of this study.

BIBLIOGRAPHICAL NOTE AND
LIST OF ABBREVIATIONS

This book is published in two editions, which are identical except that one has fuller documentation. In the partially documented edition, references are cited in both the text and footnotes. In the fully documented edition, there is, in addition, a separate section of notes, keyed to the text by numbers. Thus the numbers occurring throughout the text refer to notes that appear only in the fully documented edition. A bibliography including all the material to which there is repeated reference appears in both editions of the book. The following is a list of abbreviations used in the footnotes and text citations. References and the abbreviations for official compilations, annuals, reports, and other documents pertain to the state of Wisconsin unless otherwise specified in the citation.

A	Assembly bill
Archives	Archives Division of the State Historical Society of Wisconsin, Madison
Assembly J.	*Assembly Journal*
Comm'r	Commissioner
FUA	Fire Underwriters' Association of the Northwest
Hist. Soc. Library	Library of the State Historical Society of Wisconsin, Madison
ins.	insurance
Laws	*General Laws*
Laws (P. & L.)	*Private and Local Laws*
LRef. Library	Wisconsin Legislative Reference Library, Madison
Ops. Att'y Gen.	*Opinions of the Attorney General*
Senate J.	*Senate Journal*
S	Senate bill
SS	Special session
Stat.	*U.S. Statutes at Large*
Wis., in case citations	*Wisconsin Reports*
Wis. Blue Book	*Wisconsin Blue Book*

CONTENTS

INSURANCE AND PUBLIC POLICY

Chapter One

INTRODUCTION

Insurance is largely the product of an advanced market society. The important developments, both in the industry and in the legal doctrines that gave it protection and support, occurred in England in the two centuries after the accession of Mansfield to the Lord Chief Justiceship in 1756. It is also true, however, that significant roots of the insurance enterprise are traceable to commercial activities in the European city-states at the beginning of modern times, and that insurance of some kind existed at very remote periods. In the form of the marine contracts of bottomry and respondentia, commercial insurance of a sort seems to have existed earlier than the third millenium before Christ. Mutual benefit or fraternal life insurance appears to have existed among both the Greeks and the Romans, and it is possible that the Romans had a kind of commercial life insurance.* It is significant that the early manifestations of the urge to insure appeared in the commercial societies of the ancient world. Insurance is the characteristic response of a market civilization to the universal human search for security. It finally came to full flower only in the complex industrial society of the twentieth century.

Throughout the history of man there has been an awareness of an aleatory element acting unpredictably to bring him good luck or, much more often, to inflict bad luck upon him. Many social and economic institutions have resulted from human efforts to replace that aleatory element with some degree of certainty. William Graham Sumner even placed the origin and meaning of religion in the striving of man for security against these unpredictable turns of fate. Man propitiated the gods by sacrifice or worship to avert evil and attain good. Sumner regarded religion as but a form of "insurance," which he described as

. . . a generic conception covering the methods of attaining security, of which the modern devices are but specific, highly elaborated, and scientifically tested examples. . . .

Insurance is a grand device and is now a highly technical process; but its roots go farther back than one would think, offhand. Man on earth, having always had an eye to the avoidance of ill luck, has tried in all ages somehow

*Trenerry, *passim.*

3

to insure himself—to take out a "policy" of some sort on which he has paid regular premiums in some form of self-denial or sacrifice.*

Even though insurance might be looked on as a response to fundamental psychological urges of the human being, there are several reasons why it only came into its own in recent times. Successful operation of insurance as a large scale commercial enterprise depended to some extent on a level of technical knowledge and experience which did not exist until recently. Incidence of loss, for example, had to be predictable; this depended on the availability of statistical information about losses, and some understanding of the laws of probability. Again, with noteworthy exceptions such as Lloyds of London, successful and widespread operation depended on an organizational structure of considerable permanence, i.e., on the development of the modern corporation. More important, insurance involved, in its modern commercial form, the handling of large amounts of money, and could operate only with difficulty in a society poor in fluid capital. Perhaps most decisive of all, the role of insurance has traditionally been played by other agencies. In various cultures, kinship obligations or age-grade loyalties or secret society affiliations also provided mutual aid, which served to insure the individual against many of the vicissitudes and uncertainties of life. In feudal society, the intricate web of interpersonal relations gave some of the same assurance to lord and vassal alike. The social revolution that accompanied the rise of capitalism, and especially the urbanization of modern life have either destroyed or reduced the effectiveness of many established devices for "insurance" of the individual. For a long time, the drastic dislocations of human life incident to the change in the social order prevented achievement of such security, but at length the basic demand produced an elaborate and costly system of commercial insurance. The size of the industry was some measure of the magnitude of the needs, both economic and psychological, to which it ministered. It is striking that an enterprise which produced nothing tangible and supplied mainly a sense of security should achieve such gigantic proportions. In the 1950's life insurance companies in the United States owned about a hundred billion dollars of assets, and other insurance companies owned lesser but substantial amounts. Premium income of life companies for 1955 was sixteen and a half billion dollars, and fire and casualty premium income was comparable. These amounts were ap-

*Sumner & Keller, 2:737–70; Id., p. 749.

preciable shares of the national wealth and the national income. In Wisconsin alone, half a billion dollars a year went for insurance premiums in mid-twentieth century. In the 1950's nearly every responsible citizen insured his house against fire, had a substantial life insurance program to protect his family against his premature death and to provide for his own retirement, had some kind of health insurance, and had liability insurance on his car. That insurance had become compulsory in such fields as workmens' compensation and all but compulsory for automobiles indicated how much a part of the prevailing ethic it had become.[1]*

For the purposes of this book, insurance may be defined as any formally organized scheme for the distribution of an adventitious economic loss over a large number of persons subject to the risk of such loss, with a view to replacing the uncertain risk of loss by a predictable cost. The loss is distributed by transferring the risk to an insurer, who may be an independent entrepreneur or may be simply the group of persons insured, operating through some corporate or agency device. The loss may be distributed in advance by charging a premium, or after the event by assessment, or by a combination of the two. For the enterprise to be commercially successful, the incidence of the loss should be reasonably predictable for some class of persons from which the participants will be drawn, and therefore for any sufficiently large number of such participants taken at random. Much difficulty in the early development of fire insurance grew out of the inadequate predictability of the incidence of loss because of the catastrophic burning of large cities. No more precise definition of insurance would be useful for this book, for it is an historical critique dealing with a large number of related phenomena, and any more restrictive delimitation of the insurance enterprise might so circumscribe the study as to preclude some useful observations.

Although this is an historical treatment of the relations between public policy and the insurance business, the structure is logical rather than chronological, but logical as considered from the vantage point of the business rather than from that of the conceptual framework of the law. The writer has adopted a point of view which regards the law as instrumental in character. It sees the law as a system that takes

*This book is published in two editions, which are identical except that one is more fully documented and includes a section of notes. The note numbers occurring throughout the text refer to notes which appear only in the fully documented edition.

its initial premises from the life of society outside the law and it ultimately justifies legal decision in terms of the social goals and moral standards. In short, this study is a "functional" analysis of insurance law, and its principal focus is the actual functioning of the insurance enterprise as an aspect of the life of society. Technical legal concepts are relegated to the level of mere instruments by which the law implements the social goals. The major divisions of the book treat the various ways in which the public policy of our society, as determined by courts, legislatures, and other legal agencies, impinged upon the insurance enterprise.

In the following outline, the second, third, and fourth topics have a close relationship to one another, for they all deal with the law's concern for the internal operation of the insurance business. On the other hand, the first topic, dealing with validation of the insurance enterprise, and the fifth, dealing with the impact of insurance on society at large, treat of broader aspects of the relationship between public policy and the insurance business.

First, there was a basic problem of the validation of the enterprise. It was not beyond question that insurance should be a legally valid activity, in all the broad sweep of its possible ramifications or, indeed, in any part of it. Pious judgments about interference with divinely ordained events, pragmatic judgments about the tendency of insurance to harm society by encouraging policyholders to cause the loss insured against, moral judgments about the effect on character of the elimination of risk, political judgments about the collateral effects of the insurance industry upon the larger society, all might conceivably operate to invalidate all insurance contracts. In fact, they merely limited the sphere of legitimate operation of the insurance business in minor ways.

Second, the insurance enterprise depended upon the creation of an adequate insurance fund to pay the losses incurred. The policy of the law impinged upon the insurance enterprise in determining the kinds of organizations that might be created to act as insurers, the legitimacy of their corporate practices, the way in which capital was mobilized, the way in which rates were made, and the way in which funds were collected. Sales methods also came within the scope of the law's legitimate concern with the creation of an adequate insurance fund.

Third, the integrity of the fund had to be protected against dissipation by the persons charged with managing it. This required detailed regulation of investments, and control of many other internal business practices.

Fourth, the public policy embodied in law was concerned with the determination of the persons entitled to share in the insurance fund. The law sought a rational adjustment of two important public policies —the preservation of the integrity of the insurance fund against improper raids by persons not entitled to participate and the satisfaction of the reasonable expectations of the insured. The latter policy was threatened by the attempt of the companies to use unwarranted protective devices to preserve the fund. Adjustment of these conflicting policies required a procedure and a doctrinal structure for the administration of claims.

Finally, the insurance enterprise as it matured, by virtue of its size and strategic position, had great impact upon the larger society of which it was a part. It became a major mobilizer of capital, which might be used to broaden the tax base and for economic expansion. In the twentieth century its effect on economic expansion became significant and called for a re-examination of established doctrines about proper controls over insurance investments. Indeed, after the late nineteenth century the vastness of insurance assets created political balance-of-power problems, arising from the danger of economic domination and of improper influence upon legislatures and other legal agencies. Throughout its history in America, insurance was involved in the conflict between localism and the economic forces tending to erase state lines. Again, as it developed, not only did insurance become industrial society's chief device for distributing risk but more and more the enterprise took on the task of eliminating the risk, through education and inspection and through the setting of legally enforceable standards. Moreover, the need for insurance became so great in twentieth-century society that insurance tended to become a kind of public utility. Not only was it subject to extensive regulation but there was a developing public attitude that insurance companies might properly be required to supply their services to all who sought them. In the twentieth century, the insurance principle became a dominant theme of American law, leading to significant impact even upon traditional branches of the law. So much did the insurance idea become one of the organizing principles of industrial society that the mid-twentieth century might very aptly be called the "Age of Insurance."

Chapter Two

VALIDATION OF THE INSURANCE ENTERPRISE

The most fundamental decision law had to make regarding the insurance business was to delimit its legality. In theory the law might refuse validation to any part, or to major parts, of the insurance enterprise. The breadth of the accepted limits of validity was cogent testimony to the importance of the social needs satisfied by insurance.

In this chapter, we shall examine the extent to which the law gave approval to insurance. The problem of validation had two diverse aspects. On the one hand, there was a positive validation of the enterprise as it grew—a legal declaration of approval. Grants of corporate charters were, in effect, licenses to do business; general resort to the corporate form inherently required the law's positive approval. Moreover, as the business grew the legal agencies of society modified existing legal dogma to facilitate the conduct of the enterprise. This also represented positive validation—explicit approval of the expansion of the enterprise even against opposing legal rules. On the other hand, there were some restrictions upon the scope of legitimate operation; some legal rules did serve to restrict the area within which the insurance business might lawfully operate.

POSITIVE VALIDATION

In the early nineteenth century insurance received general acceptance. So favorable were the connotations of the word "insurance" that the term even found its way into advertising copy for patent medicines. The readiness with which Wisconsin legislatures from 1838 to 1871 granted special charters to insurance companies testified strongly to the acceptability of the business. The most striking illustration, however, was the organization of the Wisconsin Marine and Fire Insurance Company in 1839. In the panic of 1837, previously-chartered Wisconsin banks had failed disastrously, and it was politically impossible to organize a bank in the state, which was in the control of hard money Jacksonian Democrats. Canny Scotch financiers nevertheless saw real opportunity for a banking enterprise and were able to obtain a charter from the legislature by veiling the undertaking, rather thinly, as an insurance company.* The strategy and its success point up the basic acceptability of insurance in this frontier community as compared with the hatred felt for banks. Similar incidents in other places reinforce the point. Not until the Granger agitation in the 1870's did popular feeling link insurance companies with railroads and banks as part of an evil conspiracy for the exploitation of the western farmer. Even then insurance companies escaped the worst of the obloquy directed at the railroads. Although insurance never lost its aura of respectability, it is interesting to note that an early twentieth-century life insurance company used the word "bankers" in its title, which suggests that by then banking had achieved such status that its respectability could advantageously be appropriated by an insurance company.[1]

Approval of Lines of Business

The institution of insurance brought by the settlers pouring into Wisconsin in the middle decades of the nineteenth century was as yet in its formative period. Despite some ancient roots in the Old World it was not yet a basic financial institution of American society, even on the settled and commercially advanced seaboard.

Among the few lines of insurance then extant, marine insurance was the oldest, the best known, and the one most completely integrated into the commercial life of the time. During the two decades after 1840, when Wisconsin was being settled, the Yankee clippers dominated the seas, and both the American merchant marine and American marine insurance enjoyed a prominence never repeated since. In these years, the notion that insurance was an essential element of maritime commerce was quickly extended also to include inland waterway shipping. In Wisconsin, though some conservative eastern companies were reluctant to operate in this field before the Civil War, other eastern companies made such insurance available in Milwaukee in the late 1830's, and the agents of transportation companies on the lakes advertised that their operations were fully insured. In the 1850's and 1860's the charters of many Wisconsin transportation companies also authorized them to issue marine insurance.[2]

During this period, too, the insurance institution was extended from marine risks to include land transportation. In Wisconsin, for

---

*The fascinating story of the bank is told in Andersen, pp. 7–13; Butler; Krueger, pp. 41–51; Kuehnl, pp. 129–37.

example, an 1857 charter expressly authorized insurance on railroad transportation, and the 1866 charter that permitted organization of the American Overland Transportation Insurance Company (with an authorized minimum capital of $1,000,000) empowered the company to insure wagon trains bound for the far west. This ambitious projection had among its incorporators Alexander Mitchell, S. F. B. Morse, Horatio Seymour, and George Bancroft.[3]

Historically, fire insurance was of later origin than marine. It received its initial impetus from the great London fire of 1666. Before 1800 its development was somewhat spasmodic and exploratory, but in the middle decades of the nineteenth century, when Wisconsin was in its first growth, fire insurance was rapidly becoming an accepted and nearly universal concomitant of the ownership of property.[4]

Life insurance in the modern sense was new when Wisconsin was settled. The earliest life insurance society based on modern actuarial principles was established in London in 1762, and in America life insurance was still in its experimental stages in the second quarter of the nineteenth century. Rapid expansion began only with the organization of the Mutual Life of New York in 1843 and the development of an aggressive selling organization. In the 1840's, when the first serious efforts were made to popularize life insurance on the east coast, much of the sales effort was directed to refuting religious objections. Elaborate arguments were constructed to show that the purchase of life insurance did not "tempt Providence" (Stalson, ch. 6, esp. at pp. 103–4). Public acceptance of life insurance had proceeded far enough, however, that there are no discernible traces of such religious scruples in the explicit public policy of Wisconsin. Indeed, three of the eight territorial charters of Wisconsin companies authorized a life insurance business, though the life insurance issued under these charters was very limited. From a modest beginning, life insurance in Wisconsin grew rapidly. When statistical reports first were made to the Secretary of State about 1860, total life insurance premiums were only a tenth of fire and marine premiums. A decade later they had become two-thirds as large.[5]

Mutual benefit societies providing a form of assessment life insurance were of ancient origin. In Wisconsin there were such societies from the time of its early settlement, but rapid development began in the 1860's. The law never doubted the validity of mutual benefit societies, and even encouraged them by tax exemption and freedom from restrictive regulation.[6]*

Other lines of insurance hardly existed in 1840, but in the succeeding years, special charters in Wisconsin and elsewhere made numerous experimental ventures into new lines and extensions of old ones. Health insurance may be found as early as 1853, guaranty and storm by 1853, accident and lightning as early as 1865, livestock in 1866, fidelity in 1869. Livestock insurance was seriously offered for a year or so in the late 1860's by out-of-state companies, and steam boiler insurance and railroad passenger insurance were also tried.[7]

After 1871 new lines were introduced into Wisconsin by general acts authorizing incorporation rather than by special charters. The legislature authorized hail insurance companies in 1876, admitted out-of-state surety companies in 1885, permitted incorporation of title insurance companies in 1887, permitted insurance of property against hazards other than fire and lightning from 1891. It authorized mutual plate glass companies in 1905, after an unsuccessful attempt in 1895. In 1897 it authorized casualty insurance, including insurance of bicycles; this was the transitional decade when bicycles became for a short time the standard means of transportation of urban America. In 1899 the legislature authorized mutual companies to insure bankers, loan companies, and county treasurers against burglary, robbery, or the loss of money or securities in the mail.[8]

The insurance idea was extended rapidly from the very few lines authorized at the beginning of Wisconsin development to the new forms demanded by an evolving market society. There was some feeling that there must be explicit legal validation of new lines; thus the Attorney General ruled in 1896 that credit insurance and insurance against loss of money by theft were unauthorized since there was no validating statute. However, the legislature showed little reluctance to give legal validation, and the limited availability of new lines in the market reflected economic experience rather than legal limitation.[9]

The legislature in 1909 systematized the designation of legitimate lines of insurance, authorizing insurance corporations to be formed for fifteen purposes: insurance against fire (including lightning, hail,

*See, e.g., Trenerry, pp. 171–219, and "Friendly Societies," 9 *Encyc. Brit.*, pp. 843, 844 (1956). See Handlin (1951), ch. 7, for their role in the adjustment of immigrants to American life.

tempest, and explosion), marine, life, disability, liability for personal injury, steam boiler (including both insurance of the policyholder's own property and against his liability to others), fidelity, title, credit, burglary or theft, plate glass, sprinkler leakage, elevator, livestock, and other casualty (injury to insured's property). The final catchall classification facilitated the free expansion of the insurance concept to meet new market and personal needs. The legislature was also quick to give explicit recognition to new developments. In 1911 it redefined credit insurance to include deposit insurance and liability to include property damage and authorized companies to issue combination fire, liability, collision, and theft policies on automobiles. It created workmen's compensation liability and authorized insurance against such liability. In 1917 the legislature authorized fire companies to issue extended coverage insurance, automobile collision, property damage, burglary and theft, and liability for personal injury. In 1919 it expanded and made more explicit the content of the suretyship business, which had been included in 1909 under the heading of fidelity insurance. In 1921 consequential loss, including loss of rents, leasehold interests, profits or commissions, and business interruption loss, was brought within the legitimate scope of the fire insurance contract. In 1947 the legislature permitted the endorsement of a fire policy covering sprinklered mercantile risks or governmental, manufacturing, or institutional risks, to insure the difference between the actual value of the property and the amount actually expended to rebuild it with like material. The value of such insurance to policyholders was especially evident in days of inflation and uncertain building costs. In 1956 the Attorney General ruled that the business of insuring mortgage lenders against nonpayment by the borrower was valid, though curiously, he classified it as "title" rather than as "credit" insurance. The 1957 legislature, at the request of a Milwaukee company, which was one of the pioneers in the field in America, broadened the definition of "credit" insurance to cover insurance of mortgages, in order to facilitate the company's entry into other states. Despite the disaster of the 1930's, private insurers were thus edging into this field, left for a quarter century to the federal government. The opening resulted from the tight money market, which made many people willing to pay higher interest than was allowed by the rules of the Federal Housing Administration or the Veterans Administration.[10]

These extensions of the valid area of the insurance enterprise were virtually automatic responses of the legislature to the growth of society and the invention of new forms of insurance coverage. The legislative record shows almost no unsuccessful bills—mute testimonial to the readiness of the legislature to validate the new coverages as an accomodation to the companies and the public. When the 1931 legislature passed a bill to specify permissible coverages for fire insurance companies and by implication forbid others, the bill did not represent a basic policy of restriction of the authorized scope of the business, for it gave the Commissioner discretion to permit coverage of other risks. Moreover, the Governor vetoed the bill, because he thought that all insurance should be valid unless specifically prohibited.[11]

The Rise of Suretyship.—The increasing complexity of government and business in late nineteenth-century America multiplied the situations in which fiduciaries and officials, whether dealing with money or not, were required to supply surety bonds to guarantee performance of their duties. The business of compensated corporate suretyship began to develop because the individual surety was inadequate to the new demands.

In 1885 the Wisconsin legislature authorized out-of-state surety companies to do business in the state, thus making corporate suretyship available to private contracting parties, at their option. A companion act authorized corporate bonds to be received where bonds were required by law. In 1895 the legislature said that fiduciaries required to give a bond might claim credit in their accounts for a premium paid to a corporate surety. Subsequent statutes continued the process of making corporate, rather than individual, suretyship the normal form. This sometimes involved authorization to public agencies to pay the premium, as when the legislature authorized the state to pay up to a quarter of one per cent of the amount of the Insurance Commissioner's required $100,000 bond.[12]

Validation of Group Life Insurance.—There was one significant exception to the virtually automatic response of the Wisconsin legislature to demands for new forms of insurance. Concern about sound underwriting of group life insurance led the legislature to validate it with considerable reservation and many limitations. Initially it appeared to require no validation, for it *was* life insurance. Group life insurance was developed about 1912 and for many years was sold in the state without special statutory authorization (Witte, Part I), although the Commissioner assumed some control over its scope. Limiting it according to a definition of group insurance formulated by the National Association of Insurance Commissioners in 1917, he permitted only issuance of policies covering the employees of a single employer.[13]

In the 1920's the Wisconsin Insurance Commissioners were hostile to group life insurance; they regarded it as illicit cut-rate insurance which resulted in price discrimination against holders of ordinary policies. It was wholesale insurance run riot—a form of insolent competition with which no honest company could compete, which would according to Commissioner Johnson (1926c) "steer the business of life insurance into the whirlpool of scandal and disrepute." The hostility of administrators to group insurance made express statutory validation imperative.[14]

The issue came to a head in Wisconsin in the late 1920's, focused on the validity of group insurance issued to labor unions. In 1925 the American Federation of Labor, critical of extravagance of existing companies and their refusal to issue group policies through labor unions, sponsored the Union Labor Life Insurance Company. In 1927 that company asked the Wisconsin Commissioner to permit group life to be issued to labor unions, arguing that group insurance issued to single employers was a paternalistic device which tied the worker to his job, decreased the mobility of labor, and reduced the ability of the worker to cope with the power of aggregated capital.* Unions desired their own insurance in order to break the ties that bound the worker to the individual employer.[15]

In 1928 the chief of the Wisconsin Legislative Reference Library found by inquiry that while many states adhered strictly to the 1917 definition, many permitted sale of insurance to unions, usually by acquiescence rather than by legislation or affirmative ruling of the Commissioner. The arguments in favor of extension of group life to include unions were, he said, (1) that it would enable unions

---

* "It is a scheme to hold him in the plant," said a painter in an animated debate in Milwaukee's Federated Trades Council.—Milwaukee *Leader* (Wis.), Oct. 6, 1957.

to counter the use of group insurance as an antiunion device, and (2) that present union benefit funds were not sound. The arguments against it were (1) that it would lead to indiscriminate extension of group life to other organizations, and (2) that it would nullify antidiscrimination laws.[16]

In 1929 the Wisconsin legislature expressly validated group life insurance for employees of a single employer and for members of labor unions. The enactment was a verbatim copy of a part of the New York definition of group life insurance, though the New York legislature had already gone much further. Once labor union group life insurance was validated, there was little resistance to further expansion in the scope of group insurance. In 1931, at the insistence of teachers' organizations, the legislature added associations of public employees; in 1937 it approved such insurance for members of, and borrowers from, credit unions and borrowers from financial institutions; and in 1939 it added members of coöperatives. In 1939 the legislature also authorized group accident and health insurance and family expense accident and health insurance; in 1943 it permitted labor union group accident and health insurance, and in 1945 authorized "franchise" group accident and health policies—for groups of three or more employees or members of groups formed for other purposes than to obtain insurance. Virtually the only remaining step for expansion of group accident and health coverage was to authorize it for groups formed specially for insurance purposes. This was proposed in 1949, with a safeguard requirement of the Commissioner's approval, but the bill failed.[17]

In 1949 the legislature reorganized the validating statute for group life and added groups formed by combinations of two or more employers in the same industry, or by one or more labor unions, or by one or more employers and one or more labor unions. In 1951 an unsuccessful bill introduced at the request of the First National Savings Foundation would have extended group life to a group of "savers" on the instalment basis.[18]

Thus by 1955 the definition of group life was very broad; combinations of employers not in the same industry represented one of the few possible extensions. This had been proposed in 1945 and 1949; in the former year a bill authorizing group life insurance on employees of employer members of an association formed for other purposes passed the legislature, only to be vetoed by Governor Goodland because it was untried and had not yet received the recommendation of the National Association of Insurance Commissioners. In 1955 the proposal was made again.[19]

The Milwaukee representative of the Travelers Insurance Company was the sponsor. He argued that group life, which was a vital "fringe benefit" in the existing labor market, should be made freely available to more firms, and particularly to small ones. Various small business men and their trade associations also supported the bill. In opposition were the Wisconsin and national insurance industry organizations, the organized insurance workers, the Insurance Commissioner, and the Wisconsin Farm Bureau Federation. They argued that group insurance could already be obtained under the existing definition by anyone who really wanted it. The Commissioner urged that it was actuarially unsound to combine the experience of different industries, that good companies would drop out, that rates would go up, and that the enterprise would collapse.[20] The Milwaukee *Journal* (June 2, 1955), in a story on the legislative hearing for the bill, reported that local companies and local agents were urging the danger of monopoly —that all the members of the Wisconsin Manufacturers' Association could drop out of their small group policies and combine in one big policy with a single company. It would be possible under the bill for "the universe to be written up in one group policy." Further, a spokesman for the International Union of Life Insurance Agents warned that "The WMA [Wisconsin Manufacturers' Association] wants to swallow all these associations and one insurance agency wants to swallow all the agents who write group insurance." The same story reported a Beloit agent's allegation that the "octopus is trying to put me out of business." The bill passed easily in the Senate, but was overwhelmingly defeated in the Assembly, thus preventing the ultimate broadening of the legitimate scope of group insurance. Still the Attorney General had to rule in 1958 that a policy on key personnel of firms which were members of an association of employers was not legal. He also held invalid in Wisconsin a nation-wide group policy on members of the American Legion.[21]

Social Insurance

The willing extension of the insurance enterprise to novel fields reflected society's basic acceptance of the insurance principle of distributed risk. In this extension the role of the law was passive—it merely acquiesced in the search of economic man for new forms of insurance to satisfy his personal and market needs. About the turn of the century, in America the law began to play a significant active role in using the insurance enterprise to achieve new social goals. This, in turn, reflected the increased concern of public policy with the incidence of social costs attendant on private economic activity (Kapp, p. 14).

The eighteenth-century classical economists described a supposed natural order in economic life, in which processes uncontrolled by government tended toward an equilibrium that would maximize satisfactions. The mechanism of the market would assure that all were paid what their contributions were worth in economic terms.* These self-contained systems of theory ignored the marked extent to which the entrepreneur was able to transfer to other individuals or groups significant elements of cost (Kapp, pp. 2–12). The social costs of polluted atmosphere and streams, denuded forests and eroded fields, and the human suffering consequent on industrial accidents, unemployment, and technological change were ignored in the pricing of commodities and, therefore, in economic theory. The assumed maximization of satisfactions was therefore a distortion of reality. The difference between "marginal social net product" and "marginal private net product" was the basis of much criticism of the economic system, especially by Socialists. Some neoclassical economists, notably Pigou (Pigou, pp. 151–81), gave more attention to social costs. In mid-twentieth century there were attempts to reconstruct economic theory to bring social costs into a central position. The law anticipated this economic analysis by shifting to the producer, and through the pricing mechanism to the ultimate consumer, some of the costs that the producer had formerly cast on the general public or on selected individuals through the unrestricted operations of the free market economy. But usually law operated only where the balance of political power shifted from those responsible for the transfer of the costs to those who had previously borne them. No articulated theory heralded this development; the law merely reflected the underlying forces operating in society, and theory followed in the wake of the reality of changed institutions. Insurance provided a mechanism for bringing social costs,

*"The Classicists often confused the entrepreneur with society, shifting their point of view from one to the other; for there was no clear appreciation of the distinction between the idea of ultimate social costs and the expenditures of the business undertaker," Haney, p. 912.

especially those of adventitious incidence, into the private cost accounting of entrepreneurs.*

Not only did the advancing technology create new costs but the rise of the market economy destroyed prior mechanisms for solving problems incident to human existence in any economy. In feudal society a tightly structured social system sheltered the individual from the worst effects of life's uncertainty. The coming of the market economy destroyed feudal status relations and substituted the cash nexus as the principal bond between man and man. The individual, still subjected to the force of events beyond his control, was left alone; he and his family were dependent in case of sickness, accident, premature death, or old age on the casual assistance of persons under no personal obligation to him. By the early twentieth century, however, men had organized new relationships to supply the security needs which the average individual could not supply for himself. Characteristically the security needs of twentieth-century society were met by application of the insurance principle; some risks were universal risks, and they were met by spreading the risk broadly through society.

In Wisconsin the Progressivism of Robert M. LaFollette triumphed within the Republican party and achieved control of the state at the turn of the century. As a political movement, it emphasized the control of large corporate enterprise in the public interest. The main interest of LaFollette was in the regulation of railroad rates. The long continuance of his faction as a major political force within Wisconsin Republican party ranks and at the polls enabled the state to play a part in the formulation of the new social security structure of the twentieth century. From an early date there was a broadly based and persistent effort in the state to extend the newly created social obligations to new fields.

Old Age Insurance.—The free market supplied no universal way to provide security against an impoverished old age. In ways anathema to classical economists, concerted action, through labor organizations or the political organs of society, led to treatment of the economic burdens of old age as an element of social cost and a proper charge upon the whole society. In Wisconsin as early as 1889 there was an unsuccessful proposal to create a rather generous pension for public school teachers, and in 1891 pension funds began to make headway.

*See Kapp, pp. 26–46, for a summary of earlier discussions of social costs. See also Galbraith.

Fire and police department pensions came first, and pensions for teachers soon followed. Unsuccessful efforts were made to end teachers' pensions in 1913 and 1915, but the principle was too well established. By mid-century the principle of adequate pension and annuity provisions for all public workers was fixed beyond possibility of serious controversy.[22] The only remaining concern was over amounts and the actuarial soundness of the pension funds. The latter question occupied the legislature in the 1940's. Numerous special investigations were capped by the creation in 1947 of a survey committee on retirement systems, which made many inquiries into retirement problems and kept the legislature informed.[23]

The broader problem of providing for the old age of all citizens received early attention as well. In 1905 a proposed constitutional amendment would have inaugurated a comprehensive system of old age pensions under state auspices for "superannuated laborers, workmen, teachers and public officials." Another 1905 proposal recognized the difficulties of an adequate system of old age pensions at the state level and proposed to memorialize Congress to act.[24] Though these proposals received short shrift in the Assembly, in an eloquent minority report of the Assembly Committee on Manufactures, Milwaukee's Brockhausen protested that commercial insurance was inadequate to meet the old age problems of working class people. The minority report clearly foreshadowed development of a sentiment for obtaining social security by action of the federal government. Though Brockhausen's main emphasis was on humanitarian considerations, his unsophisticated and impressionistic argument yet forecast a later generation's stress on consumer-focused economics. Like an untutored Keynes, he argued that ". . . when this indifferent lawmaker advises frugality he utterly fails to observe that commercialism by which he thrives would suffer if we all started on a diet of crackers and cheese. In such an event, it would be but a matter of a week when the whole commercial class of parasites would seriously begin to look for a souphouse themselves."* This argument, based on the functional importance of a mass market, seems to express less a Marxist forecast of the inherent contradictions of capitalism, than a social engineer's concern to make the market economy work. However, Brockhausen

---

*Assembly J., 1905, pp. 1075–77. Cf. Keynes, p. 373: ". . . measures for the redistribution of incomes in a way likely to raise the propensity to consume may prove positively favorable to the growth of capital."

indicated that he spoke for a powerless minority; the majority, he accused, did not bother to hear arguments against his proposal, but automatically voted it down.

Insurance Against Industrial Accidents.—The recognition in America of the social cost of industrial accidents led to the workmen's compensation law, with a twofold application of the insurance principle. The law transferred the risk of industrial accidents from the single worker to the employer and thence through the pricing mechanism to the entire body of consumers. Moreover, employers must, by insurance, secure the payment of their obligations against the possibility of a high incidence of accidents in a single plant. Only an employer whose business itself provided a wide distribution of the risk might become a self-insurer.

Wisconsin was one of the pioneers in this development. In the 1909 legislature an elaborate bill proposed a system of workmen's compensation; another bill and a joint resolution proposed investigation of the subject for report to the 1911 session. In 1911 a workmen's compensation law was enacted. Initially the legislation permitted, but did not require, the employer to insure against the new range of liability, but the 1913 legislature made insurance compulsory. Once enacted, the compensation system so quickly won popular acceptance that there was never any real threat to its continuance.[25]

Two subordinate features of the Wisconsin compensation law illustrate the use of the insurance enterprise to solve social needs. In 1932 the legislature created a state fund to provide additional death benefits where there were dependent children in addition to the primary beneficiary. The other feature of the compensation law solved a problem created by the system itself. The greater compensation burden on employers and insurance carriers in the event of a second injury handicapped disabled workers in getting jobs. To offset this, a state fund paid to disabled workers injured in subsequent accidents the additional compensation otherwise payable by the employer's insurer. In theory this made disabled workers fully employable for any jobs within their capacities.[26]

Health Insurance.—In Wisconsin the problem of sickness received early and persistent attention. One 1913 bill proposed insurance against occupational disease and industrial sickness as an adjunct to workmen's compensation; another proposed a broad system of sickness insurance for everyone. The legislature passed neither, but did pass a bill and a joint resolution providing for an investigation of "insurance against accident, sickness and invalidity, and the prevention of pauperism and dependency." The Governor vetoed the bill with its appropriation for reasons of economy; but he showed no adamant opposition to the principle of broad social insurance.[27]

The new attitude favoring social insurance was not strictly limited to the more "liberal" political groups. In 1917 (*Senate J.*, p. 28) Stalwart Republican Governor Philipp recognized "the obligation of society as a whole to those unfortunate members of the community who suffer from sickness, accident, unemployment or old age."* He recommended a legislative investigation, which the legislature provided. An elaborate health insurance bill was introduced in the Assembly by a Socialist and in the Senate by a Republican. Similar acts were introduced in 1919 and 1921, both times by Socialists.[28]

The terms of reference of the 1917 committee were broad, but the committee at once limited its inquiry to health insurance. The committee claimed it found no substantial demand for the proposed legislation, nor did it find any necessity for the paternalism it saw in such a measure. Moreover, contributions by the state would be unconstitutional, or so the committee was advised by the Attorney General. A Socialist Assemblyman, whose roots were deep in Milwaukee's labor movement, entered a blistering minority report.[29]

The committee was wrong in its finding that there was no substantial demand for social insurance, as the continuation of proposals and inquiries attested, but the demand was of a minority, for it failed to achieve substantial success. The uncertainty consequent on the World War brought reluctance to take forward steps. A special committee report to the 1919 legislature on postwar reconstruction thus pleaded for delay. Yet this same committee showed a generally favorable attitude, for it did not seize on the unfavorable 1917 report to recommend that the whole matter be dropped. Instead it urged the appointment of a commission to continue the inquiry until the 1921 session, then to report tentative bills. However, this proposal failed of enactment.[30]

In 1933, in the more favorable climate created by the Great Depression, Socialists once again introduced an elaborate bill for social insurance, including mainly medical and hospital insurance and sickness

---

*The Stalwart wing of the Republican party was the anti-Progressive wing, i.e., the group that opposed the LaFollette faction.

and maternity benefits. Contributions were to be made by the state, by employers, and by the employees. The bill was decisively defeated. Except that the handful of Socialists were unanimously for the bill, there was no party line vote; there were Republicans and Democrats on both sides of the issue in both houses. Elaborate health insurance measures were also proposed and decisively beaten in 1939, 1941, 1943, and 1945.[31]

Unemployment Insurance.—Wisconsin pioneered in unemployment insurance in the United States. A bill authored by Professor John R. Commons of the University of Wisconsin was first introduced in 1921. It was decisively defeated in that year. A similar bill lost narrowly in 1923. Similar bills were defeated again in 1925, 1927, and 1929. Three bills were introduced in 1931 but were withdrawn in favor of the appointment of an interim committee on unemployment, which reported to a special legislative session in the same year.[32]

The 1931 committee recognized that irregularity of employment was "a distinct social waste." The solution of the long-run problem lay not only in a better relief system but in the reorganization of industry to iron out the unevenness of employment. "To accomplish these ends we recommend the enactment of a statute which will require industry to set up reserves for unemployment as it now sets up reserves for depreciation, taxes, interest and dividends."* The emphasis was clearly on compelling the individual employer to plan his operations better and to that extent the insurance idea was not involved; implicit in the evolution of the unemployment compensation system was the principle of risk-spreading, however.[33]

A minority of the committee opposed enactment of a compulsory unemployment compensation law on the ground that it would retard re-employment, especially since the system must be financed by a payroll tax. Moreover, it was argued, Wisconsin could not afford to act independently of other states. Opponents cited disagreement of economists on the economic effect of unemployment insurance as a reason to delay any action until full consideration could be given the matter. The minority were self-appointed spokesmen for the liberties of workers, too. They professed to fear that the growth of widespread bureaucracy would destroy workers' employment freedom.[34]

Finally, in 1932, a decade after the idea first reached the level of

*Rept. Wis. Legislative Interim Committee on Unemployment (1931), pp. 34, 35.

legislative proposals, the Wisconsin legislature in special session enacted the first American unemployment compensation law, on the employer's reserve principle. An Assembly vote of 64 to 20 in favor of the bill showed the overwhelming support for it. Conservatives consoled themselves that they had won some victories in obtaining alterations from the original Commons-Huber bill, especially in a provision exempting employers who established voluntary plans. Thus a spokesman for the Milwaukee Chamber of Commerce and the Wisconsin Manufacturers' Association dedicated a published collection of materials on the new law "To those public-spirited individuals, who for ten years endured obloquy to save the State of Wisconsin, and the Nation, from compulsory unemployment insurance, and thus paved the way for the present unemployment reserve law, with its provisions for voluntary plans . . . " (Hoar, p. *v*). The legislature realized that enactment of such a law by Wisconsin alone might put the state at a disadvantage in competition with states of lesser enlightenment, and a joint resolution memorialized Congress for a nation-wide unemployment compensation law. Furthermore, the legislators realized that the depth of the depression was not the best time to launch an unemployment compensation program, and the 1933 legislature postponed the effective date of the act until business recovery should be well under way; the date was to be determined by the Industrial Commission on the basis of a prescribed formula.[35]

Insurance and the Automobile Problem.—By the second decade of the twentieth century, the destructive capacities of the automobile had created a major social problem with two aspects; first, the tragic cost in actual suffering, and second, the financial distress resulting from automobile accidents, which was relieved only by the unwieldy lawsuit for negligence. Insurance principles had little relation to the first aspect of the problem but much to the latter aspect.

Compulsory insurance was early proposed to solve the problem of financial distress—to make certain that every motorist could answer in damages if he were legally responsible for an accident. However, fierce insurance company resistance and the reluctance of legislators to use compulsion on constituents delayed adoption of strong methods. As early as 1915, a proposal was made that the Wisconsin legislature require operators of motor vehicles for hire to have $4,000 liability insurance. In the same year a "jitney law" was passed, requiring a bond or an insurance policy with $2,500/$5,000 limits on automobiles operated for hire on the streets. The principle of compulsory insurance was soon accepted as applied to a variety of commercial vehicles. In 1927 the legislature required that automobile common carriers have insurance coverage or supply a surety bond on every vehicle used for the transportation of passengers, with limits of coverage depending on the size of the vehicle. Freight carriers must have a similar policy or bond in the amount of $2,000. The legislature extended the compulsion to mail-carrying automobiles and rented cars in 1929 and to school busses in 1937 and 1939. Once the principle of compulsory insurance for some commercial vehicles was established, there was merely disagreement as to its scope; a bill in 1939 would have extended the compulsory hired automobile insurance to cover trailers, and another in 1941 would have required insurance on all trailers over a certain weight, except farm trailers. In 1945 the legislature required persons furnishing hayrack, sleigh-ride, or other similar transportation for hire in Milwaukee County to have liability insurance. The required amounts of insurance also tended to increase.[36]

The principle of compulsory insurance for noncommercial vehicles was more difficult to establish. Compulsory automobile insurance on a principle analogous to workmen's compensation was proposed in other states before 1920. It was introduced in the Wisconsin legislature in 1927, 1929, and 1931. All automobile owners were to make contributions and compensation was to be paid to injured persons irrespective of fault. The bill was supported by the Wisconsin State Federation of Labor and by the Chairman of the Industrial Commission. It was bitterly opposed by the casualty insurance companies. The bill nearly passed the Senate in 1929, but this was high tide for the idea and after 1931 it was not introduced again.[37]

A more persistent proposal was compulsory insurance on the liability principle, i.e., insurance against liability for negligence. This proposal, too, was current in the early 1920's. Massachusetts adopted it in 1925 but was alone for three decades; not until 1956 did advocates finally break through fierce company resistance, and then New York joined Massachusetts in requiring insurance as a condition of automobile registration.[38]

In Wisconsin this kind of compulsory automobile liability insurance was proposed as early as 1921. Thereafter almost every session of the legislature saw one or more unsuccessful bills to compel automobile drivers to have insurance. Even the enactment of a financial responsibility law in 1931 did not stop the flow of compulsory insurance bills. Most lost by overwhelming majorities, sometimes by an unrecorded voice vote. Occasionally a bill passed one house only to lose in the other. The sentiment for compulsory insurance was persistent and fairly strong, especially among Socialists, but not nearly strong enough to prevail. In 1933, however, pressure was strong enough to cause creation of a joint legislative interim committee to study the problem of compulsory automobile insurance. The resolution even suggested the advisability of a law like that on workmen's compensation, though this proposal had not been much in evidence for several years. The committee was rather passive and despite one continuance, never presented a substantial report. Enactment of the New York compulsory insurance law in 1956 led to a renewed interest in Wisconsin. Insurance Commissioner Rogan made a special study of the problem and evidenced considerable interest, though he took no official position on the matter. However, when compulsory insurance was proposed in 1959, he gave premium rate data to the legislature which, together with an indication that the cost of enforcement might approach a half million dollars a year, seriously handicapped the bill and it was killed in the Assembly.[39]

Indirect compulsion, or financial inducement, was proposed also. Bills in 1935 and 1937 would have denied state, county, or city employees reimbursement for the use of personal cars on public business unless the owner supplied either a surety bond or an insurance policy. A 1939 bill would have reduced the automobile registration fee for insured automobiles.[40]

The resistance of legislators and insurance companies to compulsory measures led to the widespread adoption of a substitute, the financial responsibility law. Under this act, compulsion was applied only to those motorists against whom there was an unsatisfied judgment for damages. Such persons must supply proof of ability to respond in damages in the future, which would usually be satisfied by filing an insurance policy. In effect, the law was a compulsory insurance law for unsuccessful defendants, but it did not exercise effective compulsion on financially irresponsible persons, who would seldom be sued to judgment. Though undoubtedly useful, it was an inadequate solution for the pressing problem of automobile accidents.

A bill of this kind was introduced in the Wisconsin legislature in 1927 and passed in 1931. Some observers, as reported in the Milwaukee *Journal* (Aug. 16, 1931), greatly overestimated the effect of the act, thinking "the law really amounts to compulsory insurance." The 1945 legislature added an additional element of compulsion by requiring all operators and owners of cars involved in an accident to supply proof of financial responsibility. Though this made the risk of operating without insurance even more substantial, it did not solve the problem of the irresponsibles, especially juveniles, who could still drive unimpeded until involved in an accident. The motor vehicle department, on the basis of the new law, sought to educate the public to the necessity for liability insurance. And the companies welcomed the new market. They sent direct mail advertising to lists of registered drivers, obtained from the motor vehicle department, and posted billboard warnings of the new liability. Some resentment was created by their methods, if not by their objective of selling more insurance.[41]

Not everyone was satisfied that the financial responsibility law was a complete solution to the automobile accident problem, though its passage in 1931 forestalled investigation of the whole problem by an interim committee. In 1951 the legislature directed the legislative council to study the problems of motor vehicle accidents, and included for specific attention the operation of the Massachusetts compulsory insurance law. In 1953 it directed the legislative council to create a committee to study the problem of financial responsibility of motor vehicle operators, with particular attention to compulsory insurance, an unsatisfied judgment fund, the assignment of risks, and the insurance of special risk cases. A proposed joint resolution in 1955 would have instructed the Commissioner to institute conferences with the companies to frame coverage for the insured driver against the uninsured driver. This extension of the scope of coverage would make compulsory insurance less necessary. Concern over the problem had become a permanent anxiety by mid-twentieth century, and compulsory insurance in some form was still a much-considered solution to the problem.[42]

The 1945 safety responsibility law required the Commissioner of Motor Vehicles to suspend the driver's licenses of all operators of cars involved in an accident and the car registrations of the cars involved, sixty days after receipt of the accident report, unless there had been a deposit of security to satisfy possible judgments. This sanction did not apply if an automobile insurance policy covered possible judgments, provided within the sixty days the insurer filed with the Commissioner a written notice that the policy was in effect at the time of the accident. The filing of this so-called SR-21 form provided the Wisconsin Supreme Court with an opportunity to express its views about the purpose of financial and safety responsibility laws. In 1955 *Laughnan v. Griffiths* (271 Wis. 247) came before the court. To the questions in the form, asking whether the policy applied both to the owner and to the operator in the accident, the company answered "yes." Later the company contended that the policy did not cover the accident and that the form had been filed by mistake. On a motion for summary judgment by the defendant company, the court (two justices dissenting) held that filing an SR-21 form might be admissible in evidence against the interest of the company. On the question whether it might be even more conclusive than that, the court refused to rule. It contented itself with holding that a company could make itself liable if "after investigating the facts, it, acting through a duly authorized agent or employee, voluntarily files with the commissioner an SR-21 form admitting coverage as to the accident described in such SR-21 intending to be bound thereby, even though without the filing of the SR-21 there might not be liability" (p. 259). The case went back for trial.

Early in 1956 *Prisuda v. General Casualty Company* (272 Wis. 41) came on for decision. The trial court had refused to admit evidence of the filing of the SR-21, and the Supreme Court sent the case back for a new trial on the ground that the evidence was admissible against interest under the *Laughnan* doctrine. In 1957 a new situation was presented in *Pulvermacher v. Sharp* (275 Wis. 371). The plaintiff was the named insured, and was a passenger in his own car at the time of the accident. He sued the driver of the other car and the insurer of the latter, who then impleaded the driver of plaintiff's car and plaintiff's insurer. The latter had filed an SR-21. The issue was whether the filing of the SR-21 overrode a clause in the policy excluding coverage for personal injuries to the named insured. The court pointed to the legislative purpose to protect third persons as the reason for the *Laughnan* doctrine. It followed, therefore, that the doctrine did not operate beyond the confines of the statutory requirements, and there was no requirement that the insured's injuries be compensated.

Later the same year the court decided *Behringer v. State Farm Mutual* (275 Wis. 586). The company probably had a valid defense, but it had filed the SR-21 before it discovered the availability of the defense. Now the court began to feel doubts about the admission-against-interest rationale. It held that after the company had filed the SR-21, it could not deny liability on the basis of any "act occurring, or fact existing, as of the time of such filing, which it then knew, or could have known through the exercise of due diligence" (p. 593). What started out to be, apparently, a mere evidentiary admission of a party was thus transformed into a conclusive liability imposed by statute upon the voluntary filing of the form. It had become a kind of judicial (as opposed to evidentiary) admission (McCormick, p. 504). The court also said that intention to be bound, required by the *Laughnan* formula, was satisfied by the mere filing of the SR-21—that is, it was meaningless. Meanwhile the *Laughnan* case came up again (1 **Wis.** 2d 113), and the court reaffirmed its new position. The filing, which the court had said in the first *Laughnan* was *at least* an admission against interest, was held to be a conclusive and irrevocable admission of coverage in the second. Moreover, the coverage extended to the policy limits, which were greater than those required by the statute.

The *Prisuda* case, too, came up again (1 Wis. 2d 166), and the court upheld its SR-21 doctrine against constitutional attack on due process and equal protection grounds.

It seems clear that the court was motivated in this development by more than a concern for the technical meaning of language. It went beyond necessity in maximizing the effect of the safety responsibility law to give protection to persons injured in automobile accidents. The 1957 legislature appeared to have some misgivings about the lengths to which the court had gone; it provided (*Laws* 1957, 545, § 3) that no expansion of the company's liability based on the SR-21 filing should take place when there was fraud. The basic outlines of the SR-21 doctrine now seemed fairly stable, though cases continued to be decided by the Supreme Court on various novel applications of the doctrine. For example, in 1959 the court held in *Kurz* v. *Collins* (6 Wis. 2d 538) that filing of the form did not preclude the company from raising the defense of failure of the insured to coöperate after the date of the filing.

Insurance as a solution to the automobile problem was at first useless for publicly owned cars because of the doctrine that the state was immune from suit. In Wisconsin the Attorney General ruled in 1942 that since the state could not be sued, no official might pay out state funds for liability insurance. Sovereign immunity, however, was inconsistent with developing twentieth-century notions of the responsibility of government to the public, and as early as 1925, the legislature authorized cities and villages to procure liability insurance covering both the corporation and its officers and employees. As early as 1929 the legislature provided a procedure for making claims against cities, arising out of negligent use of automobiles in municipal business. Thereafter there was persistent and sometimes successful pressure to modify the doctrine of sovereign immunity at least to permit public agencies to buy liability insurance to protect injured persons. In 1932 the Attorney General modified the 1924 declaration of governmental irresponsibility, ruling that a school board might require liability insurance of contract carriers of school children and then pay the increased cost of transportation entailed by such insurance, though it might not pay the cost directly. Only five years later insurance was not merely permitted but required for school buses.[43]

However, permission to buy insurance was only of value if the law by implication removed the defense of sovereign immunity, or if the insurance company did not raise the defense. But the companies apparently sometimes did insist on the defense, and the 1949 legislature felt it necessary to eliminate this barrier in the case of school bus insurance, since the real purpose of permitting such insurance was not to indemnify the state against a liability to which it was not subject, but rather to provide a fund to reimburse injured citizens. A 1953 bill sought to abolish altogether the remaining remnants of the "archaic" doctrine of sovereign immunity. A brief for the bill argued that it was "meaningless, if not a fraud," to authorize school boards and other governmental subdivisions to procure insurance if the mantle of immunity were not removed.* The bill received some consideration but died without a vote.[44]

The contributory negligence doctrine, too, was unsatisfactory in the automobile age. It prevented recovery by any injured person who was himself negligent in any degree. Though applied erratically by juries, it often prevented recovery by injured persons whose negligence was minor and whose need was great. The insurance-and-security-focused attitudes of the twentieth century found such doctrines unpalatable, especially in automobile cases. In 1931 a comparative negligence statute was enacted in Wisconsin, under labor union

*Floyd E. Wheeler, *Reasons Why Wis. Bill No. 272 A Should Be Passed.* [Brief in LRef. Library.]

sponsorship. Contributory negligence of the plaintiff was no longer an absolute bar to the action; it merely reduced the amount of damages recoverable.[45]

The Insurance Age

The use of insurance to solve some of the major social problems of the twentieth century was only the most conspicuous illustration of the beginning of an "insurance age." William Whyte in *The Organization Man* points out the extent to which Americans of mid-twentieth century were security-conscious. Insurance, whether private or governmental, was the chosen machinery for achieving security against most risks. Even outside the field of social insurance, a host of measures offered impressive evidence of the high degree of approval accorded insurance in our society.

For example, after the first World War there was an insistent drive, in Wisconsin at least, to cause Congress to return to veterans the premiums for war risk life insurance or to have the state or the counties subsidize the continuance of such insurance. This effort still had political potential as late as 1931, when a legislative joint resolution urged the reimbursement of premiums, on the "fundamental principle that employers must insure their employees against hazards of injury." Thus early had the workmen's compensation idea become a postulate of the legal order![46]

More striking, because compulsion was involved, was a miscellaneous group of situations in which the legislature required insurance coverage, or was asked to do so. In 1925 it required insurance on property on which building and loan associations held mortgages; in 1955 it required medical and hospital insurance on boxers; in 1929 it required that school boards keep buildings and equipment amply insured. It was also asked to require liability insurance on portable feed grinding mills and on financially embarrassed railroads and malpractice insurance on doctors employed by local relief units.[47]

More numerous were statutes which authorized insurance in situations where it might otherwise have been unlawful. The legislature may have liberalized the insurable interest doctrine when it authorized corporations to insure the lives of directors, officers, and agents; at least the action emphasized how extensive was the accepted use of insurance.[48] In 1929 the legislature authorized the State Annuity Board to insure its negotiable securities against burglary, robbery, theft, and in 1947 extended similar authority to the State Treasurer. In 1933 the legislature permitted investment of trust funds in single premium endowment or annuity policies. In 1949 and 1951 legislatures validated athletic insurance plans of the Wisconsin Interscholastic Association; in 1955 the legislature authorized school boards to provide for accident insurance on pupils; beginning in 1929 it permitted county boards to provide group insurance for employees. In 1957 the Governor recommended, and the legislature enacted, a major program of group insurance for state employees; a 1959 proposal would have extended the program to local units of government. The 1959 legislature added group health insurance to the program. In 1947 the legislature created a marketing authority for Milwaukee, and so much a part of prevailing attitudes was the insurance idea that not only did the statute provide for all kinds of insurance to protect the authority against loss but it also authorized group insurance and a retirement fund, almost as a matter of course. The 1957 legislature authorized the Department of Veterans' Affairs to purchase mortgage cancellation life insurance for its mortgagors, if 60 per cent of them wanted it. Sometimes, too, the Attorney General permitted purchase of even unusual forms of insurance, despite the absence of specific statutory authority.[49]

The law most clearly acknowledged the public interest in insurance by granting exemption from execution or taxation to the proceeds of insurance policies, preferring the social value of insurance over customary claims of creditors and the public treasury. The 1851 legislature provided that any life insurance policy for the benefit of a married woman "shall enure to her sole and separate use and benefit and that of her children if any independently of her husband and of his creditors and representatives" (*Laws* 1851, 158, copied from *Mass. Laws* 1844, 82). By investing funds in life insurance, husbands might use this protection to married women to insulate money from the claims of their creditors. The 1862 legislature felt that it should limit this privilege, lest it be used in fraud of creditors, and provided that only so much of the proceeds should be exempt as represented the insurance that $300 of annual premium would purchase, unless the woman herself supplied the funds. In 1870 the legislature subjected insurance proceeds to a claim by creditors for the amount of premiums paid in fraud of creditors, plus interest. The revisors of 1878 took an intermediate position. They left the first $150 of premium free of inquiry as to the intent of the payor, and therefore absolutely exempt; beyond that figure, premiums paid with intent to defraud were recoverable by the creditors. This solution was disturbed again in 1931 when the $150 stipulation was eliminated so that defrauded creditors might claim the whole premium. This last statute represented a slight regression from exemption of life insurance proceeds, but the 1933 legislature extended the exemption principle to exempt claims of the wife's creditors, to a limit of $5,000 of insurance proceeds.[50]

Legislation granted other exemptions of insurance proceeds from execution. In 1862 life insurance on a minor payable to his parents was made exempt from the parents' debts, though not the minor's. Proceeds of mutual benefit or fraternal policies were made exempt, within limits; so also were certain pension funds and payments made from them. In the Great Depression, the 1933 legislature decided that persons seeking poor relief need not liquidate all the cash values of their insurance policies before becoming entitled to aid.[51]

Insurance proceeds also received a variety of exemptions from income and inheritance taxes, both state and federal. This favored treatment had deep roots, for the English income tax act of 1798 provided for a broadly framed deduction of life insurance premiums from income. The Wisconsin tax exemptions were less sweeping than the English, but there was some effort to broaden the exemption.[52]

RESTRICTIONS UPON VALIDATION

Insurable Interest

Use of the insurance contract as a gambling device was not unknown in the twentieth century but was relatively uncommon. By then costs of operation were so substantial and actuarial techniques so advanced, that the gambler had no reasonable chance unless he ceased to gamble and deliberately brought about the loss. In an earlier day, insurance was as much a guess for the underwriter as for the insured, and insurance was easily used as a gaming device.

In the eighteenth century a lax English public policy which permitted enforcement of gambling contracts underwent revision. By statute, the requirement of insurable interest was engrafted onto the law of insurance, limiting the legitimacy of the insurance undertaking. In 1746 Parliament invalidated marine insurance contracts if the insured had no interest in the subject matter of the insurance. This judgment of Parliament sprang both from morals and from the observation that a gaming use of insurance increased the loss ratio. Later in the century, a ghoulish practice of speculative insurance on the lives of well-known persons who were ill led to a 1774 statute which forbade wagering on lives and required an insurable interest in the life insured. In both cases an expressed reason was to counter the introduction of "a mischievous kind of gaming."[53]

Both statutes were too late in time to be generally "received" in the United States as a part of the common law. Nevertheless, American cases and textwriters generally accepted the principle of these acts, either on the historically questionable ground that the statutes were declaratory of the common law, or on the ground that they bolstered independent determination of judicial policy with respect to wagering contracts.[54]

The courts monotonously repeated two reasons for imposing the requirement of insurable interest in life insurance: the pragmatic need to minimize any temptation to cause a loss deliberately, and the moral evil in wagering contracts. Cases dealing with property insurance added a third reason: the contract of insurance was in its very nature an indemnity contract, i.e., a contract to reimburse the insured for loss actually suffered. The indemnity principle and the desire to minimize temptation to destroy the property or life were best implemented by a requirement of insurable interest at the time of the loss, while the desire to forbid wagering contracts on moral grounds suggests, rather, a requirement of insurable interest at the time of issuing the policy. The English law required insurable interest at *both* times.[55]

The insistence on an insurable interest at the time the policy was issued was not a serious handicap to an insurance industry which mainly protected fixed, unchanging property, such as homes or commercial real estate. But with the elaboration of commercial activity and the development of new forms of coverage, the doctrine became prejudicial to the performance of the services demanded of the industry. Thus fire insurance on the fluctuating stock of goods of a merchant or manufacturer would be invalid almost as soon as written.

In 1875 the Supreme Court of Wisconsin examined the problem thoroughly in *Sawyer* v. *Company* (37 Wis. 503). A fire insurance policy covered a farmer's wheat in stacks. After the policy was issued the insured acquired additional land, and wheat raised on the new land burned. The court saw that application of the strict doctrine to this case would render the policy ineffective to achieve the legitimate objectives of the policyholder. In an elaborate and perceptive opinion which recognized the wide economic implications of the decision, Chief Justice Ryan pointed out that the convenience of business demanded open insurance of fluctuating stocks of property. Ryan came down squarely in favor of a more liberal doctrine; he held that insurable interest was only necessary at the time of loss. Open fire insurance policies on the fluctuating stock of merchants had been sold in Wisconsin for many years, and although earlier cases involving such policies had gone up on appeal to the Supreme Court, in no earlier case was the defense of want of insurable interest raised, for to raise it successfully would have invalidated much of the business written by the companies and would have embarrassed them in their sales promotions. In the instant case, however, the company raised the defense as a substitute when its more substantial defense as to scope of coverage had failed.

In 1890 the Wisconsin Supreme Court was faced with a basic choice in the essential nature of insurable interest in property. A married man was in possession of and making beneficial use of a farm belonging to his wife, with her consent. The court held he had an insurable interest. Forsaking pursuit of an abstract legal logic, the Wisconsin Supreme Court tied its decision to economic reality rather than to the existence of a technical legal interest in the property. In its choice between alternative authorities the court recognized that the insurance enterprise existed to perform a legitimate economic function, and that it was the task of the law to facilitate its performance, not to advance captious objections.* Though the court decided nearly twenty more cases on insurable interest in property, it only worked out details and did not have to make any more fundamental public policy decisions. In no case did the court find insurable interest to be lacking.

In life insurance, it was the requirement of an insurable interest at the time of the loss that was inconsistent with the legitimate needs of policyholders, for if the holder of a valid policy might not assign to a person without insurable interest, he might not be able to realize its value before his death. This was especially true in the nineteenth century when policies did not always provide for cash surrender values. On the other hand, to eliminate the requirement would re-

---

*Horsch v. Co., 77 Wis. 4 (1890); followed on similar facts by Kludt v. Co., 152 Wis. 637 (1913).

move a doctrine which might be deemed useful to discourage murder. Of course the chance of murder was slight; lack of close relationship would subject the homicide to serious risk of detection when he collected the insurance. In the few cases dealing with insurable interest in life, the Wisconsin Supreme Court required insurable interest only at the issuance of the policy. This only screened out gaming contracts; on incentive to murder, the court merely asked, "Can there be anything against public policy or the law which will prevent the unfortunate holder of the policy from selling the same for the best price he can. . . ?"[*] On the other hand, in a late case the court held that at least under certain circumstances a creditor was limited in the amount of his insurable interest to the amount of his debt.[56]

There was a special danger in the insurance of young children. The common practice of insurance companies, and positive legal doctrine in some states, imposed the requirement that an adult policyholder consent before another might take out insurance on his life. This precaution could not be applied to the child. No statistics could show the frequency of infanticide for insurance proceeds, but often there was concern about the matter. As industrial life insurance became popular in the 1880's and 1890's, sentiment grew in Wisconsin to protect children from evil parents or guardians. Bills were introduced in 1901, 1903, 1905, and 1909 to invalidate insurance of children or to restrict it to a limited amount on a sliding scale varying with age. Increasing familiarity with juvenile insurance in the industrial divisions of the commercial insurance companies dissipated most of the opposition; in 1917 the legislature authorized the creation of juvenile divisions in the fraternal benefit societies, and in 1925 it modified and in 1931 removed all limits on amounts of such insurance.[57]

Other Public Policy Restrictions

Other overriding public policies sometimes limited the validity of the insurance enterprise. Moralistic concern with such conduct as suicide or drinking to intoxication led to occasional provisions in special charters forbidding coverage for death that occurred under these circumstances. This result ignored the purpose of insurance—to protect innocent third persons. But when the problem of suicide was directly presented to the Supreme Court of Wisconsin in 1898, the court emphasized the innocence of the beneficiaries, to hold that suicide was

[*]*Bursinger* v. *Bank,* 67 Wis. 75, 84 (1886); but see *Laws* 1895, c. 20.

covered unless specifically excluded, despite a then-recent decision of the United States Supreme Court holding such coverage to be against public policy and void.[58]

In 1929 the Attorney General ruled that in a malpractice policy insurance against liability for intentional torts or crimes was illegal because against public policy. Only negligence might be insured against. The same doctrine would probably not be applied to automobile insurance, though the rationalization of the difference would give trouble. The real reason for the difference was the crucial importance of automobile insurance as compared with the peripheral malpractice coverage. Earlier the Supreme Court had faced the problem whether a liability insurer's defense of an action against its policyholder was champertous, and held that it was not.[59]

SUMMARY

In mid-twentieth century the insurance principle and the formal insurance enterprise were major elements in the foundations of American society. It was abundantly clear that any form of the business that ministered to legitimate economic or personal needs would receive legal approval, even if that required the modification of opposing legal rules. Legal dogma gave way before the insistent demands of a security-conscious society as commercial insurance adapted itself to meet the needs of business and as the legislature used insurance to solve the social problems of an increasingly complex and interdependent social order.

Chapter Three

CREATION OF AN
ADEQUATE INSURANCE FUND

Once the law has determined the area within which the insurance enterprise may validly operate, it must decide what range of freedom to give to entrepreneurs in the creation of a fund adequate to pay the losses incurred by participants. The legal agencies are concerned not only with the rates of premium to be charged and the process of gathering the fund together but also with determining, at the initiation of the scheme, what framework of business organization is permissible and how capital may be mobilized for the enterprise.

§1. *Organization of the Industry*

THE FORM OF PRIVATE INSURERS

Studying the American democracy at first hand in 1831, Alexis de Tocqueville saw the great significance to a democratic society of the free use of a wide variety of nonofficial associations with local roots. He noted the tendency in aristocratic England for great men to do things singly, the French tendency to call for government to do them, and in contrast the American tendency to do them coöperatively by association, whether corporate or informal. "In democratic countries the science of association is the mother of science; the progress of all the rest depends upon the progress it has made." The insurance developments in Wisconsin illustrated the American aptitude for making maximum use of a multitude of organizational devices.*

Livermore may be pointing to the same phenomenon when he

*Tocqueville, 2:114–18. Cf. Hunt, 1:139: "Merchants of Boston and Salem, of moderate fortunes, engaged in branches of business, which it was thought in Europe could only be safely carried on by great chartered companies, under the protection of government monopolies."

argues that the ancestor of the nineteenth-century American corporation was not the specially chartered "semi-political" corporation of earlier centuries but, rather, the unincorporated association of the eighteenth and early nineteenth centuries, which often aped the structure, and without legal warrant arrogated to itself the privileges, of corporate status. Livermore (pp. 295–98, 4–5) regards the early land companies as the prime example of such associations. While the earlier chartered corporation was often an instrument of state policy, the mature American corporation of late nineteenth century was an instrument of private, economic association. It developed as a consequence of the pressing need of business men "for the unique values of the corporate mechanism," which first manifested itself in unincorporated associations that acted like corporations, though well into the nineteenth century the courts persisted in denominating them partnerships.*

The Individual Underwriter

The individual underwriter of insurance was dominant in America in the colonial period but in the next generations nearly disappeared.[1] Even in England it was mostly in marine insurance that individual underwriting was significant. Generally the underwriters became grouped in syndicates, for a wider spread of risk and greater security for the policyholder. Each policy was issued or underwritten by a number of entrepreneurs who were severally liable, to the extent only of the amount of insurance underwritten by each. These underwriters became associated in a loose organization known as Lloyds' of London; any such group of individual underwriters is said to operate on the Lloyds' principle.[2]

In Wisconsin the individual underwriter was in a fringe position from the beginning. Indeed, it was only in 1895 that the Wisconsin legislature belatedly gave explicit legal recognition to individual insurance entrepreneurs. This legislation selectively admitted to Wisconsin non-American insurers operating in the Lloyds' form, as individual underwriters, or as unincorporated fire associations. Since no Wisconsin statute previously forbade individuals to engage in the business of insurance, presumably it would have been legal for such

---

*Handlin (1947), pp. 113–43 and *passim*, shows the element of governmental character in the Massachusetts charters.

groups to operate in the state without such special authorization; apparently few did.[3]

Whether the step was necessary or not, in 1901 the legislature authorized transaction of marine insurance on the Lloyds' principle, but in 1907 and 1909 refused to extend such authorization to fire insurance. The 1911 legislature withdrew the 1895 authorization to individual underwriters and unincorporated fire associations but left in effect that for Lloyds' groups. Uncertainty as to the conditions under which Lloyds' groups might be admitted led to a 1912 act permitting Lloyds' groups to do business in Wisconsin in every field except life. There were some limitations for alien underwriters.[4]

Though Wisconsin law remained the same in mid-twentieth century, this did not reflect satisfactory American experience with Lloyds' groups, which had, in fact, proved unsuccessful and virtually ceased to exist in the United States. The Commissioner's report did not list any operating in Wisconsin in 1955.[5]

The Insurance Corporation

Although the unincorporated association was on the periphery of the American insurance business during the whole of Wisconsin's history, it was the corporate device which, from a very early date, predominated. However, the wide variety of organizational forms to which corporateness was permitted, whether by special charter or by general act, point up the significant role of social needs in fixing the modern corporate form.

The longer the terms of the insurance contract, the more desirable it is that the legal existence of the insurer be continuous; in life insurance perpetual existence became virtually indispensable. This special advantage was a reason for the early predominance of the corporation in insurance, though a tendency in the first quarter of the nineteenth century to limit the life of insurance corporations minimized this advantage for a generation.[6*]

Moreover, early chartered corporations were of a semipolitical or public utility character. Ordinary private business enterprise was conducted on a small scale and hardly justified the use of the cumbersome machinery of a Parliament. Only when the organizers of an enterprise needed special powers would they seek a special charter,

---

*Livermore, pp. 259–60, blames recurrent fear of monopoly and the rise of the Jeffersonian party for circumscription of the advantages of corporations.

which thus came to be regarded as a grant of a portion of sovereignty. The extent of the grant varied. For the great trading companies of the seventeenth century, it included delegation of governmental powers over wide colonial areas. For insurance or banking enterprises in the United States, it often took the form of monopolistic privilege or the delegation of compulsive powers, such as the power to require assessments of additional capital from stockholders. The fact that banking and insurance had wide effect on the community at large and that both were beyond the financial resources of individuals or even small groups in a capital-scarce society led organizers of such enterprises to seek the advantages of incorporation by asking the legislature for a special charter. Even within the field of insurance there were differences. Marine insurance was closely tied up with ordinary, unincorporated trading enterprise. Fire insurance, on the other hand, concerned the welfare of the whole populace. This gave it an eleemosynary character, which together with the breadth of its application, was an important reason why insurance incorporation began with fire rather than marine insurance. During the 1850's and 1860's only two insurance corporations were formed in Wisconsin under the general acts, but ninety were specially chartered by the legislature. This may have been partly because incorporation under the general acts gave no sense of special status but was merely a business convenience, and partly because some of the needs peculiar to the insurance business, such as the need for large capitalization, were dependent to some extent on special powers not given by the general act. Of purely private corporations, which had no such broad-ranging effect upon the community, a much higher proportion were organized under general laws. For example, about a fourth of manufacturing corporations were organized under the general laws.[7]

The Stock Corporation.—The first insurance enterprises to operate in Wisconsin were out-of-state stock companies, selling insurance for private profit, and throughout the state's history they predominated in volume of business done. Such insurance involved the transfer of substantial fluid capital, and thus demonstrated how early even the frontier became part of the market economy.

Little need be said about the three score stock companies specially chartered in Wisconsin before 1871. Though most were abortive, the readiness to form corporations at the slightest hint of demand for insurance—in a new geographical area or to cover a newly felt risk or to protect a new industry—all reinforce Tocqueville's appraisal of the American bent for association. The projections were incredibly optimistic, with total authorized capitalization of perhaps twenty million dollars. The incorporation of stock insurance companies for private profit was in the main stream of an optimistic and rapidly developing mercantile and industrial society.

One of the most significant of the ways in which the private profit sector of the insurance industry reflected the growth of the economy was increased specialization of function. In the 1830's it was not uncommon in the East for insurance and banking to be carried on in a single enterprise. As we have noted, the Wisconsin Marine and Fire Insurance Company, which did a very small insurance business for years, was chartered in 1839 primarily to do a banking business, its form a subterfuge to escape Jacksonian prejudice against banks.[8] A number of special charters granted to general transportation companies gave them power to write marine and inland marine insurance, and in 1854 the Merchant's Mutual Insurance Company was given power to acquire and build ships, barges, and docks.[9]

In the twentieth century the tendency was to make mixed enterprises illegal, where insurance was one of the enterprises. In Wisconsin the Attorney General disapproved a combination of real estate and mercantile activities with insurance; the Governor vetoed a bill to permit "housing corporations" to issue an indefinite kind of insurance under control of the Banking Commissioner; and restrictions were placed on the prepayment of life insurance premiums since that made the insurance company also a savings bank. The close relationship of abstracting and title insurance justified combination of those two, however.[10]

Mixed enterprises in Wisconsin insurance were uncommon. From the beginning specialized insurance companies, unmixed with trust or banking or transportation activities, predominated in the industry. Indeed the strong tendency was toward a high degree of specialization within the insurance business itself, as the business became an integral and vital part of the economy. In a sense the apex of this development was reached, so far as enabling legislation was concerned, when a 1901 statute authorized the formation of reinsurance companies in Wisconsin, to do business only with other insurance companies and not with policyholders.[11]

There was also a supracorporate form for entrepreneur insurance;

groups of companies, combined as syndicates to offer insurance, called themselves underwriters' agencies. They came into existence to provide coverage too large or risky for single companies to provide, and were especially used by very small companies. In the 1890's the legislature twice expressed approval of the development, though there was criticism within the industry, on the ground that the agency itself would develop a separate marketing organization, thus multiplying the business units in the market. Again in 1927 the legislature expressed approval in the workmen's compensation field. Though the ordinary corporate form usually proved adequate for the needs of the business, and though there was some objection to combinations of corporations, they were authorized and used wherever special problems required.[12]

The Mutual Corporation.—Insurance business conducted for profit symbolized the developing market society of early Wisconsin. There were, however, local developments in the wake of this burgeoning free enterprise which illustrated the other side of Wisconsin society—the capital-scarce, near-subsistence economy that was yet optimistic and looking forward to rapid growth and enrichment and seeking to protect its wealth. The incompleteness of the shift to a market economy may be seen in the large number of mutual and coöperative enterprises devised to serve the people's needs. There was a constant tendency for these enterprises to become market-oriented; in mid-twentieth century, mutual insurance was often Big Business.

The first domestic insurance enterprises in Wisconsin were formed on a nonprofit basis as highly localized fire insurance associations. They followed a pattern then recently developed in the New York county mutuals. Sometimes the same incorporators also formed hook and ladder companies to fight fires; these fire fighting associations later grew into municipal fire departments. The basic operating method of these companies was to exact of each policyholder an assessable premium note, made a lien on the insured property. These companies perfectly illustrate Tocqueville's thesis. Slight changes produced mutual companies intended to have a wider commercial operation while still operating on a nonprofit, assessable premium note basis. Working capital requirements were minimized in various ways, as by authorizing the companies to borrow to pay losses in anticipation of assessment revenues. Though most of the successful early Wisconsin companies were assessment mutuals of this type, some mutuals became market-oriented; for example, they sometimes obtained legislative authorization to write nonassessable policies and sometimes even to convert themselves into stock companies.[13]

The Milwaukee Mutual illustrates the rapid assimilation of the frontier by the market economy. The company was chartered in 1838 as a strictly local enterprise. It lay dormant until 1845, and then began operating even beyond the limits of Milwaukee. For twenty years it had a successful career, and obtained new authority from the legislature to issue nonassessable policies in 1851, to add inland and ocean marine and accident insurance to its operations in 1868, and finally to become a stock company in 1868, shortly before its death. The growing market economy may be seen in its 1851 petition for permission to write nonassessable policies. The petition stated that policyholders would prefer to pay a larger cash premium and give a smaller note; moreover, the company was unable to collect on some premium notes, since many policyholders would go to other parts of the country before assessment day, a reflection of the continued geographical mobility of people even behind the frontier.[14]

From an early date fire mutuals tended to specialize in the insurance of a particular kind of property—to become, as it were, the insurance organ of a particular trade. As early as the 1850's, some of the abortive companies indicated in their names a specialized interest in lumber, in mercantile property, or in farms. The first successful specialized mutual was The Brewers' Mutual in 1868. Beginning with 1878, general acts authorized the incorporation in Wisconsin of manufacturers' and millers' mutuals, druggists' mutuals, retail lumber dealers' mutuals, mutuals for insurance of county asylums and almshouse property, hardware mutuals, school district and board of education mutuals, jewelers' mutuals, and liquor dealers' mutuals. Unsuccessful bills would have authorized cheesemakers' mutuals, cheese factory and creamery mutuals, threshing machine mutuals, printers' mutuals, dry goods and grocery mutuals. Most unique, however, was a special act in 1889 authorizing members of the Methodist Episcopal Church to form mutuals for the insurance of churches and parsonages. When the Supreme Court held this act unconstitutional as special legislation, the legislature re-enacted it in a generalized form with the same provisions. The powers of this type of company were extended in 1895 to include insurance on church property in other states and, also, insurance against other casualties than fire or lightning, and in 1903 the legislature extended the act to authorize insurance of the property of members of the churches, thus making these church-related general fire mutuals.[15]

The mutual fire insurance company served as the pattern for new lines of insurance. The legislature in 1897 authorized mutual livestock insurance companies to insure livestock from disease and accident, theft, and other hazards, and in 1899, mutual bicycle insurance companies to insure against theft and injury to the bicycle by accident. In 1899 the legislature also authorized the organization of mutuals to insure against bankers' hazards, such as burglary, robbery and loss of money and securities in the course of transportation. In 1909 and 1911 it permitted formation of mutuals to issue any validated form of insurance.[16]

The Town Mutual.—As the associations patterned after the New York county mutuals became commercial companies, there was need in the capital-scarce rural communities back of the lake front for mutuals of an informal coöperative type to provide cheap fire insurance requiring little fluid capital. One response to the need was the town, or more properly, township, mutual. The 1859 legislature enacted a general incorporation law for town mutuals—small coöperative associations strictly limited to local operation. Aside from their more restricted area of business, they would operate on essentially the same basis as the earlier county mutuals. There was little activity in the organization of town mutuals in the 1860's. Quickening interest in the early 1870's led to numerous petitions to the 1872 legislature to re-enact the 1859 statute to provide a general incorporation act for town mutual companies. The legislature responded by re-enacting the 1859 act in almost identical terms. It is difficult to see why the re-enactment was necessary, for the 1859 act had never been repealed and, in fact, had been slightly amended as recently as 1870 and was included in the 1871 revised statutes.[17]

Several related factors contributed to make town mutuals significant in Wisconsin in the 1870's. Capital scarcity was accentuated by the depression of the mid-seventies and was felt keenly in the rural parts of the state. The failure of commercial companies as a result of the disastrous Chicago and Boston fires in 1871 and 1872 brought the realization that commercial companies, too, were vulnerable to catastrophe losses. The drastic tightening of the commercial companies' loss settlement practices, with heavy reliance on technical breaches of warranty and conditions, created resentment in rural policyholders, who sought organizations whose loss settlement policies they could control locally. The rise of the Grange exerted a direct influence in the development of town mutuals. Profit-seeking insurance companies were often linked with railroads in Granger demonology; it was explicit Granger policy to encourage the formation of coöperative mutuals. In other states these companies were often organized under the aegis of the Grange; in Wisconsin the existence of the town mutual law led to independent organization. This may have been what assured the continuity of Wisconsin town mutuals, even after the heyday of the Grange was past.[18] Granger bulletins published the town mutual laws and advocated organization: "Patrons, you cannot afford to pay these high premiums to joint stock companies. Insure yourselves and keep some money at home." Commercial companies wasted seven-tenths of the premiums: "This immense sum is now an annual gift from the hard working people to a set of sharpers who ridicule us for our stupidity while reveling in luxury on our hard earnings."*

The pace of growth of town mutuals was greatest in the 1870's. By 1882 there were 115 companies reporting to the Insurance Commissioner. The growth then continued at a lesser pace, to 135 in 1884, to 148 in 1886, and to 149 in 1888. In 1954 there were 189. The scale of their operations increased too; in mid-twentieth century town mutuals paid over 10 per cent of all the fire losses paid in the state; their proportion of the rural business was much greater.[19]

The initial town mutual law of 1859 strictly limited the companies to local operations, indeed to single townships. However, almost immediately there was pressure to lift the localizing restrictions, but the slowness of change evidenced the reality of the need for local institutions. In 1860 the legislature allowed town mutuals to operate in any four adjoining towns; in 1875 it raised the limit to 15 and also permited insurance anywhere within a single county. In 1876 the legislature removed the limit, provided the towns adjoined, but restored the 15 town limit in 1878. Various unsuccessful bills during the 1870's would have gone to different lengths in extending the range of operation. But the limited range which they all contemplated and the lack of success of most of the bills emphatically testified to the

*See *Bull. Executive Committee, Wis. State Grange,* June, 1875, p. 4, cols. 1-2; *Id.,* May, 1875, p. 2, col. 1 and p. 5, col. 2. [In Hist. Soc. Library.]

localism inherent in the town mutual as an insurance institution.[20]

The same conflicting tendencies continued through the first half of the twentieth century. On the one hand, the more successful town mutuals wished to expand their spheres of operations, especially into the country towns; on the other, there was a pervasive feeling that town mutuals should remain small local organizations ministering to the special needs of rural communities. In 1881 towns were permitted to exceed the allotted number if all were within the same county. The 15 town limit was raised to 20 in 1885, to 25 in 1889, to 30 in 1907. By a 1927 change the allotted number of towns might be exceeded if all were within three adjoining counties. The ambivalent character of the social forces operating on the legislature is apparent from its 1939 action limiting a town mutual to a single county except as it was already operating beyond the county, which was followed by a 1943 statute raising the limit to four counties. At first the town mutual might do only farm business in the additional three counties, but in 1945 that restriction was eliminated. A 1959 bill sought to increase the permissible number of counties to six.[21]

Over the course of a century the growth of the economy, which in early Wisconsin forced the conversion of the earliest local mutuals to commercial mutuals, impelled the town mutuals in the same direction. The need for local institutions kept the tendency within bounds, but by mid-twentieth century, the town mutual had in effect become a county mutual or even a four-county mutual. A 1947 statute provided for the merger or consolidation of two or more town mutuals, and an unsuccessful 1949 bill sought to provide for the conversion of town mutuals into ordinary mutuals. The last bill was a compromise between the town mutuals, which wanted permission to insure city property, and the commercial mutuals, which wanted the town mutuals confined within narrow limits.[22]

There was also a tendency toward greater complexity of operations for the town mutuals. In the nineteenth century town mutuals were already permitted to insure against wind damage, and in 1913 to offer members fire insurance for automobiles and motor-driven vehicles. They might have become the normal medium in rural areas for the nonliability portions of the automobile insurance business, but the 1929 codifying act for town mutuals removed the authority to insure automobiles against fire, though farm vehicles remained within the language of the act. The 1957 legislature broadened the permitted coverage to include virtually any property loss, despite some resistance from commercial insurance interests.[23]

The local character of the town mutual was both its strength and its weakness: small size and limited area meant fluctuation in loss ratio and the consequent necessity of low underwriting limits. The legislature in 1909 authorized a town mutual reinsurance company; after much discussion, the Wisconsin Town Mutual Reinsurance Company was organized in 1931. State insurance department officials were active in promoting this corporation, as they had earlier promoted reinsurance treaties among the companies.[24]

The City and Village Mutual.—The rural orientation of town mutuals made them less than fully satisfactory for the needs of the inhabitants of adjacent, more thickly settled communities, where they had limited authority to operate. In 1887 a general incorporation act, patterned after the town mutual act, authorized the formation of local fire insurance companies on a mutual basis in cities and incorporated villages. Operations were limited to a single city and to detached property except under strict underwriting limits. At once there was pressure to lift localizing restrictions. In 1889 and 1891, bills sought to permit each local company to operate in all the cities and villages of a single county. In 1895 the corporation was permitted by vote of its members to extend its operations, not only to other cities and villages in the same county but to adjoining counties. An operating limit of 100 miles from the home office was proposed in 1901, but instead the limit was set at eight counties. In 1903 the restriction was lifted altogether.[25]

There was doubt of the wisdom of following the rural pattern for the urban organization, and both Commissioners Fricke and Host opposed it. They thought that while town mutuals were successful and desirable companies, city and village mutuals were too easy to organize, lacked state supervision, and invited the speculative promoter. After unsuccessful efforts at amendment of the law in 1897, the Commissioner assumed the power to examine the city and village companies, and stopped the worst speculative abuses. His 1898 report asserted they were paying commissions to agents, indicating a strong tendency to become commercial mutuals; this development was certainly not contemplated by the 1887 act. In 1909 the legislature repealed the organizing statute for city and village mutuals, and as the old companies retired from operation city mutuals gradually ceased to

exist as a class distinct from commercial mutuals. Failures, in the years
before 1909, caused by conflagration in small cities allegedly hastened
the process.[26]

The Inter-insurance Exchange

The corporate form was not the only one available for mutual (nonprofit) operation of an insurance enterprise. The reciprocal, or inter-
insurance exchange, was a notable device developed through the use
of a simple power of attorney. An attorney in fact handled all of the
business matters of the group on a commission basis. In form the
inter-insurance exchange was simply a multilateral contract, through
the attorney in fact, by which the participants agreed to insure each
other. The premiums might be collected in advance or by assessment
or by a combination of the two arrangements. Since the attorney in
fact could be a person or corporation of experience in insurance and
could act simultaneously for many groups, this device could put professional skill into the conduct of a nonprofit insurance business. The
inter-insurer was first used about 1880, by large New York mercantile
houses, in order to get lower insurance rates and because they could
not get coverage without going to European companies. It was best
adapted to single lines with large risks, though in mid-twentieth
century it was also used for widespread, small-risk operations. If any
legal authorization were needed for the use of such a device in Wisconsin, it was given by statute in 1893 for manufacturers who wished
to insure each other. The 1913 legislature authorized reciprocals to
insure all risks except life, and in that form they were still authorized
in mid-century.[27]

Life Insurance Companies

The life insurance needs of an increasingly complex society were
met in large part by market-oriented companies operating on the level
premium or legal reserve basis. Many such companies were mutual
in form. Mutuals had the same corporate structure as stock companies
except that policyholders rather than stockholders had theoretical voting control, and the companies were not operated for profit; the surplus
was returned to the policyholders in the form of dividends or retained
to make the operation more secure. Actual control of such companies
was not in the policyholders, however, and mutual life insurance companies were as much a part of the market economy as stock companies.

Real control of commercial companies, whether stock or mutual, rested by natural evolution in the officers in power, who became a self-coöpting hierarchy virtually immune from deposition. The original organizers ordinarily continued in control; the management of large funds and the prospect of high salaried jobs provided their motivation.

Mutual Benefit Societies.—At the opposite end of the spectrum from legal reserve life companies were organizations which met the need for burial insurance and mutual aid in sickness for persons of limited means. In Wisconsin from 1853, the legislative mill steadily ground out simple charters for the creation of mutual benefit societies, which typically afforded relief to members in sickness and distress, contributed to the expenses of burial, gave aid to widows and orphans, and served other benevolent functions. The charters were very quickly reduced to a pattern and were very nearly identical. Four score special charters were granted by 1872, reaching a yearly rate of seventeen in 1868 and 1869. No method of operation was specified, but such an association would presumably do business by assessment of members. Some unincorporated benefit associations existed in Milwaukee a decade before the first corporate charter. There must have been many, for it is difficult to see tangible advantage in incorporation. It would not be needed for capital mobilization, nor would it provide for continuity of management, for discipline of members, nor for enforcement of assessments. These organizations were most often church-related societies, though often they were primitive labor unions; sometimes they were organized for charitable, as well as mutual aid, activities, and sometimes had no other apparent purpose than mutual aid. Handlin ([1951] ch. 7) sees in these associations a significant aspect of the adjustment of the uprooted European peasant to conditions in America.[28]

The informal nature of the societies was emphasized by nine statutes and twenty-nine unsuccessful bills during the 1880's, all of which were directed to exempting specified mutual benefit societies from the insurance laws. After 1882 the Commissioner might exempt such associations by certificate, but statutes continued to be passed. Since the complications in obtaining a special statute must have been greater than in getting a certificate, the continued efforts for special legislation may indicate that the Commissioner frequently refused certicates. Some other mutual benefit organizations remained even further outside the formal insurance establishment. The general corporation law permitted incorporation for mutual support and maintenance in case of sickness, misfortune, poverty, or death, or for contribution to the expenses of burial. Though these were really insurance purposes, the exemption from the insurance laws freed such organizations from the control of the insurance code.[29]

Fraternal Societies.—The informal mutual benefit societies shaded gradually into more complex noncommercial life insurance companies of great variety. Town mutual life insurance companies were proposed in 1872 and county mutual life companies in 1899. Most noncommercial life insurance companies, however, developed in connection with the ritual-practicing fraternal societies that grew so rapidly in the late nineteenth century* Some were as simple as mutual benefit societies; others had elaborate operations of the assessment type, with provision for some reserve funds. They flourished on misunderstanding of legal reserve life insurance. Thus The Patrons Benevolent Aid Society of Wisconsin, a Grange-related fraternal begun in 1875, inveighed against "the exorbitant premiums charged by the old line stock and mutual life insurance companies; the many intricate and complicated conditions imposed upon policy holders; the excessive and unreasonable salaries which the managers appropriate to themselves, and the hord [*sic*] of general, district, and subagents with handsome salaries who are sent into every hamlet in the land" (Patrons Benevolent Aid Soc. . . . , p. 1). It alleged that seventy eight cents of every premium dollar paid to the old line companies was either squandered or pocketed. The Patrons' society reached a peak almost at once and then dwindled and became moribund in the late 1880's.[30]

In several ways, the Supreme Court emphasized the peripheral and noncontractual nature of these companies. It was reluctant to interfere in such internal affairs as expulsion of members, though important contract rights might be involved. The status relations of the societies outweighed their contract obligations. The court at an early day also denied the insurer power to lend to the insured on security of the policy, thus preserving its value for burial purposes; this destroyed any investment function of such policies and limited them to protection alone.[31]

There was a long-run tendency to upgrade these companies, to make them virtually ordinary legal reserve companies. A 1945 statute extended permissible operations to include annuities and endowments.

*Kip, pp. 31–35, and Basye, pp. 9–40, give a brief history of the fraternals.

With their operations on a legal reserve basis, and thus extended, they were but another variety of commercial company.[32]

Commercial Assessment Companies.—Between the fraternals and the commercial life companies there was a kind of life insurance operation which was primarily speculative. It represented an effort to capitalize on the innate desire for "cheap" insurance, but lacked the stabilizing factors that gave real value to the fraternals even when they were not actuarially sound.

In the early 1870's, Wisconsin's Secretary of State Breese complained about two Illinois coöperative life companies. Their advertising created distrust of legitimate companies, for they alleged that the receipts of legal reserve companies above disbursements represented overcharges. They guaranteed a fixed amount of insurance only for an initial period of three to five years, after which the amount paid depended on what the assessments produced. Their lapse rate was high—80 to 90 per cent as compared with about 12 per cent for ordinary companies. Exclusion of these companies from the state would have been difficult, for they conformed to the letter of the law. By 1874 one of them had become insolvent.[33]

Life insurance failures in the 1870's, together with the economic naiveté on which the success of propaganda against legal reserve companies rested, led to the formation of numerous assessment societies—not fraternals, but commercial companies operating on an assessment basis. In 1878 a number of such companies, both domestic and out-of-state, were doing a thriving business in Wisconsin but were not complying with the regulatory laws for life companies. Commissioner Spooner in 1878 reported preparation of a test case to subject these companies to state regulation. After several attempts to bring them under control in the late 1880's, eventually, an 1891 statute regulated all fraternal and other assessment life and casualty companies. The persistent official hostility to the commercial assessment companies finally resulted in a 1907 statute compelling them to change to a sounder mode of operation. They were required to value policies as yearly renewable term policies if they wished to continue on an assessment basis; Wisconsin companies might convert to legal reserve operation. The improved actuarial standards removed them from the speculative arena but also destroyed the incentive to organize them. By 1915 Commissioner Ekern reported that the last assessment company had withdrawn from the state.[34]

One step nearer to legal reserve companies were the stipulated premium companies, which charged a set premium but retained the right to assess in case of necessity. The authorizing act of 1899 provided for minimum premiums and some reserves. It was repealed in 1907.[35]

GOVERNMENT INSURANCE

Tocqueville's thesis was richly illustrated by the profusion of organizational forms developed during the nineteenth century to satisfy insurance needs. Few of these organizational forms had any connection with government beyond an authorizing charter. As the twentieth century arrived, however, the American people began to place heavier reliance on government.[36]

The Chicago and Boston fire disasters of 1871 and 1872 showed the inadequacy of private profit fire insurance as then operated, and strengthened the tendency toward local coöperative associations of the town mutual type. These events also set in motion forces leading to government insurance. In Wisconsin an 1872 bill (A 85) proposed a "cheap and safe plan" of fire insurance. It would have put county boards of supervisors into the fire insurance business, limiting their liability to the amount of the fund accumulated. The tax collection machinery would have been used to collect premium assessments. The bill was eventually enacted for Grant county alone. Though this was government insurance, it was limited to the resources and capacities of local government. But in 1874, a resolution directed that the Assembly Ways and Means Committee inquire into the establishment of a system of state fire insurance and report by bill or otherwise. Nothing happened—perhaps the supporting sentiment was too weak. However, two forces that probably did support this relatively ineffective countercurrent pushing for state insurance in the very decade that saw industrial capitalism triumph were the traumatic effect of the big fires and the agrarian radicalism of the Granger movement. Though the Granger movement demanded only regulation, it seems likely that the notion of government operation of certain businesses would not be anathema to it. Industry spokesmen who feared state supervision as a prelude to state operation, and local mutuals as tending in the same direction, may not have been entirely wrong.[37]

Sentiment for local-focused government insurance was stronger in the 1880's. In 1881 the Assembly passed a bill permitting any rural township to set up a township insurance scheme, connected mechanically with the tax assessment process. The bill was never sent to the Senate. Sentiment for such organizations is not inexplicable, even in an age not yet ready to contemplate state-operated business, for there would be little difference between a privately run town mutual and a governmentally operated township insurance scheme. The same persons would be insured; the same persons would run it. However, when in 1887 a bill was introduced "to create a state fire insurance," the proposal did not survive even until a rough draft was prepared; the bill was changed to deal with another subject and only the title remained intact. A portion of the incomplete rough draft gives some clear insights into a minority attitude: "As Fire Departments and other preventives against fire benefit exclusively the Insurance Companies, while the Public at large has to pay for [sic], and whereas the Insurance Companies like other monopolies have combined and do combine right along to charge exorbitant rates, we deem it wise of the State, to create a State Fire Insurance Company (possibly on the mutual plan) which would secure to a large number of men a perfect safe and much cheaper Insurance than the private companies. Such insurance is in operation in every province of Germany and has forced the other companies to low rates, in no proportion at all to the rates charged in our country."* This seems more than mere agrarian radicalism; it suggests rather a doctrinaire socialism. The proponent was a Milwaukee representative, and in the metropolis, socialism was already a force of some consequence. In 1893 a Milwaukee representative introduced, and in 1895 one reintroduced, a bill which would have put the state directly into the business of insuring privately owned property. In both years the legislature summarily disposed of the bill.[38]

In 1907 sentiment for a broad scale state fire insurance program, countered by arguments to the Wisconsin constitution, produced a joint resolution for a constitutional amendment to permit a system of state fire insurance under which premiums were to be collected with taxes. This proposal lost in 1907, but in 1911 and 1913 joint resolutions urging a constitutional amendment broadly authorizing the legislature to create state insurance against any risks whatever passed. The

---

*See handwriting on back of ms. bill A 684 (1887). [In Archives.] The bill was introduced by Mr. Riemer, of Milwaukee, who ran on the People's Party ticket. Its platform suggests some influence of Socialist thinking. See Wis. Blue Book, 1887, pp. 502, 373–74.

amendments were submitted to the people, and failed by votes of about 3 to 1. There was vigorous opposition to the amendment in insurance quarters, usually taking the high ground of fear that state insurance was but an entering wedge for the socialist in state activities, and would be a step destructive of individual effort.[39]

An even more striking innovation was proposed in a 1913 joint resolution memorializing Congress to set up a federal fire, life, and accident insurance business. It passed the Assembly on a voice vote before losing in the Senate, 26 to 3.[40]

The State Fire Insurance Fund

Meantime, the problem of fire insurance coverage for state buildings eventually produced a limited form of state fire insurance. From an early date, county boards of supervisors had the power to insure county buildings. Later village boards and school boards acquired the same power. The powers and duties of state officials were less clear-cut.[41]

The State Board of Control of Reformatory, Charitable, and Penal Institutions fell into the practice of not insuring the buildings in the institutions under its governance.* In 1898 a large building at the industrial school for boys at Waukesha burned. The uninsured loss of $50,000–$60,000 caused financial inconvenience to the state, and as a consequence the Board began at once to insure its buildings—at 1 per cent for a three year term for most of the buildings and at 2.5 per cent for three years on the state prison. The total premium for the Board's property was $11,500. Much had to be placed in out-of-state companies. The Governor also insured the State Capitol at a premium cost of $2,000. The sudden shift in policy from no insurance to full insurance dramatized the large amounts involved, and in 1901 Governor LaFollette questioned the economy of paying profit-seeking companies to carry this risk, in view of the abundant resources of the State.† He urged the legislature to clarify public policy with respect to insurance on public buildings. A 1901 bill to make the state a self-insurer, by prohibiting the payment of insurance premiums from state

*The practice was based on an oral tradition of prohibitory legislation, which, however, the Board was unable to show when questioned. *Rept. Wis. State Board of Control*, 1898, pp. 12–13.

†*Assembly J.*, 1901, p. 54. LaFollette followed a more vigorous precedent of Governor Lee of South Dakota, who urged state insurance in all lines.—*S. Dak. Assembly J.*, 1901, pp. 65–66.

funds, was much discussed and variously amended but eventually was sidetracked. A similar proposal succeeded in 1903, and the state was made a self-insurer. An insurance fund, on which the Insurance Commissioner might draw for the payment of losses, was set up on the State Treasurer's books. The overwhelming sentiment in favor of this limited kind of state insurance is striking testimony to the change in the political climate of the state under the impact of LaFollette and Progressivism.[42]

When the Stalwart regime returned to power, Governor Philipp seized on the early instability of the fund to urge the legislatures of 1915 and 1917 to wind up the state fire fund. Over a decade earlier, a severe fire loss at the Capitol had exhausted the fund and had made it necessary to borrow about $80,000 from the general fund to pay the loss. By the time Governor Philipp sent his messages to the legislature, however, the general fund had been repaid, but the fire fund was still vulnerable to another large loss. The administration bills to wipe out or limit the operation of the fund were for the most part successful in the Assembly, but not in the Senate.[43]

After its initial difficulties the fund proved a remarkable money saver to the state and to local government units, which were permitted to insure in the fund after 1911, and its reserves proved of great utility to the state (and to the Governor's party) in subsequent decades.* Its success was achieved even though the premium rates were much lower than commercial rates. They were 60 per cent of commercial rates at first, raised to 75 per cent in 1917, but reduced again to 60 per cent in 1929. In 1947 the premium rates were put in the Commissioner's discretion, and in 1957 they were 50 per cent of bureau rates. Not the least of the advantages of the state fund was that for the state and for many municipalities it eliminated the perennial political headache involved in distributing the public's insurance business among agents of the fire insurance industry. Some of the attempts at limiting operation of the fund had involved efforts to take municipalities out of the fund, and that insurance agents were behind at least some of these

*The self-serving criticism of the fund, in Hanson, p. 37, and in Krier, is wide of the mark. Even without a fund operating on insurance principles, there is a wide spread of the risk in the fact of public ownership and the spread of the special tax burden after a large loss over all taxpayers. An insurance fund gives the added dimension of time to the spreading of the risk. Moreover, the 1917 legislature authorized the use of reinsurance to spread the risk still further.

suggests that the motivation was not entirely to ensure the integrity of American institutions.[44]

Conflicting pressures continued, on the one hand to expand the scope of operations of the state fund, and on the other to contract it or eliminate it altogether. Beginning in 1923, there were unsuccessful bills to make state insurance compulsory for local government units, to permit insurance of private property in the state fund, to appoint agents to sell state insurance on commission. On a third attempt, a 1937 bill, which sought to extend coverage of state property to all risks, was successful. At the same time, there were bills to limit the coverage of the fund to state property, with proponents sometimes plaintively admitting their reasons: "It isn't fair for the state to be in the insurance business because the state can sell insurance at 51 per cent less than the standard companies can" (*Capital Times* [Madison, Wis.], Sept. 19, 1935). There was also another attempt in 1935 to wind up the fund, but it failed ignominiously. Most of these bills received careful consideration, and on a great many the votes were quite close, suggesting that the issues were live ones. In mid-century, the pressures continued but apparently at a low level of effectiveness. The mid-century position seemed to be one of substantial equilibrium. At least a revision of the statute dealing with the state fund produced no important changes in basic principle.[45]

The State Life Insurance Fund

In the life insurance field, too, for a time forces operated to produce attitudes favorable to state insurance. The competitive spree begun in the 1870's by the Mutual Life, New York Life, and Equitable Life produced enormous growth of insurance company assets. It also produced wholesale subversion of the New York legislature, extravagance with surplus funds which should have been regarded as trust funds, and the shocking use of accumulated assets of the largest companies as pawns in the Wall Street chess game, to be used for the benefit of whatever groups could control them. When an internecine struggle took place for control of the Equitable Life, the audible rumblings and the sleuthing of reporters for Joseph Pulitzer's New York *World* led to the appointment of a committee, the Armstrong committee, to make a thorough investigation of the big life insurance companies in New York (Sullivan, 3:49). Simultaneously the same facts led the Wisconsin Senate in 1905 to appoint a committee to inquire into the practicability of government insurance. After reciting the sins of the Big Three, the resolution appointing the committee declared, "WHEREAS, Governmental life insurance has been found to be absolutely safe, cheap, free from oppressive conditions and coöperative in character, *Resolved,* That a committee . . . investigate into the practicability of the successful operation of governmental and state life insurance. . . ."* In the 1905 Special Session, a joint committee was appointed to investigate the life insurance business. Though the Senate committee was swallowed up by the joint committee, the Senators belonging to the joint committee did prepare a separate report on state insurance.[46]

The state insurance committee surveyed existing systems of state life, accident and health, and related forms of insurance. It found a generalized system of government life insurance only in New Zealand; Florida alone, among American states, had seriously considered instituting such a system.† The committee made the finding that government management ensured reasonable salaries, low commissions, economical management, and fairness to policyholders, but felt these conditions were also possible under private management, if the corrective legislation recommended by the joint committee were passed. The majority recommendation was, therefore, that such laws be passed and given a fair trial before the experiment of state insurance be attempted.[47]

Socialist Senator Rummel of Milwaukee dissented. He castigated the inefficiency and immorality of private life insurance, as disclosed in the Armstrong investigation. Even in the Northwestern Mutual, a Wisconsin company, he alleged, there were excessive salaries, nepotism, unfairness to policyholders, and unjust discrimination. He also found the premiums grossly excessive, but in this assertion there was a strikingly naive failure to understand the actuarial basis of legal reserve life insurance. He recommended employment of experts to prepare bills for a system of state insurance to cover sickness, accident, invalidity, old age, and death. He also recommended memorials to

*Resolution 26S, in *Senate J.,* 1905, pp. 421, 441. See also Resolution 33S, in *Senate J.,* 1905, pp. 927, 948; *Senate J.,* 1905SS, pp. 76–78.

†The Florida proposal was based on the naive notion that since loss payments were currently about a third of premiums, the difference might be appropriated by the State to relieve the pressure on tax revenues.—*Fla. Assembly J.,* 1905, 43–45 (Governor's message.)

Congress urging the adoption of a national system of insurance in the same fields.[48]

In 1907 Senator Rummel and an assembly colleague introduced bills in both houses to implement his recommendations, but they were summarily defeated. Such proposals made no progress in 1907 because favorable sentiment was diverted into the regulatory channel by the recommendations of the majority report. The sentiment for state-supplied life insurance continued very much alive, however. Interest was again aroused by the investigations of a 1909 joint committee to inquire into compensation for the injury or death of workingmen, and a bill to create a state life fund passed virtually unopposed in 1911. The fact that the state's liability was limited to the fund itself suggested that the objective was to create a yardstick for measuring the adequacy of performance of private companies rather than to achieve the social security objectives that became public policy in the next decades. There was also a hope that the state fund would help keep more life insurance funds in the state for investment in Wisconsin enterprises. It was a state life insurance company, in direct competition with private companies.[49]

The absence of serious company opposition to the creation of the fund is difficult to understand, especially since the press castigated the fund as "socialistic" (*Evening Wisconsin* [Milwaukee], Nov. 27, 1913). The reason may lie in the fact that no provision was made in the statute for active solicitation of business. Life insurance must be sold against significant buyer resistance, and commercial companies were not likely to fear serious competition from a state company selling across the counter.[50]

Periodically proposals were made to provide an aggressive selling mechanism for the state life fund, whether by mail solicitation of all voters or the creation of an agency organization on a commission basis or by newspaper advertising or by creating a $10,000 nonlapsible appropriation for publicizing the fund. In 1919 the legislature passed a bill to create an agency organization, only to have it vetoed by Stalwart Governor Philipp. This bill was a reaction to Governor Philipp's bill, proposed to the same legislature, that the state life fund law be repealed. The Governor's bill had lost after a heated controversy, in which Progressive charges that the Stalwarts represented big business were met by Stalwart charges that Progressives were disloyal and disreputable.[51] The Stalwarts also sought to undermine the state fund

from the inside; Commissioner Cleary forbade his employees to be press agents "for the LaFollette Socialistic theories at State expense."*
The growing sentiment for state funds was now met by the massive resistance of a well-established commercial business, which had roots in every hamlet in the land; the lowliest soliciting agent had a vested interest which opposed the intrusion of the state, especially in the form of a general fund subsidy for publicizing the insurance fund. "I don't know why the state should advertise an agency in competition with private enterprise," complained a life insurance agent, who was also an Assemblyman, in 1951 (*Capital Times* [Madison, Wis.], Apr. 4, 1951).

Proposals for Other State Funds

There was strong and persistent sentiment for state automobile insurance, too. Fear of such state funds underlay the opposition of the companies to compulsory insurance, which would lead, they said, to assigned risk plans, to supplementary state funds, and eventually to a monopolistic state fund. There was some basis for the fear, as was shown by three 1927 bills dealing with compulsory automobile insurance. One would have established a competitive state automobile liability fund, one a monopolistic state fund, and the third a fund of the compensation type under the Industrial Commission. The compensation fund bill was again offered in 1929 and 1931; a supplementary fund for uninsured motorists was proposed in 1937, and a similar one in 1949. A state fund not associated with compulsory insurance was proposed in 1935 and 1937, and had strong support. Skyrocketing casualty rates led to an unsuccessful suggestion of a yardstick state fund in 1947, and a state fund law nearly passed the Assembly in 1949. At mid-century automobile insurance in Wisconsin was still completely within the private sector of the insurance business, though there was significant sentiment for government operated insurance, as attested by the persistence of attempts to establish it and the narrow margin of defeat for some of the bills.[52]

Most workmen's compensation insurance was supplied by private carriers, though in some states, state funds, either monopolistic or competitive with private insurance, were initiated and proved successful. Occasional efforts were made to establish state funds in Wiscon-

Wisconsin State Journal (Madison), Aug. 5, 1915. Cleary was later President of the Northwestern Mutual.

sin, whether for all accidents, or for occupational disease, or for public employees, but in mid-century Wisconsin had a state fund only for peripheral aspects of workmen's compensation. There were special state funds to provide additional death benefits for the support of minor children and compensation for pre-existing disability, but these were as much in the nature of poor relief as of insurance.[53]

Whether government insurance could dominate or even obtain a foothold in a line of insurance, depended in part on the degree to which the development of private insurance preceded recognition of the social interests that demanded expansion of the field. Thus in automobile coverage, which was the classic example, private insurance appropriated the field before the automobile accident problem made the universalization of insurance imperative. In part the situation depended also on the extent to which private insurance was profitable. Thus unemployment insurance must be a government enterprise, though the field of mortgage insurance, surprisingly, was being invaded by private insurers in the 1950's. The case also depended on rates of premium, and skyrocketing rates in the 1940's contributed to the demand for state automobile insurance. High rates and small loss ratios on official bonds led to demand for a state bonding fund, which failed in 1927 by a vote of 42 to 33, and in 1929 by 35 to 27. In 1931 such a bill passed the Assembly, 40 to 33, after a stormy history including twelve roll-call votes, many close, only to lose out in the end-of-session rush.[54]

The reforming 1907 legislature saw broadly formulated proposals for investigating the state insurance systems of the world, with the objective of establishing state life, old age, invalidity, and sickness insurance. These propositions came to nothing because reform sentiment was exhausted in the regulation of private life insurance. The idea of broad social insurance was not dead, however; in 1911 a bill to provide social insurance was prepared but not introduced, and in 1913 the legislature provided for an investigation, but the appropriation for the bill was vetoed on economy grounds. An elaborate health insurance bill in 1917 would have created semi-independent funds, organized both by locality and by the kind of trade or business, to be under the control of the state. There were still remnants here of the early nineteenth-century tendency to organize on a local and nonofficial level, though this approach was now submerged in the state domination of the proposed enterprise.* Similar bills were introduced in 1919, 1921, and 1933. A state fund under control of the State Board of Health was proposed in 1939, 1941, 1943, and 1945.[55]

Meanwhile, as a partial solution, the legislature provided for coöperative funds under control of the state and county medical societies to provide sickness care for indigents and low income groups. It also permitted organization of nonprofit hospital service corporations, for prepaid hospital care. Other bills sought to encourage coöperative associations to provide medical and hospital care. These activities were outside the formal insurance establishment.[56]

Though it would have been quite possible to provide pensions for public employees by purchasing annuities from private insurers, no doubt ever seems to have appeared that a public fund was the proper method. Nor was there any doubt about unemployment compensation, even though the first proposal in Wisconsin would have created a mutual employers' compensation company, competitive with any private insurers wishing to enter the field. It was hardly likely that any private insurers would contest the field with the public agencies; indeed even the state could hardly act alone, and the legislature memorialized Congress for a national system of unemployment compensation.[57]

In the searing depression of the 1890's, a depositor's insurance fund to protect bank deposits was proposed by the Populists, but it was not until after the relatively minor financial panic of 1907 that any action was taken. Changing attitudes with respect to the role of the state in providing security against life's mishaps produced eight state funds between 1907 and 1917; in 1909 Wisconsin's legislature saw an unsuccessful bill to create a depositor's insurance fund under control of the Banking Commissioner. When banks began to fail in the Great Depression of the 1930's, it was assumed to be the proper role of government to solve the problem; the only question was one of mechanics. Even the most conservative recognized it to be Wisconsin public policy to protect depositors "to the utmost," but conservatives sought to keep "business and government separate in accordance with established democratic principles," by extending the validation of private

---

*Ops. Att'y Gen., 1918, p. 502, expressed the view that it was unconstitutional for the state to pay part of the cost of health insurance, as an appropriation of public funds for private purposes, or to compel employers to contribute, or to provide decentralized control, which would be an invalid delegation of legislative power.

credit insurance to include building and loan association deposits and by encouraging private enterprise in this undeveloped line of insurance.* There was little support for the conservative approach. A broader proposal to provide deposit insurance in a state fund, for all depositors, was in a fair way to be passed by the Assembly when the special session of 1931–32 ended. However, since 1925, there had been a voluntary state deposit insurance fund for public deposits, as an alternative to surety bonds, and the legislature now made this compulsory.[58]

Failure of the state to take action in the special session forfeited the state's chance to solve the problem. But, perhaps the matter so depended upon the national economy as to preclude resolution by the state. In 1933 Congress passed the Glass-Steagall Banking Act, and the legislature quickly passed enabling legislation to permit Wisconsin banks to acquire stock in the Federal Deposit Insurance Corporation and to subrogate the new agency to the rights of closed member banks.[59]†

SOURCE OF THE INDUSTRY'S ORGANIZATION

In its earlier period, Wisconsin depended to a striking extent on New York as the source of its insurance law, including the form, content, and even the phraseology of both general laws and special charters. Thereafter there was some tendency to borrow from nearer sources, notably Illinois, and in the twentieth century Wisconsin became itself creative and more catholic in its borrowing, perhaps because of the national character of the insurance business and the effectiveness of the National Convention of Insurance Commissioners.

The manuscript bills in the state archives show clear proof of direct borrowing. For example, in the manuscript draft of a livestock insurance company charter, the scribe erroneously copied "Northern New York Live Stock Insurance Company," which he then lined out and corrected. The original draft of an 1856 bill to revise the general incorporation law for fire insurance companies was a printed copy of the New York act, with a few changes. Textual comparison also is often conclusive of direct or indirect borrowing.[60]

*Cf. bill A 52 with A 12 (1931–32SS).

†Laws 1919, 527, § 1627, created the most curious of government insurance funds. It set aside a part of dog license fees for the counties to disburse to animal owners whose animals were injured by dogs. And see McCahan, p. 270.

A conflagration in New York City in 1835 was disastrous to most of the New York companies, which had not adequately understood the danger of catastrophic loss. Shaken confidence in private profit insurance led to a flood of mutual charters. From two in 1834 and none in 1835, New York county mutual fire insurance company charters numbered 36 in 1836 and 13 in 1837. The charters were all of a pattern, similar to an 1826 Massachusetts mutual charter which may have been the original model. The charters of 1837 for the Milwaukee and the Racine Mutual Fire Insurance Companies borrowed both form and language from the New York county mutuals. The Massachusetts model probably also lay before the drafters. The same legislature authorized the Wisconsin Insurance Company at Green Bay, and its charter was based on the 1816 New York charter of the Utica Insurance Company; some provisions the Wisconsin draftsman copied verbatim, some he omitted. The next session saw the chartering of the Wisconsin Marine and Fire Insurance Company, which was to disturb the political peace of the state for a decade; its charter copied that of the Wisconsin Insurance Company, adding only the power to receive deposits and make loans, in order to authorize banking activities.[61]

A decade later the organizers of the Merchants' Mutual Insurance Company chose another New York model—the 1841 charter of the General Mutual Insurance Company, a more sophisticated and commercially-oriented document.[62]

From the Milwaukee Mutual, and thence remotely from the New York county mutuals, were derived the charters of most of the temporarily successful insurance companies of early Wisconsin, such as the Madison Mutual, the Milwaukee Mechanics' Mutual, the Dodge County Mutual, and the Brewers' Mutual. A few, like the Vernon County Scandinavian Mutual, retained the local coöperative nature of their ancestors, but most operated as market-oriented mutual companies.[63]

The Mutual Life Insurance Company of Wisconsin (later the Northwestern Mutual) was patterned after the Mutual Life of New York, for which the organizer of the Wisconsin company had worked. Several unsuccessful companies also adopted essentially the same charter in the special charter period.[64]

The early Wisconsin general laws owed their origin also in large part to the creative efforts of New York legislatures. The 1850 general incorporation act for insurance companies followed an 1849 New York act very closely. The 1849 New York 2 per cent tax on fire insurance premiums, payable to local fire departments, was copied exactly in Wisconsin in 1852. The 1859 Wisconsin statute providing for the incorporation of town mutual insurance companies was virtually identical with the 1857 New York statute.[65]

By 1870, however, there was a significant departure from this pattern of borrowing. That year, after an unsuccessful earlier attempt in 1856, the Wisconsin legislature passed an act based on the more modern 1853 New York act regulating fire and marine insurance companies. The 1853 New York act, as amended up to that time, was substantially enacted, but there is also clear evidence, in the original draft, of direct borrowing from Illinois, which had enacted the New York law in 1869. The companion law to regulate life insurance was also borrowed from Illinois; thus Illinois was joining New York as a source of insurance statutes.[66]

The dominance of New York as the source for insurance legislation in Wisconsin's first generations clearly did not result from the superior availability of New York legal materials, for even before 1840 the State Library began to accumulate current statutory materials of the other states, though only later were the earliest materials picked up. In 1841 there were available in the official state collection the revised statutes of Massachusetts, Illinois, Indiana, New York, and Arkansas, as well as many volumes of session laws from those and other jurisdictions. The selection of New York rested on other grounds than mere availability of models. Though the seminal character of some of New York's legislation and the prominence of New York's insurance industry may have been factors in the choice, it seems probable that the primary reason was the natural affinity of migrants for the legal institutions of their native states. By 1860 Wisconsin had a population of three-quarters of a million, of whom about one-third were born in Wisconsin (and were under thirty), one-third in other of the states, and one-third abroad. Half of the second group, the group that by age and nativity was dominant in the public affairs of Wisconsin, came from New York, and half came from all other states combined. The dominance of New York in Wisconsin immigration sufficiently explains the direction taken by Wisconsin statutory borrowing. As the Wisconsin-born generations came into power in the state, there was a tendency to turn to states with which there was closer contact, since other-state loyalties were no longer important. In addition, Wisconsin had achieved some degree of maturity, and there was less slavish adherence to the models and even some striking out in new directions, as with the valued policy law in 1874. By the turn of the century, Wisconsin was a part of a national community, and its insurance law making was not dominated by any other state or section. But Wisconsin still borrowed freely in the twentieth century, sometimes from New York. The National Association of Insurance Commissioners also originated much legislation, and Wisconsin used it often.[67]

§2.   The Legitimacy of Corporate Structure and Practice

Various prevalent attitudes, recognized by the lawmaking agencies and embodied in "public policy," whether articulated or undeclared, played upon and modified the corporate structure and practice of the insurance business.

Anticharter Policy

The "anticharter" policy of early nineteenth-century democratic ideology opposed the creation of corporations, because they derogated from the rights of the sovereign people, because they tended to monopoly, and because they were destructive of "individual enterprise."[*] Only when corporations learned to appropriate the symbols of this democratic theory, to claim rights as "persons," and especially to claim standing as instruments of "individual enterprise" did opposition based on this doctrine cease to exist.[†]

The democratic ideology singled out banks for special attention; there were periods in early Wisconsin history when it was impossible to obtain a bank charter from the Wisconsin legislature. Consequently, in 1839 the Wisconsin Marine and Fire Insurance Company was chartered as a transparent subterfuge to evade the democracy's prej-

---

[*]This notion was of respectable antiquity. By 1700 it was felt in England that incorporation was needed only for the grant of monopoly privilege, which was of a political nature. Livermore, pp. 65, 67, 247, 253.

[†]Hartz, p. 79. See also *id.*, pp. 69-79, for relationship of "anticharter doctrine" to Pennsylvania political life.

udice against banks, for the intention of the charterers was to engage in the banking business in Milwaukee. This patent deceit practised on the legislature by responsible and conservative business men strikingly illustrated the nineteenth century's instrumental attitude toward law.[1]

Though the bank was a sound and responsible institution which contributed greatly to the development of Wisconsin, the prevailing ideology did not accept such flaunting of the authority of the state and people. For over a decade the company was engaged in a running fight with the state government; the fight was ended only when the company reorganized under the free banking act of 1853. In 1846 the legislature even repealed the charter, but the company ignored the action, contending it was beyond the constitutional competence of the legislature.

In the 1846 session of the legislature, two Council bills for the chartering of insurance companies failed, and the House Committee on Incorporations reported adversely on petitions for the creation of several mutual insurance companies. The anticharter doctrine, intensified by resentment at the Wisconsin Marine and Fire Insurance Company, thus prevented the incorporation of more insurance companies in that one year than were granted charters during the entire decade.[2]

Though the anticharter policy was prevailing doctrine wherever Jacksonian democracy was dominant, theory had little influence on the actual granting of charters; Democratic legislatures the country over responded as readily as did Whigs to the pressures of evolving capitalism.* As it became apparent that the proliferation of corporations could not be stopped, the emphasis of the dogma shifted from opposition to incorporation to the prevention of monopoly and the assertion of state control. In 1849 Governor Dewey recommended legislative action to make the corporate device generally available: "If any advantages are to be derived from the use of these powers every citizen should have the opportunity of availing himself of their benefits without the expense of procuring special acts of legislation" (*Senate J.*, 1849, p. 12). In 1850 the legislature adopted a general incorporation act for insurance companies. The terms of the act were stringent. Incorporation might be open, but it was not easy. Stock life companies must have $100,000 cash capital, and other stock companies $50,000. This was strict policy in a capital-scarce society. Con-

---

*Hartz, pp. 62–64. Schlesinger, pp. 334–39, treats Jacksonian attitudes toward corporations.

sequently, until 1871 large numbers of special charters continued to be ground through the legislative mill, invariably permitting operation with but a small amount of cash capital, the remainder subject to mobilization under assessable stock notes. From 1850 to the end of special chartering in 1871 there were about ninety special insurance charters; only two companies were chartered under the general act.[3]

The economic pressures operating on the legislature were too great to be opposed in the name of an ideology, though periodically the ideology put a temporary brake on the flow of special incorporations. In 1850 and 1851 a number of special charters were refused passage, because of the recent enactment of the general incorporation law. In 1858, Governor Randall vetoed many special charters, including one insurance company charter, on the ground of the availability of general acts. The legislature followed his lead and ten insurance charters failed of passage in that year, in direct response to the anticharter policy, now turned into an anti–special-charter policy. The effect of the Governor's crusade against special charters was only temporary. In 1859 there was one special charter and in 1860 there were two.[4] During the war period no insurance companies were chartered, but there were no requests. After the war a large number of special charters were again passed, and only one bill failed of passage between then and 1870, when pressure to end special chartering began once again.[5] A constitutional amendment of 1871 (*Laws* 1872, 305) represented the final legal triumph of the anti–special-charter doctrine, which had long since ceased to contain any anticorporation bias, however. Incorporation was not made easier, but the accumulation of fluid capital made the requirement of the general acts more reasonable.

Though opposition to corporations never ceased altogether, by late nineteenth century the prevailing attitude was favorable to them. When in 1893 and 1895 the Wisconsin legislature authorized various unincorporated insurers to operate in the state, the enactment involved either a tacit assumption that noncorporate groups must have authorization to engage in even an unforbidden business, or else it emphasized the desire of unincorporated venturers for assured status such as the corporations had. Either explanation helps show the degree to which the corporation had attained legitimacy and become the normal form of insurance organization.[6]

Prohibition of Trading Activities

Hostility to corporations and the fear that they would unfairly prejudice private, i.e., individual, enterprise by the competitive advantage of aggregated capital was reflected in a clause, common both in special charters and general incorporation acts, forbidding any insurance company to "deal or trade in buying or selling any goods, wares, merchandise or other commodities" (*Laws* 1870, 56, § 5). Though the process of business specialization had long since made it academic, this remained in mid-twentieth century as a vestigial remnant of a once violent attitude of hostility to aggregations of capital.[7]

Control of Charter Terms

It should not be assumed that during the special charter period enactment of requested charters was automatic; the legislature did exercise some control over economic policy. It is true that the legislature was driven by the force of developments it did not understand and could not resist, and that logrolling was an accepted part of the process of special incorporation, though the need for logrolling was slight in insurance. Where transportation charters were in issue there were often subsidies to be divided but insurance charters involved no such prizes for sectional or interest group bargaining. Despite the existence of some logrolling and the absence of serious resistance to chartering of insurance companies, there is evidence of real legislative concern for the details of charter provisions, especially during the earlier part of the special charter period. Thus the legislature insisted upon an addition to the proposed charter of the Wisconsin Marine and Fire Insurance Company, which made the president and directors personally liable on policies issued when the capital was impaired in certain ways.[8] When the North-Western Insurance Company (a fire company, not the Northwestern Mutual Life) sought in 1857 to change its name to the Aetna Insurance Company, for obvious reasons, and the Milwaukee agent of the Aetna and other insurance men objected, the Senate Committee on Incorporations reported unfavorably on the proposal. These are but two examples of the surveillance exercised over the provisions of insurance charters. The scrutiny was real, even though exercised only occasionally and haphazardly. Control was more insistently exercised in the early period than it was later, but it was always present in the background. Promoters were usually careful to choose accepted models. Much significance may be concealed in the cryptic 1854 report of the Assembly Committee on Incorporations approving the Potosi Mutual Insurance Company charter, because it was "in the usual form," i.e., it was patterned after the Madison Mutual charter of 1851 (*Assembly J.*, 1854, p. 644).[9]

The legislature proved willing to permit change in charters, where necessary. By 1915 difficulties had apparently been felt with the process of amending mutual company articles; in that year the legislature passed a law with unusual speed, with rules suspended in both houses to facilitate immediate passage, to provide for the amendment of mutual articles by a three-fourths vote, and to validate past amendments made without conformity to formal procedural requirements. This act required mailed notice to members; in 1945 the legislature permitted notice by publication, thus making amendment possible to a controlling group, virtually without notice to the majority of members. In this action, taken to facilitate necessary modifications, the legislature acted inconsistently with the principles of democratic control usually espoused in intracompany affairs; in 1947 it gave the Commissioner power to require additional notice.[10]

The Scope of Permitted Operations

For a variety of policy reasons, the legislature must set limits to the proper scope of corporate operations, but to suggest, as many courts have done, that acts beyond those limits must necessarily be void as *ultra vires* may do serious injustice. The Wisconsin Supreme Court dealt with the problem of *ultra vires* acts of insurance companies in too few cases to hammer out a systematic and well-considered doctrine, and in mid-century the problem was largely open. The court tended, however, to treat policies issued beyond the scope of authorized powers as absolutely void, though when a standard mortgage clause was used by a town mutual, the mortgagee was held covered even when the property was converted to a form the company might not insure. So also the court held a policyholder liable for assessments of an imperfectly organized *de facto* hail company insuring crops of tobacco *ultra vires*.[11]

Mortmain Policy

From the earliest insurance company charters in the United States, strict limitations were imposed upon acquisition of real property. These restrictions long antedate the law's real concern for the security of insurance company assets; rather, they seemed to effectuate a policy like that of the English mortmain acts, to keep real property out of the control of institutions which might enjoy perpetual life. An early New York charter limited real estate acquisitions of the United Insurance Company to its immediate needs and, since real estate mortgages were permissible investments, also to additional property acquired in the enforcement of the company's claims, whether by foreclosure of mortgages, satisfaction of debts, or at judgment sales. Property acquired because of bad debts and not because of need must be sold within five years. In Massachusetts, where real estate mortgages initially were not authorized investments, it was more common to specify a maximum sum that might be invested in real estate; thus the Cumberland Marine and Fire Insurance Company was limited to $20,000 of such investments. Such a precise limitation was an unrealistic curb upon a growing and dynamic industry, and a large number of charter amendments in the first decades of the nineteenth century permitted Massachusetts insurance corporations to purchase more real estate than was originally allowed them. Pennsylvania charters sometimes limited real estate acquisitions by putting a ceiling on the income from such property, and one Virginia charter put a limitation of two acres on real estate acquisitions of the company.[12]

In Wisconsin the limitation of real estate purchases to a specified value was found in mutual benefit charters, where the figure ranged mainly from $5,000 to $50,000, occasionally going higher. Sometimes there was need to increase the amount. Regular insurance company charters generally followed the New York pattern and permitted the companies to hold real estate mortgages as security for loans, to foreclose such mortgages, to take real estate in satisfaction of debts, and to purchase real estate on judgment sales. In addition the companies were empowered to acquire necessary real estate, usually a home office building. These provisions were also contained in the general incorporation acts of 1850 and the fire and marine act of 1870. An unusual clause in the Milwaukee Mutual charter of 1837 suggests the occasional violence of the mortmain policy; it escheated to the territory real estate acquired in the collection of bad debts and not sold within six years.[13]

The legislature set a period of six years within which the Northwestern Mutual Life must dispose of real estate acquired in the enforcement of debts; the necessity of quick disposition must often have caused loss to the company. From 1883 to 1885, conditions for disposal of special real estate were unfavorable, and on petition of the North-western Mutual, the 1885 legislature extended the permissible period for retention of real estate to ten years. The Commissioner was given power to permit postponement even further if forced sale would cause the company loss.[14]

Democratic Control of Local Mutuals

A priori one would expect the 1859 town mutual act to be the ulti-mate in democratic doctrine. It is surprising, therefore, to find voting rights determined, not on the democratic principle of one vote per person but on a property-oriented principle of one vote for each $200 of insurance. The property orientation of the voting privilege in farm mutuals was clearly in accord with the prevailing attitudes of rural Wisconsin, for it long remained intact in the law, despite the efforts of a vocal and insistent minority to establish the democratic principle. At least nine bills in the 1880's and 1890's and another in 1909 sought to end multiple voting. A handwritten petition in 1885 stated the ground as the democratic ideal of equal suffrage. At length, the 1911 legislature recognized the democratic ideology enough to permit town mutuals to adopt a democratic voting principle by two-thirds of the votes cast at an annual meeting. When registered town mutuals were authorized in 1929, the democratic voting principle was adopted.[15]

There is some indication that practice may have been more demo-cratic than legal provision. In 1934 the district attorney at Portage inquired of the Attorney General whether former officers of a town mutual might question the validity of the election of present officers because they were elected under the democratic voting principle. The Attorney General ruled they might not, because they had acquiesced in it; the property-oriented voting rule had been ignored for forty years.[16]

Quorum requirements for town mutuals also had implications for democratic control, but the practical problem of getting participation in company affairs made a democratic solution difficult. The 1917 legislature set a quorum requirement of fifteen policyholders. That was evidently too many for practicable operation of many companies, for it was reduced to ten in 1921.[17]

City and village mutuals were further removed from agrarian atti-tudes than town mutuals were, and they came more quickly to a democratic principle of voting. When they were authorized in 1887, the property principle was copied from the town mutual laws, though an alternative bill proposed the democratic form. The democratic rule was proposed unsuccessfully in 1889, but prevailed in 1891. Most local or industry mutuals adopted the property-oriented rule; so also did school district mutuals. When the legislature revised the general provisions for incorporation of domestic mutuals in 1909, it provided for one vote to each policyholder. This included unspecialized commercial mutuals, for which there was no statutory provision with respect to voting prior to 1909.[18]

Despite the property-oriented voting provisions, town mutuals were democratic in their general outlook. The democratic focus was maintained, in part, by prohibition of proxy voting; control of the company by small cliques was thus made more difficult. The 1878 legislature made a concession to the home ties of women in nineteenth-century rural America and permitted women to vote by proxy. Some pressure to remove the restrictions on proxy voting came presumably from managements which wished a clear path for the perpetuation of control. After some unsuccessful attempts to permit proxy voting, one succeeded in 1895, but the pendulum returned in 1901. Thereafter pressures persisted, from the one side to permit proxies for everyone, from the other to deny proxies even to women. This last change was achieved in 1959. The proxy rule varied for other types of mutuals.[19]

The requirement for town mutuals that the whole of the annual statement be read to the annual meeting was another effort in the direction of democratic control. However, it might also keep members away; hence an 1883 amendment permitted the annual meeting to dispense with any part of the statement it wished, but the full statement must still be filed with the town clerk.[20]

Democratic Control of Commercial Mutuals

The pursuit of the democratic objective for local mutuals was straightforward; for commercial mutuals the problem was more complex. New York's Armstrong investigation made clear what the Wisconsin insurance department had pointed out at least a decade earlier, that control of large mutual life insurance companies was normally in the hands of a self-coöpting cabal and that policyholder control was a pious fiction. Hence the stage was set so that when the Wisconsin investigating committee recommended elaborate reforming bills to the 1907 legislature the most significant of them were adopted.[21]

The first reform was to make all proxies theretofore given absolutely void.[22]

The most elaborate bill regulated in detail the election of directors, to preserve so far as possible actual policyholder control. Each policyholder was entitled to a single vote for each director to be elected. Cumulative voting enabled minority groups to concentrate their strength in order to obtain minority representation on the board of directors. Any one hundred policyholders were entitled to nominate directors, and the company was required to print the names of such nominees on the ballot. The company must furnish, at its expense, lists of policyholders. Voting was to be by mail for contested elections. Though there was no express prohibition of proxy voting, it was inconsistent with the mail vote provision, and was later explicitly prohibited in 1925. On the other hand, stability was assured and marauding management groups discouraged by staggered terms for directors, though this also meant added difficulty in removing corrupt management from power.[23]

The bill passed after a bitter fight. The Wisconsin Life opposed the single vote for each policyholder, the no-proxy rule, and the requirement of company assistance to dissenting factions. Its arguments were that the measure spelled loss of stability, availability of policyholder lists to competitors and consequent twisting, and possible proxy fights to control the great assets of mutual life companies.[24]

The Northwestern Mutual also vigorously opposed the reforms, through its general counsel and through special lobbyists. The bitterness of its fight was not the result of abstract notions about company stability, but of experience. In the years from 1869 to 1873, there had been a bitter struggle for control between the management group and a group of agents. Moreover, there was a serious attempt in 1906 to get an opposition voice in the councils of the company. A policyholder vigorously sought election as one of the trustees of the company; the company countered with an organized campaign for enough proxies to prevent the impertinent invasion of the company's councils. The policyholder had no real chance under existing election laws, but the incident gave management real reason to fear liberalizing election law changes, especially cumulative voting.[25]

The Northwestern Mutual argued that many of the procedures

would be expensive and unwieldy; the democratic principle of voting was unfair; cumulative voting was experimental and would introduce factionalism and discord into management; assistance to opposition candidates would lead to a political system within the companies; broad policyholder participation in elections was undesirable, as "a small vote is likely to be more intelligent and therefore more representative of that which is desirable" (Noyes [1906], p. 18); to outlaw proxy voting would make it more difficult for agents to amass votes to overturn management (Noyes [1907], p. 43). The Northwestern also attacked, as an unwarranted interference with the details of management, a recommendation of the committee that the Governor appoint one director of domestic mutual life companies. Management, it claimed, should have maximum freedom for decision-making, with publicity as the chief means of control, in accordance with the English system (Olin [1909], p. 24).*

The development of group life insurance created new problems in democratic control, and in 1943 the legislature authorized any domestic mutual limited to writing insurance on groups of members of labor unions, credit unions, coöperatives, or associations of public employees, to provide for proxy voting by representatives or delegates selected from specific districts.[26]

Democratic Control in Stock Companies

The legislature's concern for voting procedures in stock companies, where the property principle was accepted, extended only to the assurance of fairness. In 1917, however, the legislature forbade proxy voting by persons who had been stockholders less than a year, perhaps to confine to some degree attempts to acquire control of companies by proxy fights. Some administrative control over the transfer of shares of stock was given to the Commissioner, and the policyholders were given the option of mutualizing the company whenever the sale or transfer of control of the stock involved the transfer or reinsurance of the business of the company.[27]

---

*Milwaukee *Free Press* (Wis.), June 16, 1908, tells of continued company complaints about election expenses, but *Ops. Att'y Gen.*, 1910, p. 428, ruled the statutory procedures were only necessary for contested elections. Provision for a gubernatorial director was in bill A 680, S 322 (1907), which was Bill No. 3 recommended by the committee in *Rept. Wis. Joint Committee of Senate and Assembly on the Affairs of Life Insurance Companies* (1906), p. 243.

§3. *Provision of the Initial Capital Fund*

In its very nature insurance is a mutual enterprise.* Even when organized as a profitmaking business, it is in essence a scheme for the distribution of fortuitous losses among a large number of persons subject to similar risks. Though individual losses are unpredictable, in society at large there can be some approach to scientific predictability. The requisites for a successful insurance business are operation on a large enough scale to take advantage of the laws of probability, and a reliable rating and premium collection technique. The provision of an initial capital fund plays a subordinate role.[1]

If there were very few risk units in an insurance scheme, a few losses might destroy the company. Thus if only ten persons were insured by a fire insurance company, there would be but slight chance of any loss, but if one fire should occur, the incidence of loss would bankrupt the company. The law has approached this uncertainty of small scale operation in two divergent ways. For stock companies the law has provided security to policyholders by insisting on a capital fund, to be drawn on in the event that losses should exceed the normal before the enterprise has grown to size. For mutual companies, the law has provided security by permitting an enterprise to begin operations only on a large scale, after it has attracted enough participants to take advantage of the certainty inherent in large numbers of risks.

The primary role of a capital fund in insurance is thus to provide security to policyholders in the initial stages of operation. Even after the enterprise has grown to size, however, there remains a secondary function, for there is always the possibility that catastrophic losses may occur. Policyholder security requires a cushion for that event, whether provided by initial capital, by surplus, or by both or provided by charging premiums in excess of predicted needs and returning the excess as dividends at the end of the accounting period or by making policies assessable, so that additional premiums may be collected in the event of extraordinary losses.

The Primary Role of Capital—Profit-Seeking Entrepreneurs

Limited liability of stockholders early became a characteristic of

*A leading fire insurance man spoke of "the essential mutuality of all insurance."—FUA, *Proc.*, 1896, pp. 29, 32.

American corporation law. Indeed, the very first insurance charter granted by New York contained a limited liability provision. When stockholders were not personally liable, the capital necessary for safe insurance operation must be supplied by a fund, and its adequacy was of crucial importance.[2]

In Wisconsin's special charter period, before the 1870's, the stock insurance company charters authorized capital stock in amounts that varied from $20,000 to $2,000,000; $100,000 and $500,000 were the most common figures. The general incorporation act of 1850 required $100,000 for life companies and $50,000 for others, actually paid in, but in a capital-scarce society such as Wisconsin in the 1850's and 1860's, accumulation of such sums of money was difficult, and the general act was virtually unused for lack of a technique of capital mobilization. The special charters, however, mobilized the capital by permitting the company to begin operations when only a fraction of the capital was paid in. From $2,500 to $10,000 was usually required but as little as $200 was stipulated in one case. The remainder of the capital was to be in the form of amply secured stock notes.* The required security was usually real estate, though sometimes hypothecated stocks or bonds were mentioned, and sometimes the nature of the security was left largely in the discretion of the promoters of the company. This system was reasonably satisfactory only if stock subscriptions were adequately secured; otherwise there was but the illusion of a capital fund.[3]

The stock note technique was intermediate between the unlimited liability of the partnership and the liability limited to investment, familiar in the modern corporation. The stockholder was liable for more than his actual investment but not to an unlimited extent. It was a useful way of providing capital needed not for use but as a buffer against the unexpected. Through assessments on stock notes, a lever was provided to mobilize scarce capital on a compulsory basis as needed by the business.

In its American origins, the corporation was used more for the sake of compulsory capital mobilization than for limited liability; the limitation of liability to the par value was a later development. Eventually the corporation came to be used as a "mere contrivance

---

*Even this mobilization technique did not always provide enough capital. The Rock River Insurance Co. was chartered by *Laws* 1851, 195, with required paid-in capital of $5,000, which was reduced to $2,500 by *Laws* (P. & L.) 1853, 387, when the company was still unorganized two years later.

for avoiding the inconveniences of partnership."* Semicompulsory capital mobilization by stock notes came to an end with the end of special chartering in 1871, for the 1870 general incorporation acts for insurance companies (*Laws*, 56, § 6; 59, § 1) followed the principle of the 1850 act by requiring a substantial minimum paid-in capital. Capital was less scarce and the stock note technique, especially suited to a frontier society poor in cash, was no longer necessary.

Until 1933 fire, life, or accident insurance companies might be organized with capital stock of only $100,000; thereafter $200,000 was required. This basic requirement set a standard from which there were but few departures, and then only for special reasons. For example, a lower figure of $50,000 was set for stipulated premium companies, which charged a "stipulated" premium but retained the right to assess if necessary.[4]

Even in the beginning of the twentieth century, there was pressure to reduce capital requirements. It is doubtful whether capital was too scarce for legitimate needs, but not every chartered company was able to get off the ground. A 1903 bill to reduce the required paid-in capital stock from $100,000 to $10,000 passed the legislature, but was vetoed by Governor LaFollette, who pointed out that the purpose of a capital fund was to guaranty performance of the company's contracts: "There is great danger that the capital fixed by this bill would tend to the incorporation of companies to do the business authorized on a speculative instead of a sound basis" (*Senate J.*, 1903, pp. 1219–20). Only four senators voted to override the Governor's veto; such ready acceptance of the veto suggests that the legislators had given no great thought before passing the bill.[5]

The overall trend was toward more stringent, not less strict, capital requirements. As early as 1899, the legislature began to require the accumulation of surplus. In that year it limited the amount of dividends that might be paid by fire companies before a specified surplus was accumulated. In 1909 it required a surplus of a fourth of the capital stock, which in effect merely increased the capital requirement

*Handlin (1947), pp. 98, 133, 144–72; quotation at p. 194. The corporation was originally the body politic—a government agency; multiplication changed it into a mere business form. Some unincorporated land companies, too, used assessments to raise money, both for capital and for current expenses.—Livermore, p. 230–31. Wisconsin charters sometimes provided for application of profits to reduce subscription liability, or the conversion of profits to interest-bearing scrip, with retention of the money for additional stability.—See, e.g., *Laws* (P. & L.) 1856, 49, § 9.

by that amount. In the late 1920's there was pressure to increase the requirements to conform to the standards set in other states. In 1927 and 1931 bills failed, but the principle of increased capital requirements were finally successful in 1933, when the required capital under the general organizing statute was doubled. Thus the high point of capital requirements was reached in the depth of the depression; thereafter there was some tendency to make concessions to capital scarcity. For example, in 1935 the legislature repealed a special surplus requirement of ten times the maximum single risk.[6]

The legislature sometimes imposed heavier requirements on out-of-state companies. The 1850 fire and marine act required non-American companies to deposit with the State Treasurer an amount equal to the capital required of Wisconsin companies. The 1870 act was satisfied if such companies deposited approved securities to an amount of $200,000 with some insurance commissioner or trustee. In 1877 the legislature required that out-of-state fire companies have that much capital, though it did not require American companies to make a deposit in Wisconsin.[7] The non-American companies resented the aspersions cast upon them, even if they were not inconvenienced by the deposit requirement. The Milwaukee Chamber of Commerce in 1878, in a petition to the legislature (Petition A 310), pointed to the superior record of the alien companies in the Chicago and Boston fires, and stated that many of them were backed by the unlimited liability of their stockholders. The alien companies opposed successfully an 1879 bill which would have required them to deposit securities with the Wisconsin Commissioner, and at the same time would have put out-of-state company capital requirements on a parity with Wisconsin companies. Opposition to the bond deposit requirement outweighed the sentiment for reduction of capital requirements. Eventually, in 1895, the legislature reduced to $100,000 the capital required of out-of-state fire companies.[8]

Wisconsin had little experience with unincorporated profit-seeking entrepreneurs in the insurance business. The 1895 legislature admitted non-American Lloyds', individual underwriters, and fire associations on compliance with the applicable domiciliary laws. This transferred the policy-making responsibility of the legislature to unspecified non-American governments. The problem was difficult. Lloyds' underwriters contracted as individuals, and each was liable only severally and not jointly. The security of the policyholder thus lay in the integrity and solvency of a number of individuals. The 1901 legislature authorized Lloyds' underwriters to write marine insurance and made an attempt to provide security by requiring that at least twenty-five underwriters join the syndicate and deposit $500 each with the attorney for the syndicate. Curiously, no provision was made for bonding the attorney. In 1912 the legislature permitted American Lloyds' underwriters to do business in Wisconsin, without capital stock, but imposed the equivalent of a capital requirement by forbidding any single risk in excess of 10 per cent of net worth. Non-American Lloyds' groups were included in 1913.[9]

Primary Role of Capital—Nonprofit Enterprise

The insecurity inherent in a small number of risks was most often overcome for nonprofit companies by insistence on a minimum scale of operations at the outset, rather than by capital requirements. This initial spread of the risk, together with the assessability of members, was intended to give assurance that from the start the insurance fund would be adequate.

The first Wisconsin mutual fire insurance charters required applications for a specified amount of insurance, either $20,000 or $100,000 or $200,000, before operations might begin. The 1850 general incorporation act shifted from a specified amount of insurance to a basis more apt to assure the existence of an actual fund; it required that before business might begin a specified sum must be paid either in cash or in premium notes. Since the premium notes were for amounts largely in excess of expected needs, they constituted a guaranty fund which played the same role as capital stock.[10]

The collection of premium notes ended up in the courts, where the Wisconsin Supreme Court did not display perceptive understanding of the role of the premium notes and a minimum scale of operations as a substitute for capital stock. For example, one company divided its policyholders between the farmers' department and the merchants' department, and operated the two as if they were separate companies. In 1862, in *Allen v. Winne* (15 Wis. 113), the company's receiver sued on a premium note, and the Wisconsin Supreme Court, in effect, abandoned all responsibility for the satisfactory working of the insurance institution. It acquiesced in the compartmentalization of the operation and excused the policyholder from contributing to the losses in the department to which he did not belong: "If there is any difficulty in doing business upon this system . . . it is a matter for which the courts are not responsible. The parties have seen fit to enter into such contracts with these conditions, and the courts must enforce them as the parties have made them. . . . I know of no principle of law or public policy which has been violated by them" (*Id.*, pp. 118–19).[11]

The 1850 act was easily evaded; speculative promoters complied with it by supplying large notes signed by straw men. If the enterprise succeeded, they withdrew the initial notes as they obtained bona fide premium notes. If it failed, the initial policyholders were abandoned by the irresponsible promoters. To overcome this weakness, the 1870 Wisconsin act combined a required amount of premium with a required number of reliable applicants. No notes from any single person or firm might exceed $500, and the notes must be accompanied by a certificate of the county judge of the maker's residence, attesting financial responsibility.[12]

The 1909 legislature put its faith in a specified number of applicants and their assessability. No amount of premium was specified, so long as one full annual premium was received from each of the 100 applicants required for the beginning of operations. From 1909 to 1935 the same 100-applicant requirement applied also to stock companies. This made it clear that assessability of the 100 policyholders was a major part of the substitute for capital.[13]

For inter-insurance exchanges, the 1913 legislature combined all the bases theretofore used and required 100 separate risks aggregating at least $1,500,000 and a premium deposit of at least $25,000. The 1949 legislature authorized an inter-insurance exchange to accept reinsurance only when its surplus, exclusive of surplus notes, reached 50 per cent of the capital and surplus required of stock companies.[14]

But aggregate amount of risk had no significance in assuring an adequate initial spread of risk, and the 1937 legislature agreed with the 1909 legislature in omitting any such requirement for the formation of mutual companies other than life companies, but gave new significance to the amount of premium paid in, treating it as a temporary capital fund. In these mutuals, $20,000 must be paid in cash by the applicants. Part might be contributions returnable after a $20,000 surplus had been built. The amount was raised to $50,000 in 1941, and the increase even applied to existing automobile mutuals; Commissioner Duel sponsored this reform because the department was engaged in liquidating thirteen companies and preferred preventive regulation.[15]

The minimum starting requirement for local and specialized mutuals was usually couched in terms of the amount of insurance rather than of paid-in premiums. Thus millers' and manufacturers' mutual fire companies might be formed when there were twenty-five policies of at least $1,000 each on property worth in the aggregate at least $100,000. An 1887 amendment permitted such associations to do a general fire business whenever the amount of cash and premium notes in possession reached $100,000. This shift in basis suggests the reason for the initial choice of the more modest requirement. So long as the company was a local or industry mutual, public policy could be content with minimal controls because policyholders were close to management, but as soon as commercial operation was contemplated, management and clientele were separated and more rigorous control became necessary.[16]

During the 1850's and 1860's the legislature chartered about twenty commercial mutual companies with no provision for a guaranty fund or minimum scale of operations. One was the Vernon County Scandinavian Mutual, which began operations in 1870 with annual premium income of a few hundred dollars and continued at that level for years. The 1872 income for the company was $156. A single loss of any consequence would have shown its policy to be worthless. The legislature may have felt that these companies were neighborhood mutuals, subject to the bare minimum of state control, but some of them, notably the Madison and Dodge County Mutuals, had successful commercial operations from the outset. The failure to require a guaranty fund probably reflected economic naiveté and inadequate understanding of the nature of the insurance enterprise. It also pointed up some of the inadequacies in special legislation as a technique of government.[17]

Sometimes, in addition to the other requirements, mutuals were also required to have a guaranty fund. Until 1907 mutual life insurance companies, like stock companies, had to have a guaranty capital of $100,000, but there was no requirement of a minimum scale of operations. The provision seemed altogether reasonable. And yet the requirement was sufficiently strict that it compelled the Wisconsin Life to organize first as a mutual assessment company in 1895, under the 1891 law. In 1902 it had accumulated enough assets to reorganize as a legal reserve company. The 1907 legislature eliminated the guaranty capital requirements and imposed more elaborate requirements: 500 persons must subscribe for at least $1,000 of insurance each, aggregating at least $1,000,000, and each must have paid one full annual premium in cash.[18]

In keeping with the informal structure and limited objectives of mutual benefit societies, their early charters made no provisions for guaranty funds. The life insurance laws did not generally apply to them, but the 1891 legislature required that 500 applications be on hand before local companies might begin operations. Out-of-state companies must have a safely invested fund equal to one assessment on each member. An optional guaranty fund might be created. Thereafter there was a tendency to increase the requirements for mutual benefit societies, but they were always of a minimal character.[19]

The Secondary Role of Capital

Once the insurance enterprise had grown to scale, the primary role of capital was completed and it was no longer needed for that purpose. By the turn of the century that fact was well understood; indeed, it had been known by many in the early nineteenth century. Commissioner Host recommended a law compelling redemption of the capital stock and mutualization of the companies. He thought that would lessen the incentive to financial manipulation of the enormous aggregations of insurance funds. An unsuccessful bill in 1905 would have required the retirement of capital stock out of profits; another in 1927 would have authorized the voluntary mutualization of life companies. The legislature finally authorized conversion of stock life companies into mutual companies in 1955 on a voluntary rather than a compulsory basis. Elaborate provisions protected nonconsenting minority stockholders.[20]

There was need for a surplus, however, even after the enterprise had grown to size. There must be a cushion for disastrous loss experience. A minimum fixed sum of capital or a minimum required scale of operations might serve the initial need for capital but could not adequately perform the secondary role of supplying a contingency reserve, for the necessary size of the latter increased as the scale of the business increased. Expertly run capital stock companies might increase capital stock as the business expanded, either by stock dividends or by additional flotations of capital, or might maintain voluntary surpluses which increased in size with the scale of the business. The contingency reserves of assessable mutuals might lie, like capital, primarily in the assessability of policyholders, but the law reflected an attitude that even such companies should create reserves to avoid the necessity of assessments. Thus when the 1919 legislature permitted mutuals to write nonassessable policies on the accumulation of surplus equivalent to the capital and surplus required of stock companies, it recognized the secondary role of capital as a contingency fund by requiring that the surplus be at least 20 per cent of the premium income.[21]

The most significant problem of contingency reserves, and the earliest to arise, developed out of the conflagration hazard of large cities. In 1875 the Wisconsin legislature responded to the Chicago and Boston conflagrations with an optional catastrophe reserve law. A special reserve fund deposited with the State Treasurer, in effect, constituted a new capital fund; together with the unearned premiums on still outstanding policies, it continued into the future as virtually a new company. All other assets were applied to pay the catastrophe losses. Persons not involved in a catastrophic fire thus were assured continued protection from a solvent company; those suffering loss in the catastrophe would have a fairly good chance of payment. In 1877 Secretary of State Doyle reported that the law had yet to be used by a Wisconsin company, though the corresponding New York statute had been used by some New York companies.[22]

The catastrophe fund idea was apparently dormant in Wisconsin until the turn of the century, but then, and as early as 1904, Commissioner Host insisted on the necessity of a compulsory conflagration reserve. In 1907 Commissioner Beedle reported that no Wisconsin company had failed as a result of the San Francisco fire, though some had been inconvenienced. Apparently one unidentified company took advantage of the safety fund law after the San Francisco fire.[23]

The essence of the safety fund law was twofold: (1) the special reserve, and (2) the deferment of loss claims to the unearned premium reserve. In 1912 Commissioner Ekern noted a recent ruling by the New York Attorney General, that on dissolution unearned premiums took precedence over losses. This put a new light on the conflagration problem, even without the safety fund law, for since losses would only be payable out of surpluses and capital, those funds attained greater importance. On recommendation of the Legislative Fire Insurance Investigating Committee that rule became the law of Wisconsin in 1913, except where the policy was endorsed to provide that unearned premiums were not held in trust for the policyholder. In that case he would be only an ordinary creditor and would share pro rata on insolvency. This rule only applied to fire insurance, however. As to other kinds of insurance, the unearned premiums were not preferred claims but ranked with other debts.[24]

In 1947 an elaborate compulsory catastrophe reserve law was introduced into the legislature. The State Treasurer would hold the funds. Payments out of the fund might exceed accumulations, to be repaid by future contributions, thus making the state a limited reinsurer. The bill did not pass, and in mid-twentieth century the catastrophe reserve problem remained where it had been three-quarters of a century earlier, except for the precedence given unearned premiums by the 1913 statute. In the interim, increased underwriting skill, sounder management practices with respect to surpluses, and decreased conflagration hazard in well protected steel and brick cities made such a provision less important. But catastrophes of another kind had begun to concern insurers, who were beginning to think about pooling resources to handle catastrophe losses in the event of atomic warfare.[25]

Conversion of Mutuals to Stock Companies

Sometimes provision for a guaranty fund was a first step in the conversion of a mutual company into the stock form. Such conversion might represent a legitimate effort to put a faltering company on a sound basis, but more often it represented a scheme of a controlling cabal to raid the treasury of a prosperous mutual for personal benefit, either by a subsequent dissolution and distribution of the surplus or simply by appropriating the enhanced value of the stock resulting from the existence of the surplus. Such raids once were common; in Wisconsin a classic example occurred.*

For a quarter century the Madison Mutual Insurance Company, chartered in 1851, was the most successful of the Wisconsin fire insurance companies. By 1870 it did a larger Wisconsin business than even the great eastern companies; its 1869 cash premium income was $141,000. Dangerous practices, such as taking notes for even the cash portion of the premium, and years of heavy losses, necessitated assess-

*Rept. Ins. Comm'r, 1879, pp. 10–15, gives the history of this raid on the Madison Mutual Insurance Co.

ments in 1871 and 1875. The first was for 25 per cent, but in 1875 the officers made a 50 per cent assessment, much larger than necessary, which created a surplus. These two large assessments put the company in a bad competitive position, and business began to fall off, especially in the assessable category.[26]

In 1877 the legislature authorized a fateful charter amendment. The board of directors might create a guaranty fund of $100,000 or more; when the securities constituting the guaranty fund had been deposited, the board of directors might reorganize on a stock basis. Guaranty fund depositors had one vote for each dollar subscribed, but mutual policyholders one vote for each hundred dollars of mutual, i.e., assessable, insurance outstanding. This would give the guaranty fund depositors clear control. Pursuant to the amendment, subscriptions to the guaranty fund were made by William F. Vilas, subsequently United States Senator from Wisconsin, and five other prominent Madison citizens; closely associated with them was the secretary of the company. They deposited no money but only securities, from which the statute permitted them to receive the income.[27]

Everything was now set for the final act. In the 1879 legislature, the secretary, now the chairman of the Assembly Committee on Insurance, Banks, and Banking, introduced a bill to authorize the board of directors to wind up the company and distribute any surplus to the depositors of the guaranty fund. The bill passed the Assembly and was in course of passage in the Senate when the Insurance Commissioner, Mr. Phillip L. Spooner, Jr., called attention of the Senate committee in charge of the bill to a surplus of $41,410 (later he calculated it to be $54,721) contributed by the mutual policyholders, especially those who paid the 1875 assessment. Dissolution would give the guaranty fund depositors a large windfall, though they deposited only securities from which they continued to receive the income, and ran no risk, in view of the surplus.[28] Commissioner Spooner suggested the surplus be returned "to those who are entitled to receive it," i.e., the 1875 policyholders (*Rept. Ins. Comm'r*, 1880, p. 10). The Senate committee reported the dissolution bill, so amended. It failed to be enacted. One cannot be sure whether it was lost in the end-of-session rush, or was scuttled by its proponents, who preferred no law to a statute amended as the Commissioner had suggested. Even without the bill, the company reinsured with Westchester Fire Insurance Company and was dissolved. The disposition of the surplus remains uncertain.

Commissioner Spooner had no doubts about the affair. His 1879 report gave a detailed history of the transaction, in which he alleged that it was merely a raid on the surplus. The guaranty fund was unnecessary, for with a large surplus, the company was perfectly sound. He urged the original members to take legal action to determine whether the 1877 act had taken away their rights, and promised the help of his department. In September 1879 a Madison farmer, seeking to participate in the surplus assets, began an action against the company and the guaranty fund depositors.* His own stake was small, for he had paid total assessments of $33.75 in 1871 and 1875, but he brought a class action on behalf of all the similarly situated policyholders who contributed to the expense of the suit. After delays of over a year the case was settled out of court and the cause of action released. Despite urging by the Commissioner, no other action was ever initiated, probably because the share of any policyholder was too small. In 1881 a joint resolution requesting the Attorney General to investigate and take action to prevent payment to the guaranty fund depositors was killed by an unfavorable report of the Committee on Insurance, Banks, and Banking.[29]

So much is conceded fact, but the interpretations vary. His biographer acquits Vilas of sharp dealing, arguing that this was a legitimate business transaction in which the guarantors sought to preserve a local institution and put it on a sound footing, but finding that the company's business was beyond preservation, they liquidated it (H. Merrill, pp. 23–28). This view accepts at face value the defense that the company retired without failing to pay a single claim in full. This defense missed the point, as the defendants must have realized. No one even alleged that the company defaulted on any claims, but that the defendants raided the surplus of a sound mutual company and appropriated it to their private benefit. Vilas paid a great price for his involvement in the affair, for he was attacked viciously for his part in it for the rest of his life.

William Welch, a Madison attorney, was an unsuccessful Republican politician with a grudge against the world. He spent much of his life in blistering and relatively ineffective attacks on the citadels of power; few political leaders of his generation escaped his vitriolic

---

*Bartlett v. Co. [In Dane County Circuit Court files, Drawer 185, Microfilm 89.]

pen. His vehicle was a family publication, the *Home Diary*, circulated to his family, his friends, and presumably his enemies. The unrestrained political gossip it retailed must have made it widely and quite avidly read. For years he criticized the Madison Mutual, which to him was an adjunct of the "Madison Regency," the dominant clique of the Republican party. In 1881 Welch launched his attack on the company's conversion to stock form, publishing the exposé in the *Home Diary* as *The History of a Crime*. Elaborately he discussed control of the company by the Madison Regency, and labelled the 1877 act a "daring scheme . . . concocted" to raid the surplus. The farmer who brought the action and his "high-priced lawyers" were well paid. Commissioner Spooner failed to act with sufficient vigor to protect the rights of the policyholders. Later Welch retracted this last charge.[30]*

The main target of Welch's vituperation was Vilas. After the initial excitement the matter was quiescent for a number of years. Vilas then became Postmaster-General in President Cleveland's first cabinet, later was Secretary of War, and was sometimes considered for the Vice-Presidency. Welch, by then removed to Minneapolis, conceived it to be his moral duty to expose the villainy and destroy the public career of the distinguished Madisonian.†

According to the standards of the Gilded Age, as seen by Mark Twain and Charles Dudley Warner, even a deliberate and carefully planned raid on the surplus of the Madison Mutual would not have been especially immoral. The social conscience that would regard such conduct as a breach of fiduciary obligation was emerging, as the opposition of Commissioner Spooner and the attacks of Mr. Welch illustrate, but it was not yet clearly dominant. The moral attitudes of 1880 were perhaps as sympathetic to the raider as to the raided. The raid was conceived and executed within the framework of laws designed to serve as the instrument of the occasion. While the court,

*For the exposé, see 4 *Home Diary*, No. 186 (Aug. 15, 1881) and following issues. No. 190 (Sept. 9, 1881) retracted the charge against Spooner.

†On one occasion Welch was prosecuted for criminal libel in Minnesota, but for the most part Vilas ignored the charges.—H. Merrill, p. 25. As the years went by, Welch picked up additional details. For example, he said the farmer who had brought the action and his backers were bought off for $3,000, of which the farmer got $1,000. No trace of the settlement terms remains in the file of the case among the papers of Vilas' law firm. [In Archives.] No final report of the company was ever filed with the Comm'r, and the principals never gave any information about the disposition of the surplus. See 4 *Home Diary*, No. 225 (Feb. 16, 1887) and issue of June 7, 1890.

properly solicited, might have used its visitatorial power over corporations to distribute the surplus on an equitable basis, the inherent
limitations of judicial power prevented the court's interference when
its help was not sought.[31]

For decades, the legislature retained an interest in the problem of
raids on surplus, and sought to protect policyholders by a wide variety
of measures. Thus in 1883, when the Milwaukee Mechanics' Mutual
converted to the stock form, the legislature amended the introduced
bill to prohibit division of any part of the assets among the members.
The bill also gave the policyholders proportional pre-emptive rights
in the stock and theoretically closed the door to a raid of the Madison
Mutual type. In practice, however, stock purchasers would be benefited by the appreciation in the value of stock resulting from the failure
of most policyholders to take up the stock to which they were entitled.[32]

The Madison Mutual raid was made possible because the large
assessment of 1875 built up a surplus wholly disproportionate to need.
The 1897 legislature struck at this method of accumulation by requiring mutual fire companies immediately to notify the Commissioner of
all assessments and to show the necessity for them.[33]

The inadequacy of a notification provision was quickly shown, for
it only applied to surpluses built by the assessment process. It did not
help with respect to surplus built by slow accretion. The Germantown
Farmers' Mutual Insurance Company began in 1854, and by 1902 it
had accumulated a surplus of over $200,000. The officers conceived a
scheme for raiding the surplus for their own benefit. There was to be
conversion to a stock form, followed by continued operation as a stock
company, owned by the erstwhile officers of the mutual company.
Contrasted with the crass vulgarity of the Madison Mutual raid, the
Germantown raid was planned with considerable finesse, and very
nearly succeeded. Public revulsion against the more obvious forms of
chicanery typical of the Gilded Age made subtlety necessary. To
implement the plan a bill was introduced in 1903, providing for conversion of any mutual fire insurance company to the stock form. It
contained elaborate provisions for notice to policyholders, for written
consent by two-thirds of them, for pre-emptive rights of stock purchase in the policyholders for thirty days, and provided that the assets
of the mutual company should not be divided among the policyholders
but should be transferred to the stock company for its ordinary opera-

tions. The legislature insisted on one amendment—to permit any policyholder within ninety days to request distribution to him of his equitable share of the surplus. So unobjectionable did the bill, as thus amended, seem to the legislators that it passed routinely. But beneath its benign face it concealed a corrupt heart, for the formula defining the quantity of stock to which policyholders had a pre-emptive right gave them such an insignificant amount of stock that if all policyholders had exercised the right they would have subscribed only $1,500. In this unfair formula the officers overreached themselves; both they and the legislature were unrealistic if they supposed that many policyholders would exercise a pre-emptive right within thirty days or even request a return of an equitable proportion of surplus in ninety days. In fact, a munificent total of $57 was paid out to policyholders who requested it. Acting on the statute, the new Germantown Insurance Company took over the assets of the old mutual. The stock was closely held. The secretary of the mutual subscribed $80,700 out of $200,000 and another person of the same surname an additional $10,000. Directors of the old corporation held another $24,000. Shortly thereafter a policyholder instituted an action against the new company as well as some of the individual officers of it, asking an accounting of the assets belonging to the old company and asking also for the appointment of a receiver for the old company. In 1906 the Supreme Court of Wisconsin seized upon the shortness of the pre-emptive period and the one error of the officers, the unfair pre-emptive formula, to strike down the act of 1903, as an unconstitutional taking of the property of the policyholders, the beneficial owners of the assets (*Huber* v. *Martin*, 127 Wis. 412). Despite the court's technical analysis, it is clear that the judges mainly felt a revulsion characteristic of the new age:

The very statement of the position which must be maintained in order to defeat the complaint . . . so shocks the moral sense that one is inclined to enter upon a study of the subject with the impression that no substantial basis can be found for it in the law. . . . The very thought that such a result would be possible . . . suggests the existence of such serious infirmity in our constitutional guarantees as regards property rights that one could not well conclude that they exist, except in the face of some unmistakable demonstration (*Id.*, pp. 422–23, 426).

The court declared the Germantown Farmers' Mutual to be still in existence.[34]

The old company resumed its operations and at once distributed $50,000 of the surplus to policyholders. Litigation in 1907 determined that the distributed amount should be divided among those persons who were members as of the date of distribution, in proportion to the total amount of premiums they had paid.[35]

The 1907 legislature struck at the heart of the problem of excessive assets. Mutual fire companies, whenever surplus exceeded 3 per cent of outstanding risks, must reduce the surplus to 2 per cent by distribution to policyholders. The act would have required the distribution of about four-fifths of the Germantown's assets, but the officers of the company had no intention of dissipating the assets prematurely. The 1907 decree of distribution had provided new possibilities, for if most policyholders could be frozen out, the insiders who remained might appropriate the surplus. Distribution under the 1907 law was stalled for two years. When a policyholder complained to the Insurance Commissioner, the company answered that the act did not apply to the Germantown, which issued policies only on the nonassessable basis, rather than on a mutual plan. The Attorney General agreed; earlier he had ruled that the Germantown might refuse to renew policies of members, without any reason.[36]

As a result of the supposed threat to freeze out policyholders, the 1909 legislature considered a bill forbidding any mutual company to refuse to renew a policy except for cause. A substitute, which passed, only to be vetoed, forbade payment on dissolution to any member of a domestic mutual of any sum in excess of the payments made by him with compound interest at 6 per cent. Any remaining surplus went to the school fund as a dissolution license fee. The substitute bill also sought to repeal the 1907 act requiring the distribution of surplus.[37] Superficially this bill seemed to solve the Germantown problem, for it would prevent dissolution as a method of raiding the surplus, but it had serious loopholes which the Governor used as the basis for a veto.* He argued that the eight months delay before the bill went into effect might give the Germantown Mutual officers time enough to squeeze out the policyholders, that the bill surreptitiously repealed the 1907 act, and that the forfeiture to the school fund applied only on dissolution, which would not be necessary to a raid. The Governor had little

*Assembly J., 1909, pp. 997–1000 (veto). The Assembly passed the bill over the veto.—Assembly J., 1909, p. 1034. The Senate did not.—Senate J., 1909, p. 981. See Milwaukee Free Press (Wis.), June 3, 1909, for a story on the attempt to pass over the veto in the Senate.

doubt that the object of the bill as passed was to facilitate, rather than to hinder, the raid. However, the Commissioner's reports show no evidence of a serious effort to freeze policyholders out. Risks in force dropped only gradually from 1903 to 1907, probably as a result of unsettled conditions during the attempted conversion. Beginning in 1908 the risks in force steadily increased.

Quite aside from the specific problem of the Germantown surplus, the direct approach of the 1907 statute had serious disadvantages, for it made it difficult for companies to accumulate the surplus necessary to begin a sound advance-premium, nonassessable operation, which might be highly desirable in certain cases. It might be better to seek to prevent raids by more apt means than by preventing the accumulation of surpluses. The 1911 legislature, therefore, repealed the 1907 act and closed off dissolution as an avenue for raiding by forbidding payment to any member on dissolution of any sum in excess of the payments he had made plus interest at 6 per cent, the remainder to go to the school fund. Reorganization as an avenue for raiding was closed off by explicit prohibition of the reorganization of a domestic mutual as a stock company. Despite effectual elimination of dissolution and reorganization as raiding devices, there still remained the possibility of squeezing out policyholders and distributing the surplus to the insiders who remained. This would doubtless be impossible to do so quickly that the legislature could not take corrective action. With the legislature apparently alert to frustrate any raid, however subtly conceived, all effort to raid the Germantown apparently was abandoned. The company's scale of business grew constantly till mid-century, and its surplus grew also, though more gradually, to $753,181 in 1953.[38]

A case of reinsurance of a fraternal society with the total loss of the interest of old members led to public control of consolidation or total reinsurance agreements. The 1905 legislature forbade either, for life and disability companies, without approval of an ex officio commission responsible to protect policyholders by making a just and equitable order for the distribution of surplus assets. The legislature in 1937 applied a similar control to all domestic mutuals and made it the responsibility of the Commissioner. In 1947 the legislature extended the control and gave an important role to an ex officio commission consisting of the Governor or his deputy, the Attorney General, and the Insurance Commissioner.[39]

Enforcement of Capital Requirements

The basic sanctions for the enforcement of capital requirements were the refusal to out-of-state companies of a license to do business and administrative action against local companies to terminate their operations. The surveillance was real. In 1906 the National Casualty Company of Michigan, a stock company, sought admission to the state. Commissioner Host learned that the company was formed when the officers of the National Protective Society reinsured its business in the new company, looted the surplus, and themselves appropriated $40,000 of stock for alleged services in the reorganization. The Commissioner, with the approval of the Attorney General, refused a license on the ground that potential liability of the new company to account for the assets to the old policyholders impaired the capital. The company subsequently filed a new application accompanied by a certificate from the Michigan Insurance Commissioner that the new company had faithfully carried out its part of the reinsurance contract to the satisfaction of all 20,000 members of the earlier society, as evidenced by payment of new premiums in excess of $80,000. The Wisconsin Attorney General was less sure that all the members were satisfied, but concluded that they had ratified the reinsurance contract by the payment of premiums, that the capital therefore was no longer impaired, and that the Commissioner must issue a license. The power of surveillance was not directed to moral questions nor even to the integrity of management but only to the ministerial question whether there was, in fact, capital to the required amount and in the required form. Similarly, when the Old Line Life Insurance Company of America was organized under the Wisconsin laws, large sums were diverted for promoters' fees, but the Attorney General ruled that the Commissioner could not keep the company from doing business, for the remaining capital met the requirements of the law.[40]

This technical approach was not entirely satisfactory. The ruling of the Attorney General about the Old Line Life led Commissioner Beedle to ask for legislation controlling stock flotation; he pointed out the immorality of squandering 25 per cent of the funds paid in the process of organizing. In 1911 the legislature regulated stock flotation and limited the commissions paid on stock sales to 10 per cent, which it increased to 15 per cent in 1915.[41]

A favorite promotional device in the initiation of new life insurance companies was the sale of "profit-sharing bonds," usually in connection with life insurance policies. A limited class of bond holders was thus formed, and for a specified period one dollar per $1,000 of insurance written was set aside to be divided among the members of the class. Such bonds were used in Wisconsin, despite the strictness of the state's insurance laws.* Commissioner Beedle and Deputy Ekern sought to have such a bond declared a gambling contract and illegal, but the Attorney General ruled it to be merely a hypothecation of a portion of the profits of the company and perfectly valid. The Supreme Court also upheld it.[42]

The capital fund, once created, must be preserved against improper dissipation by the managers of the company. The 1850 general act provided that dividends which impaired the capital of the company would subject the directors and the stockholders receiving the dividends to joint and several liability in double the amount of the dividend. Many special charters had similar provisions. The 1870 fire and marine act provided for forfeiture of the charter if dividends exceeded those permitted by the act; in addition the stockholder was liable to the extent of the dividends received. Under some circumstances directors were personally liable for losses on risks insured while the capital was impaired. From the 1870 fire and marine act also came provisions giving to the Commissioner power to order stockholders to make up deficiencies in impaired assets, on penalty of dissolution of the company.[43]

§4. *Rate Making and Premium Collection*

The Regulation of Rates

Fire Insurance.—Rate making and premium collection were crucial to the provision of an adequate insurance fund. As a scheme for the distribution of losses among many persons subject to similar risks, insurance had an essentially mutual character, even when organized for private profit. The essential mutuality of insurance gave the policy-

*On April 29, 1909, the *Eastern Underwriter* (N. Y.; Boston) editorially twitted the state for its ambivalence in permitting these bonds while otherwise being so strict that it drove 23 companies from the state in 1907.

holder a stake in the adequacy of the premium, so that the fund would be sufficient to pay all losses. He also had a stake in seeing that the premium was neither unreasonably high nor discriminatory between classes of policyholders. Until rather late, however, the law left it to the forces of competition to see that premium charges were neither excessive nor discriminatory, and relied on capital and surplus requirements for stock companies and assessability for mutuals to guarantee the adequacy of the fund. Not until well into the twentieth century was more than passing attention given to the direct regulation of premium rates. Previously rates were made in the market place; companies might charge "such premium or consideration . . . as may be agreed on between the said corporation and the party or parties agreeing with them."*

Early Wisconsin fire insurance rating was very simple. The companies charged flat rates of perhaps one dollar per $100 for brick construction, and two dollars for frame. Later, local agents or field men made inspections, and developed a rough rating schedule.[1]

Losses seemed to follow cyclical patterns. A low loss ratio and high profits attracted newcomers by the prospect of quick riches. Insurance companies were easy to start, for a rented office, a few clerks, and some solicitors on commission would suffice. Moreover, if it did not set up adequate reinsurance reserves, a new company could enjoy an illusion of large profits even if the business were potentially insolvent, since the delay from premium payment to claims payment meant that income of even an unsound company would greatly exceed outgo so long as the business was expanding. Hence the frequently excessive competition forced premiums down to uneconomic levels and ultimately drove companies out of existence. Insiders claimed that there were long periods in fire insurance history when the whole business was carried on at a loss.[2]†

Faced with periodic threats to the integrity and the profitableness of their business, insurance men sought to organize the industry to eliminate anarchy. The first stage of organization, beginning as early as 1819, was the formation of local boards, whose members undertook

*Laws 1838–39, 36, § 2. Cf. Laws 1947, 487, § 203.32(3) (a) (2): "Rates shall not be excessive, inadequate or unfairly discriminatory."

†A company spokesman said, in FUA, Proc., 1877, p. 17, that 4,000 insurance companies had come into existence, but that only 1,000 remained, most of them local. Another said, in FUA, Proc., 1890, p. 91, that 700 stock companies, with $150 million in assets, had failed since 1860. FUA, Proc., 1874, p. 31, asserted a loss in fire insurance over the whole period from 1791 to 1850.

not to depart from established premium rates. At first these organizations were ineffective. The National Board of Fire Underwriters was born in 1866 and sought to systematize rate making, but because many industry representatives felt that the largest companies dominated it, it soon became moribund. Perhaps nothing more would soon have developed in the rationalization of the industry but for the Chicago and Boston conflagrations of 1871 and 1872, which destroyed scores of companies. The traumatic effect of these fires gave real impetus to the formation of combinations to make rates, and though competitive forces continually reasserted themselves, there was thereafter a continuous history of concerted rate making.[3]

The National Board came to life. Regional organizations were formed. During the 1870's the national and regional organizations emphasized the formation of state and local boards throughout the country. Though effectiveness varied a great deal, the industry quickly became highly organized. The control of rate making shifted from the national to the local boards, and on the local stage the drama of price fixing was played out in American insurance. In insurance, as compared with railroads and other public utilities, it may have had great significance for the legal validation of price fixing by the industry, that it was not industry-wide, nationally oriented "trusts" but local bodies that did the price fixing.[4]

No one ever doubted the purposes of these organizations. The promotion of "harmony and correct practice among the profession" was the stated object of the Northwestern Association, for example. Members were to report to the secretary all instances of "wanton reduction of rates among Local Agents." There was never a meeting thereafter without some attention, and usually protracted attention, to the problem of rate making and the creation of machinery to police the rates (FUA, *Proc.*, 1871, 2d. Reg. Meeting, pp. 11, 13).

In the view of the industry, these combinations were not to gouge the public. From a very early date, insurance men took the position that the business was a kind of public utility, existing to give an important service at a reasonable price. They insisted on the professional character of fire insurance underwriting and even classed it with medicine as a learned and liberal profession. People who consider themselves engaged in a public service profession, even if it is only in their more solemn and dedicated moments, must rationalize their conduct as in the public interest. The insurance men quite early developed a sophisticated theory: if insurance was to provide its intended protection, rates must be fixed and adequate, and prevention of rate competition was a necessity of sound operation of the business and should be sanctioned by forfeiture of corporate charters.[5]

A combination to fix rates was difficult to maintain intact and effective. The ease with which companies could be organized provided potential competition which made monopoly profits impossible, and the existence outside the boards of an enormous number of mutual companies, both commercial and local, provided actual, constant competition which kept rates down. Sometimes competition from the mutuals forced the board companies to abandon rate fixing on certain kinds of property. Nor were all of the stock companies necessarily amenable to the board discipline. The board companies were in competition with independents, and had to rely on the customer who wanted indemnity *"for the sake of security* and *not for speculation."* Competition sometimes even erupted into rate wars.[6]

Difficulties with enforcement of rate fixing compelled a constant effort to create new methods. In the 1880's the compact system developed. This involved heightened emphasis on the locality as the scene for agreements among local agents to respect rates set by compact managers, employed to carry out the agreements. Since competition made itself felt most keenly at the local level because of the commission method of compensating agents, it could best be controlled at the local level. Compacts began in Missouri in the early part of the decade and spread rapidly throughout the northwest. The effectiveness of the technique was suggested by the early enactment of anticompact legislation in various states.[7]

The new compact system of the 1880's created little interest in Wisconsin officialdom. In general the Insurance Commissioners were sympathetic to concerted rate making by the companies. In 1887, however, the Governor expressed mild concern with the "growing tendency of insurance companies to combine in fixing the rates of insurance and the division of business" (*Assembly J.*, 1887, p. 25). A bill relating to board rating was introduced; presumably it was an anticompact law. As a reaction to the growth of combinations, a Milwaukee representative started to draft a bill to create a state fire insurance company, but he abandoned his purpose before completing the draft.[8] In 1889 an anticompact law was introduced. Another bill would have made it unlawful for an agent to reduce existing fire rates and would have appointed a fee-compensated assistant commissioner in every village and city to collect all premiums and to fix rates for the locality. No new agents and no new companies would be permitted. In combination these two laws would have put insurance rates under a degree of social control not achieved till much later.[9] From 1893 until 1905 the antitrust sentiment was persistent, and antitrust bills were introduced in every session of the legislature. All failed, except an 1897 bill which forbade combinations to fix prices, except at the local level; it explicitly authorized local boards and local associations of insurance agents to fix rates. The persistence of anticombination sentiment in the 1890's is shown by the fact that this bill passed. It was a concession to such sentiment, but the weakness of the sentiment is clearly shown, too, for the 1897 law could have had little repressive effect since the normal method of rate making was at the local level. From 1899 to 1909, there were repeated efforts to eliminate the local exception from the 1897 act. Despite the growing strength of Progressivism in the state, no action was taken; usually there was no serious effort to press for passage of the bills. In 1903 the three bills put in the legislative hopper induced several local associations of fire insurance agents to send petitions opposing the legislation, but it is doubtful whether their concern was jusitified.[10]

The first proposal for centralized state control of insurance rates was made in 1899. The bill would have set up a board consisting of the Insurance Commissioner, the Secretary of State, and the State Treasurer, with power to set rates for accident insurance. When the bill was reintroduced in 1901, the rate fixing provisions were omitted. It was too early for such strong measures.[11]

The progressive administration of Robert M. LaFollette gave primary attention to the regulation of railroad rates. Such attention as insurance received was focused on the dramatic possibilities suggested by the 1906 life insurance investigation. The more fruitful but less newsworthy field of fire insurance rate regulation was left uncultivated. Though other western states had taken earlier action, the first indication of Wisconsin concern with the question was a 1911 letter of a "consulting fire insurance expert in the public interest," who sought professional employment on the ground that the Wisconsin rates were 25 per cent too high. Four months later the Wisconsin legislature passed a resolution calling for the appointment of a joint legislative investigating committee to survey the entire field of fire insurance, with special reference to rates, agency commissions and marketing methods, investments, and loss prevention.[12]

The committee held hearings for fourteen weeks and took 3,250 typewritten pages of testimony. It found that antitrust agitation had destroyed the compacts, and that in their place the industry had developed independent rating bureaus. Since the local boards were the only authorized rating authorities under the 1897 law, they were superimposed on the rating system in effect in other states. Milwaukee, Superior, and Madison local boards made their own rates; in practice the other local boards performed largely nominal functions, merely adopting the rates fixed by the Wisconsin Inspection Bureau, a private rate making body supported by subscriptions of the companies. The local board represented the interest of local agents—an interest in maximum commissions (and therefore in maximum premiums). Its local nature made it susceptible also to the pull and haul of local pressures for favored treatment of large risks. Its interests were adverse to preventive measures that would decrease the rates.[13]

The committee did not propose an enforced return to competition; it seized upon the public nature of fire insurance and the fact that competition increased acquisition cost and made rates higher, to recommend instead publicly controlled coöperative rate making. It proposed compulsory membership of all companies in rate making bureaus. Member companies should share the cost of operation and the control of the bureaus. Bureau membership must be open to any authorized company. An *ad hoc* commission to be appointed by the Governor should review the rates.

If the latter provision became law, the concept of a fair profit would be important. The committee took a middle position on profits, suggesting that it was misleading to parade alone the ratio of dividends to capital stock for the exceptionally successful companies, but that misleading also was the assertion by companies that they were poverty stricken because their underwriting profit (i.e., premiums less losses and expenses) was small or even negative. A large part of the assets of the companies consisted of unearned premiums, which were in reality trust funds belonging to the policyholders; investment income from such funds were properly a part of underwriting profit. A 1911 New York joint legislative committee had devised a special formula for computing underwriting profit. Though the Wisconsin committee discussed the New York formula and made suggestions for its modification, it was not prepared to decide whether the 10 per cent profit that the formula would yield in Wisconsin was excessive.[14]

The investigating committee recommended fifteen bills, of which eight became law. However, the basic proposal, to bring the rating process under social control, went down to smashing defeat. Its opponents demonstrated their strength by suspending the rules and disposing of the bill summarily; one of the opposition characterized the bill as "the most radical and drastic insurance measure ever offered to a legislature" (Milwaukee *Free Press* [Wis.], May 22, 1913). The insurance companies opposed especially the power of public representatives to review the rates. Compulsory bureau membership was another matter, and some company men strongly urged the system the committee recommended, except for the power to review rates.[15]

A committee of the National Convention of Insurance Commissioners, chaired by Wisconsin's Commissioner Ekern, recommended a similar system of control in 1914. By 1915 a dozen states were regulating the rating process, but Wisconsin, often a progressive leader, was not one of them.[16]

One of the Stalwarts in the legislature introduced a similar regulatory bill in 1915. It would have given the Commissioner power to determine whether rates were discriminatory or unjust, and if they were, to fix nondiscriminatory rates. The National Board of Fire Underwriters led the company opposition to the Commissioner's power to review and fix rates. Company representatives expressed fear of the growth of a bureaucratic octopus—the creation of a Commissioner's office with legislative, executive, and judicial powers. The companies said they would be forced to go into politics, something they claimed they had not done before. Some professed fear that rate regulation would drive all the small companies out of business, giving a monopoly to a few big companies. The companies were not making money in Wisconsin, some said. Some asserted that the failure of policyholders to complain in large numbers proved that rates were not excessive and that there was no demand for rate regulation. On the other hand, the Stalwart proponent of the bill expressed belief that rate regulation would save Wisconsin policyholders $2,000,000 a year, and emphasized the public utility character of insurance. The Commissioner pointed out that Wisconsin paid

$226 in premiums for each $100 loss, Kentucky $171, Kansas $156, Texas $143. The other states had regulatory laws while Wisconsin had none. He charged discrimination among cities, designed to drive out the mutuals. "Their methods in these towns are the methods of Standard Oil, of cut-throat secret cutting of rates" (Wisconsin *State Journal* [Madison], May 26, 1915). The companies made an unsuccessful effort in the Senate to emasculate the bill, and in the Assembly they succeeded in defeating it. Insurance men who were legislators supplied the leadership for opposition to the bill.[17]

The bill's defeat was dramatic; it plunged the issue of rate regulation into partisan politics. The Progressives castigated the Stalwarts for their lack of solicitude for the welfare of the people; they hit the Governor for his failure to reappoint Progressive Commissioner Ekern, who had achieved national recognition for his work as Insurance Commissioner. The Stalwart Governor replied that the Progressives, during ten years in power, had done nothing about high fire insurance rates but make political capital of them, and that his appointee, without compulsive legislation, had obtained agreement for a 20 per cent reduction in dwelling rates. The Stalwart author of the 1915 regulatory bill called the roll on the Progressives and showed that many of them had opposed the bill. The truth was that on the insurance issue neither Progressives nor Stalwarts could claim a monopoly of virtue.[18] Characteristically, the great leader of the Progressive movement joined the fight for adequate regulation of fire insurance rates only when its dramatic possibilities became sufficiently clear.*

The penchant of the Progressives for oversimplifying and dramatizing the conflict between good and evil was clearly shown in the 1917 legislature, when the Stalwarts once again introduced a regulatory bill similar to the one of 1915. Discriminatory or unreasonable rates were forbidden, and the Commissioner was empowered, either upon written complaint or upon his own motion, to review rates and order the bureau or insurer to substitute a reasonable and nondiscriminatory rate. Existing rates might continue until revised by the bureau. Though the bill receded a little from the strong position of 1915, critics undoubtedly went too far in declaring that its objective was an insurance monopoly. A compromise gave to the Commis-

---

LaFollette's Magazine (Madison, Wis.), Aug. 1916, editorialized that the "insurance scandal is a boil on the end of the administration's nose; it is red ripe; keep your eye on it."

sioner power to fix a reasonable rate after a finding of unreasonableness and removed the protection from existing rates. If the Commissioner should find that the rate was discriminatory, he could not fix the rate but could only order it corrected by the bureau. The bill had smooth sailing and passed both houses unanimously.[19]

The law represented attainment of two basic objectives: recognition of the public character of the insurance business and social control of insurance rate making. The control was substantial in extent. The new law compelled every company to be a member of a rating bureau. Membership must be open to all companies, and bureau control must rest on the basis of one vote for each company, though expenses were to be borne in proportion to Wisconsin premium income. The Commissioner might examine the rating bureaus. Risks might be specially rated only after inspection, and all rates were to be filed for permanent record in the bureau's office. The bill forbade unreasonable or discriminatory rates. Insurers might depart from bureau rates by a percentage uniform for all risks of a class, by filing such deviations with the bureau and the Commissioner. Upon hearing, the Commissioner might find rates discriminatory or unreasonable, and order changes, and in the case of unreasonable rates might himself fix a reasonable rate. Coöperatively the companies must maintain a stamping office; all policies must be stamped and violations noted, and instructions for corrections sent to the offending company. The rating bureau must fix rates for increases in hazard permitted by rider. The companies must classify risks as ordered by the Commissioner.[20]

The regulation was not merely a paper regulation. Indeed, at times it was fairly effective. On various occasions Commissioners suspended the bureau's rulebook, denied a war-motivated plea to increase premium rates, ordered the bureau to cease its criticisms of policies not in violation of law, ordered lower rates on Milwaukee dwellings, and permitted an increase in farm insurance rates to encourage firms to write rural policies.[21]*

The rulebook was the focus for extensive controversy. Some of the larger agents, especially in Milwaukee, had been accustomed, in palmier days, to use their stronger bargaining position to get favored treatment for their clients. They objected to the bureau's attempt, through the rulebook, to control rates, rules, forms, and

*Deputy-Commissioner Timbers, who was with the department as early as 1915, says that "the law had good administration from 1915 to 1923 under the terms of Commissioners Cleary and Whitman."—Letter to Author, Nov. 21, 1957.

riders, and sought to enjoin the enforcement of the rulebook. The court refused to reach the merits of the controversy, and held that the agents had no standing to complain, since their rights were derived solely from their companies, which wanted the rulebook enforced.[22]

On the other hand, the companies objected to the Commissioner's attempt to disapprove some of the rules in the book. In 1928 after an initial Circuit Court decision adverse to the Commissioner's power over forms and rules, the Supreme Court, in *Bureau* v. *Whitman* (196 Wis. 472) gave sweeping recognition to the realities of the twentieth-century administrative process: "Certainly if we are to have any regard for prior decisions or for 'common sense and the inherent necessity of governmental co-ordination,' we cannot hold the power . . . an unconstitutional delegation of legislative power" (*Id.* at p. 505). The decision gave the Commissioner effective power over rules and forms, as well as rates, despite the breadth of the language with which his powers were conferred.[23]

By 1929 there was dissatisfaction with the way the regulation system was working. In that year mutual insurance companies objected to a rate reduction filed by the Wisconsin Inspection Bureau, the local fire rating bureau, on the ground that they had not been consulted. This event led to a vigorous but not well-organized attempt to repeal the requirement that companies be members of a rating bureau. Compulsory membership, the leading advocate argued, placed smaller companies under domination of the larger and resulted in monopolistic practices. He contended further that a single bureau had complete control of fire insurance rating in Wisconsin, and that whatever the intention of the legislature may have been, the companies meant from the start to establish a fire insurance monopoly. Since 1917 no stock company had filed rates varying from those of the Wisconsin Inspection Bureau, whose very name he claimed misled policyholders to think the rates were fixed by the state. The bill had a stormy and brief existence and was defeated by steamroller tactics. A circular prepared by the Wisconsin State Association of Mutual Insurance Companies conjured up the spectre of unfair and cut-rate competition and wild-catting by nonbureau companies. It urged legislators to protect local agents and mutual companies by killing the bill.[24]

A resolution, also presented in 1929, to inquire into the Wisconsin fire insurance business fared better. The same advocate who had urged an end to compulsory membership in rating bureaus now alleged that the price fixing monopoly was gouging the state by over $3 million a year. He alleged a corrupt political bargain between stock company and mutual company managers to preserve the existing situation. The resolution provided for the appointment of an interim joint committee with broad powers to investigate rate making in fire insurance. The investigating committee held extensive hearings and reported to the 1931 legislature. Unlike the committee appointed in 1911, this one showed an attitude of deep suspicion of the motives of insurance men. The committee thought one purpose of the 1917 law was to provide a protective screen of legality for price fixing by a private monopoly controlled outside the state. The privately owned Western Actuarial Bureau actually determined the rates. "The theory of the rating law was to regulate the fire insurance companies, but the actual effect of the law is a price-fixing monopoly under foreign dictation."* The committee concluded that the powers of the Commissioner were largely ineffective; the bureau had almost uncontrolled power to make rates, and through the making of rules, had even materially affected the meaning of the standard fire insurance policy. It pointed out that there was no definition of "reasonable rates," and no statistics available for setting them, and that the accounts of the companies were not in such condition that the Commissioner could determine underwriting profit.[25]

The committee made drastic recommendations. The existing law should be repealed. All rates should be filed with the Commissioner and should be effective only after prior approval by him. The burden of proof on the question of reasonableness should be on the companies. The Commissioner should have power to review rates on his own motion and order them changed, subject to court review. Bureaus might be organized and must be open to any authorized company, but membership must not be compulsory nor might any bureau adopt a name likely to mislead the public into supposing the bureau to be a state agency. A stamping office must be maintained for control purposes. Alternative to its full recommendations, the committee urged voluntary rating bureau membership.[26]

Despite some industry opposition to even the existing degree of state control, the legislature enacted a modified version of the com-

*Rept. Wis. Legislative Interim Committee on Fire Insurance (1931), p. 29.

mittee's recommendations in 1931. The new law repealed the previous rating law. It continued to prescribe compulsory membership in rating bureaus, but a single company might operate its own bureau. Rating schedules must be filed with the Commissioner and must be reasonable and nondiscriminatory, and the burden of justification rested with the insurers. Though no precise definition of "reasonable rate" was given, reasonableness must be determined for the whole business, not for each insurer. The statute did not require prior approval of rates by the Commissioner, as recommended by the committee, but was firmer in tone than the previous law. At least it was widely thought that the Commissioner now had real rate-making powers. After a hearing he was to "order a change in any rate . . . if he finds such rate . . . to be unreasonable, unfair to the insured or the insuring public, or unfairly discriminatory" (Laws 1931, 437, §203.39).[27]

A 1935 bill to reduce fire premiums 25 per cent suggested some persistent dissatisfaction with the Commissioner's activity under the rate laws. Nevertheless, the statute did enable the Commissioner to prevent some discriminatory rating practices. Thus in 1936 the Commissioner ordered that companies cease to evade the rating law merely by altering the form of their policies; they must comply with their filed rates. Some companies were issuing fire insurance policies in the inland marine form, thus seeming to evade the established controls on fire insurance. The Northwestern National, a Wisconsin Company, issued a $90,000 policy covering the paintings in Milwaukee's Layton Art Gallery. The policy was in the inland marine form and was written at rates substantially below those filed by the company for similar fire risks. It was clear that the marine form was merest pretense, for hazards in transit were excluded. After the Commissioner gave formal notice demanding correction of the policy, the company sought to enjoin the bureau and the Commissioner from compelling corrections. The litigants smothered the trial judge with over a thousand pages of reading matter, but he thought the matter was very simple. Marine insurance involved transportation; hence this was fire insurance and subject to the rating law. The Supreme Court agreed; the company must adhere to its filed rates. It might file a deviation from the bureau rates but must do so for an entire class of risk. The evil seen by the court was not competitive rate reduction, but discrimination in favor of particular policyholders.[28]

The large reduction in rates offered the Layton Art Gallery by the

Northwestern National, a sound and reputable company, suggested that perhaps bureau rates were excessive. Sentiment again built up for a thorough investigation into the reasonableness of fire insurance rates. The attitude was based on the wide gap between premiums received and losses paid; a 1943 joint resolution stated that premiums collected in the six years from 1936 to 1941 amounted to $128 million, while losses in the same period were merely $52 million, thus raising clearly the issue of the meaning of "reasonable rates." Opponents of the probe urged that the figures did not take into account the high costs of operation. The resolution failed, on a vote that tended to follow party lines; Republicans opposed and defeated the investigation. In 1945 the Insurance Commissioner sought unsuccessfully to broaden the rating law to include substantially all property insurance. The key reform requiring prior department approval of filed rates was not proposed, but some additional assistance would have been given in the determination of a "reasonable rate."[29]

Meantime, in the fall of 1942 the United States Department of Justice obtained an indictment of 198 fire insurance companies and 27 insurance executives in Atlanta, Georgia, for violation of the federal antitrust laws. The elaborate structure of concerted rate making by company-dominated bureaus was probably in violation of the Sherman Act, protected only by the specious dictum, in the seventy–eight–year–old case of *Paul* v. *Virginia*, that insurance was not "commerce." Wisconsin joined with most of the states in filing briefs opposing the prosecution, contending that subjection of insurance companies to the Sherman Act would "result inevitably in Federal regulation destroying the sovereignty of the States in this field." The United States Supreme Court held that insurance was "commerce"; Congress then passed the McCarran-Ferguson Act, which preserved the basic structure of state regulation of insurance but specified that to the extent that the states chose not to regulate, the Sherman, Clayton and Federal Trade Commission Acts were applicable.[30]*

The 1947 Wisconsin legislature adopted the "All-Industry" bill, advanced, as a uniform law to satisfy the requirements of the McCarran Act, by a joint committee of the industry and the National Association of Insurance Commissioners. Under the new law, membership in an actuarial bureau was made voluntary. The new law

Paul v. *Virginia*, 8 Wall. (U.S.) 168 (1868). *U.S.* v. *Southeastern Underwriters*, 322 U.S. 533 (1944); 59 Stat. 33 (1945); 15 U.S.C., §§ 1011–15 (1952). See also Kimball & Boyce and references cited therein.

contemplated that administrative supervision be substantial, though there was no basic change from the former Wisconsin law. Rates were still in effect unless disapproved within a specified time by the Commissioner; it followed that the effectiveness of rate control still depended largely on the aggressiveness and qualifications of the Commissioner and his staff and the degree to which pressure could be exerted by crusading journalists or local politicians.[31]

In addition, many factors made adequate regulation difficult. The limited budget of the insurance department severely hampered its activities in rate regulation. Thus in 1948 the press reported that the department had recently approved an increase in automobile insurance rates without reviewing the supporting statistical data, simply because it lacked the personnel to conduct such a review. Also, until the legislature defined "reasonable rate' in more precise terms, there was room for disagreement over the legitimacy of various expenses and over the proper amount of underwriting profit. The Commissioner's attitudes on these questions would depend on his political philosophy and, perhaps more important, on whether he had a background in the insurance business and whether it was in the mutual or the capital stock side of the business. Conceivably his reaction might even depend on a venal conflict of interest resulting from stock ownership or hope of employment in the insurance business.[32]

In 1950 a new factor influencing the adequacy of regulation of fire insurance rates became apparent; in that year the Mayor of Milwaukee sought special reductions for his city, which had a loss ratio below the state as a whole. The Mayor's demands forced a broad scale hearing, and though the Commissioner did not feel there was justification for separate treatment for Milwaukee, he did order substantial rate cuts for the whole state. Not everyone was satisfied with the extent of the reduction, and politicians seized on the question for campaign ammunition. One candidate for the Republican nomination for Governor denounced the cuts as "pathetically small" and as "purely a political move" by the "big business interests supporting my opponent." Madison's *Capital Times*, too, seized on the issue for a crusade, which it continued year after year. Much of the controversy revolved around determination of a "fair underwriting profit." The Commissioner espoused a 2.5 per cent figure; the companies pointed to the 5 per cent which was standard elsewhere. Compromise was reached in 1950 when the companies accepted the Commissioner's proposed rate cut, in return for which he deleted specific reference to a 2.5 per cent underwriting profit. In the 1950's that issue was still alive and discussion of it was acrimonious, for the companies sought to eliminate the Wisconsin salient. Rate cuts in the early 1950's were almost an annual event, as a result of informal conferences between the bureau and the Commissioner's staff, but there is some reason to suppose that during most of that time the Commissioner was not making very strenuous efforts toward real regulation. In 1955 an inept Commissioner approved a rate increase over the vigorous protests of his staff. This ill-considered action threatened to blow up into a major political issue, but a timely resignation and the substitution of a strong Commissioner of the same political party, with a stronger sense of obligation to the public, undercut the political arguments on the subject. In mid-twentieth century Wisconsin, fire insurance rate regulation was in process of becoming effective; the attitudes of the public and hence of men in public life were generally favorable to it, but rate regulation was not yet sufficiently an administrative tradition to escape involvement in political and personal controversy. Every sign pointed to more effective regulation of rates as the years passed. Perhaps the most notable fact was that support of stringent regulation was becoming institutionalized, especially through municipal politics; the League of Wisconsin Municipalities took more than passing interest in the problem of fire insurance rates in the 1950's.[33]*

Rate regulation was less important for the highly localized mutuals; at least there was a tendency to exclude from the rate regulatory statutes town mutuals, domestic mutual cyclone companies, factory mutuals, and inter-insurance exchanges.[34]

Workmen's Compensation Insurance.—Social control of rating for workmen's compensation insurance developed simultaneously with that for fire insurance, at the very inception of the compensation insurance business. The need for regulation was at once apparent, for the premium cost to industrial policyholders was great. As early as 1913 the legislature required insurers to file classification and rate schedules with the Industrial Commission. The rates must be adhered to, without discrimination among policyholders. The 1917 legislature imposed a regime of control on compensation insurers even more

*The story of rate regulation in the 1950's was reported fully in the newspapers; a clipping file in LRef. Library makes many of them readily accessible.

rigid than it imposed on fire companies. All companies must belong
to a single bureau. A "Compensation Insurance Board," consisting
of the Insurance Commissioner, a member of the Industrial Commission, and an appointee of the Governor must approve a minimum
adequate pure premium for each class of business, a system of
schedule or merit rating, and minimum and maximum expense
loadings. Each company must file its rates with the Compensation
Insurance Board; rates must be nondiscriminatory. The long period
during which a company might continue liable to injured workmen
put a high premium on solvency and hence on adequacy of rates.
The legislation, following a recommendation of the Governor, showed
clear evidence of that concern.[35]

Schedule rating in compensation insurance applied debits and
credits to a basic rate through a set formula, and thus avoided discrimination. But the enormous sums sometimes involved created
sentiment for giving credits to the individual policyholder for his
favorable experience. To the extent that such experience accurately
reflected effective preventive practices of the individual policyholder,
it did not violate the principle of nondiscrimination, but to the extent
that favorable experience was merely adventitious, experience rating
frustrated the basic purpose of insurance—spreading of the risk. In
1921 the Governor vetoed a bill to provide experience rating, on the
ground that it would have an adverse effect on employment practices,
for to improve experience policyholders would crowd out older
employees in favor of younger men more agile at avoiding harm.
Moreover, employers would try to minimize compensation payments
in order to improve experience. The result would be to put people
on the level of the machine. In the Governor's view, although merit
rating was consistent with the humanitarian purposes of the compensation law, experience rating was not. However, the 1925 legislature
authorized experience rating for compensation insurance. It met the
Governor's objections by providing that, on determination of the
Industrial Commission, any employer applying an oppressive plan
of physical examination and rejection of employees should forfeit the
advantage of experience rating.[36]

Liability and Surety.—The 1919 legislature required liability companies to file rates and rules with the Insurance Commissioner; rates
must be reasonable and nondiscriminatory. The Commissioner might
review and disapprove discriminatory or unreasonable rates, and in

the latter case might fix a reasonable rate. No provision was made in 1919 for rating organizations, but the 1923 legislature forbade any insurance company to subscribe to such a rating organization unless its membership were open and it came under mimimal control of the Commissioner.[37]

Real control of liability rates, and especially of automobile rates, was slow to develop. An attempt in 1925 to require prior administrative approval of rates was opposed on the ground that actual prior approval was not practicable and that perfunctory approval would bias the Commissioner against later disapproval. In the mid-1930's there were attempts to subject automobile liability to definite control of the Commissioner, but the efforts were unsuccessful. In 1938 the Commissioner publicly criticized an increase in rates but was reluctant to assume power to do anything about it. A resolution to investigate automobile liability rates in 1947 might well have passed, and an investigation might have resulted in regulation, but the contemporaneous pressure of the McCarran-Ferguson Act made such action unnecessary, for Wisconsin passed the "All-Industry" casualty-surety bill as a counterpart to the fire rating bill. The provisions were closely parallel, but as of fire insurance rates, regulation did not thereby become real. In 1948 and 1951 the department approved automobile rate increases without hearing and without even a check of the statistics, simply because of inadequacy of staff. On the other hand, a rate increase was denied in 1957. The fire insurance rate regulation that was becoming effective in mid-century, had as yet no counterpart in the liability field. Regulation to prevent excessive rates might be less important in liability than in fire insurance, because of the greater significance of mutuals, which returned excessive premiums as dividends; on the other hand, regulation to ensure the adequacy of rates was as necessary for mutuals as for stock companies.[38]

For surety companies, the Commissioner was given power only to order the removal of discriminatory rates; reasonableness was not required by the 1919 statute. But the public had special concern with the reasonableness of premium rates for the bonds of public officials, since premiums on bonds were paid from public revenues. Some degree of control was exercised by a statutory limit of a quarter of one per cent on the amount of premium the state would pay. The Governor in 1921 vetoed a bill to remove that limit, in order to protect the public treasury against charges set by an unregulated non-competitive business. A joint resolution to investigate the cost of official bonds narrowly failed in 1945; then the 1947 rating act brought suretyship too, under public control.[39]

Life Insurance.—Life insurance rate making was altogether different. When Wisconsin insurance law was formed, the level premium method of operation was standard among commercial life companies, whether mutual or stock. Premiums did not increase with age as the risk of death increased (the so-called natural premium basis); instead they remained constant. In early policy years premiums were higher than the natural premiums, and the excess went into a reserve fund which was accumulated at interest. A concern furnishing level premium life insurance was thus a combination savings bank and life insurance company.

Generally the law relied on competitive forces to prevent excessive or discriminatory charges. In mutuals, at least, excessive premiums tended to return to the policyholders in the form of dividends; low net cost to the policyholder, rather than low premiums, was the desideratum. Wisconsin, virtually alone among the states, made a serious effort to place a maximum on life insurance premiums. The 1906 legislative committee investigating life insurance felt that in practice dividends returned by higher premium companies did not bring the net cost down to levels comparable to lower premium companies, and that, in any event, there was no guarantee that they would. The committee's consulting actuary violently opposed any premium limitation, however. The committee's own data, he said, showed the lowest net cost to be in the two highest premium companies investigated. The 1907 reforming legislature followed the lead of the committee and limited the maximum premium to the sum of a pure premium based upon the mortality table and interest rate assumed by the company, and an expense component which might not be more than a third of the net single premium on an ordinary life policy at the same age, on the 3 per cent American Experience Table.[40]

Theoretically the maximum premium provision might compel companies, in order to provide margins for contingencies and extra money for acquisition expense, to assume a rate of interest and adopt a mortality table that would unreasonably increase their reserve requirements for early policy years, thus preventing the companies from returning true surplus to the policyholders as dividends. The

1947 legislature gave more flexibility to the maximum premium; the pure premium component, which theretofore had been calculated on the basis of the interest assumption and mortality table used by the company for valuation purposes, now might be larger, so long as it did not exceed a premium which would mature the policy on the basis of the American Experience Table and 2 per cent interest. Because the American Experience Table showed unrealistically high mortality, especially at the lower ages, and because actual interest earnings never fell near 2 per cent, this rule gave the company substantial leeway to work out sales inducements and to provide a margin for contingencies, while still keeping maximum premiums under some control. This provision was still in effect in mid-century in Wisconsin, though there was no similar provision anywhere else.[41]

In fact, however, competitive pressures kept premiums well below the maximum. Indeed, the real problem for the law was that of putting a floor under premiums. This was done indirectly by requiring a "legal reserve" of funds which, together with future premiums, all accumulated at an assumed rate of interest, would be sufficient to meet the company's future obligations as predicted by mortality tables chosen by the legislature. The problem was complicated because the mortality tables chosen were always too conservative, i.e., they did not take sufficient account of the constantly lengthening life span of Americans. Competitive forces led the companies to use their own more realistic tables based on their own experience for computation of premiums, thus enabling them to charge premiums less than those they would need if the statutory tables were accurate. So long as the reserve requirement was met, the law was not generally concerned to ask how the premiums were arrived at. However, it not infrequently happened that the gross premiums (net premiums plus expense loading) computed on the companies' own realistic tables could safely be lower than the net premiums on the basis of the mortality tables used for valuation purposes. At this point, since the company apparently would not be receiving enough money to make up the tabular reserves, even completely ignoring the expenses of operation, the legislature called a halt by requiring a "deficiency reserve," which must come out of surplus.* Thus, unless the company was an old, well-established one with large surpluses, the deficiency

---

*See "Informal Discussion on a New Mortality Table," *Trans. Actuarial Soc. of America*, 1957, p. 212, for the actuarial theory of the deficiency reserve.

reserve law made it difficult to reduce premiums below this level, and the law tended to set an inflexible rate minimum; the company could hardly afford to set its gross premiums below the net premiums computed on the valuation table, lest it be required to provide a deficiency reserve out of surplus. In fact, however, competition did lead many companies to reduce premiums even below that line and to set up deficiency reserves out of surplus.[42]

Fraternal Life Insurance.—Initially fraternal societies collected assessments upon each death. Later they collected assessments periodically, and also graded assessments on the basis of the age of the member at entry. This straight grade plan was only slightly better; a step grading plan that increased assessments with age was more satisfactory because it approximated a natural premium basis. The only nineteenth-century legal limitation on the freedom of the fraternals to devise their own schemes was an 1895 statutory requirement that each assessment be large enough to provide $1,000.[43]

As the average age of the fraternal membership increased, the latent weakness of assessment operation in life insurance became apparent, and attention was given to the rates of premium. In 1898 the National Fraternal Congress recommended as a safe basis for premium computation a mortality table based on fraternal experience. To the older societies, which dominated the Congress, the problem appeared in the form of a competitive advantage of newer societies with younger members; older members thought new blood should join the old societies and take care of them, as expected in earlier decades. They proposed legislation which would require that new societies collect higher premiums based on the National Fraternal Congress table, with interest at 4 per cent. The older societies might continue on the lower rates, thus restoring to them a competitive advantage they had lost. The hope was that this would correct the age trend. The newer societies reacted violently to this recommendation. They formed the Associated Fraternities of America, and fought the so-called "Force Bill" bitterly and for the most part successfully. In Wisconsin, however, after unsuccessful attempts in 1901 and 1905, the 1907 legislature adopted the "Force Bill"; thereafter actuarially sound rates must be collected by fraternals subsequently organized or subsequently admitted to the state.[44]

Premium Collection

Legal regulation of rates was focused on the commercial companies; legal implementation of premium collection was concerned mainly, though not exclusively, with the assessment mutuals. Commercial companies, on the whole, were left to their own devices and the pull and haul of the marketplace, though eventually discriminatory practices led to some legal concern for premium collection problems of commercial companies.

The first mutual charter granted in Wisconsin, in 1837, provided that the insured should give his premium note for an amount to be determined by the directors and should pay a portion, not to exceed 7 per cent, in cash, the remainder to be payable on assessment whenever needed. Besides, the company might assess for an additional 1 per cent of the amount insured, beyond the premium note. The potential liability of the insured was thus greatly in excess of the amount of cash premium he paid.[45]

The principal weakness of the premium note plan lay in the small cash payment, which resulted from the pressure of capital scarcity in a frontier society. There was a constant tendency toward even greater reduction of the cash premiums, through short-term notes. This practice, common in times of financial distress, depleted reserves and necessitated frequent assessments. But assessments created uncertainty and destroyed confidence in the efficiency of the mutuals and by adverse competitive effect put limits on the tendency to smaller cash premiums. Conservative commissioners like Secretary of State Breese, in 1870 and 1871, urged the advantages of operation without assessments on premium notes. He pointed out that such practices had led once-large mutuals like the Madison and Dodge County Mutuals to the verge of insolvency, when hard times made assessments difficult to collect, as in the depression years of the mid-seventies.[46]

The pure assessment basis authorized for town mutuals and millers' and manufacturers' mutuals was used especially for purely local or highly informal organizations, where the closeness of control and intimacy of relationships would not only minimize the need for substantial sums of money for loss payments but, in theory, would facilitate collection of assessments without legal action. It was not often that pure assessment operation was justifiable, however, and some cash premium was nearly always contemplated. Operations on an assessment basis could be facilitated by charging separately a policy fee for the cost of issuing a policy. The 1909 legislature authorized such a charge up to $1.50 for city and village mutuals.[47]

Frequent uncollectability of premium notes created the most serious problem. When registration of town mutuals was conceived as a means of upgrading these important local companies, they were encouraged to operate by charging an advance "stipulated" premium, which was supposed to be sufficient for normal operation, but they also retained assessability of members as additional security for the adequacy of the fund. But even when it was not practicable to eliminate assessability, the law contributed in various ways to make the assessments collectible. For example, it might "void" the policy, or more accurately suspend it, if after 60 days an assessment remained unpaid.[48]

The law might also give the company a lien on the insured property to secure the premium note. At first the legislature required the filing of a memorandum with the county registrar of deeds, but later the lien was made automatic. Beginning in 1854, most of the charters of the Madison Mutual pattern, which had earlier contained the lien provision, omitted it, and a general act in 1855 repealed the lien for all previously granted charters. No explicit evidence explains this change in policy, but it is not unlikely that the resulting complication in real property titles was a reason. There were many unsuccessful efforts to revive the lien device; their persistence suggests the difficulty of adequately sanctioning assessment collection, but with few exceptions the lien device was not used in the twentieth century.[49]

Policyholders, too, were subject to risks inherent in the premium note technique. Company managers might negotiate the notes to holders in due course, so that the policyholders would be liable to the full face of the notes, even though the company did not need the money. The 1877 legislature minimized this risk by compelling companies to insert in premium notes language which would destroy negotiability, and thus would preserve the policyholder's defenses. The note was also made wholly void with respect to premiums accruing after insolvency or bankruptcy of the company. In 1883 an additional, and more subtle, safeguard was proposed. Exclusive original jurisdiction of suits to collect the notes would be given to the justices of the peace in the locality of the maker's residence.[50]

The premium note method of operation minimized the cash

required for insurance protection. On the other hand, frequent assessment was costly and unwieldy; assessment for each loss would dissipate what was saved. Two devices were developed to make such frequent assessments unnecessary. One was a provision authorizing mutuals to borrow money to pay losses. There were restrictions on the amount that could be borrowed, the duration of notes, the interest to be paid. The other device was a provision permitting mutuals to assess in advance of losses, thus lessening the number of assessments and reducing the costs and complications of operation.[51]

Over the long run, as it became less difficult for policyholders to find ready cash to pay premiums, the tendency was for mutuals to charge adequate original premiums and return any excess as dividends. In this they had the constant encouragement of the Commissioner. The change reflected the shift from a capital-scarce, near-subsistence economy to a market-oriented, cash-nexus economy. Despite this shift, a large proportion of policyholders in mid-twentieth century were still enough concerned with ultimate cost to purchase mutual, rather than stock, insurance. Moreover, even in the 1950's, a reduction in farm income in the state was important enough to lead to the organization of at least one new assessment company for windstorm insurance.[52]

Difficulty in collecting premiums from agents was a problem common to stock companies and the commercialized mutuals. Agents collected premiums and remitted them to the companies. Delaying premium remissions enabled the agent to use in his own business substantial sums of money belonging to his principal. Some money never reached the company, but even if it did the company lost the interest earnings. Pressures from the companies sometimes reached the level of legislative proposals in aid of the agency contract, but the legislature never actually interfered. Thus the 1913 legislature saw a proposal to require the agent to account to the company for each month's premiums within 45 days of the end of the month; in 1915 and 1917 bills sought to punish an improper taking by the agent as larceny; in 1933 a bill would have provided for revocation of an agent's license for misappropriation of premiums. None of the bills was necessary to make the agent accountable for his principal's funds, but all illustrated concern with the collection problem. However, the companies could protect themselves; often they required agents to furnish surety for payment of premiums collected.[53]

§5. *Marketing of Insurance*

The story of insurance marketing is primarily a chapter of entrepreneurial history. Legally declared public policy was little concerned to control or confine the way in which insurance was sold. On the other hand, the way in which the business set up its marketing structure played a significant, even decisive, role in shaping the law of claims administration. The development of a commission-compensated agency system was largely responsible for the vast increase in the insurance business in the nineteenth century; at the same time it created serious tension between the self-interest of the agent and his fiduciary duty to the company. Upon this tension was focused a large part of the litigation over the administration of claims.[1]

The earliest statutes had little specific to say about marketing. For example, the 1870 fire and marine insurance act only required that agents procure certificates of authority from the Secretary of State, and declared that embezzlement of funds by the agent was larceny.[2]

The Form of Insurance Contracts

Insurance contracts were relatively complicated, and from a period long before the settlement of Wisconsin, oral contracts of insurance were relatively uncommon, except as temporary binders preliminary to the issuance of a written contract. But oral agreements were always held valid if they were within the authority of the agent and if all of the terms were certain. However, with healthy skepticism, the Court tended to set an exacting standard for the proof necessary to establish the existence of an unwritten agreement.[3]

The rule that oral contracts of insurance were valid subjected the companies to the risk of adverse findings on contested and obscure facts. The companies sometimes sought protection in a statutory requirement of a writing. Bills to require that insurance contracts (or at least fire insurance contracts) be in writing in order to be enforceable were introduced in 1897, 1905, and 1909.[4]

In 1923 the Supreme Court, influenced by the uncertainties inherent in parol transactions, held that the accident and health insurance standard provisions law impliedly forbade oral contracts of accident insurance, though it did not expressly prohibit them. But in the same year, in *Milwaukee Bedding* v. *Graebner* (182 Wis. 171), the court refused to extend this doctrine to fire insurance; however, it conceded that the language of the standard fire policy statute (*Laws* 1917, 127) could not be distinguished on this question, and it pointed out the importance of oral binders in fire insurance: "It would operate as a serious disturbance of settled notions, as well as of the manner in which fire insurance business is conducted, to hold that the insured was without protection until the written policy was issued or delivered. We feel that the abolition of this long settled custom requires express legislative declaration" (*Id.* at p. 180). The court was influenced, also, by the fact that there was a single standard fire policy, to the terms of which the oral contract could be assimilated, but that there were various alternative standard provisions for the accident and health policy. Subsequently the court held valid an oral contract of automobile insurance and even expressed the view, as dictum, that an oral life insurance contract would be valid, notwithstanding the complexity of such a contract and the fact that such a transaction would be unusual.[5]

The Multiple Lines Problem

An attitude pervasive around the turn of the century restricted the scope of insurance company activities to a single line of insurance, or to a few related lines. The paucity of early insurance operations outside the basic fields of fire, marine, and life make it impossible to be certain how early the feeling became prevalent. The scope of some of the early Wisconsin special charters suggest that this view was not taken in the first half of the nineteenth century, for those companies were authorized to offer all lines of insurance then in existence. On the other hand, the practical improbability of extensive combined operations made restriction academic at that early date. In mid-nineteenth century, fire and marine lines tended to be combined, at least in the commercial companies; neither was combined with life to any substantial extent, because of the basically different nature of life coverage.[6]

The origin of the doctrine forbidding combinations of lines is a matter of speculation. Partly the attitude may have reflected lingering anticharter doctrine—hostility to and fear of aggregations of capital.

Partly it may have come from fear of discrimination among classes of policyholders. Partly it may have indicated a judgment on the efficiency of management—that operations in many lines must be less efficient than specialization in one. Partly it may have implied an underwriting judgment on the dangers of multiple line operation, especially on careless additions to coverage without additions to premiums. However, if charges were adequate, combination of lines should be desirable from an underwriting point of view, by adding a dimension to the spread of the risk. Partly the doctrine may have reflected only the case-by-case growth of insurance legislation. During the latter part of the nineteenth century, the legislature enacted separate authorizing statutes for each new kind of company, even if it were merely a specialized fire company. Thus druggists' mutuals, city and village mutuals, retail lumber dealers' mutuals, all had their own authorizing statutes. So also, new lines of insurance were authorized by special statutes, and only around the turn of the century was there a substantial effort to systematize the law and authorize all kinds of companies under a single statute.[7]

The truth probably lies in a combination of these factors, with a heavy emphasis on the last one. The tendency throughout Wisconsin experience was toward a gradual broadening of the authorized combinations, though the persistent feeling was that combinations must be specifically authorized, as the Attorney General ruled in 1896.[8]

The 1909 statute which systematized the legislation authorizing organization of insurance companies was the highwater mark of the doctrine forbidding multiple lines. It permitted three kinds of combinations, forming the fire, life, and casualty triumvirate. Companies might combine fire, marine, and sprinkler leakage, or they might combine life and disability, or they might combine the remaining validated lines, collectively called casualty; disability might be combined with either casualty or life. In this development Wisconsin law followed a pattern common in the United States. The restriction on the combination of lines was responsible for the formation of casualty subsidiaries of the great fire companies, often wholly owned and under virtually identical management. In Wisconsin, however, the Supreme Court held illegal the formation of casualty subsidiaries, because investment in the stock of its own subsidiary was outside the permitted range of investments under the strict Wisconsin law.[9]

The 1915 legislature significantly liberalized the multiple lines doctrine by authorizing any combination of lines, provided separate reserves in trust were maintained for each kind of insurance thus written. Two unsuccessful bills would have permitted the issuance of a single policy whenever the lines represented by the policy were combined in a single company. In 1919 the doctrine that required separate policies for each line of business was relaxed to permit fire and sprinkler leakage, fire and burglary, or liability and disability, to be combined.[10]

In 1947 the legislature permitted companies authorized to issue burglary policies to issue all-risk policies of the personal property floater type, and insurance against loss of securities, though both were normally regarded as inland marine. In 1951 the multiple lines doctrine was virtually repealed. The only remnant was that companies writing both life insurance and other lines must keep separate reserves in trust; one for life and one for the other lines. This remaining fragment of the doctrine reflected only the basic differences in the nature of life insurance, and its attendant management problems, that distinguished it from other lines of insurance. Nevertheless, heavy losses on automobile business in the 1950's led many casualty and fire companies to go into life insurance, to gain additional stability.[11]

Limitations on Agents

There is nothing inherent in the agency relationship or in the special problems of insurance marketing that precludes corporations from acting as insurance agents. Yet when the problem arose formally in 1903, the Attorney General ruled the incorporation of a fire insurance agency to be unlawful. He found in the general incorporation statute no specific authorization for the incorporation of an insurance agency. He read the act's omnibus approval of organization "for any lawful business or purpose whatever" by the rule of *eiusdem generis,* to include only purposes of the kinds already specified. The 1907 legislature adopted this policy and enacted that no corporation might act as a life insurance agent in soliciting, selling, or placing insurance policies. In 1911 this policy was generalized to all lines of insurance; no corporation might be agent for any company required to pay tax or license fee to the state. On a surprising number of occasions the Attorney General found it necessary to point to the 1907 and 1911 statutes and reaffirm the state's policy against incorporated agents; the number of such incidents suggests a strong tendency toward incorporation of even such relatively small and personal enterprises. In 1916 he ruled that a corporation might not act as attorney in fact for an inter-insurance exchange. In 1917 he had to make the same ruling for a fire insurance agency, and in the same year he ruled that a national bank might not act as agent for an insurance company, despite the federal authorization of the bank. An unsuccessful effort was made in 1919 to except both state and national banks from the rule forbidding corporate agents. As late as 1925 the Attorney General repeated his ruling to apply it to a building and loan association. The rule against corporate agents invalidated an assured savings and estate plan by which a bank obtained insurance for its clients and paid premiums for them through a savings account. But when the insurance was already in existence the plan was valid.[12]

However, there was inconsistency in the policy about corporate agents. The Attorney General ruled that a bank might collect life insurance premiums if it obtained an agent's license. So also, the 1911 legislature authorized commissions to be paid by agents to domestic corporations, but to prevent the formation of corporations merely to save commissions, an exception was made for the case when officers, employees, or stockholders of such corporations were also interested in the property at risk. In the latter event there was illegal rebating.[13]

Licensing and Examination of Agents.—At first the Commissioner licensed agents directly. This was an administrative task of no small magnitude. The 1909 legislature substantially lessened the Commissioner's burden by authorizing the companies to issue licenses to their agents; the Commissioner preserved control of the licensing process, since he might still revoke the licenses, but the heavy clerical burden was transferred from the department to the companies. The 1917 legislature returned licensing of life insurance agents to the Commissioner; similar bills for all insurance failed in 1919 and 1927. The 1951 legislature returned to the Commissioner the task of issuing initial licenses.[14]

Beginning in the second decade of the twentieth century, there was increasing sentiment for an examination to precede the licensing of insurance agents. The motivation for such measures was complex; partly it represented a feeling, both inside and outside the industry, that insurance agents needed professional competence, which should be assured by the state, and partly it represented a desire of agents already in business to foreclose at least some of their potential competition. The latter motivation was especially apparent in a 1913 bill proposing an examination program for fire insurance agents, for another provision of the bill would have forbidden fire companies to appoint additional sales representatives in territories where they already had agents.[15]

Bills providing for compulsory examinations for new insurance agents were offered without success in 1931, 1935, 1939, and 1943. In 1946, a Madison area meeting of the Wisconsin Association of Insurance Agents unanimously supported an adequate licensing law. In 1947 a bill sponsored by that association proposed state licensing of agents; a "grandfather's clause" would protect existing agents from subjection to the examination requirements. The Wisconsin Mutual Insurance Alliance objected on the ground that the requirement would prejudice the extensive use of part-time insurance solicitors by the mutuals. Other special interests, as well, fought the bill, including spokesmen for the Wisconsin Association of Finance Companies, who opposed unless auto salesmen were excluded. After a great deal of maneuvering the bill was defeated in the Assembly by a vote of 55 to 38.[16]

A similar bill, applicable to life insurance agents, was introduced in 1949. It was strongly supported by the commercial insurance interests, especially by the agents, but was opposed by the Wisconsin Farm Bureau Federation, which did life underwriting among farmers. There was opposition also from insurance interests other than life, although these groups would not be directly affected unless compulsory examinations should be extended to them. Despite the opposition the bill was enacted.[17]

During 1950 the fight for enactment of agents' licensing in the property insurance field was renewed. Farm organizations again registered vehement protest. Opposition to the bill was once more too strong in 1951; the bill made no progress. Though it did not become law in 1953 either, it did pass the Assembly 63 to 19; in the Senate it lost after nine roll-call votes and complicated parliamentary maneuvering. Finally in 1955, the "fence-me-in" licensing bill was passed and signed by Governor Kohler.[18]

Control of Unfair Marketing Practices

Misleading Advertising and Sales Talk.—The technical character of insurance made it possible for unscrupulous agents and companies to victimize insurance buyers. At a fairly early date legislation sought to curb the worst marketing excesses of companies and agents. In 1878 the legislature forbade publication of misleading advertising about the nature or assets of fire insurance companies; any public announcement or advertisement of assets must contain full information about cash capital, surplus, and reinsurance reserve. In 1882 the legislature added to the monetary penalties of the 1878 act the sanction of revocation of license. The 1898 revision applied these provisions to all lines of insurance.[19]

Misleading statements about dividends, especially in the case of tontine policies, were a common practice in life insurance selling. The 1907 legislature forbade advertising which misrepresented the terms of life policies or the dividends to be received thereon. The 1913 legislature forbade also sales presentations of promised or predicted future dividends or net cost unless they be mathematical calculations from the assumptions of the policy; such figures must be filed with the Commissioner.[20]

Much business was done through large general agencies, and policy-holders often assumed that the agents were the insurers. The 1915 legislature forbade advertising which tended to misrepresent or conceal the true identity of the insurer. Policies must make clear by the size of print which was insurer and which was general agent.[21]

In 1919 the legislature passed a bill to forbid wilful misrepresentation of the terms of the policy or of the financial standing or of the management of another company. Violation would be stringently sanctioned by fine or imprisonment and revocation of license. Though the bill only applied to wilful misrepresentations, the Governor thought it too drastic and vetoed it. However, a similar bill became law. It applied to wilful and malicious derogatory statements about the financial condition or solvency of some other types of financial institutions; in 1923 there was an unsuccessful attempt to extend the act to include insurance companies. It was extended in 1931 to domestic mutuals in fire, casualty, and workmen's compensation.[22]

It was natural for insurance buyers to assume that life insurance policies were on a legal reserve basis; the 1923 legislature saw an unsuccessful bill to require policies not meeting the valuation standard of the American experience table at 4 per cent to contain, printed in red letters an inch high, the words "National Fraternal Congress Reserve," "Assessment Plan," or other applicable reserve plan.[23]

Control of misleading advertising was not limited to commercial companies; the 1895 act regulating fraternal societies forbade issuance of a license to any such society whose literature was misleading and required that every such company that did not pay the full face value of its certificates explain in its literature and in its solicitations how much was paid. Names might mislead, too; the 1901 legislature required the words "Town Insurance Company" to form part of the name of every town mutual and forbade use of such words to other corporations.[24]

Discrimination Among Policyholders.—Though there was discrimination and favoritism in retailing insurance, the practice did not rise to the level of a great public issue, nor did it provide the companies with ready means to subvert the processes of government, as the use of the railroad pass did in the late nineteenth century. Still, moral revulsion at the excesses in the use of the railroad pass had its counterpart in a dislike for discrimination in insurance marketing.

Discrimination was most apparent in life insurance, where it usually took the form of rebating. Tontine policies provided huge surplus funds with which company management might play. In the 1870's this led to higher and higher agency commissions in a battle among the giants for primacy in the industry. The higher commissions gave the agents the competitive weapon of a margin of funds which they could share with applicants in the form of rebates. Rebates uniform throughout the business would not differ from a lower premium and smaller agency commission. But rebates had a highly adventitious aspect, and in application they were grossly unfair.[25]

During the 1880's there was an effort to suppress these marketing practices. Conservative insurance men were in the lead in seeking to control the excesses of their own competition. Bills were introduced in various legislatures to control rebating; in 1891 the Wisconsin legislature forbade any distinction or discrimination between insured persons of the same class and expectation of life, whether by initial rate differentials or by subsequent rebates.[26]

In the twentieth century, as rating regulation became a reality, the principle of nondiscrimination became an essential ingredient of every statutory rate standard. Commissioners and Attorneys General gave it extensive application; for example, they invoked the doctrine once to prevent back dating of life insurance policies to change the age of entry and once to require that a paid-up annuity issued at the time a policy lapsed be proportioned to the reserve instead of to the number of premiums paid. The Attorney General by his ruling on this last question in effect incorporated the whole of actuarial science into the notion of nondiscriminatory rating.[27]

Rebating was only a symptom, however. The problem was excessive commissions, which made the agency system uneconomic and necessitated legislation to preserve it. Sometimes such legislation produced unjustifiable results. Thus when in 1940 the Banking Commissioner had to liquidate a building and loan association, he sought to save agent's commissions involved in purchasing the necessary insurance on the property held by the association, by arranging for wholesale purchase from general agencies. The Attorney General ruled the plans violated the antirebating law; he thus prevented the Commissioner from making an economically justified saving. Fortunately the Banking Commissioner was able to solve the problem by buying mutual insurance. But the incident pointed up the fact that the antidiscrimination laws were helping to shore up a marketing system that in many situations was uneconomic.[28]

The pressures for rebating were not easily thwarted by mere legal proscription; those who would rebate sought legal devices to evade the prohibition. The most used device was the local advisor, or the advisory board contract, by which certain policyholders were appointed to an advisory board of limited membership, and among them was to be divided a certain sum obtained from all new contracts over a period of time. The "advisor" must furnish names of prospects to the company, and cause the company to receive premiums on a specified amount of insurance. In fact, however, such contracts were inducements to the purchase of insurance, and thus were disguised rebates. After careful analysis, the Attorney General ruled in 1903 that such a contract was an illegal rebate. In 1906 the Attorney General said that each such case must be decided on its merits, since the law was passed only to stop rebating and not to alter the marketing structure of the business; legitimate service contracts might be entered into in the free discretion of management. Nonetheless he held a "special inspectors' contract" void as an illegal rebate, since it was entered into simultaneously with the issuance of the policy and as an inducement to it. The Supreme Court, too, held void a "special agent's contract" entered into as an inducement to take out insurance, and permitted the policyholder to recover the initial premium paid on the accompanying policy, on the ground that the object of the statute was to protect policy-holders, and thus the plaintiff policyholder and the company were not equally at fault. The court also pointed out that the contract was still executory, and in subsequent cases used this as a basis for qualifying the rule; emphasizing the bad effects upon the nonfavored policy-holders of permitting the favored ones to make claims on the com-pany's surplus, the court refused a policyholder's claim to recover four annual payments already made. But the judges continued to refuse recovery to the policyholders on the special agent's contract, if the contract were shown to be a rebating device.[29]

The Des Moines Life Insurance company had issued many special agents' contracts of the kind invalidated by the Supreme Court. The company sought to keep faith with such policyholders by replacing these contracts with fifteen-payment life policies backdated to the date of the original contract. But the Attorney General ruled that this action would be an illegal discrimination and rebate, since the initial contracts were entirely void.[30]

The 1907 legislature also sought to improve the machinery for enforcing the principle of nondiscrimination. It withdrew the privi-lege against self-incrimination and, instead, granted to witnesses im-munity from any prosecution arising out of transactions in which they were compelled to testify. In 1911 the legislature substantially revised and systematized the statutes on discrimination and rebating. The new legislation made it against the policyholder's interest in security to accept a rebate, by providing that he should suffer proportionate reduction of his coverage for knowingly accepting a rebate. The legislature forbade agents to insure their own property unless they were also doing other insurance business in volume at least equal to the insurance taken for themselves. A careful specification was made of the persons with whom an agent might lawfully share commissions; he might share with any other agent licensed in Wisconsin, and under some circumstances with nonresident agents. The Commissioner was given broader discretion in determining the length of time during which a license would be suspended.[31]

Commissioner Fricke believed that rebating was not evil in itself; but that it produced other evils, such as lapsing and twisting. Twist-ing was the practice of encouraging policyholders to drop existing policies and take out new ones. In life insurance this was a vicious practice, because the initial years of a policy were those in which the policyholder got least value; much of the early premium went for agency commissions, and precisely this fact led agents to twist. Twisting in itself was never illegal; however, the 1907 legislature forbade the written misrepresentations often involved in twisting and made violation by an agent or company officer a criminal offense. The 1915 legislature made a criminal offense of all misrepresentations, oral or written, to induce any person to take out life or disability insurance or to surrender such insurance. The 1929 legislature extended this provision to all insurance.[32]

Usually antidiscrimination laws ministered simply to a generalized dislike for unfair marketing practices. But toward mid-twentieth century, an increasing concern in America to achieve a society which did not discriminate among people on the ground of race or color had its effect on insurance law. A 1937 civil rights bill, among other things, would have forbidden life or automobile insurance companies to engage in rate or other discrimination between Negroes and whites. Amended to apply only to automobile insurance, the bill passed the Assembly by the overwhelming vote of 56 to 19, but in the Senate lost in the end-of-session rush. In 1939 a similar bill applying to life insurance was introduced; the measure eventually passed in that session but in its enacted form the bill only forbade persons to refuse to sell automobile insurance on the ground of race or color, or to discriminate in rates on those grounds. Bills in 1951 and 1953 would have forbidden the state life fund to discriminate on the ground of color. Though neither passed, the Supreme Court of Wisconsin achieved the objective on policy grounds; without specifically invoking the Constitution, it forbade the insurance department to decline insurance or to make a rate distinction on the basis of race or color.[33]

Discrimination Among Agents.—Though most discrimination was among policyholders, there was a little concern, as well, about discrimination among agents. Legal regulation of compensation arrangements of companies with their agents was a much more serious intervention in management than the prevention of discrimination among policyholders, since it removed from management the privilege of determining the relative value of its employees.

A bill in 1909 forbidding discrimination in commissions among local agents and limiting general agents' commissions to a set relation to local agents' commissions, was nearly successful. A bill in 1915 also sought to forbid discriminatory commissions among agents; in addition to the forfeitures and monetary penalties that would have implemented the 1909 bill, the 1915 proposal would have permitted the lower-commissioned agent to sue for and recover at the higher rate, thus bringing agents to the support of the policy. Frequent bills to prevent tax assessors from acting also as agents for insurance companies perhaps sought to prevent unfair competition, partly by preventing the property tax assessor from making use of his superior knowledge of the property in the community to the disadvantage of other agents, and partly by preventing him from making use of his superior position as assessor to show favoritism in tax assessment to his insurance clients; combination of the roles of insurance agent and tax assessor in the same man might not only give him competitive advantage but also subvert the integrity of government processes. Such bills were introduced in 1891, 1897, 1905, and 1913; they were all unsuccessful. A bill in 1915 would have forbidden any income tax assessor to be an insurance agent. Unlike the previous bills, it was nearly successful.[34]

Likewise the 1941 legislature refused to forbid life companies to reduce the compensation of industrial agents for policy lapses; nor would it pass a bill in 1945 to require life insurance agents to be full time agents. In the latter case the political strength of rural areas, where part-time agents were common in the local mutuals, played a part in the defeat of the bill.[35]

On the other hand, when the insurance adviser developed as a purportedly impartial expert adviser to the policyholder, the legislature was willing to try to prevent his subversion through self-interest by forbidding him to receive any part of his compensation from the company, whether directly or indirectly.[36]

The 1947 legislature broadly proscribed unfair methods of competition, making more extensive the existing system of marketing regulation. It did so in order to prevent the application of federal marketing statutes to insurance, as prescribed by the McCarran-Ferguson Act. In 1957 the legislature forbade sellers or persons engaged in financing purchases of real or personal property to coerce the buyer in selection of an insurance agent; instead, the latter must be informed of his right of choice. Reasonable exercise of a right of approval was permitted. The Wisconsin Insurance Agents Association sponsored the bill.[37]

Subversion of Government Processes

From an early date it was established public policy in Wisconsin to forbid public officials at all levels of government to have any pecuniary interest in transactions with the public body they represented. Determining the scope of the proscription was a recurrent task of the Attorney General. Thus he held that a public library board might not place insurance on the library building in a company of which a board member was a director; the board might, however, place it through the insurance agency of which the library officer was a member, if he did not personally share in the commissions. It was necessary to restate the rule constantly in very obvious situations. Thus the Attorney General ruled that the county board might not insure county buildings through a member of the board, that it was illegal for the district attorney, as agent, to write insurance for the county, and that it was illegal for a city officer to solicit insurance from the city, even if he did not receive the commission. The Attorney General thought the prohibition applied even to a mere stockholder in an insurance company.[38]

In 1915 the legislature excepted from the prohibition the sale of commodities to an amount not exceeding $100 per year, and the Attorney General ruled that insurance was a commodity within the meaning of the provision. In 1922 the Attorney General changed his position on this matter, and held that insurance was not a commodity, so that the $100 exemption did not apply to insurance premiums. In 1938 the Attorney General came around once again to the view that insurance was a commodity.[39]

In 1924 the Attorney General expressed the opinion that a policy issued in violation of the statute would not be void, but would protect the county, notwithstanding a Supreme Court holding that sales of personal property were completely void under analogous circumstances. The distinction between the cases might merely be that in the sale case the seller was seeking payment, whereas in the insurance case the public body was seeking to realize the protection on which it had relied. It was not technical notions of "voidness" but underlying public policy that motivated the court.[40]

Chapter Four

PROTECTING THE INTEGRITY
OF THE INSURANCE FUND
AGAINST DISSIPATION

Level premium life insurance was, in effect, a combination insurance policy and savings account. In the early years of the policy the premiums were larger than required for pure insurance, and the excess charges were accumulated in reserves for the later years when death claims exceeded premiums collected; the increasing reserve made the policy less insurance and more savings account as it grew older. In mid–twentieth-century America, such reserves reached the hundred billion dollar mark. Fire and casualty insurance companies also collected large sums of money in advance premiums. The funds so accumulated had to be preserved and increased by wise and safe investment, so that the funds would be adequate to pay the losses as they occurred, often many years after the premiums were paid. However complete the company's legal ownership of these funds, they were in function trust funds, belonging to the whole body of policyholders, and often the courts so designated them. The preservation of the integrity of these "trust funds" became a major problem of public policy, for such enormous sums of money tempted the venal, the ambitious, or the foolish. Possibilities were legion for misuse of the funds in ways that did not transgress the ordinary criminal law, and it early became an objective of social policy to exercise more thoroughgoing control over the administration of insurance company assets than the criminal law afforded. The basic principles of social control long antedated the turn into the twentieth century.[1]

§1. *Restrictions on Investment*

Social policy and sound business practice were agreed that the basic principle of insurance company investment should be to maximize yield so far as consistent with absolute safety of the principal sum.

Even the application of the principle was never a matter of serious controversy. Thus, in Wisconsin in the first half of the twentieth century, about three out of every four introduced bills dealing with investment control were enacted into law on first introduction. Some others passed later.

Early Regulation of Investment

Two major phases can be discerned in the development of investment control in Wisconsin. Before 1870, control was relatively haphazard, highly diverse, and relatively ineffective, though the tendency was constantly to tighten the control. In the late 1860's, an attitude sympathetic to strict control of investment came to dominate the legislature. Special charters led the way in 1868 and 1869. Then the general acts of 1870 sought to bring under systematic regulation all companies organized in the state, whether formed under the general acts or by special charter. After 1870 there was a consistent tendency, relieved in nearly a century by only one or two exceptions, toward a gradual broadening of the narrow categories of investment authorized by the 1870 law, as experience and developing economic sophistication permitted. The nature of the particular insurance enterprise was always significant. Life insurance received separate treatment from the beginning, and sometimes particular forms, such as fraternal benefit societies or state funds, were singled out for special treatment.[2]

Strict limitation of insurance investment had early origins. For example, the 1795 charter of the Massachusetts Fire Insurance Company provided that its capital must be invested in the funded debt of the United States or of Massachusetts, or in stock of the United States Bank or of any incorporated bank of Massachusetts. The control extended only to capital, however, not to all assets. Similarly strict limits were nearly universal among Massachusetts charters of the period. Some charters permitted companies to invest in mortgages and in ground rents. Occasionally a charter permitted a company to invest in stocks, or in loans on such security as the directors might order. Most companies might also invest a specified fixed sum in real estate. In 1818 a general act permitted companies to invest capital in the funded debt of the United States or of Massachusetts; in the stock of the newly chartered Second Bank of the United States, or of any incorporated bank in Massachusetts; and in loans on respondentia or bottomry bonds to any citizen of Massachusetts, provided no more than half of the capital stock might be so loaned to any one person, nor more than one-tenth on any one bottom. Moreover, up to two-thirds of the capital stock might be loaned on mortgage of Massachusetts real estate; or on pledges of the public stocks of the United States, of the Bank of the United States, or of any Massachusetts incorporated bank.[3]

Haphazard and diverse investment control was characteristic of the early period in Wisconsin. The most common investment restriction was a provision forbidding the acquisition of real estate except within closely defined limits. Two kinds of real estate might be acquired; real estate for operational purposes and real estate acquired in the bona fide enforcement of lien rights in land. The second class arose out of the permission—nearly universal in Wisconsin (and in New York) though uncommon in Massachusetts—to invest to an unlimited extent in real estate mortgages. The restriction on acquisition of real estate probably reflected a mortmain policy, not an investment control. True fund-security restrictions on investment in real property appeared in the almost universal requirement of a margin of safety for mortgage investments; the mortgaged land must be worth 50 per cent or 100 per cent more than the loan. In addition, one or two mutual charters limited the term of mortgage loans to a year, with interest payable half-yearly, the debt to accelerate on default of interest payment.[4]

Before the Civil War, no other investment restriction was commonly found in the Wisconsin special charters. Usually investments might be made in whatever assets the directors felt were desirable. Thus the directors of the Wisconsin Insurance Company were authorized to employ its funds "in the purchase of public or other stock, or in any other monied transactions or operations." On the other hand, the 1850 insurance act provided a strict regime of investment control. The act was initially limited to the companies incorporated under it, but an 1857 amendment extended it to all Wisconsin companies. Under the act, companies might invest their assets in mortgages with a 50 per cent safety margin or in stocks of the United States, or might make collateral loans secured by such stocks or mortgages. Marine companies might also lend on respondentia or bottomry bonds.[5]

The most important special charter in Wisconsin was the 1857 charter of the Mutual Life of Wisconsin, later the Northwestern Mutual Life. It limited real estate acquisitions to those requisite to provide premises for the transaction of the company's business and such as should come to it in the bona fide enforcement of debts. Half the premiums might be invested in public stocks of the United States, of Wisconsin, or of any incorporated Wisconsin city. The remainder must be invested in real estate mortgages on Wisconsin real property with a 100 per cent margin of safety. Thus the investment control of Wisconsin's most important insurance company was strict from the very beginning. The company's first report to the State of Wisconsin in 1859 showed premium notes as its sole earning asset, however. This reflected the difficulty a new concern had in selling insurance. If kept well below the policy reserve, premium notes were perfectly safe investments and rather remunerative, at about 7 per cent. "Bills receivable," a type of premium note the Northwestern Mutual accepted when there was not an adequate margin in the policy reserve, brought 10 per cent. These kinds of investments were products of the marketing policy of the company and not results of investment policy. With increasing availability of money, such investments became less important.[6]

About 1867 there was a change from the general laxness of investment control. The legislature began to insert into nearly all special charters strict limitations like those in the Mutual Life charter, and like those that were put into the later 1870 act for fire and marine companies.[7]

The 1870 legislation separated life from fire and marine insurance companies. For purposes of investment control newer types of insurance were assimilated to fire and marine, and life remained separate down to mid-twentieth century. The reasons are apparent. Legal reserve life insurance accumulates gigantic quantities of money; thus investment control for life insurance companies acquires an added element of social importance because of the very size of the accumulations. Moreover, size itself creates special difficulties that do not exist with the more modest accumulations of other insurance companies.[8]

Control of Life Insurance Company Investments after 1870

The 1870 life insurance act imposed a strict investment regime on all companies—on those already chartered and on those to be incorporated thereafter under the act. The list of authorized investments was short. It included stocks of the United States, of Wisconsin, or of any incorporated city or town in Wisconsin; first mortgages with a safety margin of 100 per cent; and policy loans to policyholders of not more than half the annual premiums on the policies. Sanctions were no problem; for example, the Attorney General ruled in 1895 that mortgages without the required margin could not be scaled down in computing assets for solvency purposes—they could not be counted at all. There was little litigation about investments, but the Attorney General often had to interpret the statutes.[9]

The 1870 act finally established a principle of strict control over investments. Thereafter the trend was cautiously to broaden the authorized list. The legislature in 1882 authorized investment in county bonds; in 1893 in village bonds, school district bonds, first mortgage bonds of Wisconsin railroads, and in collateral loans secured by any bonds in which the company was authorized to invest. It also authorized policy loans to 95 per cent of the surrender value of the policy. In 1901 the legislature added street railway bonds, and in 1903 it extended the geographical scope of permitted investments to include investments in the territories and the District of Columbia as well as the states. In 1905 it added mortgages on twenty-five-year leaseholds or on the fee simple subject to a leasehold. The 1893 authorization of railroad bonds came late, for in the 1880's the large eastern companies were investing heavily in them. The Northwestern Mutual could not, nor did it seem to wish to, for it made no effort to have the law broadened.[10]

When the legislature called for the investigation of life insurance companies in 1905, it included in the scope of the inquiry "the nature and condition of their investments, methods of making such investments, and the manner in which their funds, securities, and assets are safeguarded" (*Laws* 1905SS, Jt. Resolution 1). Governor LaFollette had painted a frightening picture of interlocking directorates and of domination of industrial and transportation companies by life insurance companies. The strictures of the reform Governor against investment in voting shares bore little relation to Wisconsin problems, for investment in voting shares was already forbidden to Wisconsin life insurance companies. The investigation did not disclose any serious deviations from investment rectitude by the Northwestern Mutual. The big eastern companies were another matter. In 1903 and 1904 Commissioner Host had already called attention to interlocking directorates and heavy investments in trust companies, with particular reference to the link between the Prudential Insurance Company and the Fidelity Trust Company. For years he opposed investment in capital stock.[11]

It was a significant indication of the uniquely adequate functioning of Wisconsin investment control at that date that the 1906 committee made no recommendations for tightening the system. On the contrary, though the committee did not recommend legislation, it did mildly criticize the Northwestern Mutual for allowing a large percentage of its investments to slip into the bond category, when mortgages were more profitable.* The committee called attention to the steady drop in the interest earnings of the company, from 5.91 per cent in 1890 to 4.64 per cent in 1904, and also pointed to changes in the portfilio during this time. The percentage of bonds increased from 7 per cent to 37.25 per cent and the percentage of mortgages decreased from 83.74 per cent to 47.88 per cent. The company's answer illustrated the principal economic force behind the development of life insurance investment law: it was difficult to find high-yield investments without keeping money idle in bank accounts while waiting for opportunities. The company found it better to accept the lower yield.[12]

The 1911 legislature resumed the cautious advance in liberalizing the authorized list when it increased the permissible policy loan from 95 to 100 per cent of the surrender value.[13] It also permitted the acquisition of "apartments to rent as a source of income, the value of which shall not exceed twenty per cent of its admitted assets" (*Laws 1911, 157*).

In 1917 the legislature re-enacted the investment statute for life insurance companies, and made significant changes. It authorized investment in mortgage bonds of public utility corporations in Wisconsin cities of 10,000 or more, in mortgage bonds of the farm loan banks authorized under the Federal Farm Loan Act, in loans on collateral security of any authorized securities with a compulsory margin of safety of 10 per cent, and in bonds of the Dominion of Canada or any Canadian province or city. A new dimension was added to investment control; many of the authorized investments must satisfy qualitative standards. For example, the public utility bonds must meet several exacting standards; standards of earnings in relation to

---

*The committee also mildly criticized the Northwestern for failing to invest in Wisconsin farm loans, but no legislation resulted. In Texas, on the other hand, local protectionism resulted in the Robertson law.—*Texas Laws* 1907, 170.

interest charges, of value of the physical property in relation to the indebtedness, and of date of maturity.[14]

Thereafter the process of liberalization continued. In order to facilitate loans on newer farms, the 1921 legislature permitted the value of unimproved land to be considered in determining how much could be loaned. It declared a long list of easements, liens, and other minor outstanding interests in land not to be encumbrances within the meaning of the 1917 act. It authorized investment in the bonds of such special government divisions as sewer districts and drainage districts with a population of 50,000 or more, and approved Canadian railroad mortgage bonds. Companies with an unassigned surplus of a million dollars might invest up to a third of it in evidences of indebtedness eligible for discount, for rediscount, or for purchase or sale by Federal Reserve banks. This had the objective of authorizing investment in a variety of short-term obligations, to permit a high degree of liquidity at better yields than bank balances would produce. Also the 1921 legislature extended the 1917 authorization of investment in public utility mortgage bonds to companies supplying any American city of over 25,000, and reduced the quality standards to require only that the interest have been paid on the bonds for at least the preceding three years. The 1925 legislature added to the public utility bond list companies supplying Canadian cities, and authorized investment in equipment trust obligations on railroad rolling stock. The 1931 legislature added interest-bearing notes of any Wisconsin building and loan association.[15]

In 1933, for the first time since 1870, the legislature contracted the scope of authorized investment. Because of the disastrous history of mortgage foreclosures and bankruptcies in the Great Depression, it withdrew permission to invest in mortgages on leaseholds, and limited investment in the securities of any one corporation to 10 per cent of admitted assets. Even in 1933, however, the overall tendency was to expand the authorized list; a statute approved investment in the debt of municipally-owned Wisconsin utilities whose book value was at least twice the amount of the bond issue.[16]

The 1935 legislature permitted companies to invest up to 2 per cent of admitted assets in the secured debt of any solvent American corporation that had not defaulted on any debt within five years. In 1937 it added bonds of municipally-owned utilities in other states, adequately secured by mortgage or lien or by specific pledge of revenues.

It made similar provision for bonds secured by pledged revenues, issued by the United States or any state, or a commission, board, or other instrumentality of one of them. The 1939 legislature extended the approval of public utility bonds to those of smaller cities. The most striking liberalization of all was permission to acquire the unsecured debt of any solvent American company that met an earnings test. No more than one-half of one per cent of the insurance company's admitted assets might be invested in any single such issue, nor more than 5 per cent of assets in all issues under this authorization. The 1941 legislature reduced from 50,000 to 5,000 the required population of the miscellaneous governmental unit provision of 1921. It also permitted fifteen-year amortized loans to 60 per cent of value on real estate mortgages, instead of 50 per cent.[17]

The 1937 statute suggested the development of an area of free investment. That was realized more fully in 1945 when the legislature permitted up to 5 per cent of a company's assets to be invested in unqualified securities. The 1947 legislature permitted investment in preferred stock that met earnings tests, to a total of 5 per cent of assets, though no more than one-half of one per cent might be invested in a single company. It also approved investment shares of federally-insured building and loan associations, and shares of corporations chartered under the home owners' loan act of 1933. The postwar housing shortage offered an opportunity for profitable investment that would also be beneficial to the community, and the 1947 legislature permitted investment in the development, ownership, and operation of housing projects, or in the mortgage bonds of any housing authority or redevelopment company. The 1953 legislature removed the limit on the 1939 authorization to invest in bond issues of solvent companies, except for the limitations on single issues; gave permission to invest in income-producing real property up to 5 per cent of the company's admitted assets; and also permitted lending on mortgage up to two-thirds instead of one-half of value. This last change was very helpful to the Northwestern Mutual, then seeking to expand its mortgage lending against the competition of companies subject only to a "two-thirds of value" restriction. The 1955 legislature added equipment trust obligations on motor vehicles and commercial aircraft, and in 1957, at the request of the Wisconsin Farm Bureau Federation, the legislature authorized equipment trust obligations without limitation on the kinds of equipment. The 1957 legislature also authorized investment of up to 2 per cent of admitted assets in the debt of the International Bank for Reconstruction and Development.[18]

In 1959 Wisconsin joined a national trend and at the request of the Wisconsin Life Convention authorized investment of up to 5 per cent of admitted assets in selected common stocks, and up to 3 per cent in various kinds of equipment and machinery. The same act also provided that the leeway provision of 1945 might be used in such a way that when more was loaned on mortgage than the statute permitted the excess amount was charged to the leeway provision, and the authorized two-thirds was not. This, in effect, reversed the 1895 ruling of the Attorney General that mortgage loans without the required safety margin could not be counted as assets at all. Thus, over the eighty-nine-year period from 1870 to 1959, the trend was consistently, steadily, and almost without retreat, toward the liberalization of permitted investments. This reflected a number of forces. It undoubtedly reflected the increasing sense of responsibility of insurance company management as administrative control became more effective, and a resulting willingness in the legislature to give freer rein to management decisions. It reflected an increasing measure of economic sophistication that found safety in diversification as well as in property liens. It reflected during inflationary periods a sense of frustration with fixed-dollar obligations, when preservation of the dollar quantity of insurance company assets was at the expense of its value relative to commodities. Most of all, however, it reflected the increasing pressure of enormous aggregation of assets in the hands of companies required by law to make safe investments. In addition to insurance companies, there were savings banks, trust companies, building and loan associations, and others. The assets of all these companies constantly pressed on the available fixed-dollar investments, and drove down the rate of interest. Trustee investments became poor investments because too many buyers competed for them in the market. A constant search for permitted investments created pressures the legislature could not resist. Only relatively radical requests were refused, such as a 1927 bill to authorize investment in the securities of investment companies. In mid-twentieth century, the problem of enormous aggregates of capital that must be safely invested continued to distort the capital structure of the nation and harass insurance executives. The compulsion it exerted toward top-heavy debt financing was one of the major problems created for twentieth-century society by the growth of the insurance enterprise. In the creation of the problem, the life insurance companies played the biggest part. In the late 1950's the variable annuity was in a process of development, as a reflection of continued concern with inflationary pressures; in Wisconsin public retirement systems were overhauled in 1957 to make use of it. On the investment side this involved an increasing investment in equities.[19]

Control of Other Insurance Company Investments after 1870

Investment control of other insurance companies roughly paralleled that of life companies. Though such companies contributed relatively little to the burgeoning assets that made it necessary to expand the authorized list, they too suffered from any decline in the rate of interest.

The 1870 fire and marine act imposed a strict regime of control on the investment of capital; investment of surplus was less rigidly restricted. The distinction really meant only that a part of the company's investments must satisfy higher standards than the remainder. Capital must be invested in real estate mortgages with a margin of safety of 50 per cent, in Wisconsin state or municipal stocks, in stocks and treasury notes of the United States or in collateral loans on such securities. Surplus might be invested in the assets authorized for capital and also in the public stock or bonds of any state or in the stock, bonds, or other evidences of indebtedness of any solvent dividend-paying institution incorporated under the laws of Wisconsin or of the United States, but it might not be invested in the companies' own stock. Loans secured by such paper were also authorized, provided that the market value always remained at least 10 per cent above the amount of the loan.[20]

Title insurance companies might be organized under the general incorporation laws in 1887. Approved investments were similar to those for other insurance companies. The provision was made a part of the insurance code in 1927, without essential change, and there it remained in 1955, independent of other insurance company investment restrictions. When the legislature provided for organization of casualty and surety companies in 1897, the investment control closely paralleled that of other companies; they were assimilated to fire and marine companies in 1909.[21]

Pressure to broaden the list of authorized investments also came from insurance companies other than life from an early date, but the need was not felt so quickly, partly because the return on investment was less crucial than for life insurance companies, partly because of the broader initial authorization for such companies. The 1909 legislature thoroughly revised the authorized list for all companies not otherwise regulated. It preserved the distinction between capital and surplus, but made it less important. It broadened the authorization for investment of capital funds to include the bonds of all states; the county, city, town, village, or school district bonds of any state or territory; and first mortgage railroad or other public service corporation bonds. It only extended the authorization for investment of surplus to include the new municipal bonds also authorized as investments for capital. It forbade the company to invest more than 10 per cent of capital and surplus in the securities of any one corporation or to hold more than 10 per cent of the capital stock of any corporation or to invest in the stock of any insurance company.[22]

The 1911 legislature departed from prior anti-mortmain principles to authorize purchase of "apartments to rent as a source of income, the value of which shall not exceed twenty per cent of its admitted assets." The 1913 legislature revised the law once again. It slightly extended the capital list, especially to include Canadian government and utility bonds. It extended the restrictions on surplus to include all assets, and for certain investments created quality standards concerning dividend payments and the relation of paid-up equity to funded debt. It permitted assets other than capital to be invested in real estate mortgages anywhere in the nation and approved mortgages of unencumbered building leases with at least twenty-five years to run. It eliminated the 10 per cent margin of safety for collateral loans and provided that the investment remained legal so long as the market value was at least equal to the debt. In 1921 the legislature added mortgage bonds of the farm loan banks authorized under the federal farm loan act, bonds of Wisconsin land mortgage associations, and foreign government bonds in an amount not exceeding 25 per cent of capital stock; in 1931, interest-bearing notes of Wisconsin building and loan associations; in 1933, interest-bearing notes of town mutuals, whether ordinary or registered; in 1939, investment shares of local building and loan associations, shares of corporations organized under the home owners' loan act of 1933, and single premium life and endowment policies of authorized life insurance companies. The 1943 legislature limited foreign government bond investments to 1 per cent of admitted assets, instead of 25 per cent of capital, and imposed quality standards upon the investments in bonds and stocks of solvent dividend-paying corporations. Such corporations must meet earnings tests which became more stringent as the acquired paper descended from bonds to preferred stocks to common stock. The legislation permitted some relatively free investment in stocks of American corporations that could not meet the exacting tests here set up, to the extent of 3 per cent of admitted assets. In 1945, the legislature restricted investment in building and loan associations investment shares to the extent to which they were federally insured, but resumed the expansion process by eliminating the qualification that they must be local associations. It also added a new category of bonds secured by pledged public revenues. In 1947 it increased the free stock and bond investment provision of 1943 from 3 to 5 per cent of admitted assets and permitted 5 per cent of the assets to be invested completely free of restriction. In 1953 it increased the completely unrestricted investments from 5 to 10 per cent of assets. The 1955 legislature added income-producing real estate to the extent of 5 per cent of admitted assets and equipment trust obligations on railroad rolling stock, on motor vehicles, and on commercial aircraft. The 1957 legislature expanded the latter authorization at the request of the Wisconsin Farm Bureau Federation. The 1957 legislature also permitted investment in mutual fund shares, provided the fund met certain diversification requirements in its own investments.[23]

Early town mutuals had no surplus assets for investment. More often they borrowed to pay losses pending the collection of assessments. Later some of the town mutuals operated on an advance premium basis, and accumulated assets for which investment outlets were necessary. The 1915 legislature applied to town mutuals essentially the law applicable to other fire companies.[24]

As early as 1921 there was some effort to assimilate all domestic insurance companies to trusts for investment regulation. Such a measure would have greatly simplified legal control. In 1935 and in 1939 the legislature began to develop such generalized control of trustee investment, but it did not at once affect the control of insurance investment.[25]

Investment Control for Public Insurance Funds

Special problems were created by the development of state and other public insurance funds. For example, a 1907 act authorized police pension funds in second and third class cities, and the boards of trustees were to invest accumulated assets in United States, Wisconsin, and Wisconsin municipal bonds. The 1903 act setting up the state fire insurance fund made no provision for investment. In 1917 the legislature provided that the State Treasurer, who had custody of the money, should credit the state fire insurance fund with the average rate of interest earned by all state bank deposits during the preceding year, but that the Insurance Commissioner, with the approval of the Governor, might cause the assets of the state insurance fund to be invested as were the assets of domestic life companies. In 1911 the state life fund was created, and the State Treasurer was instructed to invest its assets, subject to the general direction of the Insurance Commissioner, in investments appropriate for domestic life insurance companies. In 1913 the legislature gave supervisory powers over the investment of the assets of the state life fund to a board consisting of the Secretary of State, the Attorney General, the State Treasurer, and the Insurance Commissioner.[26]

Efforts at systematic investment control began when the 1911 legislature created a teachers' insurance and retirement fund, managed by a board of trustees. The statute instructed the board to invest the assets as state trust funds were to be invested. In 1921 the legislature revised the law and authorized a newly created board to invest in the securities appropriate for domestic life companies, with preference given to small loans on improved farm property amortized over long terms not exceeding fifty years.[27]

In 1927 the Governor recommended that control of the state fire insurance fund investments be given to a new board under the Governor's supervision, to consist of the State Treasurer, the Attorney General, and the Insurance Commissioner. He urged that preference be given to the securities of local communities that insured in the state fire fund, and that investments be made only in Wisconsin. The legislature appointed a committee to investigate the haphazard and inconsistent control of the various funds. It found eight distinct investment boards, using complicated and inadequate machinery to invest $30,000,000 of state insurance and trust funds. The committee recommended a central state investment department, operating under the law applicable to domestic life companies. Accordingly the 1929 legislature gave to a new annuity and investment board control of the assets of the state retirement system, the state life fund, the state fire insurance fund, and other funds. The laws to be applied were those appropriate to domestic life companies, though in 1955 the legislature assimilated the state fire insurance fund to insurance companies other than life, thus differentiating it from the other state trust funds.[28]

The committee did not consider the possibility of using state trust funds to achieve special public objectives. Not everyone was blind to such possibilities, however, and in 1929 the legislature took a first significant step. The state fire insurance fund surplus had grown to approximately $2,000,000. The legislature appropriated $600,000 from the fund to construct a state office building. It made provision for the amortization of the loan at 5 per cent over a twenty-year period. It appropriated $300,000 in the same way for the construction of an orthopedic hospital for children, to be amortized over a ten-year period. The 1931 legislature appropriated additional funds, and also conveyed title of both the office building and the hospital to the Insurance Commissioner to be held in trust as an asset of the state insurance fund. In 1935 the legislature set up a special plan to retire the loan by making the state office building self-liquidating. In that same year, the creative possibilities inherent in the fire insurance fund became apparent once again when the fund was used to purchase a tract of land for use as a fish hatchery by the Conservation Commission. The property was to be sold by the fund to the Conservation Commission on a lease-purchase agreement. In 1937 it was natural for the legislature to go to the fire insurance fund as a ready source of $800,000 of additional money for an addition to the state office building, in order for the state to take advantage of matching federal monies under the New Deal recovery program. The loan was to be amortized over twenty years at an interest rate of 3 per cent. In 1951 the orthopedic hospital loan of 1929 was finally paid off and title conveyed from the Commissioner to the state. In spite of Governor Goodland's 1945 recommendation that the state retire the obligations to the state fire insurance fund, the state office building remained an asset of nearly a million dollars on the balance sheet of the fund in the mid-1950's.[29]

The ultimate utility of the surplus accumulated by the state fire insurance fund was only demonstrated in 1955, however. The surplus had then grown to nearly $9,000,000, in spite of the fact that premium rates were only 60 per cent of commercial rates. Governor Kohler recommended that five million dollars be transferred from the state insurance fund to the general fund. The legislature did so on almost a straight party-line vote. Ultimately, therefore, Wisconsin exhibited in mid-twentieth century the delightful anachronism of the use of the profits of "socialistic" enterprise to shore up the political fortunes of a conservative Republican administration.[30]

In 1933 the legislature also made use of state controlled trust funds to achieve desired social objectives. It declared an emergency arising out of the depression, and pointed to the dire need for credit by farmers, home owners, and various other citizens and institutions. It then provided that not less than 70 per cent of the assets of all the funds under the control of the annuity and investment board be invested in Wisconsin. Preference was to be given, first, to small loans on improved farm property, at a rate of interest not exceeding 5 per cent, and with authorization to arrange terms of payment that did not require payments on principal during the first three years; second for mortgage loans to coöperative associations and mutual organizations. The large accumulation of assets in the funds was thus harnessed to the achievement of social objectives other than the original investment objective of safety and maximum yield for the fund itself.[31]

§2. *Statutory Restrictions on Underwriting Policy*

From an early date the statutes placed a few scattering limitations on underwriting. But even in mid-twentieth century, the determination of the risks to write and the conditions under which to write them were regarded as largely a matter for decision by management, with which the state should not lightly interfere. The complexity of underwriting practices made effective public control difficult, and the solution was left primarily to a process of education of the companies. Of the few limitations that were imposed, some compelled an adequate spread of the risk and others sought to maintain high quality in the risks selected.

If a fire insurance company unduly concentrated its risks, as by writing a large proportion of its total fire insurance within the congested area of a single inflammable wooden city, it subjected its assets to the danger of a catastrophe. A long succession of catastrophic fires, culminating in the San Francisco fire of 1906, helped teach the companies to limit the proportion of their total risk subject to a single fire. Though the competitive motivation encouraged the companies to take chances, the lesson was eventually learned. Where he could, the Insurance Commissioner discouraged concentration of risk. In 1920 and 1922 he opposed the extension of town mutual operations to include tornado. When town mutuals were fully authorized to sell windstorm and hail insurance, in 1951, the legislature required reinsurance of at least 90 per cent of the coverage, as a precaution against catastrophe.[1]

An undue concentration of risk might be effected also by writing single risks of large size, especially with small companies. Limitations on the maximum amount of a single risk were both early and fairly common, though far from universal. An 1853 health insurance company charter specified $400 per year as the maximum coverage any insured might obtain. Among the general laws, maximum risk limitations were most commonly imposed on the local mutuals. Thus the 1859 town mutual law limited risks to $2,000. That limit was lifted altogether in 1870. In 1876 the legislature permitted town companies to insure a variety of nonfarm buildings, such as country stores and schoolhouses. On such buildings, it imposed a risk limit of $1,500. There was after 1870 no risk limit on the farm buildings whose protection constituted the *raison d'être* of the town mutuals. As the town mutuals grew in size and stability and as the value of country property increased, the legislature raised the limit on nonfarm buildings and in 1953 removed it altogether. As the legislature authorized organizations of other trade and local mutuals, it set risk limits for each. In 1909 it assimilated these mutuals to the general fire insurance companies and the risk limits ceased to apply.[2]

The legislature limited the state fire insurance fund to $500,000 of insurance on the state capitol building, and $200,000 on the state historical society building; the Commissioner might reinsure above $100,000 with the consent of the Governor. A 1927 proposal would have limited the state fund to $100,000 on any risk. The legislature removed these limits in 1951, though the Commissioner might still reinsure above $100,000, with the Governor's approval. In 1917 the alleged impossibility of an adequate risk spread led to a gubernatorial recommendation that the state fire fund be liquidated; in 1919 the same Governor urged the same reason for eliminating the state life fund. The argument may have been only window-dressing; Governor Philipp was the leader of the Stalwart Republicans, and state insurance funds smacked of socialism. Both proposals failed. Another 1917 proposal would have created a board, consisting of the Attorney General, the Secretary of State, the State Treasurer, and the Insurance Commissioner to reinsure the risks in the state life fund if necessary to protect the interests of the policyholders. It may have been either a subterfuge to enable the Stalwarts to terminate the state fund, or a legitimate precaution in the event the state life fund became too small for actuarially sound operation.[3]

The legislature also considered maximum risk provisions in life insurance from time to time. An unsuccessful bill in 1891 would have limited fraternal benefit society policies to $5,000 on any one person; one in 1907 would have set $25,000 for commercial life insurance; and one in 1923 would have limited the state life fund to $5,000 on any one person. The 1937 legislature set a limit of $2,000 for group life on borrowers from credit unions, though it raised this to $5,000 in 1943 and to $10,000 in 1947. The 1949 group life statute set various maximum risk limits.[4]

Absolute risk limits were generally unsatisfactory; the determination of a sound risk limit necessarily depended on many factors, including the scale of operations and the existence of special reserves. More realistic statutes sought to individualize risk limits in terms of such factors as these. One method was to relate the risk limit to the assets of the company. This was especially satisfactory for stock companies. It probably originated in Massachusetts, where various charters set 5, 7, 7.5, 8 or 10 per cent of the capital of the company as the maximum for a single risk. The 10 per cent limit became the standard and was adopted in Massachusetts by a general statute in 1818. In Wisconsin the legislature put the 10 per cent risk limitation in the 1850 and 1870 general acts, but rarely in the special charters. The 10 percent limit became general in 1909. In 1909 the legislature changed the maximum risk limit for livestock companies from $250 on one animal to 5 per cent of the paid-up capital; in 1912 and 1913 it set the maximum for Lloyds' underwriters and for reciprocal subscribers at 10 per cent of net worth. In 1913 the Governor vetoed a bill permitting single bank-deposit insurance risks up to 100 per cent of the assets of a casualty company, but not over 10 per cent of the total risk carried; he said it was not sound practice because a single loss might wipe out all the assets of a company. Oddly, the Governor signed a companion measure that permitted mutual casualty companies to write such risks with no other limit than was specified in the bylaws.[5]

There was uncertainty whether percentage risk limits should be limits on gross risk before reinsurance or on net risk after. Commissioner Fricke ruled that any company taking a risk larger than the statutory limit might reinsure the excess only in authorized companies; thus he terminated the practice by which out-of-state companies took very large risks and reinsured the largest part of each risk in unauthorized companies. An effort was made in 1917 to double the gross limit by making the limit a net one with a 50 per cent limit on reinsurance. The 1919 legislature permitted surety companies to take risks in excess of 10 per cent of capital and surplus to the extent that the excess was protected by reinsurance or co-suretyship of a company satisfying certain tests, or protected by pledged or mortgaged property.[6]

A percentage-of-assets risk limit was less appropriate for assessment mutuals, though the 1903 legislature set 10 per cent of assets as the maximum risk of accident societies writing death benefits. For mutuals a more satisfactory way of individualizing the risk limit was to relate it to the total insurance in force or to the average risk. Thus in 1905 the legislature set a limit of 2 per cent of the total insurance in force for school district mutuals. In 1909 it permitted city and village mutuals to write policies above the $1,500 limit but not in excess of $3,000, provided they did not exceed 10 per cent of the surplus nor one-eighth of one per cent of the insurance in force. For other mutuals, it set the maximum at one-eighth of one per cent of the insurance in force or three times the average policy, whichever was greater. There were several efforts to increase the limit, one successful.[7]

In 1911 the legislature set the risk limit for the new state life fund at $1,000, until there should be 1,000 insureds; at $2,000 until there were 3,000; and thereafter at $3,000. It limited annuities to $300. In 1925 the legislature changed the risk limit to one-half of one per cent of the risk in force.[8]

The statutes often imposed limits on the length of time for which policies might be written; the fact that only mutuals were so restricted suggests that the purpose was to confine underwriting errors within reasonably narrow limits where the profit motive would not do so. The 1859 statute limited town mutual policies to terms of five years. This same period was set for most other mutuals, but the legislature set three years for lumber dealers' mutuals, two years for livestock mutuals, one year for bicycle mutuals. In 1909, it reduced city and village mutuals to three years, and made the five year rule general where there was no special provision. In 1923, 1925, and 1941 unsuccessful bills sought to eliminate the time limit for mutuals and give unlimited discretion on the matter to management; the reform was achieved and the limit removed in 1943.[9]

The most rigorous control of the qualitative selection of risks was naturally applied to the local mutuals, where the absence of the commercial motive and the local character of the operation might be expected to lead to difficulty. The chief instance of statutory limitations on underwriting was on the insurance of nonfarm property by the town mutuals. A majority vote must authorize the extended business, and the 1876 act limited such coverage to country stores, schoolhouses, churches, town and society halls. The legislature added country hotels and water mills in 1881, cheese factories in 1887, blacksmith shops in 1905; buildings of agricultural societies in 1929; country taverns, social halls, garages, oil stations, and feed mills in 1935; country grain elevators in 1939; buildings, equipment, materials, and supplies of rural electric coöperative associations in 1943. In 1949 it added fourteen additional classes of buildings. It was at length apparent, if it were not previously, that the legislature would authorize any additional classes of country buildings for which there was demand; the logical next step was to empower the town mutuals to insure any property within their authorized territory, and the legislature took that step in 1953. The legislature had never done much more than delay slightly the addition of requested country buildings as the demand was made, and the legislative surveillance therefore had little long-term significance. A majority of town mutual members might extend operations to farms and detached dwellings in adjoining towns, but insurance of such property was forbidden unless the insured property were removed "from exposure" by a distance of 200 feet. The minimum distance for permitted exposure was reduced to 100 feet in 1880; numerous unsuccessful bills sought to raise it or to lower it. In 1903 the stipulation was eliminated altogether. In 1905 and 1907 bills sought to reinstate it.[10]

Various restrictions sought to protect the quality of the insured risks in life insurance. In 1895 the legislature required the 500 initial applicants for fraternal societies to be recommended as insurable by a reputable physician, and in 1911 made it clear that the physical examination was required for subsequent admissions as well. In 1917 it required "medical examination or inspection" for juvenile insurance, but since a full-fledged medical examination would have made such insurance prohibitively expensive for the industrial classes, a liberal administrative interpretation of "inspection" made examination by a doctor unnecessary. There was an attempt in 1915 to require a medical examination for all life insurance except industrial, and several efforts to require it for some group life. Another effort to screen out undesirable risks was the 1895 provision that fraternals might insure only persons between the ages of 18 and 61.[11]

The invention of group insurance created new problems of underwriting control; there was much fear that sound underwriting would not be possible and that uninsurable risks would be covered in large numbers because of the blanket basis on which such insurance was written. Control could only be directed at the group itself. The initial control was in a narrow definition of the integrating facts around which groups might permissibly be selected, based usually on employment or organization membership. There were some limitations of a distinctively underwriting character, such as rules for the minimum size of the group and the percentage that must be insured. Characteristically the 1929 statute required coverage of at least fifty employees, written on some plan precluding individual selection, representing not fewer than three-fourths of the employees in a common employment. The long-term tendency was to permit writing of smaller groups, as strangeness wore off and fear was replaced by confidence. In 1949 the legislature revised and systematized the requirements for group life, with underwriting restrictions still directed to preclude individual selection and obtain a representative group of participants.[12]

The underwriting limitations already considered were relatively systematic; there were also miscellaneous restrictions, which appeared as isolated exceptions to a general policy of noninterference with management prerogative. The legislative decision to intervene was largely fortuitous. Most often the concern was with underwriting control, as when the legislature forbade an 1867 horse insurance company to insure horses under three years of age, and "very old ones"; each horse must be examined and appraised before the insurance might be written. Sometimes, however, more basic public policy might be involved. Thus a divided Wisconsin Supreme Court ruled that the Commissioner might not refuse to insure Negroes in the state life fund on the ground that their mortality experience was worse than that of whites; he must work out a classification not based upon race or color, unless he could show that race itself was the decisive factor in the unfavorable experience. In the absence of paramount social considerations, race was a sound, if primitive and crude, underwriting consideration, but it must yield to more important policy.[13]

§3. Control of Other Management Practices

One of the difficult problems of insurance law was how to control management enough to prevent wasteful or venal handling of the insurance fund, without depriving society of the benefit of wide dispersion of decision making. One method early found useful for this purpose was the imposition of personal liability upon directors responsible for the granting of dividends that impaired capital. This device appeared in many special charters and in the general acts of 1850. It was a common variation to impose personal liability upon directors who knowingly issued policies when capital was impaired, whether the capital impairment was due to unwise or illegal payment of dividends or some other cause.[1]

Reserve Requirements

The Unearned Premium Reserve.—More frequently, however, the legislature imposed, directly on management, rules of practice to safeguard the fund. Thus in 1870 it required that before fire and marine companies might distribute profits, they must first set aside in an unearned premium reserve a sum equal to 100 per cent of the premiums on unexpired policies. Except for the field of life insurance, the unearned premium reserve is the basis of modern control of insurance companies, for it ensures that companies which find it preferable to liquidate their activities can reinsure all of their outstanding risks in solvent companies, with no loss to policyholders. It also ensures that all companies keep books on an accrual rather than on a cash basis. Because of delay between premium payment and claims payment, a company whose books are on a cash basis may have the illusion, without the reality, of prosperity, so long as it is expanding rapidly. This was understood quite early by the responsible men in the industry.[2]

Even earlier, in 1862, the legislature required out-of-state fire and marine companies to report to the Secretary of State the amount required to reinsure all outstanding risks. But the earlier statute set a mere reporting requirement, not a reserve requirement. The absence of compulsive sanctions was not the only difficulty in control through reports. Estimates of the cost of reinsurance varied from $1.42 per thousand dollars of risk for the Madison Mutual, the largest local fire insurance company, to $9.76 for the German Mutual, one of the smaller concerns. The uncertainty led the Commissioner to obtain more uniformity of practice by setting a reporting standard of 40 per cent of fire premiums on unexpired business, and the full amount received on marine and inland marine risks; this was the basis approved by the insurance fraternity.[3]

A percentage-of-premium basis for the reinsurance reserve had the weakness that the reserve was least for those companies that charged the least adequate premiums. A more subtle reserve requirement, which adjusted the reserve to an adequate measure of the risk undertaken, would be better but would be difficult to work out. Such a reserve requirement would also be good protection to the industry against rate-cutting, an advantage the companies were not slow to see.[4]

For want of a better formula the percentage-of-premium basis continued to be used for reinsurance reserve requirements for insurance other than life. As new kinds of insurance or new organizational forms were authorized, a reinsurance reserve was often set, most often at 50 per cent of premiums on policies in force at the time of computation. Sometimes the legislature gave the Commissioner some discretion to increase the reserve beyond that figure; once it permitted him to compute unearned premiums on each single risk. A residual provision, supplied by the 1911 legislature and applicable to cases not otherwise provided for, gave him very broad discretion in setting a basis, but specific provisions were so frequent that the residual provision was not often needed. In 1929 the 50 per cent basis was applied to all lines of insurance for which no other provision was made. The 50 per cent reserve was a rough averaging on the assumption that business was fairly constant; it would have been inadequate if the business were rapidly expanding. In 1949 the legislature introduced more flexibility into the reserve computation; the new legislation gave the companies the option of calculating reserves on a monthly pro rata basis if they wished, and granted the Commissioner the discretion to require the monthly pro rata basis, or even a computation on each separate risk, if he thought the reserve produced by the 50 per cent basis was not sufficient.[5]

Approval of the requirement of adequate reserves was overwhelming; there was little support for a 1923 bill to reduce reserve requirements of domestic mutuals. The strong sentiment for reserves was a major factor in a lengthy and acrid dispute, which served as a vehicle for the expression of political and personal animosities spanning most of the second quarter of the twentieth century. The State Farm Mutual Automobile Insurance Company of Illinois, organized in 1922 by a group which included Herman L. Ekern, former Insurance Commissioner and long-time prominent Wisconsin Progressive politician, sought admission to Wisconsin several times from 1923 to 1931, but was refused each time. Commissioner Mortensen, campaign manager for one of Ekern's political campaigns, issued the license in 1939 over the opposition of the State Farm Mutual of Madison, organized in 1934, and the Wisconsin Mutual Insurance Alliance. The contesting companies then sued to compel the Commissioner to revoke the license, making use of the similarity-of-names statute which, they urged, was intended to protect local companies, not out-of-state companies, even though the latter were organized first.[6]

The Illinois company operated on the basis of a life membership fee plan, which was the substantial object of attack. In 1932 the mutuals of the state had unsuccessfully sought cancellation of the license of the Workmen's Mutual of Milwaukee, another of Ekern's automobile insurance firms which charged a $15.00 life membership fee; the ostensible ground was discrimination among persons of different ages, but the real reason for opposition was the competitive advantage given to the Workmen's by the different method of operation. The $15.00 was available for initial promotion expenses, and no reserve was set up for it. The objecting companies revealed their strategy in a 1939 bill to require all membership fees or other like fees collected in any state to be included in the premium, for the computation of reserve liabilities. This would probably prevent operation of the Illinois company in Wisconsin, because it would hardly wish to change its whole scheme of operation in order to be admitted to the state. The bill quickly passed the Assembly by a vote of 83 to 4. In the Senate, the opposing forces were evenly balanced and the bill was lost in the end-of-session rush. Charges and countercharges were intemperate. Lobbyists for the two sides were accused of exercising improper influence on state officials; the Insurance Commissioner who issued the license was charged with expecting employment as the payoff for his coöperation.[7]

In 1940 a new Commissioner refused to renew the company's license. While court action was pending to determine whether he was justified in so doing, a legislative attempt was made in 1941 to permit automobile insurance mutuals to charge limited membership fees which would be regarded as part of the initial premium, for taxation and reserve purposes. The Mutual Alliance lobbyist attacked the bill as a relaxation of the Wisconsin insurance laws; he wanted to require that the fee be allocated to several years in order to compel an increase in the reserve requirements of the Illinois company. Again intemperate charges of venal conflict of interest were made.[8]

The Wisconsin Supreme Court refused to consider the soundness of the life membership method of operation, but it did hold that the membership fee was a part of the premium and that the reserve requirements applied to it. Thus the Commissioner was right in refusing the license. The Court made it clear, too, that domestic companies might not operate on the life membership fee plan.[9]

The State Farm Mutual stopped using the life membership plan in Wisconsin, and again sought admission unsuccessfully. The Wisconsin Supreme Court declared that Wisconsin law required the company to set up unearned premium reserves on the life membership fee in all states, and the United States Supreme Court found no federal constitutional grounds for upsetting this ruling. In 1945 the company changed its entire business practice to set up an unearned premium reserve on its life memberships, but a license was still denied. Finally, in 1950, the battle which had raged for so long and which was waged with vigor and tenacity, came to an end with the issuance of a license by a new Commissioner, who announced that "all differences between the state and the company have been worked out" (Milwaukee *Journal*, Jan. 26, 1950). During all this time, the company never ceased to operate in the state, under injunctions which it managed to keep alive because of the litigation that was always pending. Finally, in 1957, at the request of the State Farm Insurance Companies, the legislature regularized the use of the membership fee plan.[10]

Reinsurance reserves had little meaning for assessment companies, and the percentage-of-premium method of computation effectively excluded them from application of any such requirement.[11] The Attorney General thought that "a company operating on the assessment plan is in the very nature of things not required to carry any reserve" (*Ops. Att'y Gen.*, 1931, pp. 148, 150).

Legal Reserve in Life Insurance.—Control of policy reserves for legal reserve life insurance companies had two functions; a direct and primary one to require the companies to carry as liabilities, rather than as surplus, sums adequate to meet probable obligations, and an indirect and secondary one to compel adequate premium rates. We have already discussed the secondary function. In the other role, such a fund was a true unearned premium reserve.[12]

The legal reserve was essentially the "value" of the policies in force, i.e., the discounted or present value of promised benefits, less the present value of future premiums. Computation of the reserve depended upon adoption of a mortality table to predict future premiums receivable and future obligations payable, and assumption of a rate of interest to be earned, for discounting future benefits and obligations to the date of valuation. Once the rate of interest was assumed and the mortality table adopted, calculation of the value of the policies was technical but arithmetically precise; any good actuary might perform the computations, which did not involve policy judgments. Legal reserve requirements were met if assets equalled the actuarially computed "value" of the policies; administrative surveillance likewise required no policy judgments, only actuarial computations. The policy judgments were performed in limiting the company's choice of mortality table and assumed rate of interest.

Selection of the mortality table had much less effect on the calculation of the reserve than did selection of the rate of interest. The reason was that though a more favorable mortality table would justify smaller premiums, so that each future premium would have a smaller present value and thus tend to increase the reserve requirement, at the same time, the reserve would earn interest for a longer time, and need not be so large. Put another way, since the reserve was the difference between the present value of future benefits and the present value of future premiums, a better mortality table would decrease both the present values, and thus the difference between them would be less than if the present value of benefits remained constant. As a matter of fact, the shift to a more modern mortality table for valuation purposes would not result in much reduction in premium either, for reasons explained elsewhere.

Because of the accelerating impact of a high rate of compound interest, the important factor in the regulation of the legal reserve was the selection of the permissible limits of the assumed rate of interest. The higher the interest assumption, the lower could be the reserve, for higher interest on the company's assets would make up the difference. But if the interest assumed in the calculations were higher than the company actually earned on its investments, premiums might be inadequate and the company become insolvent, or the deficiency might be made up out of new business, the new policyholders partially carrying the old.

Pressure for a higher assumed rate of interest came from companies that desired rapid expansion. With little concern for security, such companies wanted low premiums as a selling point.[13]

For valuation of policies, the general life insurance act of 1870 adopted the American Experience Table of Mortality, with interest assumed to be at 4.5 per cent. This interest assumption was the New York standard. Massachusetts was at 4 per cent. Actual earnings of the companies on invested assets then substantially exceeded those figures. In the early 1870's some companies urged the increase of the assumed rate to 5 or even 6 per cent, but Secretary of State Breese recommended in his insurance reports a reduction from the New York to the Massachusetts level. Breese showed insight into this basic problem of life insurance by pointing out that it was entirely uncertain how low the rate of interest might sink during the long period of the life insurance contract.[14]

A quarter-century later, Commissioner Fricke called attention to the dropping interest rate. He criticized the prevailing assumption of high rates of interest in reserve valuations, and suggested a reduction to 3 per cent. Economic naiveté may well explain the failure of the legislature to act on several bills to reduce the interest assumption to 4 per cent.[15]

The 1906 report of the Joint Committee on the Affairs of Life Insurance Companies also recognized the long-term decline in the interest rate on high-grade securities, but recommended that management have wide discretion in assuming a rate of interest. It, however, suggested that the companies should be required to assume an interest rate between 2.5 and 4 per cent. One renowned actuary thought 2.5 per cent too low a minimum; such a figure tied up assets unnecessarily. He failed to anticipate the extent of the long-term decline in interest. The committee's bill did not pass. But this particular measure was part of a complex program of legislation recommended by the committee, and failure to pass it resulted in repeal by another act of any specified valuation standard. However, the 1909 legislature passed a valuation law requiring that assumed interest be between 3 and 4 per cent; the law also set a minimum standard of mortality similar to that recommended in 1907. One serious mistake was to determine solvency, not according to an inflexible minimum standard but according to the company's own assumptions. Theoretically, this might result in technical insolvency for a strong company whose reserves did not meet its own excessively high standards. As a practical matter the emphasis on the company's own assumptions as the standard provided a way for a sound company to hide surplus in reserves and thus evade statutory requirements that surplus be distributed.[16]

Interest continued to drop. In 1941 the legislature reduced the minimum permitted interest assumption from 3 to 2 per cent; and in 1943 it reduced the maximum permitted interest assumption from 4 to 3.5 per cent, but recognized more favorable mortality experience by choosing the recently compiled Commissioners 1941 Standard Ordinary Mortality Table as the minimum permissible mortality assumption, i.e., any table used for valuation purposes (other than certain specified tables) must not exhibit at any age a lower death rate than the C.S.O. table. The legal reserve must be not less than that calculated on the basis of the C.S.O. table at 3.5 per cent interest.* The 1943 legislature also permitted companies to strengthen reserves by revaluing certain existing policies on a lower interest assumption. In 1959 the legislature brought the law up to date by adopting the Commissioners 1958 Standard Ordinary Mortality Table.[17]

Before the strict legal regulation of valuation, companies often computed the gross valuation, which gave the company credit for future gross premiums, including the loading for expense; but after the development of legal control of valuation in mid-nineteenth century, the value computed was the net value, and the company only received credit for net future premiums. Before the 1907 legislation, the value for the legal reserve was on the full level net premium basis, i.e., the same contribution to reserve was called for in the initial years of the policy as later. The 1907 legislature recognized that increased expense in the early policy years necessitated modifications in the full level net premium basis; this matter is discussed elsewhere.

Control of the accumulation of reserves was at first deemed unnecessary for mutual benefit and fraternal companies. Thereafter such regulation became nearly a political impossibility, because fraternalism spread during the last third of the nineteenth century until a large percentage of voters were members of a lodge; naturally, restrictive legislation was unpopular, and was opposed as an effort by the old-line commercial companies to freeze out competition. By the end of the century, the only reserve requirement was that there must be a reserve or emergency fund not less than the proceeds of one assessment and at least equal to the largest outstanding certificate. Permission was given to societies to build a larger reserve, if they wished.[18]

Latent in the assessment technique when used in life insurance was a serious weakness not present when it was used for the insurance of

*Huebner (1950), part II, gives a simple explanation of actuarial science, adequate for most purposes.

property. Assessments could be kept at a constant level only if the average age of the society could be kept constant. Once recruitment lagged and the age structure changed, the mortality rate climbed, and the assessments must be increased or benefits cut, or else the organization faced bankruptcy. With one society after another, the early faith that regular infusion of "new blood" would keep the association financially healthy, proved fallacious.

During the 1870's and 1880's, this latent weakness was concealed under a flood of new memberships as the institution spread and sank deep roots into American life. In addition, there were numerous failures of legal reserve companies at the time, and the latter were under aggressive attack as an expensive and wasteful method of supplying life insurance; the effective motto of the fraternals was "keep your reserve in your own pocket." Secretary of State Breese early saw the weakness in assessment life insurance: "Something of this sort may do well enough as a channel for neighborhood benevolence, while the project holds together, but it cannot pretend to have a scientific basis or financial stability" (*Rept. Ins. Comm'r*, 1870, p. 65, quoting the Mass. Comm'r). But he was a prophet without honor, and in the depression of the 1870's, the need for cheap insurance reinforced the deep suspicion of the capital aggregations involved in legal reserve life insurance.[19]

By the 1890's a more sophisticated understanding of life insurance led to an attitude sympathetic to some rating and reserve requirements even for assessment companies. An 1895 bill would have compelled the fraternals to collect 25 per cent in excess of their average mortuary requirements as measured by standard mortality tables, i.e., the companies would no longer have been able to make assessments only when losses occurred, but would at least have to charge policyholders collectively 25 per cent above the natural premium. This regulation at least recognized the problem created by an ageing membership.[20]

A source of the difficulty, as Commissioner Fricke recognized in 1898, was the assumption that there were any basic differences between the reserve needs of commercial life insurance and fraternal companies. In both cases the problem was one of computing accurately the present value of future promised benefits, using dependable mortality tables, and making sure that accumulated reserves plus the present value of future premium receipts were at least as large.

Fricke criticized the distinction in form of valuation; a properly formulated law would take care of both the natural and level premium companies, if premium rates responded to actuarial realities.[21]

By the turn of the century, many people in the fraternals were anxious to remedy the situation, but the natural disinclination of old-timers to accept less than the face value of their policies slowed down reform. They could not understand that they had paid less than they should for their certificates; a whole generation was convinced of its vested rights in promised benefits. Despite the feeling of some old members that they were being robbed, a satisfactory solution of the problem demanded that new members not be burdened by old mistakes.[22]

It was not only the old members who were obsessed with their vested rights. The Wisconsin Supreme Court at the turn of the century, especially Justice Marshall, could see only a legal person reneging on its promise. The reality of the insurance business—a mutual fund, which could pay out in benefits only what it collected in premiums—seemed not within the court's grasp. When fraternal companies sought to convert to a sound method of operation, whether by scaling benefits down or by increasing premiums or by converting from an assessment to a legal reserve basis, the court unrealistically put roadblocks in the path, in the name of sanctity of contract, sometimes bolstering its position by reference to the contract clause of the federal constitution. There was actually no basic hostility to a change-over in method of operation, however, if there was no conflict with freedom of contract, as when the policyholder paid premiums on the new basis and thus acquiesced, and the court was then ready enough to hold him estopped to allege breach of contract.[23]

Wisconsin legal agencies were largely content with a voluntary and gradual approach, for it was feared that drastic measures would convert the fraternals into regular life companies or else kill them off. The main need was for fraternals to recognize the existence of mortality tables and put rates on a realistic basis. But rate competition and pressures from older members kept many of the fraternals from up-grading their operations. Commissioner Host recommended to the legislative investigating committee in 1906 that the legislature compel all new societies to collect adequate rates, all societies to collect adequate rates from new members, and all societies to keep the funds from members paying adequate rates separate from the funds of old members.[24] The first recommendation was adopted in 1907; it was the "Force Bill" recommended by the National Fraternal Congress, which represented the older societies, and opposed by the Associated Fraternities of America, which represented the newer societies, which would be put at a competitive disadvantage by it. The 1911 legislature enacted the rest of Host's 1906 recommendations. It set as a valuation standard the National Fraternal Congress table, at no more than 4 per cent; each company might use its own table if the table covered twenty years and 100,000 lives. This valuation was not made the test of legal solvency; that still depended on ability to meet current obligations. But the valuation did make information available so that actuarial solvency might be tested. The 1913 legislature made clear that the actuarial requirements did not prevent operation on a natural premium basis, without reserves, so long as the rates were sufficient on that basis.[25]

The valuation method provided by the 1911 legislature was the prospective method which was applied to legal reserve companies. It was satisfactory for such companies, since legal solvency for them was dependent on actuarial solvency. But for the upgrading of fraternals, where legal solvency depended only on ability to meet current obligations, actuaries worked out a more satisfactory valuation method. It was a retrospective method or "accumulation basis," which credited each member with the amount contributed and interest, and charged him with his share of losses and expenses. Mathematically the two methods would produce the same results on the same assumptions concerning experience. But the advantage of the accumulation basis was that it focused on actual, not assumed, experience. Thus if actual mortality experience were better, or expenses lower, than the assumed rates, even unsound operations would show a credit to the accounts of old members; this gave old members an inducement to transfer to an actuarially sound operation, since it gave them some equity to transfer. The accumulation, or retrospective, point of view permitted a free choice on the changeover, and made the society at once solvent, because it focused on the individual equity in the assets, and thus made the contract whatever the premiums would purchase in fact. So long as the transfer was not made, the assets would be available for death claims, thus avoiding the court's objection that the amount of the contract might not be unilaterally reduced. The 1913 legislature made this valuation method a permissible alternative. The 1915 legislature completed the process by authorizing the formation of separate classes of members with separate funds, and enacted provisions to encourage transfer from low-rate to high-rate classes and thus encourage upgrading of the operation.[26]

With these enactments, the mechanism for conversion of the fraternals to a sound basis of operations was complete. In 1913 and 1915 efforts to repeal the law were unavailing; some of the fraternals themselves rallied to prevent repeal. The process of upgrading under the voluntary conference method was fairly rapid. From 1913 to 1925 domestic fraternals operating in Wisconsin increased solvency (the ratio of assets to the net value of outstanding certificates or required reserve) from an average of 40.6 per cent solvency to 70.4 per cent; only seven fraternals were not yet solvent. Out-of-state fraternals operating in Wisconsin improved from an average of 13.3 per cent solvency to 55.8 per cent. There was great variation, however; in 1925 the Wisconsin societies ranged from 21.7 per cent to 158 per cent solvency.[27]

Thereafter the legal problems were primarily of two kinds: the court had to handle in litigation application of the adjustment provisions to particular fraternals, and the legislature had to accommodate its policy to the pressures of societies demanding special treatment.

In 1922 the court was faced with a complex adjustment problem. The United Order of Foresters had a typical history. At first it issued policies that promised far more than the rates justified; later it made several insufficient modifications of its contracts in attempts to save its solvency; and finally it made an extensive readjustment under the statutory provisions, including such changes as division of policy-holders into classes, retrospective valuation, permissive transfer between classes, and rerating of old members. The Supreme Court showed that it had learned much since the end-of-century days when it was obsessed with abstract notions of freedom of contract; the wrecks of fraternals strewn across the decades taught the court that sanctity of contract put no money into the fraternal treasury. Not only did the court give its approval to restructuring of the company's operations, but it refused to approve precisely those portions of the reorganization in which concessions were made to old members. The court insisted that the old members must get only so much as they were entitled to get on a retrospective valuation, give and take a little because of the rough approximations necessary to solve the extraordinarily complicated actuarial problem. With this decision the court seemed to recognize the mutual reality beyond the contract facade, and to adopt the principle of the mortality table as the social policy of the state. But the old attitudes were not yet dead. In 1925 the court held that conversion to a legal reserve operation did not justify scaling down the benefits on old assessment contracts which had matured; the court compelled precisely what it denounced in 1922—the transfer of funds from surplus created by policyholders who had paid sufficiently large premiums, to the old members who had not. In effect, notwithstanding the sweeping language of the 1922 opinion, whether the court would enforce its realistic policy on adjustments among members of a company on the basis of contributions made depended on whether the company acted under the authorizing statutes, and whether the contract right had matured.[28]

Pressure began at once for special treatment of individual fraternals or for postponement of the effective date of the act, to permit newly organized or admitted companies to operate on the old assessment basis. A 1917 statute permitted societies which had continuously operated in the state since 1907, but for any reason had failed to obtain a license in the interim, to obtain a license on the basis of the pre-1907 law, but subject to the later acts for future operation.[29]

Meantime, small benevolent societies on a primitive assessment basis again became popular in southern and western Wisconsin. The Attorney General at first ruled such societies to be exempt from the insurance laws. Then he reversed himself. Thereupon the Commissioner asked district attorneys to drive such companies out of existence. But when the companies were well-established, district attorneys were reluctant to proceed. Three existing societies sought legal exemption from the insurance laws in 1931 and 1945. Both times the Governor vetoed the enacted bill on the ground that the plan of operation of such societies was unsound. However, the very next day after the second veto, proponents slipped the same provision into an omnibus correction bill as an amendment, and it became law without any objection from the Governor. The 1947 legislature saw a proposal to reinstate the Dane County Mutual Benefit Association. This concern had been operating continuously in the state since 1931, but its charter had been annulled in 1944 for failure to comply with the insurance laws. Again the legislature succumbed to the special pressure, and again the Governor vetoed the bill; he saw no reason to increase the number of such manifestly unsound enterprises. The process of excluding assessment life insurance companies from Wisconsin was substantially complete.[30]

Reserve for Pending Claims.—The inevitable delay between the incidence of loss and its settlement also concealed the true financial position of insurance companies. As early as 1903 unsuccessful bills proposed a reserve for pending claims, to be based upon average figures to be supplied by the Commissioner on the basis of the experience of all companies. The 1917 legislature imposed complicated loss reserve requirements on liability and workmen's compensation insurers. For liability insurance, the loss reserve was 60 per cent of earned premiums less loss payments and loss expense for policies issued during the three preceding years, but, on policies issued in the first of the three years, the loss reserve must be not less than $750 for each outstanding liability suit. A fixed sum was required for suits pending on older policies, on a scale that increased with the age of the suit. The provisions for compensation insurance were differently formulated, but had the same basic objective. The 1919 legislature imposed a very flexible suretyship requirement. In all three cases the legislature gave the Commissioner wide discretionary power to compel upward adjustment of the reserve.[31]

Valuation of Assets.—Once solvency became dependent on the constant preservation of an excess of assets over reserve requirements, the companies became vulnerable to fluctuations in the value of assets. Strict investment limitations prevented the extreme fluctuations in value that would have accompanied the purchase of equity shares, but there was some fluctuation in the market value of even fixed-dollar obligations, such as bonds. Any rise in the rate of interest depressed the market value of long-term fixed-dollar obligations. On request of the Northwestern Mutual the 1903 legislature permitted averaging of bond prices over a six-month period. This step was sufficient for normal times. The critical events of 1907 in the securities markets led the National Convention of Insurance Commissioners to resolve that securities be valued as of the 1906 market value, to avoid the unrealistic deflation of 1907. The Attorney General thought the Commissioner would not be justified in so valuing securities, but he reached almost the same result by holding that the Commissioner had reasonable latitude in determining the present market value for 1907 valuation.[32]

When insurance companies bought long-term fixed-dollar securities, they did so with no object of speculating on the short-run fluctuations of the market, and it was unwise to penalize them for such fluctuations. Rigid valuations of bonds caused some insolvencies in the 1870's and 1880's. On the other hand, limitations of the amount of surplus a company might retain could cause difficulty in the event of a sudden and dramatic rise in bond prices. The 1915 legislature realistically permitted valuation on an amortization basis for life companies; so long as the securities were not in default, the value was adjusted to keep the effective rate of interest constant, and to bring the value to par at maturity.[33]

Control of Internal Management Practices

In theory, the policyholders controlled, and were entitled to benefit from, the operations of a mutual company. In practice, mutuals other than those strictly local were operated by a self-coöpting inside group which might have its own interests more in mind than those of the policyholders. A 1905 contract for the sale to a doctor of a half interest in the Wisconsin Health and Accident Company and the transfer of its principal office from Fond du Lac to Wausau involved the crass assumption that a mutual might be bought and sold as private property. Though the court held the agreement illegal as contrary to public policy and good morals, the incident shows how little the policyholders exercised even a residual control; the only effective restraint upon the greediness of corporate officers might be the officials of the state government. But regulation of internal management practices was difficult and was not attempted before it was felt to be absolutely necessary.[34]

A first abortive effort at regulation of internal management affairs came in 1885, when a proposed bill would have limited the total of all officers' salaries for mutual life companies to $25,000 unless a committee of policyholders appointed by the Commissioner should decide otherwise. Membership of the committee would be drastically restricted to forestall official domination. This proposal probably represented a particular policyholder's resentment at management practices of the Northwestern Mutual, rather than any broadly-based sentiment.[35]

In the Progressive period there was less reluctance to interfere with management prerogatives. In 1905 the Wisconsin legislature appointed the Joint Committee on the Affairs of Life Insurance Companies. That committee supplemented the exhaustive study of New York's Armstrong committee with a thorough examination of the practices of the Northwestern Mutual, the Wisconsin Life, and the Union Central of Cincinnati, especially with respect to lobbying activities, political contributions, internal management practices, investment policy, and marketing methods. The critical report showed real understanding of the economics of life insurance, and with the possible exception of the controversial "actuarial bills" its recommendations were realistic and practicable. They were directed to the suppression of the tontine; the control of management expenses, especially agency commissions; and the suppression of various corrupt practices found less in the Wisconsin investigation than in the Armstrong inquiry. However, there were findings of some Wisconsin practices offensive to the heightened moral feeling of the Progressive era. Despite an assumption that nothing of significance would be discovered, some of the press, at least, thought that the public had been "treated to a succession of surprises" (*Evening Wisconsin* [Milwaukee], April 28, 1906). The sentiment for close regulation was fed by the findings.[36]

Suppression of the Tontine.—The tontine contract originated in mid-seventeenth century in a suggestion of Lorenzo Tonti, a Neapolitan banker, to Cardinal Mazarin. In its original form it was a scheme for floating government loans for military purposes on peculiarly advantageous terms. Tontine contracts were first issued in the United States by the Equitable Life in 1867. They provided for the accumulation of dividends over ten, fifteen, or twenty year periods; the dividends were then divided among those whose policies were still in force. Premature death or lapse meant forfeiture of all share in the deferred dividends, though not usually of the principal sum.[37]

The tontine appealed to the gambling instinct of the insurance buyer, and it was a leading factor in the fantastic growth of the life insurance business in the late nineteenth century. The Equitable Life was the pioneer and leader in the field, and rode the tontine from insignificance to first place in the industry. Other leading companies were but little behind in this appeal to avarice. In Wisconsin the Northwestern Mutual was also affected by the fever and beginning in 1881 wrote tontine for some years. Its original charter, issued in 1857, permitted quinquennial distribution of surplus, and amendments in 1863 and 1887 gave the trustees permission to distribute annually or once in two, three, four, or five years, as they might determine. The company interpreted the provision to permit longer deferments. By the turn of the century, however, the Northwestern Mutual was not pushing the tontine, and sold rather little of it.[38]

The primary evil of the tontine was the accumulation of large sums beyond the legal reserve. Control of such sums, for which legal accountability was both limited and postponed, was a heady draught to the managers of the large eastern companies, and the funds were used in extravagant contests for new business, in subversion of the New York legislature, and for high salaries and wasteful expenses. They were sometimes diverted to the benefit of annual dividend policies to maintain the dividends. These evils were well known; the facile assumption that the Armstrong committee hearings first brought the information to light is inaccurate. The service of the Armstrong committee was, rather, to give widespread publicity to facts already known to the informed.[39]

In 1899 an attempt at suppression of the tontine sought to make use of differential taxation. A next effort in 1901 and 1903 pointed straight at the misuse of deferred dividends; it would have required deferred dividends to be set up annually as a liability to the policyholder, and would have forbidden misuse of such sums. Another 1903 bill would have made use of publicity; the companies must report to each policyholder his share of the deferred dividends. A more direct proposal would have required annual distribution of surplus. Another would have compelled annual accounting of deferred dividends, and would have given the policyholder an absolute right to his share. Another 1905 bill would have forbidden all forfeitures of policyholders' equities. All this legislative activity came before the Armstrong committee investigation.[40]

Efforts were also made to suppress the tontine under existing law. In 1902 complaint was filed with the Commissioner against the Equitable Life Assurance Society for its failure to distribute surplus at least every five years under the section of the 1870 life insurance act providing that "every life insurance corporation doing business in this state upon the principle of mutual insurance, or the members of which are entitled to share in the surplus funds thereof, may make distribution of such surplus . . . annually, or once in two, three, four or five years, as the directors thereof may . . . determine." The issue before the Commissioner was simple: was the section mandatory or permissive? Commissioner Host decided that the section was mandatory. To give it a permissive meaning would mean that the statute was nugatory, since it gave permission to do an act that was already permissible without the statute. The Circuit Court agreed with the Commissioner, despite the company's technical arguments on the meaning of the statute and the disingenuous argument that the retained surplus was a "safety fund," needed to give the policyholder additional security. On appeal the company added a threat that an adverse construction would drive the leading companies out of the state or bring chaos to the business. The Supreme Court dealt almost exclusively with the technical problem of statutory construction and concluded that the statute was merely permissive and hence, that deferred dividend policies were lawful.[41]

When the Equitable case was decided, the legislature was still in session. The Attorney General and the Commissioner proposed a bill to forbid deferment of dividends beyond five years. The bill passed with ambiguous amendments added in committee, and the Commissioner at once informed the companies he would enforce the law.[42]

Thus before the Armstrong committee began its work, the Wisconsin legislature had taken a long step toward suppressing the tontine by limiting it to a maximum of five years. Commissioner Host wanted to go even further—he advocated heavy taxation of undistributed surplus and a required annual accounting or distribution. The next legislature had before it the elaborate recommendations of the 1906 Wisconsin investigating committee, contained in twenty-four bills; many of the bills were passed, including those suppressing the tontine. One of the bills required annual apportionment to each class of deferred dividend policies and forbade diversion of apportioned funds to any other purpose, with an annual accounting to the Commissioner and an annual statement to any policyholder requesting it. Another required annual apportionment of surplus to participating policies, and except for existing deferred dividend policies required that the apportionment be made to each individual policy, with an annual statement to the policyholder. The Armstrong laws in New York had finished the tontine for the big New York companies, but there was strenuous resistance, even so, to legislative interference with insurance policies already in force, sometimes on the high moral ground of the sanctity of contracts. The suggestion that management control of deferred dividends might not be interfered with did not prevail with the reforming legislature.[43]

Control of Agents' Commissions.—Though the agency system was intrinsically wasteful, it was the marketing system best calculated to expand the insurance business rapidly in the nineteenth century. The dynamic of the system, however, was to encourage vigorous competition among companies for the better agents, with a constant increase in commissions. In 1860, John Rountree of Platteville was selling fire insurance for 10 per cent commission, plus occasional expenses. In 1871 company men were deprecating payment of more than 15 per cent commission. An 1887 report to the Fire Underwriters Association of the Northwest pointed out that average commissions had risen in twenty years from about 11 to nearly 18 percent, creating one of the grave problems of the business. In 1911 Commissioner Ekern criticized commissions as high as 40 per cent in the fire insurance business. In the twentieth century commission rates continued at levels unjustified by the service performed, and direct writing through salaried agents was one of the competitive answers of mid-twentieth century.[44]

In the life insurance business, too, commissions increased. Tontine policies were especially responsible for the increase, which took place in the 1870's and 1880's; the availability of large sums of money above the legal reserve, for which there was limited accountability, provided a ready source of funds with which to play the competitive game. As commissions increased, competition of agents for business became more keen and rebating became common. High commissions tended to concentrate expenses in the first year of the policy. Excessive first-year expenses might be paid for in two ways: by an initiation or life membership fee, or by absorption in surplus. The latter was more practicable for life insurance, but it tended to favor established companies and to concentrate the life insurance business, for only established companies had the surplus with which to pay heavy first-year expenses and still provide the required reserves on the full level premium basis required by early valuation laws. New small companies had difficulty in competing with the giants on first-year expenses.[45]

The evil of excessive expenses was understood in the state, and efforts at reform were made, long before the investigations, though effective control awaited the dramatic revelations of 1906. In 1897, 1901, and 1903, bills sought to limit the expense of new business by relating permissible commissions to expense loading, or to the face of the policy. Though no success was achieved earlier than the legislative investigations, sentiment for the limitation was evidently persistent. The Armstrong-triggered reforms led to control of commissions in life insurance before there was serious thought of control in other lines. This was a by-product of the dramatic corruption in the life insurance business, rather than of any greater need for control; the problem was a half-century old in fire insurance, too.[46]

Discovery by the Wisconsin committee that some general agents of the Northwestern Mutual were receiving incomes larger than the company's president led the 1907 legislature to require life insurance companies to report in detail to the Commissioner all expense charges contained in premiums, and forbade participating companies to pay expenses that exceeded the expense charges, whether on a single policy, as commissions or advances to agents or, in the aggregate, on first year business or on total business. No agent for a participating company might be paid any compensation not determined in advance, nor might bonuses, prizes, or rewards, based on the volume of business produced, be paid. The principle of expense limitation was not entirely unacceptable to the insurance interests, but this statute fixed an inflexible rule, setting aside a definite portion of each premium of each policy for expense purposes. Company actuaries argued that this was so unacceptable that a company should withdraw from the state rather than submit to it. A companion bill limited the permissible total expense loading to a third of the net single premium on an ordinary life policy issued at the same age, on the 3 per cent American Experience Table. This measure passed without serious objection from the companies and was still law in mid-century.[47]

The committee wanted to limit not only the aggregate of expenses, but also the yearly distribution of expenses. The old, well-established companies, customarily valuing on the full net level premium reserve plan, distributed the expense over the life of the policy. What this meant in practice, since initial expenses could not in fact be paid on this basis, was that a substantial part of acquisition cost was treated as a part of the general cost of doing business, chargeable to old, as well as to new, policies. The excess came out of surplus. This was only possible to companies with surpluses, and the fact that the existing valuation laws virtually compelled the practice was a handicap to new companies. Since new companies could not possibly recoup first-year expenses out of first-year premiums, the result was that even new companies must begin operations with substantial surpluses.[48]

The statutory solution of the problem of heavy first-year expenses was a primary concern of the Wisconsin committee, as well as of the Armstrong committee. One solution was to treat the first year of each policy as written on the term basis; no reserve need be set up, but all the premium above the mortality cost was available for first-year expenses. This might be done legally by actually writing the policy on a preliminary term basis. This was a mere device to evade reserve requirements, since a policy written in this way provided exactly the same benefits. Company and consulting actuaries were concerned with the problem too, and there was not a little professional jealousy among the proponents of various plans. Various modifications of the preliminary term plan were devised and adopted. Another plan, popular at its inception, though not entirely satisfactory because it did not provide a wide enough margin in early years, was the select and ultimate plan. It was partly developed by Miles M. Dawson, former employee of the Northwestern Mutual and consulting actuary for the Armstrong and Wisconsin committees. The select and ultimate plan took cognizance of the fact that medical selection of applicants produced a select group of policyholders whose mortality experience for a few years was more favorable than an unselected group at the same age. Ultimately the selective effect of the medical examination wore off, and the mortality experience of the selected group became comparable to that of an unselected group. Mortality tables constructed on this basis showed low mortality in the first years, thus freeing more of the premium for expenses. This select and ultimate table became the basis of valuation in New York under the recommendations of the Armstrong committee, for which Dawson was consulting actuary. Not unnaturally he also thought it should be adopted in Wisconsin, and especially objected that the committee's plan was a preliminary term plan, modified by some elements of the select and ultimate table. Professional jealousy probably explains Dawson's extreme statements about the proposals and his petulant refusal to be questioned by the author of the committee's plan.[49]

The valuation proposal finally made permitted preliminary term, select and ultimate, or full net level premium valuation with equal tolerance; Dawson criticized the bill for its undue latitude, for it seemed to permit "as great a variety of minimum standards of valuation as there were different forms of schedules which companies might conceivably adopt" (Dawson [1907b] p. 7). He thought the variety of valuations would unduly burden the Wisconsin insurance department. Actuaries of well-established companies professed to think the reserve requirements for early years inadequate; they were undoubtedly partly motivated by the desire to compel full net level premium valuation as a protection against the incursion of new companies, as they, in effect, admitted when they complained of the "excessive first year's commissions" permitted in the bill. It was not excessive first-year commissions that really bothered them, but a provision for valuation that permitted *new* companies to pay such commissions. Among signers of the statement were actuaries of companies which were serious offenders on first-year commissions. In fact, the way to prevent high acquisition cost was to forbid it, not to prevent new companies from indulging in it while permitting it to old. The bill lost narrowly in 1907 but passed easily in 1909.[50]

The basic valuation law was not seriously objectionable to the companies. But the provisions for expenses were anathema. The expense limitation was uniform in amount for a given age, regardless of the type of life insurance written. The company actuaries objected to this as permitting the largest percentage of expense on the least desirable forms of policies. More important, the actuaries objected to the recommended requirement that each policy contain a table showing an expense charge and mortality charge for each year of the policy. They said such a table would be misleading. Sometimes the companies were more frank; they objected to providing full information on the ground that policyholders would not take the policies if they knew how much they were paying for expense, perhaps an admission that expenses were uneconomically high. Dawson pointed out that it was illusory to suppose there could be any such neat distribution of expenses and mortality charges to individual years and individual policies as the original bill contemplated; it would be misleading. He also thought such a rule would encourage rebating, because of public knowledge of high first-year commissions. The illusory precision of this method of distribution was so serious a defect, the actuaries said, that companies should not remain in the state if it were required by law. The bill requiring this disclosure was narrowly beaten.[51]

The companies made strenuous and expensive efforts to defeat the 1907 legislative program, with little success. They objected most to the proposals dealing with expense and premium limitation, against which their charges were intemperate. Thus former Commissioner Fricke, lobbying for the Northwestern Mutual, pointed out that the author of the valuation plan was a "junior" professor of mathematics, that the proponents of the bills could claim no "practical" experience in life insurance, and that many companies had threatened to leave the state if the bills were enacted. The proposed legislation was sheer folly, a *pet theory and unworkable ism*" (Fricke [1907]). Many criticisms were undoubtedly justified, but the intemperate formulation must have prejudiced the industry's case before a reforming legislature suspicious of the good faith of insurance companies. At an early stage in the hearings, many insurance men began to threaten withdrawal from the state. But both sides could play the same game; comparison between Fricke's views as spokesman for the Northwestern Mutual, and some views he previously expressed when his opinions were not paid for, was devastating. Nor did management threats to withdraw frighten the reformers; they countered with the suggestion of state insurance.[52]

Once the bills were passed, threats of withdrawal came with added frequency and vehemence, in an attempt to club the Governor into vetoing the bills. Many suspected a "bluff"; the state had the example of the valued policy law to show that withdrawal did not necessarily follow adverse legislation. But this time the companies were not bluffing. In November they began to announce their withdrawals, and finally twenty-three of them left the state. The limitations on expense were the part of the new laws most criticized by the companies, but they were also the part most necessary to prevent diversion of surplus funds and to keep premiums down. Two years later, Commissioner Beedle reported a marked decrease in company expense.[53]

The new laws could be lived with, however. Not only did the Northwestern's departure never materialize, but the New York Life, the Aetna Life, the Prudential, and others stayed and made the necessary adjustments. Stock companies were readier to stay than were mutuals. Eventually many of the retiring companies returned, making their peace with the new order in which even life insurance companies were accountable to society for the details of their management. It was more difficult to take a philosophical view in the stress of battle, and many business men regarded the departure of so many companies as an emergency. They urged a special session to get rid of the "obnoxious laws," but the Governor was not so easily frightened by the "crisis." Even before the year was out, it was apparent that the jeremiahs had been too hasty. The companies that remained in the state prospered, and the state did not suffer.[54]

Many of the withdrawn companies were eager to get back, and made their plans accordingly. Progressives charged that insurance money was poured into the political campaigns of 1908, in an effort to bar re-election of the leading reformers in the legislature. But there was no real chance to repeal the laws, even though eastern insurance men came to Madison to testify.[55]

In 1915 the first-year expense provision was modified in a number of ways. The amendment represented no concession by the state of any basic principle of control insisted on by the 1907 legislature. There was still control of maximum expense, of minimum premium, of expense loading, and of distribution of the expense among policy years. But it was a practicable compromise by which the companies could justify their return to the state. By 1917 ten of the withdrawn companies had returned; thereafter returns were infrequent, though one occurred as late as mid-century.[56]

Control of Management Salaries.—In the Progressive period, one of the focal points for resentment against insurance companies was the high salaries paid to officers. The Governor mentioned high salaries of life companies in his 1905 message to the legislature. The bill of the Committee of Fifteen* in 1907 sought to limit salaries in domestic life companies to $5,000 except by vote of the board of directors. The bill that passed was the Wisconsin committee's bill; it limited salaries for domestic life companies to a maximum of $25,000, unless a greater maximum were fixed by a majority of the policyholders voting at a regular election of directors, after notice that the question was at issue. The necessity of appeal to policyholders apparently proved inconvenient to management, for in 1915 unanimous vote of the board of directors was made another way to raise the maximum. In 1927, 1929, and 1931, bills to eliminate the directors' vote as a way to raise the maximum manifested resentment at this avenue for evasion. The 1927 bill also would have eliminated the policyholders' vote as a method of raising the maximum, which it would have increased to

---

*An interstate committee resulting from a conference of Governors, Attorneys General, and Insurance Commissioners called at the instance of President Roosevelt because of the Armstrong investigation disclosures. See Buley, 1:264–68.

$35,000 to make the change more palatable to industry sentiment. The 1915 law was still in effect at mid-century.[57]

Opposition to high salaries was a tenet of the liberal faith; it revived in the depression period, and the 1933 legislature memorialized Congress to forbid Reconstruction Finance Corporation loans to corporations paying any salary in excess of $17,500 per year. The legislature also requested the Insurance Commissioner to supply information about insurance salaries. Though his exhibits showed that the eleven hundred or more principal executive officers of insurance companies operating in the state received average salaries of about $15,000 per year, the legislature did nothing further to limit salaries. Unexampled prosperity and wider distribution of the benefits of American productivity at mid-century lessened the urgency of the traditional demand for more equality.[58]

A 1939 bill had a related objective—to forbid payment of commissions to officers for supervising sales or for selling. A 1953 bill to forbid management of mutuals by corporate managers had the same underlying purpose—to prevent the manipulation of the company resources primarily for the benefit of management rather than of policyholders.[59]

Other Restrictions on Management.—The legislature also restricted the management of life insurance companies in other ways. The findings of the Armstrong committee in New York created concern about the basic morality of insurance management; many of the limitations were therefore directed to the prevention of corrupt or discriminatory practices. One bill would have forbidden disbursement of $100 or more by a domestic life company except on a voucher signed by the recipient. If the expenditure was for lobbying, the voucher must specify the matter in question. Fear that management of life insurance companies could not be trusted to hold an even balance between participating and nonparticipating policyholders led to a prohibition against issuance of both kinds of policies by the same company. Reporting requirements sought to give the Commissioner some surveillance over the determination of the surplus to be apportioned to participating policies. A bill in 1909 sought to forbid loans to officers or employees of companies except at standard rates and with security fixed at double the amount of the loan. In 1937 the legislature finally took direct action to prevent officers of the companies from misusing their power for personal benefit; it made it illegal for officers in a position to influence investment to receive any fee, brokerage, commission, gift, or other consideration other than the regular fixed compensation. Nor might they be pecuniarily interested in any such transaction. Though this evil was one of those at which the Governor had inveighed most vigorously in 1905, its correction was longest delayed.[60]

§4. *The Development of Administrative Control*

Development of an Independent Insurance Department

Techniques of administrative supervision of business gradually developed in the second half of the nineteenth century, perhaps as much in the regulation of insurance as of any other economic activity. Administrative control of the insurance business was early; it began with the general act of 1850.[1]

In keeping with a strong mid–nineteenth-century tendency, the 1850 statute assigned to existing state officials such administrative duties as it created. The State Treasurer, the Secretary of State, and the Governor were all given tasks, mostly ministerial and hardly burdensome. The Secretary of State had the largest assignment; it was out of his office that the insurance department grew. The 1858 legislature briefly cast on the Governor heavier duties, some discretionary, including the power to initiate an examination into the affairs of a company. It also gave the Attorney General the duty to apply to the court for dissolution of a company, under certain circumstances. In fashion typical of the times, these two mid-century acts distributed new governmental tasks to four existing officials, with no attempt at rational concentration of responsibility for insurance regulation.[2]

The weakness of the scattering technique was soon recognized. In 1866 both the Governor and the Secretary of State urged that powers over insurance be concentrated in the office of the Secretary of State; the Secretary also called for the state to take "more perfect control" over insurance companies, and in 1869 suggested a "system more in harmony with that of Massachusetts, New York, Illinois, and California, based upon national as well as local considerations" (*Rept. Sec'y of State*, 1869, p. 27). Inferentially, though not explicitly, this suggestion called for a separate insurance department and Commissioner such as already existed elsewhere.[3]

Meantime legislative attitudes were developing in the direction of a rationalized system of insurance regulation. An 1868 bill would have created an ex officio administrative board to prescribe uniform policy forms. Then the 1870 revision of the insurance statutes concentrated regulatory power in the Secretary of State and greatly expanded his power. It established a separate insurance department in the office of the Secretary of State. It gave him power to examine the books and inquire into the affairs of insurance companies in order to exercise effective control over them. It limited expenses of the office to $5,000, but it cast the expense of the examinations of the companies on the companies themselves. This gave some independence to the Secretary, who in his examination of insurance companies need not rely entirely on the coöperation of the legislature in supplying funds.[4]

Reliance upon the Secretary of State as ex officio Insurance Commissioner was unfortunate, however, because he carried so many other duties. The special interest which Secretary of State Breese took in his insurance duties concealed the mistake temporarily, but it became only too evident during the years of service of his successor, Peter Doyle. Doyle's consistent failure to make recommendations to the legislature and his unwillingness to take positions in a period when exciting issues were before the industry and the legislature highlighted the need for a separate Insurance Commissioner who could devote full time to his task. As early as 1872, the legislature had considered two bills radically altering the administrative structure of insurance regulation. The first would have created a separate insurance department, with a Superintendent as its chief officer; the other would have given remarkably broad discretionary powers to an ex officio board of Insurance Commissioners. Then when Secretary of State Doyle complained of the burden of his ex officio duties, his protests impressed the Governor, who recommended to the 1878 legislature that the Secretary be relieved. The Governor's message nonetheless reflected the motive of economy which played a large part in the imposition of ex officio duties, for he recommended that the Secretary's insurance duties be shifted to the Railroad Commissioner. The Senate Committee on Finance, Banks and Insurance, however, thought the insurance duties should be separated from other tasks and proposed to the same legislature a separate department of insurance. But the committee did not abandon economy as an objective, for economy was an important consideration at the time, during the long-drawn-out and severe depression of the seventies. Rather, the committee argued that its bill would result in a saving over the existing arrangement. A serious attempt was made to amend the bill to combine the duties of the Insurance and Railroad Commissioners in a single person, but this proposal was false economy, as was subsequently shown. The legislature created a separate department of insurance, and the new Commissioner, through the collection of back taxes, soon proved he could pay his way, as the Governor himself conceded in his 1879 message to the legislature.[5]

Notions of economy were not easily overcome. An 1891 bill would have abolished the Insurance Commissioner's office and returned his duties to the Secretary of State. As late as 1915 an economy bill would have made the State Treasurer supervisor of inspectors of illuminating oils, and the Secretary of State ex officio Insurance Commissioner, but the overwhelming defeat of the bill proved that a separate insurance department had come to stay.[6]

Selection of the Commissioner

The 1878 law originally provided that the new Commissioner be appointed by the Governor, with the consent of the Senate, to hold office for two years unless sooner removed for cause. In 1881 the legislature made the Commissioner of Insurance a biennially elected officer, and in 1891 it provided that a vacancy caused by resignation be filled by appointment by the Governor until regularly filled by election.[7]

In 1909 serious charges were brought against the incumbent Commissioner. Though the charges were largely without basis, they may have created support for the passage of a 1911 law which made the Commissioner appointive for a four-year term. The statute required that the appointee have knowledge of insurance and prohibited his participation in partisan politics. The provisions suggest some of the attitudes supporting the change. But an appointment by the Governor did not remove the Commissioner completely from the political arena. In 1913 the Governor sought to remove Commissioner Ekern, alleging improper participation in political activities. The issue was hotly fought, and the Commissioner won. Resentment at the Governor's unwarranted action led to the introduction of a bill to provide for legislative selection of the Commissioner for a six-year term. But in mid-twentieth century, the Commissioner was still appointed by the Governor.[8]

Financial Provision for the Insurance Department

Economy was the major theme in the entire history of financial provision for the Commissioner's office. The legislature was always ready to add to the duties of the department, but constantly reluctant to authorize additional expenditures for insurance regulation.

The 1878 act limited the Commissioner's salary only by limiting the total expense of the department to $3,500; in 1881 the legislature fixed his salary at $3,000 and authorized him to employ a clerk at $1,200 per year, and in 1883 authorized him to appoint a deputy at $1,500. There was reluctance even about these limited expenditures. Many bills to make modest increases in department budget were unsuccessful. But the growth in the complexity of the task assigned the Commissioner, concomitant upon the growth of the economy, periodically overcame the legislative frugality. Additions were made to the staff in 1895; then in 1897 a revising statute authorized tables of organization for all the state departments, and gave the Commissioner of Insurance a deputy at $1,500, a chief clerk and two other clerks at $1,200 each, an actuary and an examiner at $1,200 each, a stenographer at $720, and a filing clerk and mailing clerk at $900 each. An ex officio committee might authorize even more help.[9]

The Commissioner's domain was becoming a substantial one. But the political character of the Commissioner's office and the relative inadequacy of salaries made it difficult to maintain a high level of ability. Commissioner Fricke recognized the problem and recommended the institution of civil service.[10]

A factor of no small consequence in the financing of the Wisconsin insurance department was the provision of the 1870 life insurance act imposing a duty of valuing, or computing the required reserves of, all outstanding life insurance policies of all Wisconsin companies and some out-of-state companies.[11] The companies paid compensation of one cent per thousand dollars for the valuation. The fee was treated as personal compensation to the Commissioner.*

*In some states the fee system brought serious graft and corruption. See, e.g., Chicago *Record-Herald*, Feb. 4, 1906; Pittsburgh *Post*, Feb. 3, 1906, dealing with situation in Pennsylvania; the Comm'r had salary of $3,000 a year, but his "take" in fees was $52,000 in six years.

In point of fact, the pressure of work on the Commissioner and his staff was usually such that he contracted the valuation work to accountants or actuaries outside the department. About 1895 the department actuary learned the technical skills and thereafter performed the job. He received extra compensation of $1,800 out of the valuation fees, in addition to the statutory salary of $1,200. In the early 1870's, the fees amounted to about $600 per year; they began to increase rapidly about 1880, and by the mid-nineties were nearly $4,000 per year. Ten years later they exceeded $6,000. Though this additional income was not all net, it put the Insurance Commissioner on approximate salary parity with the Governor and Secretary of State.[12]

The private profit aspect of the fee system conflicted with the reform attitudes of the Progressive era and it is not surprising that a change was attempted even before the Progressive capture of the legislature in 1905. Commissioner Fricke thought the fee system "pernicious," and he sought unsuccessfully to eliminate all compensation except the salary. In 1903 a bill passed the Assembly to require payment of all valuation fees into the state treasury. Commissioner Host protested bitterly that the enactment of the bill would cripple his department. He drafted a substitute bill to direct the valuation fees into the state treasury, but also to raise the Commissioner's salary from $3,000 to $5,000, raising him above the Railroad Commissioner and the Attorney General to parity with the Secretary of State, State Treasurer, and Governor. The bill would also have increased staff and raised salaries in the department, especially the actuary's pay, increasing it from $1,200 to $3,000. Host made a very persuasive case. His own salary compared unfavorably with those of Insurance Commissioners elsewhere in the country, salaries of his subordinates were less than in other departments of the state government, work had greatly increased—department receipts had tripled in five years while expenses remained constant—and the legislature was at that very time imposing substantial additional responsibilities on the Commissioner without additional budget. Host's arguments apparently persuaded the Senate, but not the Assembly, and the session ended with no action on the problem.[13]

The 1905 legislature passed a number of measures; to meet the needs caused by the increased burden of work on the Commissioner's office, to eliminate the private compensation, and to remedy the disproportion between salaries in the insurance department and elsewhere in the state government. Governor LaFollette reluctantly signed a measure which provided that the valuation fees be paid into the state treasury and an actuary be appointed to do the valuation work at a salary not more than $2,400, along with an assistant actuary at not more than $1,500. Though LaFollette thought one actuary was quite enough, he signed the bill in order to end the payment of the valuation fees to the Commissioner.[14]

The second of the 1905 bills increased the Commissioner's salary from $3,000 to $5,000 to compensate him for the loss of revenue from valuation fees. The Governor vetoed this bill; he could not see why the abolition of the fees justified raising the salary to parity with the Tax and Railroad Commissioners. He also vetoed a bill to increase other salaries in the department of insurance. A fourth bill became law; it added some clerical assistance to the department, but its meliorating effect was greatly diminished in the Senate, which reduced to one a net addition of four. Since the Governor seemed extremely reluctant to enable the Insurance Commissioner to do a more adequate job it is rather surprising that he signed this measure without comment. He did not condescend to answer Commissioner Host's strong prima facie case for strengthening the office except in sweeping generalities which simply ignored the alleged facts. Governor LaFollette was passive toward reforms he did not originate. Railroad regulation and rate problems obsessed him; insurance regulation seemed too prosaic except when the New York insurance scandal showed the way to gain headlines through an insurance investigation in Wisconsin. The Governor's reluctance to give the Wisconsin insurance department the tools it needed must cast doubt on his merits as a reformer.[15]

The 1907 legislature began to remedy LaFollette's mistakes; it increased the Commissioner's salary to $5,000 and made other raises. The 1911 and 1913 legislatures continued the process with raises, additions to staff, and authorization to the head of each of the state departments to set salaries within his department. Only the Commissioner and the Deputy Commissioner thereafter had salaries set by statute, and those salaries kept approximate pace with the increases in other state salaries. In 1959 the Commissioner received $13,500.[16]

The persistent economy motivation of the legislature was a frequent complaint of the incumbents of the office; occasionally an outsider also recognized the needs of the department, which made it clear that the problem was more than the product of a bureaucrat's desire to expand his domain. In 1941 the Division of Departmental Research recommended an increase in the operating budget to make possible more frequent examinations, and in 1946 a report by a private firm of management consultants found no evidence of over-staffing. The periodic increase in appropriations was never equal to the increase in the complexity and volume of the work assigned; support for the insurance department was less than for some less complex operations more in the limelight. The inadequacies of the budget became most evident in the second quarter of the twentieth century, when the rate-making process came under the supervision of the Commissioner. Such parsimony was very short sighted. A well run insurance department was a good investment, if only for tax collection purposes.[17]

The Commissioner's staff might be temporarily increased under the provisions casting the expense of examination and compensation of examiners on the examined companies. This power gave a needed flexibility to the staff available to the Commissioner. The power to make examinations at the expense of the companies was subject to abuse, however, for it enabled the Insurance Commissioner to authorize expense-paid junkets for his staff as concealed bonuses. Commissioner Fricke severely criticized the examination practices, and especially the expense and compensation arrangements. He felt that while the companies should pay for admission examinations, the state should pay for subsequent ones. Fricke paid his own expenses when he could not approve a company, since he felt this left him free to pass adverse judgment upon the applicant. He may have been accurately interpreting his own reactions, but his suggestion seemed hardly to represent sound standard practice for it would bias most examiners in favor of admission, so that they would not have to pay their own expenses.[18]

The cautious practices of the Fricke administration might not always obtain in other states. Recognition of this led to an unsuccessful bill providing that whenever in the judgment of the Wisconsin Commissioner the examination of a Wisconsin company by an out-of-state commissioner was unnecessary, the company might prorate the cost of the examination among policyholders of the examining state. The 1905 legislature passed a bill which went even beyond Fricke's recommendations and would have cast the expense of examination of companies on the state.[19] Governor LaFollette vetoed the bill, declaring that "if examinations . . . are necessary, then the expense . . . should be borne by the companies for whose benefit they are made" (*Assembly J.*, 1905, pp. 1816–21).

Though it was contrary to the general policy of the law for fees to be payable as compensation to the Commissioner, it was accepted practice under the 1880 statute for examination fees, like valuation fees, to be collected and retained by the Commissioner, and the Attorney General approved. The reform sentiment of the Progressive period reinforced the general policy and when, in January 1909, the deputy Commissioner filed charges against his chief with the Governor, he seized on the retention of examination fees and expenses as a major item in his accusation. The Governor suggested that the legislature investigate the charges and take any necessary action. The problem quickly became enmeshed in all of the personal and political controversies in the Statehouse. There were demands for immediate action to recover fees collected by Commissioners in the past; proponents of this position cited as a parallel the successful suits to collect back interest on state funds from State Treasurers, which had provided a dramatic incident in the rise to power of Wisconsin Progressives.[20]

The legislature examined the charges and found that they posed a fair legal question. It instructed the Attorney General to institute suit against the present and previous Commissioners and their sureties to recover for the state all the retained fees; one of the actions was to be pressed to trial to settle the controverted legal questions. The Attorney General filed such actions against Commissioner Beedle and former Commissioners Fricke, Giljohann, and Host; two years later none of the cases had been brought to trial, and the legislature instructed the Attorney General to report at once and to proceed forthwith to trial on one of the cases. In 1914 the Beedle case was brought to trial and he was adjudged to owe the state $1,105. In 1916 the Attorney General reported the disposition of the case against Beedle; the state recovered $1,105 on proof of the fees collected and retained. The other cases were not further prosecuted despite notices to the defendants in 1914 of impending trial. In 1919 the Attorney General reported that the other three cases were still pending. In 1925 they were permitted to die quietly.[21]

Concern to prevent corruption in the department led the 1909 legislature to forbid state employees to receive from insurance companies compensation or reimbursement of expenses; the law required that such money be paid to the state. An ambiguous companion bill would have used the sums collected to pay the examiners on audited vouchers for their expenses and compensation up to the amount collected. The Governor vetoed this measure on the ground that it would allow the Commissioner compensation as well as actual expenses—in effect, giving him power to set his own salary. The result was that there was no longer provision for payment of the cost of examinations; nevertheless, the Attorney General thought the Commissioner was still under an obligation to make them. The Commissioner refused, because of the enormous expense involved. He sought a quick court test of the expense situation so he could handle the many pending examinations, and he criticized the Attorney General for refusal to coöperate. The 1911 legislature straightened out the tangle and made provision for compensation to be paid out of the treasury on voucher of the Commissioner. The statute provided that the Commissioner might require a deposit from any company to provide for expenses, that he might employ special examiners, and that the company must pay to the state all expenses of examination, including the compensation of special examiners, but not of state employees.[22]

The Commissioner's inability to charge insurance companies for the compensation of regular employees was a handicap for the regular, systematic operation of an examination program. This became more true as the use of outside examiners lessened, and by 1933, entirely ceased. An unsuccessful bill in 1927 would have remedied the matter by charging companies a pro rata share of the salary of the examiner. In the 1940's the difficulty became extreme. Depression-born budget cuts were not restored, and Commissioner Duel repeatedly sought a budget increase to permit a satisfactory examination program. Many companies, he pointed out, had not been examined in forty years. A subcommittee of the legislative council in 1948 urged more frequent examination and that the companies should bear the full cost. This basic reform was at length achieved in 1949, when a statute made the department virtually independent of legislative appropriations for examination of companies. But money was not enough; a new Commissioner declined to use his new budgetary independence to increase the examination program, contending that the existing situation was satisfactory.[23]

Reports

The dominant emphasis in the early regulatory statutes was on reporting and publicity. Other techniques of control, while often present in rudimentary form in the mid–nineteenth-century statutes, received their full development only after the earlier mechanism proved inadequate.

The 1850 act required out-of-state companies, as a condition of admission, to supply the Secretary of State with verified statements of capital and assets. The Secretary had no discretion to deny admission if the statement showed compliance with the law. Out-of-state and domestic companies must make annual reports to the Secretary and cause these to be published. Though the Secretary might sometimes order a capital deficiency repaired, the primary emphasis of the reporting requirement was on publicity, and its use as a basis for active administrative surveillance was minimal. The legislature extended the annual report requirements in 1858 and 1859. These early reports were comparatively uncomplicated; they were not designed to elicit information to facilitate administrative surveillance, but such information as might be supposed to interest policyholders. This was still true after the legislature overhauled the requirements in 1867.[24]

Sentiment for more thorough control was in the making, however. Secretary of State Allen showed uncertainty about the adequacy of reports and publicity as a technique of control when he suggested a thorough revision of the insurance laws, though at the same time, he expressed the naive view that a careful study of the published abstracts of company reports under existing laws would enable any person to form a reliable judgment about any company. The 1870 acts marked a change in point of view with respect to reports, in the direction of making them a basis for administrative control. Although the subject matter of the reports was still specified with particularity, the Secretary of State might make changes in the form of the statements to elicit the desired information. To simplify the companies' reporting, in the early 1870's, Secretary Breese adopted the forms recommended by the National Insurance Convention, but he never succeeded in getting uniform interpretation, nor did he have sanctions adequate to compel such uniformity.[25]

The use of reports as a basis for administrative surveillance depended on the adequacy of the data reported. Wisconsin led the nation in one development. The initial appearance of the gain and loss exhibit, or profit and loss statement, was made in the 1895 examination of the Northwestern Mutual, under the supervision of the Wisconsin Commissioner.* The National Convention of Insurance Commissioners that same year inserted the exhibit in the annual-statement blank for life companies, but company opposition slowed down its adoption. In 1903 Commissioner Host reported that only Wisconsin and Minnesota were using it, despite its value in exhibiting many facts about management. The Wisconsin Commissioner, under his discretionary powers, required the gain and loss exhibit from the time of its inception, and in 1907 the legislature, without opposition, made it a statutory requirement.[26]

The wide range of the information required in reports in the twentieth century gave testimony, too, to the new purpose of reports—to serve as the basis for administrative control. The legislature now required that life companies report to the Commissioner their lobbying expenditures, information about the surplus and the method of assigning part of it for distribution to participating policyholders, expenses paid in the acquisition of business, accumulations retained for deferred dividends, and complete information about stock ownership. In 1927 the legislature carried all these tendencies to their logical conclusion. The statutory particularity of the reporting requirements was eliminated; the Commissioner was merely empowered to require information "upon any and all important elements of such business . . . including gain and loss exhibit, and any matter, condition or requirement imposed by law and tending to a strict accountability of the management" (Laws 1927, 124). With this statute, reporting had become a subordinate tool available for the detailed administrative control of the insurance enterprise.[27]

Reporting and publicity requirements for town and other local mutuals were less formal, and usually emphasized that records must be available to the inspection of members. Supplementary reports were also required for the Commissioner, and as these mutuals tended to become more commercial in character, the report to the Commissioner was more heavily emphasized. In 1937 the legislature even empowered the Commissioner to prescribe the form of town mutual books, so as to exhibit the true condition of the company.[28]

*Comm'r Fricke, who introduced it, thought of it largely in terms of publicity. —Rept. Ins. Comm'r, 1896, 2: xiv. It was omitted from the Northwestern's final examination report, since the company objected to being a guinea pig.—Rept. Ins. Comm'r, 1903, 2:xxxii-xxxiii.

But reporting requirements alone were inadequate to provide satisfactory control of insurance companies. As early as 1852, the Secretary of State complained of the inadequacy of the enforcement machinery. While the public gave substantial credence to the Secretary's certificate of compliance, assuming that it meant a kind of state guarantee of company solvency, in reality the certificate only meant that if the reports were accurate the company apparently had the requisite capital and satisfied certain very superficial tests of solvency. There were sometimes failures soon after statements of full compliance with the requirements of the law.[29]

The 1858 act not only required reports; it went further and gave to the Governor a large discretionary power to initiate an examination into the affairs of a company.[30]

Examinations

That a free-ranging examination had advantages over reports as a device for obtaining information may be shown by an example. Owners of lumber mills and factories organized the Mutual Fire Association of Eau Claire in 1885, allegedly to provide cheap insurance for themselves; the Association did business until adjudged insolvent in 1890. In an effort to subject the officers and directors to claims of creditors, charges were made in insolvency proceedings that rates were substantially less than necessary for solvent operation; that the enterprise was operated so long as its insolvent character could be concealed, whereupon the organizers, having benefited from very cheap insurance for several years, permitted dissolution, leaving other policyholders and creditors to suffer the loss; and that the directors used fraudulent reports to obtain a certificate from the Commissioner showing apparent solvency, and made the certificate public to induce new policyholders to subscribe. Whether the allegations of the complaint were justified is not important; such manipulation would be easy, if the Commissioner relied merely on reports for his information about the company.*

The early examination had also a publicity purpose, for the Governor might publish the results in the newspapers. But even then it was clear that publicity was often a weak reed, so the legislature also provided that the Governor might revoke the licenses of unsound

*The actions were barred by the Statute of Limitations. *Boyd* v. *Ass'n*, 116 Wis. 155 (1903).

out-of-state companies and communicate adverse findings on Wisconsin companies to the Attorney General, whose duty it was to initiate proceedings to terminate their business. The legislature gave similar powers to the Secretary of State when it overhauled the insurance laws in 1870.[31]

The difficulty with publicity, whether based upon reports or examination, was that it was either ineffective or too effective. It had none of the subtlety characteristic of the Commissioner's direct powers. A striking example occurred in 1890. The Milwaukee Mutual Fire Insurance Company was organized in 1886 as a millers' and manufacturers' mutual; during the next four years it had a fairly successful existence. In 1887 it qualified to write nonassessable policies. On December 21, 1890, the Milwaukee *Sentinel* published a story, purportedly based upon the Commissioner's recent examination of the company, alleging virtual insolvency and representing the Commissioner as uncertain whether to proceed at once for dissolution. Policyholders quickly cancelled policies, and the company soon became insolvent and was forced into receivership.* Whether or not the *Sentinel* story was accurate, the publicity use of information acquired by examination of the company proved too crude a weapon; it destroyed the company without even the possibility of careful liquidation.

Examination was a duty which all Commissioners performed, more or less adequately. The adequacy of the performance depended to some extent on the adequacy of financial provision for the expense; it also depended on the interest and sense of duty of the Commissioner. Proper examination was involved and protracted. For example, the 1917 examination of the Northwestern Mutual, in coöperation with the departments of four other states, took over four months; in particular, there was careful inquiry into suspect investment transactions between the company and a brokerage firm run by the president's son. Though nothing immoral was shown, the trustees forced the resignation of the president as a result.[32]

Commissioner Fricke recommended examinations for life companies every three or four years, supplemented by interim reports. An unsuccessful bill in 1907 would have required the Commissioner to examine domestic insurance companies triennially; each out-of-state company must file triennial reports of examination by the insurance

---

*Milwaukee Mutual v. Sentinel, 81 Wis. 207 (1892), and Case on Appeal, 11 This was a libel suit by the receiver; the court did not reach the merits but held that the action was personal and did not survive dissolution.

department of its home state or be examined in Wisconsin. In 1919 the legislature did require triennial examination for surety rate-making organizations. Whether the Commissioner carried out the duty was another question.[33]

In 1915 the legislature gave sanction to the examination process by making it an offense punishable both by fine and imprisonment to wilfully falsify books or papers with the intent to deceive an examiner, and in 1943 deleted intention to deceive an examiner as an essential element of the crime.[34]

The Growth of Administrative Discretion

Reporting and examinations only provided information, which then had to be used, whether merely by publication or as the basis for administrative control. In the beginning, the administrator's power of control was mostly ministerial. The discretionary powers conferred on the Secretary of State were not large under the 1850 act. The 1858 act gave the Governor much more discretion, but in practice he used it rather little. The Governor, after all, had more to do than act as a Commissioner of Insurance. The 1859 act required the Secretary of State to be "satisfied" that the capital, securities, and investments of companies remained secure before he renewed certificates of authority to do business; this involved some exercise of judgment.[35]

In the 1860's, sentiment was building up for giving substantial administrative discretion to some official who could make use of it. Secretary of State Allen asked that the state assume "more perfect control" over insurance companies; he wanted power to compel the dissolution of companies in difficulties.[36] The 1870 act did give more discretion to the Commissioner, at least with respect to solvency subsequent to admission. The extent of the sentiment was best shown, however, by an 1872 Assembly bill to create an ex officio Insurance Commission and give it the "duty to determine when any such corporation or association is doing the business of insurance beyond the limits of prudent safety or otherwise conducting its business in an unsafe manner," and in such case "to revoke the license of such corporation or association . . . " (A 10 [1872]).[37]

Duty in terms ministerial might in practice result in considerable discretion. This is suggested by the terms of the 1879 act imposing on the Commissioner the "duty" of revoking the license of an out-of-state company, or reporting to the Attorney General "persistent violations" of the laws, as the basis for bringing dissolution proceedings. Casual violations were merely to be brought to the attention of the company. The ambiguity inherent in the word "persistent" gave discretion in enforcement, which used as a lever, might be effective to give some discretion in substance as well. Indeed the extent of the Commissioner's discretion seems to have depended in practice principally upon the attitude of the Commissioner. On the one hand, Commissioner Spooner complained of the inadequacy of his discretionary powers on admissions, especially with respect to reckless rate competition. He also felt unable to take decisive action to prevent the raid on the Madison Mutual surplus. On the other hand, Commissioner Fricke was inclined to refuse admission to companies he thought unsound, even when he was not sure of his legal ground. It is true that he urged that the Commissioner be given the tools to do his job, or else that his office be abolished, since the very existence of the office gave assurance to policyholders that the companies with which they did business were reliable. But Fricke was less inclined than Spooner to wait for the legislature.[38]

The tendency was constantly to give broader discretion to the Commissioner. The 1887 legislature gave him complete discretion to license assessment accident companies after a personal examination, and in 1891 also gave him power to revoke an agent's license whenever it appeared to his satisfaction, at a hearing held by him, that the provisions of the antidiscrimination laws had been infringed. In 1891 and 1895 the legislature gave him very broad discretion on admissions of fraternal and mutual benefit societies. The 1897 act to regulate casualty and surety companies gave broad discretion to the Commissioner to decide whether a company with impaired capital might reduce its capital or must repair the deficiency or dissolve, and he was given unlimited discretion in working out a reinsurance reserve formula for casualty and surety companies.[39]

By the turn of the century, the Commissioner had wide discretion with respect to a great variety of problems. The Attorney General ruled in 1903 that the Commissioner might revoke a company's license for any violation of the statutes. Such power would give large discretion in practice, even if none were formally declared in law. The twentieth-century tendency was to tie the exercise of the Commissioner's power to broad standards rather than to specific rules. Thus the legislature gave him some power to determine the proper basis for calculating reserve liabilities, a more flexible power to revoke agents' licenses, a free hand in determining the form of reports, a discretionary power rather than a mandatory obligation to revoke the license of an out-of-state company in unsound condition, and the power to revoke a license for a single kind of insurance while leaving it in effect for other kinds. In 1919 he received broad discretion in the admission of out-of-state companies; he might license such companies if he were satisfied that the interests of the people of the state were not jeopardized.[40]

In general, the statutes conferred on the Commissioner only the sanction of refusing or withdrawing a license. But the extension of his discretion with regard to grounds of action was paralleled by increased flexibility in the sanctions he might employ. An unsuccessful 1927 bill would have permitted him to hear complaints on money claims against casualty companies and issue a just and reasonable order; in effect, to this extent he would become a judge. Again, the banking crisis and holiday of March, 1933, brought hasty enactment of a law empowering the Commissioner—subject to the Governor's approval—to suspend the payment of cash surrender values or making of policy loans by life insurance companies, and to extend the time for payment of premiums. The object of the legislation was to prevent the forced liquidation of assets by the companies at ruinous prices in order to meet the policy obligation to pay cash values. The law was used for a short time during the crisis, to delay payment of both cash values and premiums. Another discretionary power not directed to the granting of a license was the power to approve rates.[41]

Notwithstanding the broad reach of the Commissioner's discretion, the Attorney General announced in 1927 that the Commissioner's power to admit out-of-state insurance companies was ministerial in nature: "an insurance commissioner is a ministerial officer and . . . cannot be given any judicial or legislative powers" (*Ops. Att'y Gen.*, 1927, pp. 167, 168). However, the facts had long since rendered the legal dogma obsolete; the same Attorney General was quite able to recognize the existence of discretion in fact, whatever he might term it. One student of the administrative process in Wisconsin, seeking to give quantitative measure to administrative discretion, found a strong twentieth-century trend toward more discretion. Because their offices were the oldest, he found the Insurance and Banking Commissioners, among administrative officials, the most significantly limited in administrative discretion. Following Freund's grading of discretionary standards into (1) precisely measured terms involving no discretion, (2) abstractions of common certainty, conferring medium degrees of discretion, and (3) terms involving a broad appeal to judgment, he thought the Insurance Commissioner's powers fell almost entirely within the first two grades; in his view the degree of discretion did not change after first enactment of a law but was carried forward from revision to revision. This does not seem to be entirely true.[42]

The growth of discretion in the Commissioner necessitated procedural rules and provisions for judicial review of his orders. The 1911 legislature provided procedures for hearings before the Commissioner and review of his orders by the court. Rights of persons affected were carefully preserved. The same legislature gave the Commissioner power to administer oaths and to compel attendance of witnesses and production of documents, and made it the duty of the Circuit Court to compel compliance with these procedural orders. Toward mid-century, concern for the preservation of due process in a new bureau-dominated government structure led to the enactment of the Uniform Administrative Procedure Act; the Insurance Commissioner was included within its scope.[43]

Dissolution of Insolvent Companies

The Insurance Commissioner had some power to initiate legal proceedings to dissolve insolvent local companies, but he also needed tools to prevent the dissolution, or at least to supervise the dissolution, of solvent companies, in order to prevent their manipulation for the purely private purposes of company officers. Such power would have enabled the Commissioner to prevent the raid on the Madison Mutual surplus.

If the Commissioner were receiver for all insurance company dissolutions, many abuses might be prevented; in particular, this device would eliminate much of the milking of corporate assets that may take place in receivership. Commissioner Spooner remarked that "a receiver seems to consider the sole object of a receivership to be, to receive" (Rept. Ins. Comm'r, 1879, p. 100). Much later, Commissioner Fricke was concerned about the long delay in the completion of the many insurance company receiverships during the depression of the 1890's, when he was in office. He suggested in 1896 that the Commissioner or his deputy be made receiver in all insurance company dissolutions. One of the reforms of the Progressive period made the Commissioner liquidator of insurance companies, and permitted him to petition the court for an order that he conduct a business, on the ground that the company was insolvent; or had refused to submit to inspection or examination; or had neglected to obey a Commissioner's order to repair a deficiency in capital; or had transferred its entire business or conducted some other similar transaction without the Commissioner's consent; or had engaged in operations hazardous to policyholders, creditors, or the public; or had violated its charter; or had suffered an officer to refuse to be examined under oath.[44]

In his capacity as liquidator of insurance companies the Wisconsin Commissioner achieved considerable success. By mid-twentieth century, he had liquidated a substantial number of companies, with full payment of claims in nearly all cases, and at low cost. Not every dissolution was trouble-free, however. In January 1941 Commissioner Duel began dissolution of the Wisconsin Mutual Insurance Company. The Circuit Court ordered an assessment of $491,000 for a deficiency of $189,000; the excess was thought justified by expenses of liquidation and probable uncollectability of a substantial part of the assessment. The order directed that the liquidator's books be maintained in such a manner as to allocate, so far as possible, each assessment collected from any policyholder to the period when he was a member.[45]

Some policyholders contended that the assessment was unlawful because it was "horizontal," i.e., made without regard to the apportioning of losses and expenses to the policyholders holding policies at the time the losses and expenses were incurred. The Supreme Court held that the initial horizontal character of the assessment was not a vice if books were kept so as to provide for appropriate apportionment. Nor was the excess assessment bad, since experience showed that the probable collection would yield about 40 per cent; successive assessments would be costly. Clearly, the court wanted to facilitate the expeditious and inexpensive liquidation of the company. (*In re* Wisconsin Mutual, 241 Wis. 394 [1942]). The assessed policyholders did not willingly accept this result. They sought to stall collection, by a legislative investigation of the adequacy of administrative controls and the failure of the Insurance Commissioner "to safeguard the interests of . . . policyholders and the people of the state" (Resolution 21 A, *Assembly J.*, 1943, pp. 271–73). The policyholders' committee supported the resolution, but the Commissioner, the creditors, and the

Wisconsin Mutual Alliance, which was concerned to get the creditors paid off and uphold the reputation of other Wisconsin mutuals, all opposed it. It was overwhelmingly defeated.[46]

One of the objections to the liquidation was the large amount of the legal fees involved. The total of these grew until it reached the figure of $76,929 by 1948. The crusading *Capital Times* (Madison, Wis.) bitterly attacked the use of private attorneys for the liquidation, instead of the salaried employees of the Attorney General's office, and also criticized the failure of the insurance department to stop operation of the company much earlier, when it was a matter of wide knowledge that it was "on the rocks" (*Capital Times*, Jan. 30, 1944). This criticism ignored the costly and unnecessary litigation forced on the Commissioner by the policyholders' protective committee, and the expense of collecting a multitude of small claims, many of which must be pursued by litigation. In the end, over $140,000 out of the original assessment was returned to policyholders, on completion of the liquidation.[47]

Delimitation of the Insurance Field

One of the persistent problems of administrative control of insurance was the delimitation of the area within which the insurance laws applied. A great variety of peripheral economic activities resembled insurance in transferring some risk of adventitious loss from one person to another for a consideration. The determination of which such activities were subject to the Commissioner's control proceeded in substantial measure on practical considerations of the importance and the effectiveness of control, though since the Attorney General made most such decisions, the rulings were usually couched in technical legal language.

The nineteenth-century statutes exempted from regulation a large number of mutual benefit societies as well as providing less formal regulation of local mutuals. This approach implied that the intimate relation between members and managers made regulation less necessary for these operations. Substantial regulation eventually developed for the larger of such operations, but small mutual benefit operations continued to be exempt from the control of the Commissioner. For exemption the terms of the statute must be met, however; merely avoiding the use of the word "insurance" did not produce exemption.[48]

In 1903 the legislature declared the payment of accident or sickness benefits to be insurance; in 1909 it brought under insurance regulation the business of paying funeral expenses of deceased members when such an enterprise was conducted for profit. In 1931 it assimilated burial insurance to legal reserve life insurance for most purposes of regulation.[49]

In 1904 the Attorney General decided that issuance of an elevator receipt agreeing to indemnify the owner for the loss of grain by fire was a fire insurance contract. In 1908 he ruled that it was an illegal guaranty insurance business for agents of city and village mutuals to guaranty members against further assessments, on their individual accounts and for a consideration.[50]

In another instance, the Attorney General ruled that a "windmill insurance policy" issued by the Appleton Manufacturing Company on the windmills it sold was an insurance policy when there was a separate consideration for the policy. He reserved judgment on mere sales warranties without separate consideration; in 1908 he held a similar sales warranty on lightning rods, promising a $500 reward, to be insurance even without mention of separate consideration. But in 1912 he held that a lightning rod warranty, which promised to refund only the cost of the rod, was not insurance. All these rulings had involved promises to pay sums of money if there were a fire.[51] In 1915, however, a new Attorney General ruled that payment of a sum beyond the cost of the article sold did not make the contract one of insurance; the amount prescribed was a mere liquidation of damages. Still another Attorney General ruled that an agreement to service machinery and to indemnify the owner for loss caused by breakdown was insurance. So also was a contract of sale under which the buyer's debt for the purchase price was discharged in case of death or disability. When the Woodland Farms Company proposed to guarantee land values for a consideration, the Attorney General ruled that this was an illegal insurance business, since the proposal permitted the guarantee of land values even when the company did not sell the land. The Company then proposed to guarantee only the value of land it sold, and in the same contract. This the Attorney General held not to be insurance, but a sales warranty.[52]

In 1906 and 1908, the Attorney General thought the contract of the Automobile Owners Defense Company to defend civil suits for negligence in the operation of an automobile was not an insurance contract but a contract for legal services. A manufacturing concern's private and voluntary accident compensation scheme was insurance, however.[53]

The Ford Car Owners' Protective Association sought to escape regulation of its business of indemnifying for fire, theft, and other casualty losses to automobiles by advertising that it merely acted as agent to distribute the proceeds of indemnity calls by members and had no interest in the proceeds. The Attorney General thought the association "sought by an adroit use of language to cover and conceal the real purposes of the organization"; he saw through the transparent veil and ruled that the organization was subject to regulation as an insurance business.[54]

The problem was perennial; in mid-twentieth century the Attorney General decided that a contract by which for an annual fee a company purchased all dishonored checks was a contract of insurance and that the business of issuing used car warranties, too, was an insurance business. The legislature decided to what extent interscholastic athletic benefit plans were subject to the insurance laws, was urged to subject labor union health and welfare plans to the insurance laws, and partially exempted from insurance regulation nonprofit sickness plans for indigents.[55]

Revision of the Law

One of the advantages of the concentration of responsibility for insurance regulation in a single official was that it provided a responsible person to recommend desirable changes in the law. In the long run, that part of the Commissioner's role had great significance, because of his influence exercised not only through official reports and recommendations but also through informal and backstage effect upon legislative activity. It is impossible to measure the extent to which various Commissioners were able to guide the growth of insurance law, but it was considerable. Through the whole history of the Commissioner's office, the Commissioner was one of the driving forces for change in the law; though many Commissioners were of conservative political orientation and showed a markedly friendly attitude toward the companies, their recommendations were most often in the direction of more adequate control. Implicit in the bureaucrat's position was concern for the public interest as he saw it, and it would be misleading oversimplification to suggest that the industry "took over" the insurance department, as some critics were wont to declaim.

In addition to a steady flow of administrator's suggestions to the legislature, there were some efforts by Commissioners to achieve thoroughgoing revision of the insurance law. Commissioner Fricke was the prime mover in the first major attempt at codification. In 1895 the legislature enacted a law providing for a commission to revise the insurance laws, which by then were in a confused state after fifty years' haphazard growth; the Commissioner with two others constituted the commission. After a thorough study, the commission reported to the legislature an extensive revision and systematization of the insurance laws in 106 printed pages. After the Senate postponed the major revision, many of the bill's innovations were introduced as separate bills, but they too came to grief. The Senate was not in a reforming mood, even though most of the changes were moderate. The reasons for the failure of this revision effort were probably inertia, a multitude of vested interests in established procedures, and the disinclination of the legislature to enact substantive changes in a general revision bill; it was becoming accepted practice for the legislature to enact changes individually, and to use revision bills only for changes in the form of the law, not its content.[56]

Thirty years later, the Commissioner made another major attempt at wholesale revision of the insurance laws. In 1925 Commissioner Smith spent a great deal of time in preparing a codification of the insurance laws of the state. He pressed into service the technical staff of the department, and obtained the collaboration of former Commissioner Fricke. To avoid the charge of political motivation, he left taxation provisions out of the revision. After months of work, with the aid of the Revisor of Statutes and the Legislative Reference Library, and such insurance interests as responded to his invitation to assist, he introduced a revision bill. Committee hearings produced many corrections, but some changes proposed by the companies were not accepted by the Commissioner or the committee. The committee unanimously reported the bill, despite what Smith called "crude and unwarranted attacks by representatives of certain insurance interests who maintained an expensive and powerful lobby for that purpose (Rept. Ins. Comm'r, 1925, pp. 9–10). He did not further identify the "interests," but he may have meant the mutuals and fraternals which had been represented by Herman L. Ekern, Attorney General and former Commissioner. Ekern opposed the bill and out of that opposition came a bitter fight between the two men. The fraternals also opposed the bill. After a tempestuous life, it died by a close vote of 14 to 13.[57]

Ekern's main line of attack on the bill was that it made substantive changes in the law, contrary to the proper scope of a revision bill, and that the measure failed to explain the changes made. Smith then appointed former Commissioner Fricke to a position in the department, to prepare another codifying bill for presentation to the 1927 legislature; they planned to make full explanation of all changes, to obviate the objections made by Ekern. Joint resolutions for insurance law revision were introduced in each house of the legislature in 1927, but neither resolution made any substantial headway. An extensive revision of the statutes on insurance passed the legislature in 1931, but the Governor vetoed it because it made changes of substance. The 1933 legislature finally made very extensive changes in the organization of the law, but no changes of substance. In 1943 a joint resolution to study the need for a new revision of the insurance laws was defeated. In 1957 the Commissioner expressed some interest in a new codification, but nothing came of it.[58]

Effectiveness of Administrative Surveillance

The evaluation of the prosaic day-to-day administration of the Commissioner's office is beyond the scope of this study. Adequate evaluation must await a detailed examination of the records of the Commissioner's office; though incomplete, these are yet of daunting bulk. Evaluation of early Commissioners must be based upon the official reports of the office, which must be taken with caution as sometimes self-serving. Here no more can be done than to sketch the activities of the Commissioners from official reports and other easily accessible sources, to some extent suggesting possible directions for further inquiry.[59]

One thing is very clear from the record: the quality of administrative control was closely dependent upon the character and personality of the Commissioner. Like most institutions, the insurance department was no better than the people in it. From the beginning, some Secretaries of State took an interest in insurance problems. Even in the 1850's and 1860's when administrative control was minimal, some Secretaries made recommendations for changes in the law in the direction of more adequate control. Others were content to do little more than report statistical information.[60]

For its first ex officio Insurance Commissioner, after the 1870 statute created a department, Wisconsin had the good fortune to have Mr. Llewellyn Breese in the office of the Secretary of State. Breese had no particular background in insurance and he was very young, but he was a man of marked ability. During his four years in Madison, he was twice vice-president of the National Insurance Convention and then its president. He demonstrated in his reports an incisive and comprehensive, if somewhat conservative, understanding of the problems of the industry. He showed what could be done by an energetic and intelligent use of the limited powers at hand, but he also made clear in his reports the main defects in the laws.[61]

His conservative attitude was reflected in insistence that insurance funds be kept secure. He made frequent examinations of local companies. He responded promptly and decisively to the insurance crisis after the Chicago fire by calling at once for reports from all companies operating in Wisconsin and revoking the licenses of thirty-nine of them. Events proved him to have taken an indefensibly conservative position on local mutuals; he recommended immediate repeal of the authorizing acts, on the ground that such associations could provide neither an adequate distribution of the risk nor a sufficient accumulation of reserves. He also criticized coöperatives and mutual benefit companies in the life insurance field: "Something of this sort may do well enough as a channel for neighborhood benevolence, while the project holds together, but it cannot pretend to have a scientific basis or financial stability." He strenuously opposed a pair of Chicago coöperative life companies that operated in the state in the 1870's on the basis of a nonguaranteed policy value. His vigorous opposition to these unsound operations, even though they were technically legitimate under the law, was in noteworthy contrast to his successor's equivocation on the same question. Breese clearly recognized the weaknesses of mutuals, and with insight, he criticized inadequate reserves, which led to frequent assessments, which destroyed public confidence. Mutuals, he pointed out, left an undue amount of their cash assets in the hands of agents, making impossible a quick payment of losses, and they risked insolvency by taking promissory notes for the cash portions of the premiums and by taking unsecured premium notes for the assessment portion of the premiums.

He urged the legislature to eliminate anomalies in the tax laws and rationalize the revenue purpose of taxation; to reduce insurance costs by eliminating unnecessary publication of information; to ban such unfair trade practices as agents' misrepresentations of other companies. To the companies he recommended shorter policy terms to minimize the moral hazard derived from a drop in property values. He urged a separate insurance department and better enforcement machinery. He was not only able, but willing, to think problems through clearly and express his views in his reports in competent prose.[62]

Breese's successor, Peter Doyle, took much less interest in his insurance activities. Though he faced problems of equal import and interest, he avoided taking positions on most insurance issues during his period as ex officio Commissioner. His long reports were models of grandiloquent equivocation, and the growth of insurance law suffered from lack of direction during his years in office. He did make systematic examinations of companies in 1877—almost his only noteworthy reported act as Commissioner.[63]

The first full-time Insurance Commissioner was Philip Spooner, Jr., brother of United States Senator John Spooner. He was first appointed to the office, then elected, and served a total of eight years. Judging from his written reports, his first years were the most productive. He kept close watch on legislative activity, recommended increased discretionary power in the Commissioner, an increase in the reinsurance reserve requirements, and repeal of the valued policy law. He collected back taxes; he arranged cases to test unauthorized doing of business in the state by out-of-state brokers, and noncompliance with insurance laws by semicommercial fraternals and mutual benefit societies. He also initiated what action he could to prevent the Madison Mutual raid.[64]

During Spooner's last four years in office, his reports were purely statistical. The change may indicate a tendency for the office to recede from its creative role into one of passive gathering of data and issuing of licenses. The passive role seemed to continue under the succeeding administrations of Philip Cheek, Jr. and W. M. Root, though the latter managed to make a few suggestions in his 1892 report. With the annual report of July 1, 1895, a new energy was exhibited in the Commissioner's office. The newly elected Commissioner, William A. Fricke, saw the dynamic possibilities of the office in a way matched only by Secretary of State Breese and the early Commissioner Spooner. Under Fricke's administration, the office became a vigorous and significant part of the state government.[65]

Commissioner Fricke was a curiously ambivalent man in his relation to the insurance business. Essentially his philosophy seems grounded on laissez faire principles, but woven into the basic pattern of his thought was also a clear recognition that the insurance business had a public utility character. He sought to free the companies from a multitude of conflicting regulations by recommending national regulation. He criticized antirebate laws on the ground that the solution to rebating and twisting was to require that the policy publish the amount used for expenses, which would force commissions down to a competitive level and end rebates and twisting. This was another ambivalent position, reflecting basically a laissez faire attitude, somewhat tempered by willingness to require that full information be supplied to policyholders. He also opposed nonforfeiture laws, but insisted that policies supply full information of the rights existing under the policy. His opposition to valued policy laws as well as to legislation against coinsurance and compacts also reflected considerable confidence in the efficacy of publicity and competitive forces to keep prices down. Through the statement of his laissez faire philosophy, Fricke acquired the confidence of the industry. He spoke frequently at industry meetings, chiefly in vigorous opposition to premium taxation as a tribute on the thrifty. He also urged that company examinations be paid for by the state, since they benefitted the policyholders, not the companies.[66]

However, Commissioner Fricke only partially worked out his theoretical views in specific measures. In his actual administration of the office, he was usually a vigorous interventionist. He complained of his inadequate discretionary powers with respect to admission, and was inclined to exclude companies without clear warrant of law, when they were unsound. He recommended changes in the law to increase effective administrative control of reserves. He recommended that valuation standards be applied in fraternal insurance, that the city and village mutual organization law be repealed since it was conducive to speculative schemes, and that the Commissioner be made receiver for all defunct companies. Even with respect to premium taxation, which he strenuously opposed, he was the most aggressive Commissioner the department had seen, and took decisive action to collect back taxes in some doubtful and borderline cases. He even interested himself in internal management problems. He criticized high expense ratios, and interpreted the underwriting risk limit of 10 per cent in a way very restrictive to some companies, by reading it to limit the gross amount of risk before reinsurance, thus preventing companies from taking very large risks and often reinsuring the major parts of them in unauthorized companies, as some out-of-state companies were doing. Though he was a laissez faire theorist, in practice he was the most modern of bureaucrats, an able precursor of the highly administered society of the twentieth century. His company orientation was always evident, however; after his term was over he became an insurance consultant, and represented the companies in many legislative controversies.[67]

Emil Giljohann succeeded Commissioner Fricke, only to lapse, in the official reports, into the inarticulate pattern set by some of his predecessors. Few traces of his work remain.[68]

Zeno M. Host became Commissioner in 1903, and revived the articulate and dynamic character of the office. He pressed early and consistently for elimination of tontine insurance, for compulsory conversion of stock life companies to the mutual form, for control of expenses, and for the upgrading of fraternals. He was not unsympathetic to the companies; indeed, he followed Fricke in opposition to gross premium taxation and in advocating that the state pay examination expenses. He was more consistent than Fricke, however, for he was a state interventionist both in theory and in practice, with a bias toward mutual insurance.[69]

Host's administration of his office was aggressive and fearless. He tried to force the Equitable Life to distribute its deferred dividends, and sought to compel the Prudential to divest itself of its interlocking stock ownership with the Fidelity Trust Company.

The difference between Fricke and Host is illustrated by their careers after leaving the Commissioner's office. Fricke became an insurance consultant, and served as legislative counsel for many of the insurance companies, including the Northwestern Mutual. On the other hand, Host, after his term as Insurance Commissioner, spent twenty months in charge of insurance field work for the Knights of Pythias, during which he had much success in using the retrospective rating scheme for readjusting rates of fraternals through voluntary transfer to a sounder basis of operations. Thereafter he became director of agencies for the United States Annuity & Life Insurance Company of Chicago.[70]

The next two Commissioners were Progressive Republicans who were in the forefront of political controversy during much of their public life. George E. Beedle was the elected Commissioner during the 1907 legislature; his advocacy of the radical reform legislation of that year made him suspect in the eyes of the guardians of the status quo. Not only did the insurance companies bitterly oppose his election in 1908, but a serious effort was made to unseat him in 1909. The Deputy Insurance Commissioner charged Beedle with admitting an irresponsible company to the state without examination; with retention of examination fees; and with other misconduct in office. An investigating committee found that the charges were either trivial or not soundly based, except for the keeping of examination fees; about that there was a substantial legal question, and litigation ensued. Aside from his involvement in controversy, Beedle was not an outstanding Commissioner. He was excessively cautious as an administrator and was too fearful of deviation from the strict letter of the law; the Attorney General's opinions during Beedle's incumbency are full of opinions on relatively trivial matters on which Beedle asked for guidance.[71]

Beedle's successor was in the center of controversy during a long life in Wisconsin politics. Herman L. Ekern was a man of real ability, who was almost in the front rank of Wisconsin statesmen in the Progressive period, but never quite achieved prime distinction. As a young lawyer of marked Progressive tendencies, he was the dominant member of the investigating committee on the affairs of life insurance companies in 1906. In 1907, as Speaker of the Assembly, he pushed the insurance reform legislation through that house. In 1908 the insurance companies bitterly opposed him for re-election to the legislature; running as an independent, he narrowly failed of re-election. He was Deputy Insurance Commissioner during part of Beedle's incumbency; in 1910 he was elected Commissioner and appointed Beedle deputy. When the 1911 legislature made the office appointive he received a four-year appointment.[72]

In January, 1913, factionalism in the Republican party related to the Bull Moose split of 1912 put Ekern and Governor McGovern on opposite sides. The focus of controversy was the selection of the Speaker of the Assembly in the 1913 legislature. The Governor charged Ekern with political activity in supporting a candidate for that office, contrary to the legislature's 1911 prohibition of political activity by the Commissioner. A few minutes before nine o'clock on the morning of the day that the legislature was to convene, Ekern was served with notice of the charges against him and ordered to appear in a hearing before the Governor at nine A.M. the same day. He scarcely had time to obtain counsel, and had no time to locate witnesses or prepare his case. After a star chamber proceeding that was hurried through to completion before the legislature convened at noon (since the statutes gave the chief executive removal power only during the recess of the legislature), the Governor removed Ekern from office. All attempts on the part of Ekern's attorneys to get time to prepare a defense were overridden by the Governor, anxious to complete his political coup by the noon deadline. Ekern had only three-quarters of an hour in which to present evidence respecting the propriety of his removal from office. The Governor would permit nothing to protract the hearing beyond noon. His rulings in the course of the hearing were shocking for their lack of scruple and their gross display of political immorality.[73]

L. A. Anderson, actuary in the department, was appointed by the Governor in place of Ekern, and sought to possess the office. Ekern refused to admit the force of the removal order and appealed to the courts; a temporary restraining order came just in time to prevent forcible ejection of Ekern from his office by the capitol police. The Senate resolved itself into a committee of the whole to consider the incident, and reported that the Governor's action represented irresponsible political machination, that the charges against Ekern were untrue, and that the purported hearing held by the Governor had been arbitrary and was not even conducted in good faith. The report was adopted by a vote of 22 to 6; by a vote of 22 to 4 the Senate refused to approve the appointment of Anderson.[74]

The Supreme Court subsequently reviewed the incident with care; the printed opinions in the case are 124 pages long. Despite judicial reluctance to engage in controversy with the chief executive, the court fully vindicated the Commissioner's position. It found the notice given him to be the "merest mockery" and that Ekern's right to a fair hearing "was plainly violated." It found him to be the lawful incumbent of the office. The court also ruled that the charges against the Commissioner were without "real basis"; the extent of his political action, it found, had amounted to an expression of personal preference and a courtesy telephone call to arrange for hotel headquarters for assemblyman Johnson, whom Ekern was accused of supporting. (*Ekern* v. *McGovern*, 154 Wis. 157, esp. 279, 282 [1913]).

After Governor Philipp failed to reappoint him in 1915, Ekern practiced insurance law in Chicago, though he maintained his political residence in Wisconsin. He continued to be active in Wisconsin politics throughout his long life. He served a term as Attorney General, and unsuccessfully aspired to higher office. During his incumbency as Insurance Commissioner, he was mainly concerned with loss prevention activities and the upgrading of fraternals. He was chairman of a Special Committee on Fire Insurance Rate-making of the National Convention of Insurance Commissioners, and pushed state regulation of rate making. In his insurance practice, he was active in the organization of mutual insurance companies. He participated in the creation of the State Farm Mutual of Bloomington, Illinois, which became one of the largest casualty companies of the country.[75]

Though Commissioner Ekern was respected in insurance circles, he was also feared as an effective crusading liberal. It was with great joy, therefore, that the insurance fraternity greeted his displacement in 1915 by a real conservative, Michael J. Cleary, later to become president of the Northwestern Mutual.* A newspaper interview reported that Cleary, in keeping with the objectives of the Stalwart reaction, intended to suppress the development of the state life fund by preventing anyone in his office from publicizing it. Though the Commissioner denied having said what the press claimed he said, there was little doubt about his generally conservative orientation. Perhaps because of his conservatism, he was very successful in working with the companies and accomplished many things through persuasion. He changed the form of the annual report to make it a much more useful compilation of the comparative statistics over a five-year period.[76]

Cleary's restrictive policy with respect to the life fund was reversed by W. Stanley Smith, who was in office in the middle 1920's. Smith undertook to develop the state life fund, arguing that state insurance was the cheapest and most stable form.[77]†

Smith's tenure was marked by an effort to codify the law, which led to a politically motivated controversy with Ekern, then Attorney Gen-

---

*Cleary was unanimously approved in the Senate, despite some regret that Ekern was not reappointed.—*Senate J.,* 1915, pp. 916–18.

†Platt Whitman served between Cleary and Smith. Attitudes toward the state life fund reflected the political and social outlook of the administrator. Conservative administrators were reluctant to get legislative authorization to build a sales force. Thus Commissioner Duel said, "You know how insurance salesmen are. They would have to go out over the state and they would be hanging around taverns and backrooms and they would have a sweetie here and a girl friend there."—*Capital Times* (Madison, Wis.), editorial Nov. 20, 1945.

eral. Their difference was no less real though both were vigorous Progressives in outlook. Ekern's opposition to the revision led to strained relations between them. Smith wrote open letters attacking the integrity of Ekern's motives and also had a resolution introduced into the Assembly for an investigation. The resolution was killed after a short but sharp fight. Nothing daunted, Smith issued another open letter to Ekern making damning, purportedly documented, charges of unethical conflict of interest between Ekern's private representation of insurance interests and his conduct of his official job. Smith concluded his letter with the caustic observation, that "pure progressive politics and greed will not mix" (Assembly J., 1925, p. 1281). Ekern prevented publication of this letter by threatening libel actions against the press if they published it. Smith again had a resolution for an investigation introduced in the Assembly, but again it was defeated, this time by a decisive margin of 50 to 21; a Progressive effort was even made to expunge the resolution from the record, but this attempt narrowly failed.[78]

Ekern wrote to the Senate, denying the charges and requesting an investigation. Influenced perhaps by the unseemliness of this public controversy within the official family, and perhaps partly by less praiseworthy considerations, the Senate unanimously adopted a resolution granting Ekern's request for an investigation of the charges. Smith protested that the chairman of the investigating committee was an ally of Ekern. It may indeed be the case that Ekern had more to say than was entirely proper about the makeup of the committee.[79]

The committee hearings also were marred by unseemly behavior. A unanimous report then completely exonerated Ekern, finding that the charges were "unfounded and without justification." The report was adopted by the Senate. There were political undertones of the controversy that could only be guessed at. Observers speculated that the objective of the original attack was to eliminate Ekern as a gubernatorial or senatorial candidate; it was certain at least that the flare-up represented a deep-seated political controversy within Progressive ranks, with a split between Senator LaFollette and Governor Blaine a possible outcome. Smith's own political ambitions for the gubernatorial position were also suggested as in the background.[80]

After Ekern, the Commissioner's annual reports became a mere collection of statistical information, without explanation of the department activities. This may suggest a passive administrator, but without careful examination of the department files it would be premature to generalize simply from the absence of articulate discussion in the reports that the Commissioners were no longer creative and aggressive. The powers of the Commissioner did continue to increase, especially his rate regulatory powers, and at least some of the Commissioners sometimes used their powers.

One dynamic Commissioner in mid-twentieth century was such a striking contrast to his less articulate predecessors that he requires some mention. Paul J. Rogan served as Commissioner from 1955 to 1959 and provided a vigorous administration of the office. Despite a lack of previous experience in the business, he showed, from the first, his intention and capacity to provide effective supervision. His predecessor had resigned under a cloud, because of inept handling of the matter of fire insurance rates. Rogan made an auspicious start by taking vigorous action to reduce drastically fire insurance rates for the state. Credit life insurance was growing rapidly, and there were serious abuses in its sale. With the full backing of Republican Governor Thomson, Rogan demanded power to regulate premium rates and other aspects of such insurance, and over the bitter opposition of the affected companies was successful in getting regulatory authority from the 1957 legislature. Under his newly acquired power he then demanded, and obtained, a substantial rate reduction. Wisconsin pioneered in this aspect of administrative control, though some other states followed quickly. In the same legislature, the Commissioner also obtained a supervisory control over employee welfare plans. This, too, was a development in which Wisconsin was very early, though not first. Rogan also reorganized the department and increased its budget substantially. He subjected accident and sickness insurance companies to rules controlling advertising practices and policy forms. He urged a more aggressive investigation of misrepresentation and other unfair practices, and sought funds to carry out the proposal. In 1957 he sought to stop the unfair claims adjustment practices by which some automobile insurers were using the difficulty of litigation as a club to force unfair settlements in property damage cases. Though an adequate assessment of the Rogan administration is not possible this soon after its close, especially without an exhaustive examination of department records both during and before Rogan's tenure, it seems safe to say that the administration was one of the more effective and dynamic in the history of the office. How much the impetus given the department would continue into the future was not clear in 1959. Until after the term was over, published reaction to Rogan's administration was almost uniform in its praise, though occasionally insurance men expressed disagreement privately. Then, in 1959, when a laudatory resolution was introduced in the state Senate, some people began to see the start of a boom in a campaign for the gubernatorial office, and the resolution was tabled. One Democratic Senator was quoted by the Milwaukee *Journal* (July 8, 1959) as saying that the resolution was "highly partisan, unnecessary, superfluous and ridiculous at this time," and another as saying that "this man was a highly controversial figure. Now we are being asked to form an ecumenical council here and sanctify him." Whatever one's final judgment might be on the achievements of Paul Rogan's administration, this administration, like many others in the past, re-emphasized the fact that the vigor and success of an administrator depend very little on his previous experience in the insurance business, and very much on his quality as a man.[81]

A thorough inquiry into the modern operation of the Commissioner's office might show whether the pre-Rogan cessation of articulate discussion of accomplishments and hopes indicated a significant change in the role of the Commissioner, from that of a creative law-originating agency to that of an administrator merely carrying out the passively accepted policy of the legislature, or whether it simply reflected mediocre and unimaginative Commissioners. Equally important, though of less concern to the purposes of this book, a thorough inquiry might also enable one to make sound generalizations on the effectiveness of the Commissioners on the technical level, especially in the control of rates. On the basis of the material examined for this book, it seems justifiable to suggest that if one does not set impossibly high standards of performance, the Commissioner's job was satisfactorily done during most of Wisconsin's history to the middle of the twentieth century. There were periods when the incumbent was intellectually, or perhaps even morally, inadequate to the demands made upon him; the financial support for the department was always less than its task required; and the legal authority of the Commissioners was not always what was needed for adequate performance. On the whole, however, the insurance enterprise was under a substantial measure of social control at least during the twentieth century, and the more effective Commissioners were often able to accomplish much by persuasion and education, even with inadequate powers of compulsion.

A thorough inquiry into the actual operation of the Commissioner's office might demonstrate to what extent the policing of individual claims was regarded as a part of the role of the administrator, at various stages in history. Part of the theoretical justification for the growth of the administrative process was the inadequacy of the judicial process to police a multitude of small individual claims. If that was any part of the rationalization for the growth of power in the Insurance Commissioner, there should be evidence of much surveillance of that kind, but there is little evidence outside of the department files to indicate that the Commissioner concerned himself overmuch with such matters. In 1908, when an attorney asked the Commissioner for an opinion on the meaning of the incontestable clause, the Attorney General expressed the view that the Commissioner had no duty to give such opinions. An occasional Attorney General's opinion suggests that the Commissioner was interesting himself in claims administration, but such cases are rather rare. Commissioner Smith, on one occasion, asked advice on the interpretation of contract terms in a given fact situation, suggesting that he was policing at least one claim, probably on specific complaint.[82]

On at least one matter the Commissioners sought to police claims administration in detail. There were a multitude of complaints to the Commissioner about rejections and scaling down of claims in the accident and health business. In most such cases the companies had sound technical defenses, and the indicated direction of reform was to bring policy terms under administrative control; this Commissioner Smith sought unsuccessfully to do in 1923. Presumably the Commissioners continued to do what they could to control accident and health claims administration on specific complaint, after the Supreme Court denied to the Commissioner the power to standardize policy forms.[83]

There were frequent proposals for legislative investigations of the Commissioner. The attempts suggest the importance of political considerations and motivation in selection of a Commissioner and in controlling him. In addition to those already discussed, a 1939 resolution calling for an investigation alleged that the Commissioner was guilty of arbitrary, discriminatory, and unlawful actions in the state, that the department issued false and fraudulent statements about the condition of certain companies, that deputies used confidential information about insolvent companies for their own gain, and that department morale was bad. The resolution was before the Assembly for seven months but did not pass; a change in Commissioners made the matter moot. A similar resolution in 1943 attacked the use of management contracts for siphoning money out of the mutuals, and alleged special favors for large mutuals and careless admission practices. The frequency of such proposals for investigations and the infrequency with which anything developed from them suggest that they represented political maneuvering more often than seriously intended charges of legal wrong.[84]

Chapter Five

THE ADMINISTRATION OF CLAIMS: THE DISTRIBUTION OF THE FUND

In the process of deciding what persons were entitled to the payment of losses out of the insurance fund and how much they should receive, two basic public policies were in constant conflict. There was, first, the pervasive policy of giving effect to the reasonable expectations of contracting parties. Persons who took out insurance expected to obtain protection, and it was the concern of the law to assure them that protection. At the same time, however, it was the policy of the law to preserve the integrity of the fund by preventing unwarranted raids on it by persons not entitled to share. The conflict between these policies arose because expectations of policyholders which appeared reasonable were often in excess of the coverage the companies contemplated when the policies were written, and for which premiums were computed.

In the administration of claims, the heart of public policy making was in the courts. This was in marked contrast to the rest of insurance law, where public policy making centered in the legislature and the Insurance Commissioner. The contribution of case law to the growth and development of any branch of the law was mainly adventitious and passive, because the germinating cases were determined by the accidents of litigation. But insurance was a major subject of litigation, and consequently the court's contribution was of great, if somewhat uneven, importance.[1]

Case law was much less responsive—at least, much less immediately responsive—to economic forces than was legislation. In the first place, the traditional theory of judicial action was that the judge merely found the law instead of creating it; this tended to limit the court to analogical reasoning and excluded frank examination of public policy. Traditionally, also, law was thought to be unchanging, and this attitude made it resistant to change. Dean Pound made the point:

Tenacity of a taught legal tradition is much more significant in our legal history than the economic conditions of time and place. . . . The outstanding phenomenon is the extent to which a taught tradition, in the hands of judges drawn from any class one will, and chosen as one will, so they have been trained in the tradition, has stood out against all manner of economically or politically powerful interests. The role of economics in our legal history has not been one of dictating decision of particular causes or judicial promulgation of particular new rules, but one of raising new wants, new claims, new demands and desires. . . . There has been a gradual shaping of obstinate traditional precepts and traditional doctrines through the need of applying them to new economic conditions in the light of reshaping ideals of the legal order (Pound, pp. 82–84).

Underlying the tough taught dogma of contract law, against which the growth of insurance case law must be viewed, was the notion of the utmost freedom of contract. This attitude reached its zenith in the late nineteenth century in the application to law of Kantian free will and individualist economics (Pound, p. 114). Freedom of adults to contract as they will was recognized in 1896 as paramount public policy when Mr. Justice Marshall, for the Wisconsin court, adopted, in *Houlton* v. *Nichol,* the famous statement of an English judge:

As very truly said by Sir George Jessel, M.R., in *Printing & N.R. Co.* v. *Sampson,* L.R. 19 Eq. 462: "It must not be forgotten that you are not to extend arbitrarily those rules which say that a given contract is void as being against public policy, because if there is one thing which more than another public policy requires it is that men of full age and of competent understanding shall have the utmost liberty of contracting, and that their contracts when entered into freely and voluntarily shall be held sacred and shall be enforced by the courts of justice. Therefore you have this paramount public policy to consider—that you are not lightly to interfere with this freedom of contract" (*Id.,* 93 Wis. 393, 398 [1896]).

Ironically this notion received most emphasis after the expansion of the economy and the increasing size of business organizations had made inaccurate the notion that the major contracts of our society were expressions of free will in Kant's sense.[2]

When the court said, in *Wustum* v. *Company,* "we know of no sound principle of law or morals which would warrant a court in relieving the assured from an express stipulation in his contract to give immediate notice to the company when the building became vacant" (*Id.,* 15 Wis. 138, 143 [1862]), it was adopting explicitly the freedom of contract dogma. Nevertheless, the court was quite able to decide many such cases in favor of the insured.[3] It skillfully used the canons of construction to relieve the insured of various stipulations, and resorted often to the doctrine that ambiguity must be resolved against the draftsman of the contract. In a striking case, *Morse* v. *Company* (30 Wis. 534 [1872]), when a fire insurance policy prohibited the presence of "crude or refined coal, or earth oils" on the premises, the court held that the use of kerosene for lighting purposes did not violate the policy. The court emphasized the maxim *noscitur a sociis*, and bolstered it with no less than six other arguments derived from the law of interpretation of contracts.

Nor was the skillful use of interpretative devices the only way in which the court might counter its own dogma of freedom of contract. Beginning about 1875 the Wisconsin Supreme Court made use of equity's abhorrence of forfeitures as an explicit public-policy ground for permitting the policyholder to escape from the more rigorous conditions of insurance contracts.[4] Chief Justice Ryan made it clear in 1879 that this was a deliberate and considered course of action, when he warned:

If the crafty conditions with which fire insurance companies fence in the rights of the assured, and the subtle arguments which their counsel found upon them, were always to prevail, these corporations would be reduced almost to the single function of receiving premiums for little or no risk (*Appleton* v. *Co.*, 46 Wis. 23, 32 [1879]).

However, the pervasive influence of the freedom of contract notion often led the court to clothe even the nonforfeiture policy in interpretative dress:

It is freely admitted . . . that, to work a forfeiture of the contract, the breach must be a substantial one. . . . This rule is based on the presumption that the parties could not have intended by their contract that so serious a result should follow a failure to fulfill the strict letter of the stipulation, when the risk was not increased by such failure (*Copp* v. *Co.*, 51 Wis. 637, 640 [1881]).

So long as the freedom of contract tradition was uppermost in the mind of the court, the process of accommodating the conflicting public policies—contract freedom and reasonable expectation—was one long education of company lawyers in the drafting of forms. The industry men saw it as a game, the object of which for them was finding and using language so explicit that the court could find in it no latent ambiguity. Though in fact the courts were less hostile than company men supposed, industry committees frequently made drafting suggestions for making the contracts so airtight that even a judge with a strong bias against insurance companies could not misunderstand. For example, some thought that representations and conditions might be given added strength by expressing them as a part of the consideration, i. e., as promises of the insured. Others thought the weakness in the company position was the use of the language of promise when the contract was unilateral, and that conditions should be put more clearly in conditional language. Occasionally someone expressed a more pessimistic view—that the courts were creating liability arbitrarily outside the contract. If that were true, more careful drafting would help little.[5]

The freedom of contract doctrine was not the only bulwark of the integrity of the fund. Out of eighteenth-century England came harsh doctrines of warranty, representation, and concealment, imposing heavy burdens of accurate and complete communication upon the insured. When Lord Mansfield first enunciated these doctrines for the law of marine insurance they were satisfactory, because then the insurers, no less than the policyholders, were individuals. Moreover, they were no better informed than policyholders about the business of insuring marine bottoms and cargoes, and were much less adequately informed about the particular risks. In the nineteenth and twentieth centuries, however, the situation changed. Insurance was sold by a highly organized corporate industry, using a carefully drafted contract containing innumerable clauses to protect the insurer, and sold to a policyholder generally uninformed about the business of insurance, and often less informed about the risk aspects of his own property or business than the insurance company. The disparity in bargaining strength and comprehension of risk between individual policyholder and corporate insurer made the existing doctrine unfair. As a natural result of this conflict between received doctrine and the needs of modern society, the warranty doctrines were gradually modified, in Wisconsin as elsewhere. The Wisconsin development was sufficiently typical of that process to make it unnecessary to discuss it separately here.[6]

Despite the pessimism of the spokesmen for the companies, and despite the gradual modification of the doctrines of warranty and representation, the companies had the trump card. The doctrine of freedom of contract was pervasive and insistent; eventually, improved drafting made it very difficult for the court to misread the policy. Once drafting was thus far advanced, the legislature had to inject itself into the problem; it forbade the use of certain clauses and required the use of others. By the turn into the twentieth century, statutory control of policy terms was an important facet of the problem. To the extent that policy terms were stipulated by the legislature, there was no longer as much justification for hostile techniques of interpretation, and in fact judicial attitudes were modified by an overt abandonment of the doctrine that ambiguity must be resolved against the draftsman.

§1.   Control of Loss Settlement Procedures

Notice and Proof of Loss

Loss settlement procedures traditionally involved two principal steps which must be taken by the insured, both of which the insurance policy invariably declared to be conditions precedent to recovery. One was that the insured immediately give notice of the loss to the insurer; the other was that the insured submit proofs of loss within a specified time. Since these provisions were part of the contract, the court in dealing with them was faced with the "tough taught tradition" of freedom of contract. Moreover, in very many cases, there was at least a technical, and sometimes a substantial, failure of one of these conditions. Since the insured had no part in specifying the terms, and since his failure to recover would impose great hardship on him, there was frequent conflict between legal dogma and the practical needs of society. Viewed in this light the development of the law respecting loss settlement procedures tested Pound's thesis.

Basically, in the first generations, the loss settlement cases elaborately evaded the doctrine of freedom of contract while paying homage to it, though occasionally a court found it absolutely necessary to give effect to the doctrine. The attitude of the Wisconsin court is clear from an examination of the cases; the judges were not willing to forfeit the insured's protection by reason of his failure to perform these technical conditions, so long as they could possibly rationalize a contrary result without overtly discarding the canon that freedom of contract was a basic value. In so recognizing freedom of contract while also giving effect to the reasonable expectations of the insured, the court followed a path basically in accord with what it would do in the interpretation of policy terms. It was laying the groundwork also for the twentieth-century idea of *contrat d'adhesion,* with an overt refusal to give full effect to the freedom of contract dogma. The Wisconsin court was not alone in this approach; the same dogma coupled with the same pressures produced essentially the same result in other jurisidictions too. Especially was this true with respect to loss settlement conditions, for everywhere the courts were much more ready to find waiver of these technical conditions than they were of those relating to conduct of the insured that affected the risk. Strict construction of the clauses —indeed, even distorted construction—was used to prevent forfeitures.[1]

Around the turn of the century the court was more ready to give full effect to its respect for contract, though even Justice Marshall, the high priest of the dogma, held that physical inability to give notice of an accident, due to unconsciousness resulting from the accident, excused the failure to comply with the notice condition. He had much more difficulty in reaching the result than earlier judges would have had, however. A subsequent case refused to extend Marshall's result to a situation where notice was not given because the insured thought the injury trivial until near the close of the specified period; the time for giving notice was not extended, though the court suggested that it might have reached a different result if the notice time had entirely expired when the insured learned the injury was serious.[2]

The legislature, also, gave some attention to the notice-of-loss clause. An abortive bill in 1893 would have permitted the policyholder to give notice of loss to the Commissioner or to any agent of the company, as well as to the home office, no matter what the policy provided. In 1901 the legislature made it unlawful for an accident or casualty company to shorten the time allowed for notice of loss to less than twenty days. It also provided for the conspicuous printing of the time limit in the policy, and provided that deposit in the postoffice of a properly addressed registered letter constituted compliance with the notice requirement. More frequently, however, there were either no provisions regulating the company's freedom to contract for notice and proof of loss, or else the requirements were strict. The legislature required that immediate notice of loss be a condition in policies issued by town mutuals, millers' and manufacturers' mutuals, city and village mutuals, and church mutuals. Moreover, the standard fire policy applicable to all commercial companies required immediate notice and allowed sixty days for proof of loss. The 1911 legislature required insertion in disability policies of numerous standard provisions; among them was one specifying rather short minimum periods for giving notice. The 1913 legislature also provided that "failure to give notice within the time provided in this policy shall not invalidate any claim if it shall be shown not to have been reasonably possible to give such notice and-that notice was given as soon as was reasonably possible." Both in 1911 and in 1925 the legislature provided that for certain kinds of insurance notice might be given either to the office or agent of the company.[3]

The 1911 legislature also forbade the companies to require proofs of loss in less than ninety days, nor might they limit the time for bringing an action to less than two years. The same legislature also forbade the companies to limit the time for bringing an action to less than that specified by the statute of limitations, or otherwise authorized by law. An effort was made in 1913 to reduce the statute of limitations for insurance policies from six to two years. The bill passed but the Governor could see no reason for shortening the statutory time of suit, and vetoed the bill.[4]

Protective Practices and Devices of the Industry

The companies were primarily responsible for the tendency of the courts to destroy the efficacy of the loss settlement conditions. In the days after the big fires of 1871 and 1872, it became industry policy to tighten up loss settlement practices. Suspicion of arson seldom resulted in a defense frankly based on an allegation of criminal incendiarism; instead the companies used whatever technical defenses came to hand. Moreover, to protect the companies against fraudulent and exorbitant claims, and to give time for adequate investigation, it was industry policy to delay settlement as long as possible under the contract. Though insurance men were presumably actuated only by creditable motives, no device can be imagined more calculated to harm the industry's public relations than a set policy of arbitrary delay of loss settlement for the maximum period permitted by the law. Eventually, the industry learned the value, for public relations and competition, of speedy loss settlement except in cases of real suspicion of foul play and altered its loss settlement practices accordingly. In the compensation field, the 1931 legislature empowered the Commissioner to revoke a company's license, after hearing, for its failure to pay claims promptly. The legislature was willing, however, to help protect the companies against fraud. Although the resources of the criminal law and the principles of quasi-contract were available and perhaps adequate, the legislature showed little hesitation in designating certain new insurance crimes. Thus in 1915 the legislature made it a misdemeanor to make knowingly a false or fraudulent statement for the purpose of procuring a benefit.[5]

A more defensible effort by the companies than the one to delay loss settlement as a matter of industry policy was the effort to free adjusters from interference in loss settlement by the local agents, who, despite their legal position as agents of the companies, were often spokesmen for the policyholders. This theme was constantly played in all its variations in the industry meetings. However, the effort to prevent agent participation in the loss settlement process was never successful. The legislature helped frustrate the company effort when in 1931 it passed a bill, after heated controversy, which provided that if a fire, marine, or casualty agent induced an insured to refrain from doing, or delay doing, any act required to perfect his contract right, failure to comply with technical requirements was no defense unless the company was substantially prejudiced or there was collusion between agent and insured.[6]

As early as 1870, the statutes reflected legislative concern with undue delay in payment of judgments. The legislature forbade, at penalty of $1,000 forfeit, that any insurance company do business in the state while a judgment against it stood unpaid for more than sixty days, except where appeal was pending. An 1889 statute changed the designated time to ninety days for life insurance companies; the provision was also applied to fraternal and beneficiary societies. There was an abortive effort to repeal the 1870 provisions in 1881, but the attempt received short shrift from the legislature. On the other hand, in 1893 a proposed bill would have shortened the time to thirty days, and would have applied a new sanction by awarding 7 per cent interest on late payments; a 1911 bill would have reduced the time to fifteen days and compelled a company wishing to raise the defense of fraud to pay the money in to a bank pending suit. There were similar attempts to tighten up the law, especially by charging the company interest, in 1895, 1899, 1901, and 1913. One of the 1901 bills would also have made claims incontestable unless contested by the company within thirty days. One in 1949 would have imposed treble liability on the company for delay. These measures did not reach the basic difficulties of enforcing creditors' rights, and two 1897 bills would have specifically provided for a receivership as a method of enforcement.[7]

Not only delayed payment of judgments, but also the use of unnecessary litigation as a club to compel favorable settlement, provoked critical reaction among legislators. An 1869 bill would have taxed the insurance company with costs, including attorney's fees, if it unsuccessfully defended against payment of a policy. A clause of the 1874 valued policy law, dropped before the law was passed, would have gone much further and imposed a penalty of 50 per cent of the judgment on companies that unsuccessfully appealed to the Supreme Court. In 1943 bills introduced in both houses sought to impose attorney's fees and costs, both at trial and on appeal, on insurance companies that unsuccessfully defended claims not paid within three months from the loss. One motivation favoring the bills is suggested by a petition of the Vernon County Bar Association; though it asked for the broad provision on attorney's fees, its concern was primarily with the problem of workmen's compensation cases, where the limitation of attorney's fees to 10 per cent, together with the comparatively small recoveries, made it difficult for claimants to get adequate legal assistance. The motivation was undoubtedly mixed; partly the lawyers were concerned with their own income, and partly there was honest concern for the proper administration of justice, threatened by the fee provisions.[8]

The statutory standard fire policy required that when a loss occurred the insured must provide a complete inventory of the damaged and undamaged property. The Attorney General ruled in 1908 that the law did not forbid a clause waiving the inventory where the loss was small. He thought it absurd to interpret the law literally and require an inventory of both damaged and undamaged property in all cases. In 1911 he concluded that only the damaged property need be inventoried, on the theory that damaged *and* undamaged really meant damaged *from* undamaged. On the other hand, the Commissioner ruled that the inventory requirement might not ever be waived. The notable thing about these rulings is the apparent reluctance to countenance a departure from the standard policy provision, even for the benefit of the insured.[9]

Adjustment and Appraisal

In the insurance business, the use of appraisers and arbitrators began at an early date. Especially in fire insurance, every loss settlement involved the determination of uncertain facts about which there could not fail to be frequent dispute. There was imperative need for a mechanism for settling the dispute without the cost of litigation. As early as 1849 an amendment to the charter of the Milwaukee Mutual provided for referees to settle the amount of loss when there was disagreement. Such provisions were common thereafter in the special charters.[10]

The first general provisions for arbitration of disputes were in the town mutual statutes. In 1859 the legislature provided that if a town mutual and the claimant could not agree on damages, the claimant might ask the county court judge to appoint a committee of reference to determine the amount of the award, and its decision should be final. The legislature also provided, in 1878, for compulsory reference to referees chosen by mutual agreement in disputes involving millers' and manufacturers' mutuals. This left more room for breakdown of the machinery and necessary litigation. Agreement by the parties was encouraged by a cost sanction, for the cost of the reference must be borne by the company if the award were greater than the company conceded; by the policyholder if it were less. In the procedure worked out in 1880 for the Milwaukee Mechanics Mutual charter, reference to agreed referees was optional, but peaceable settlement was encouraged by casting the cost of suit on the company if the judgment were greater than the company conceded, and on the policyholder if less. The same encouragement to peaceful settlement, but without the possibility of reference to appraisers, was worked out for the Germantown Farmers' Mutual in 1878. Finally, the 1895 standard fire policy provided for compulsory reference to two appraisers to be selected by the parties, and an umpire to be selected by the appraisers, or by the court if one of the parties failed to select an appraiser.[11]

In 1927 the Governor suggested that it was unfair to leave entirely in the Commissioner's hands the settlement of losses to be paid out of the state fire fund. In accordance with his recommendation the legislature applied to the settlement of losses on buildings owned by local municipalities essentially the same appraisal provisions that were provided by the standard policy.[12]

The importance of the adjuster in the loss settlement process was apparent to the legislature, which brought the adjustment process under a measure of social control by requiring in 1913 that the Commissioner license fire insurance adjusters who were not also agents. After a hearing, he might revoke the license for violation of any insurance law. Upon completion of each adjustment the adjuster must file reports with the deputy fire marshal and with the inspection bureau; such reports helped in the loss prevention program. Limits were placed on the amount of compensation an adjuster might receive, and his recovery might not be contingent on the amount he obtained for the loss. A 1945 bill would have required that every newly licensed insurance adjuster be a duly licensed member of the bar; motivation was probably twofold, both to upgrade the adjusting profession by establishing a fairly high standard of professional competence, but also to carve out a private preserve for young lawyers.[13]

The Direct Action Statute

Traditionally, insurance other than life was written in the form of a contract to indemnify the insured against loss resulting from named risks. In insurance against loss from liability to third persons, this indemnity character of the contract was often reinforced by a "no-action" clause, which provided that no action might be brought against the company except by the insured, to recover for loss actually sustained by him and paid by him in satisfaction of a judgment. Whenever there was such provision in a policy, the court held that a third party claimant had no direct recourse against the company, even when the company retained the right to participate in the defense of the action, and did defend. Sometimes, however, a policy provided for direct liability to the third party claimant; thus the "jitney law" of 1915 required that a policy supplied to satisfy the law provide for direct liability to the injured party.[14]

In the absence of direct liability created by the policy or imposed by special statute, the court recognized the traditional indemnity nature of the insurance policy, adhering with tenacity to the dogma of freedom of contract. Thus it was held improper to call attention during trial to the possibility that an insurance company might be liable for whatever the defendant was called upon to pay, though the customary evasion of the insurance-reference doctrine was permitted by the Wisconsin court; on *voir dire*, plaintiff's counsel might question prospective jurors about their interest in insurance companies.[15]

This absurd pretense, by which the courts of most states preserved the appearance of the doctrine forbidding a reference to insurance while permitting evasion of its reality, was soon made unnecessary in Wisconsin, through its pioneering development of the direct action statute. The 1925 legislature enacted that any policy of automobile insurance covering liability to others was to be construed to contain a condition making the insurer liable to the injured third party claimant. The legislature also provided that insolvency or bankruptcy of the insured should not release the carrier, which should be directly liable to the insured person if judgment were returned unsatisfied against the insured. Bills in 1927 to repeal the direct action statute of 1925 lost in the Senate by a vote of 17 to 12; in the Assembly by 79 to 6.[16]

Obsession with the freedom of contract dogma led the court to interpret the direct action statute restrictively and unsympathetically, though it did give effect to the statute in situations clearly within its terms. The court made it clear that in its view the only purpose of the statute was to permit insurance companies to be joined as defendants, not to enlarge in any way the scope of the coverage. Despite the statute, it gave effect to a different kind of no-action clause, providing that no action would lie against the company until the amount of damages for which the insured was liable was determined either by final judgment against the insured or by agreement with the written consent of the company. This result, by preventing joinder of the insurance company in the original action against the insured, preserved the circuitous character of the proceedings necessary to impose liability on the company, and frustrated in large measure the remedial purposes of the 1925 legislature. The ultimate doctrine of the court was that "where the parties do not see fit to make an agreement to the contrary in the contract, the insured and the carrier may be joined as defendants in the same action."* Well advised insurers saw to it that the parties did agree to the contrary. However, it was not direct action to which the court was hostile, but interference with contract freedom, and sometimes the court might find that a policy was a liability contract even without the statute.[17]

The 1929 legislature amended the direct action statute to provide that the insurer was directly liable to the third party claimant whether the company's liability to the policyholder was immediate or was to become fixed and certain by final judgment against the insured.[18] There is little doubt that the purpose of the amendment was to over-

---

*Burkhart v. Burkhart, 200 Wis. 628, 630 (1930), quoting from Morgan v. Hunt, 196 Wis. 298, 301 (1928).

come the restrictive interpretation of the Supreme Court and permit the company to be joined in the initial action against the policy-holder, despite no-action clauses or other contractual devices. The court's subtle ingenuity was too much for the legislature, however. Chief Justice Rosenberry seized upon the failure of the legislature to enact certain other (perhaps more clearly phrased) bills as a ground for finding that the legislature had no intention to change the existing rule: "[W]e are unable to discover any purpose on the part of the legislature to prohibit such a clause being inserted by the insurer in its contracts." The court conceded its underlying bias: "[I]t is a question of how far the legislature has intended to limit the right of insurers to freely contract, a right which is a valuable, constitutionally protected right."*

The legislature's 1929 intention was made quite clear in 1931 when the unenacted 1929 bill on which Chief Justice Rosenberry had rested his argument was reintroduced and was overwhelmingly passed, after an involved parliamentary history, including clarifying amendments. It provided that an automobile insurer was a proper party defendant in any claim against the insured, if the company had an interest in the outcome adverse to the plaintiff or if it reserved the right to control the defense or if it agreed to defend or pay the costs of litigation. It is difficult to see how the insurer could escape the broad sweep of the 1931 statute. After a number of intervening cases in which the court adhered to its discredited position on "no-action" clauses, and even held a no-action clause effective to postpone action under a compulsory insurance statute for common carriers, a case was finally appealed in which the 1931 act was squarely in point; the court at length recognized the effectiveness of the 1931 statute to permit immediate joinder of the insurance company in the face of a no-action clause.[19]

The broad sweep of the direct action statute was still not sufficient to create a cause of action; the court held that it did not render the insurance company liable when the insured was dead, for the cause of action abated on his death in accordance with the traditional (although outmoded) common law doctrine on the survival of causes of action. The court was also hesitant about giving extra-territorial effect to the direct action statute, but the company might waive the clause,

*Bergstein v. Popkin, 202 Wis. 625, 631, 633 (1930). The rejected bills were S 220, 253, A 579 (1929). They were but narrowly defeated.—Senate J., 1929, pp. 767, 1191.

as by filing the SR-21 form required under the safety responsibility law. However, the 1959 legislature provided for direct action against the insurer in action on Wisconsin accidents, even if the policy was issued outside the state and even if the policy forbade such direct action.[20]

Other Loss Settlement Problems

There were a variety of other proposals to change loss settlement procedures to prevent real or fancied abuses. Thus an 1893 statute permitted an insured to join in a single suit all fire companies interested in his loss. Again, liability policies usually required the insured to coöperate in defending the action against him. Unsuccessful bills in 1937 and 1939 sought to prevent abuse of this condition by providing that the third party claimant's right of recovery should not be defeated by lack of coöperation by the insured, unless the claimant had connived with the insured for that purpose.[21]

Similarly, life insurance companies often sought to avoid the effect of the presumption of death from protracted absence, by policy provisions (or bylaws of fraternal societies) altering the evidentiary effect of the absence. The 1941 legislature nullified all such provisions and bylaws, and provided instead for notice to be given the insurer within a year of disappearance in order to stop the running of the statute of limitations. The inequitable operation of the ordinary venue statutes when applied to automobile insurance cases led to a special amendment of the venue statutes in 1943. Abusive practices of some adjusters in taking statements from injured persons led to an attempt in 1945 to require that a casualty company which took a statement from an injured person must supply him with a copy of the statement made.[22]

Not infrequently a liability insurance carrier had an opportunity to settle a claim within the policy limits, but chose to defend a lawsuit on the chance of escaping liability altogether, with the result that the recovery exceeded the policy limits. The doctrine of the Wisconsin Supreme Court at first was that the insurance company was liable beyond the policy limits only if it exercised bad faith in its decision to fight instead of settle; subsequently it required that the good faith decision not to settle must be preceded by the exercise of reasonable care and diligence in investigation. To the policyholder, however, the burden was no less because the company's error in refusing to settle was in good faith, and 1951 and 1953 bills sought unsuccessfully to make the company liable for the full amount of judgments beyond the policy limits if the company refused an opportunity to settle within the policy limits.[23]

§2. *The Relationship of Marketing Practices to Claims Administration*

Business practices in insurance marketing had much relevance for the law governing the distribution of the fund, because the way in which insurance was sold, the representations made, the waivers and estoppels to be found, determined the fairness of claims. Legal decisions in turn reacted on the marketing structure, though less significantly than business practices affected legal decisions. For the most part the law-making task was one for the court, which initially had to provide a framework of approved practice in accordance with which the insurance business could be institutionalized, and thereafter had to superintend the marketing process, in an indirect fashion, through its residual supervision of claims administration.[1]

Of the many complex problems inherent in the relationship between business practices and the law, perhaps the most interesting and important were those resulting from the conflict between the duties and the interest of the insurance agent. The marketing structure of the insurance business early came to revolve around the person of the agent. This independent businessman received his compensation by commissions on insurance sold; his own financial interests were thus largely identified with the welfare of his friends and neighbors whose good will constituted his chief business asset. On the other hand, the developing law of fiduciary obligation placed on him the duty of fidelity to the interests of his principal, the distant company. The constant tension between interest and duty, between fact and legal theory, was one of the major focal points for insurance litigation. By mid-twentieth century the Wisconsin Supreme Court had decided about 175 cases which involved this conflict in some degree. The natural defense of the insurance companies to the doubtful loyalty of their agents was an attempt to circumscribe their powers, and legal controversy swirled about the effectiveness of such attempts.[2]

These cases, like those dealing with loss settlement procedure, show the characteristic pattern of a partial and sometimes reluctant accommodation of tough dogma to the needs of an evolving economy. Here, however, the court's application of policy considerations was more frankly articulated. Moreover, here the taught tradition to be outflanked—the notion that the authority of an agent must be shown by the acts and words of his principal—might sometimes be countered by the freedom of contract principle, for the maintenance of a firm base of reliable reasonable expectations was a practical prerequisite of the workings of a free contract system. But the victory of needs over dogma was only partial, and some cases applied traditional concepts mechanically and strictly.[3]

An 1861 case showed how early the court was prepared to articulate an enlightened public policy as an expressed ground for decision. The question was how far an agent might modify an insurance policy to conform to the needs of the insured. The court relied more heavily on the reasonable expectation of the insured than on the technical authorization to the agent:

The company, however, held them out to the world as its agents, authorized to receive applications for insurance, to issue policies, receive premiums, etc., and it is little less than a downright fraud upon the public, to claim that such agents could not make a policy accurate in the description of the property insured, or insert such a clause in respect to subsequent insurance as was inserted in this policy. If insurance companies can avoid their liabilities on such ground as these, there would be no safety in dealing with them. . . . [W]e must hold that this was within the scope of the agent's authority (*Warner* v. *Co.*, 14 Wis. 318, 323 [1861]).

Though the result can be explained by an apparent authority doctrine, that is nothing but a rationalization of the victory of reasonable expectations over the principal's power to define the scope of the agency.[4]

In its early cases the court chose as its half-articulated premise a public policy imposing on the companies complete responsibility for the workings of the marketing organization. The companies chose their agents; the law would not permit them to limit agents' powers with any degree of effectiveness, because the practical needs of the evolving market economy demanded that policyholders be able to rely reasonably upon the companies as represented by the agents. These decisions transferred the burden of malfunctioning of the market system from the individual policyholder to the companies, and thence to the policyholders collectively. Thus, for example, the predominance of self-interest among the motives of the agent often led him to conceal from the company information he received from the policyholder, when it showed a breach of a warranty or condition of the policy, because full disclosure might mean cancellation and a loss of the commission. In an early case dealing with this problem, the insured made a continuing warranty concerning the fire-fighting facilities existing in his mill when it was not operating. When the agent made the survey, the policyholder disclosed that even then he was not complying with the warranty. The court held the company

responsible for the accuracy and omissions of its agent. . . . The tendency of modern decisions has been strongly to hold these companies to that degree of responsibility for the acts of the local agents which they scatter through the country, that justice and the due protection of the people demand, without regard to private restrictions upon their authority, or to cunning provisions inserted in policies with a view to elude just responsibility (*May* v. *Co.*, 25 Wis. 291, 306–7 [1870]).

The court firmly established this central doctrine by a dozen cases in the 1870's, and never abandoned it, though it might have used the parol evidence rule to rationalize a contrary result, had it wished. Other facets of the doctrine allowed the agent to modify or construe the policy to permit the breach. Even if the agent obtained the information in some other capacity, the company was sometimes charged with the knowledge.[5]

The court's action presented the companies with a serious problem in management, for it was difficult to control commission-compensated agents so as to make them behave in fact as their theoretical fiduciary obligations demanded. Though the companies might sue agents for breach of the agency contract, the paucity of such cases in the reports suggests that such suits were only practical for egregious cases, both because of the inherent limitations of the lawsuit as a corrective measure and because of the bad public relations effect of such actions on other agents. The insurance companies were constantly concerned with the problem, and made some efforts to restructure the marketing system to put the agent's self-interest on the same side of the transaction as the company's interest. Thus they tried to work out systems of compensation on a contingent basis, to give the agent a stake in the company's success, but the adventitious character of loss made contingent commissions impracticable except for the largest general agencies.[6]

Primarily, companies sought to protect themselves from venal and careless agents by limiting their authority. For example, the companies distinguished between recording and surveying agents; the former were empowered to issue policies, the latter only to solicit business. At first, in 1877, the court gave effect to the distinction and refused to let the agent pull himself up by his bootstraps; the policyholder might not rely on the agent's declarations or conduct to determine the scope of the agency (*Fleming* v. *Co.*, 42 Wis. 616, 621 [1877]). Two years later, however, a divided court took a more liberal view, holding it "unreasonable to charge the insured with notice of the precise character and limits of the agent's authority, merely because he knew that the agent thus forwarded the application for approval" (*American* v. *Gallatin*, 48 Wis. 36, 46 [1879]). For all practical purposes the surveying agent was put on the same ground as the recording agent.

The 1879 case was decided on common law "principle"; the court also cited Section 1977 of the Revised Statutes, but refused to interpret the statute. From this time forward, however, this statute dominated the cases on the powers of agents. The provision was originally a part of the 1870 life insurance act; in 1871 the legislature broadened it to include other insurance. After slight modifications in 1878 and 1880, the statute (*Laws* 1880, 240, §5) provided that

whoever solicits insurance on behalf of any insurance corporation or property owner, or transmits an application for insurance, or a policy of insurance, other than for himself, to or from any such corporation, or who makes any contract for insurance, or collects any premium for insurance, or in any manner aids or assists in doing either, or in transacting any business of like nature for any insurance corporation, or advertises to do any such thing, shall be held to be an agent of such corporation to all intents and purposes, unless it can be shown that he receives no compensation for such services.[7]

Not uncommonly an insurance agent was unable to place insurance with companies he represented; customarily he then placed it through another agent, sharing commissions with the latter. In 1880 the Supreme Court held that Section 1977 made the occasional subagent of the company an agent "to all intents and purposes," thus extending the prior doctrines of the court on the scope of an agent's authority to subagents of whom the company might know nothing. To a considerable extent the company was thus made responsible for the workings of the whole insurance agency system—not merely for its own agents: "[The statute] seems to be designed in the clearest manner to make the company responsible to the public for the acts of one whom it permits to solicit insurance on its behalf. . . ." (*Schomer* v. *Co.*, 50 Wis. 575 [1880]). Fear of the broad sweep of the statute led to an abortive effort in 1885 to limit it so that it would not apply to solicitors, clerks, and employees of the agent.[8]

The statute could be used also to strike the geographical limitations from an agency contract, so far as the policyholder was concerned. Indeed, it removed virtually all limitations from agency contracts: "The above statute makes all agents soliciting insurance, receiving premiums, or transmitting applications, *general* agents to the fullest extent."* It even gave to a mere soliciting agent the power to make an oral contract of insurance on behalf of the company.[9]

At an early date the companies sought to prevent "waiver" by agents by inserting a policy clause requiring endorsed consent or written waiver. Such clauses were ineffective to prevent waiver by reason of the agent's knowledge of a breach at the outset. In 1887, however, the court gave effect to a provision "that no officer, agent, or employee, or any person or persons, except the secretary, in writing, can in any manner waive either or any of the conditions of this policy" (*Hankins* v. *Co.*, 70 Wis. 1, 5 [1887]). It used the symbols of freedom of contract to hold the insured bound by the non-waiver clause with respect to subsequent waivers. This was a limited effect, however; two years later the court held the non-waiver clause did not apply to subsequent waivers by general agents. The company could not thus limit its own power to contract. Nor was the insured chargeable with notice of the lack of authority of the agent to waive, simply because he had another policy in the same company containing the same clause.[10]

A more subtle attempt to limit the agent's power to bind the company made use of the standard fire insurance policy law. In 1891 the legislature instructed the Commissioner to prepare a standard policy. The statute forbade attachment to the policy of printed or written matter which waived any of its provisions; this may have been the motivation of those who introduced the statute. Though the statute was held unconstitutional for improper delegation of legislative power, during the time that it was assumed to be valid the Supreme Court gave it effect to prevent an agent's oral waiver of a clause incorporated in the standard policy by the Commissioner.[11]

Mathers v. *Ass'n*, 78 Wis. 588, 593 (1891). The case permitted agent to waive clause in application postponing effective date of policy until approval by company.

In 1895 the legislature enacted a statutory standard policy, to avoid the defect of unconstitutional delegation. The standard policy included a non-waiver provision, but it was followed by a provision charging the company with any knowledge possessed by the agent up to the time of delivery of the policy.[12] In the Supreme Court, Mr. Justice Marshall seized upon the "knowledge" clause to hold that the legislature intended to preserve intact the long line of authorities on the agent's knowledge of breach. He eluded the non-waiver clause by calling the result an "estoppel" rather than a "waiver." The distinction, largely ignored in previous cases, was now seized upon to preserve this part of the established structure of marketing responsibilities: "The fundamental principle involved is that forfeitures are not favored and will be held not to have been intended in the absence of language clearly indicating the contrary. That applies as well to a law as to a contract."*

Around the turn of the century, despite Justice Marshall's reluctance to overturn the agents' knowledge cases, on other matters there was a significant retreat from the attitude exhibited in the nineteenth century on agents' powers. In 1901 the court seized on the parol evidence rule to find that there was no "waiver" of a clause delaying effectiveness of a life policy till after approval by the company. In 1902 the court went very far in putting the burden of the malfunctioning of the marketing system on the policyholder. It held that a life insurance agent might not waive the requirement that the initial premium be paid in cash, even by making private arrangements to take merchandise for it. In stating his position, Justice Marshall even conceded that the agent might be regarded as a general agent. In 1903 Justice Marshall, speaking for a divided court, denied a policyholder rescission of a life insurance policy which he had kept for months before discovering that it was not what the agent had fraudulently represented it to be. The court permitted a more timely rescission on two other policies. Though Justice Marshall justified his position by an elaborate technical analysis, he also indicated some of the considerations of public policy that underlay his attitude. To permit rescission by a policyholder who slept on his rights would place a burden on the innocent company and

*Welch v. Ass'n, 120 Wis. 456, 469–70 (1904). Deletion of the "knowledge" clause by the 1917 standard policy, Laws 1917, 127, did not change the rule.— Gould v. Co., 174 Wis. 422 (1921). Laws 1919, 248, incorporated the doctrine in the statute for fire, casualty, or marine companies.

the even more innocent other policyholders, for he had received full protection under the policy for the months it was in force.[13]

By the 1920's the court once again was inclined toward a broad interpretation of the agent's powers. In 1923, for example, it held that an unconditional delivery of a life insurance policy by the agent was a "waiver" of nonpayment of the first premium. Though the court distinguished the 1901 and 1902 cases on their facts, a significant shift in attitude from the position taken by the court two decades earlier is apparent. In 1926, too, the court characterized conduct subsequent to the formation of the insurance contract as creating an estoppel, which was not affected by the non-waiver clause of the standard fire insurance policy. However, the court declined to return to the extreme position of the nineteenth-century cases. In 1930 the court held that the statute defining the powers of agents did not give to a mere soliciting agent the authority to waive the nonpayment of the first premium; in the 1923 case the agent had broader authority. The court thus took cognizance of the fact that while fire insurance agents normally had contract-making powers, life insurance agents ordinarily were mere solicitors; in giving effect to the distinction the court ignored the nineteenth-century cases that held that the statute made all agents general agents.[14]

Subsequent cases followed the moderate position thus established; by the casuistical process of judicial inclusion and exclusion the court sought to draw the lines defining for mid-twentieth century the scope of the agent's power. The analysis was technical and considerations of public policy seldom appeared explicitly in the opinions. It was apparent, however, that in mid-twentieth century the court's arsenal of weapons was sufficiently diversified that policy considerations might affect the result indirectly, through choice among relevant analogies. The court developed with telling effect the doctrines of waiver and estoppel, and resisted all efforts to destroy their utility. Notions of freedom of contract might be used or ignored, and there were always the useful statutory provisions. With discriminating analysis and attention to subtle fact differences in the record, the court might make the insurance company, and ultimately the whole body of policyholders, bear the burden of most of the malfunctioning of the agency system, without completely freeing the individual policyholder from responsibility to respond rationally to the marketing process.[15]

§3.   Statutory Control of Policy Terms

The interaction of the companies and the courts in settling the meaning of the insurance contract could have but one outcome. As company lawyers learned better drafting techniques, the freedom of contract dogma narrowed the area within which the courts could maneuver. As a result there was pressure to correct by legislative reform any apparent injustice. When the companies tightened up loss settlement practices in the early 1870's, the public became aware that policy conditions contained real teeth, and legislatures began to react to the need.

The Standard Fire Policy

Prescription of the terms of the insurance contract was one of the earliest and most persistent forms of the reform sentiment. As early as 1868, a bill in Wisconsin would have given an ex officio board the power to prescribe initially and change subsequently the printed portion of all fire insurance policies; the written portion of the policy was to be left free of control, so long as it was written in a plain and legible manner.[1]

By 1881 the prescribed and uniform fire policy was again an issue, and remained one until a standard fire policy was a reality. The 1881 bill followed the pattern of the 1868 measure, except to give the power of prescription to the Commissioner. In his annual report, Commissioner Spooner called attention of the companies to the proposal before the legislature, and urged them to take voluntary action to reform their policies and eliminate objectionable conditions and terms. Uniformity and reform of policy forms had been suggested already as an industry objective, not to eliminate harsh conditions but rather to tighten up the policy language to preclude judicial favor to the insured.[2]

. In 1883 the Governor recommended a uniform policy, upon the Commissioner's suggestion. Two bills applicable to fire insurance were introduced, one like that of 1881, and the other a bill to prescribe policy terms by statute. A third bill went further, and would have required uniform policies for life, fire, accident, and extended coverage insurance; the Commissioner and the Attorney General were to approve and adopt the policies. An 1885 bill would have given the Supreme Court power to appoint a person who, with the Commissioner and the Attorney General, should constitute an Insurance Commission and should draft and report a uniform policy to the legislature. In 1889 three differing bills proposed a uniform policy. In 1891 a uniform fire policy law for all fire insurance companies was at last enacted. It instructed the Commissioner to prepare a printed form for a Wisconsin standard fire policy, based on the New York standard policy. An 1895 amendment corrected an oversight in the 1891 law; it exempted town mutuals, though it required them to submit blank policies for the Commissioner's approval before issuing them.[3]

In 1895 the legislature learned that the Supreme Court of Pennsylvania had held a similar uniform policy law unconstitutional, for improper delegation of legislative authority. Fearing that the Wisconsin statute might also be defective for this reason, the 1895 session enacted a standard policy by statute, thus putting the prescribed terms beyond constitutional attack on that ground. The legislature's action was soon justified, for the Wisconsin Supreme Court held the 1891 law unconstitutional.[4]

The legislative move toward a uniform policy offended the laissez faire attitudes of some insurance men, who often sought to elevate their objections to the level of constitutional doctrine. As late as 1894 one argued that the state might not interfere with the liberty freely to form one's own contract. He was willing to endure some state regulation, "[b]ut when it is asserted that the internal management and the manifold details of the business of a private corporation may be regulated by Statute, the protection of our form of government is menaced and socialism uprears its head" (FUA, *Proc.*, 1894, p. 40). On the whole, however, the industry seemed favorably disposed toward uniform laws. The favorable attitude seems implicit in the criticism made of the Commissioner, who in preparing the Wisconsin standard policy had consulted Madison merchants and had modified the New York form so carefully worked out by the profession; the assumption of the criticism was twofold, that the prescription of uniform laws was all right if the companies had a dominant voice in the drafting, and that the Commissioner's task was to work not only with, but for, the companies. Thus early the regulated had learned to seek an amicable partnership with the regulating agency.[5]

The 1895 standard fire insurance policy was a harsh contract; notable among its provisions were a number of conditions, breach of any of which rendered the policy void. For example, the policy was void if the interest of the insured were other than unconditional or sole ownership; or if the hazard were increased by any means within the control or knowledge of the insured; or if the insured had any other contract of insurance, whether valid or not, on the same property. These harsh "moral hazard" clauses were productive of great injustice in the settlement of claims, for policies might be rendered ineffective by technical breaches, despite the ingenuity of the courts in interpretation. In the second decade of the twentieth century, a movement for the amelioration of the standard policy swept the country, and the Wisconsin legislature enacted a new standard policy in 1917. The policy format and language were vastly improved, and the harshness of the earlier policy softened. Most of the conditions were made merely suspensory; only a few still made the policy void.[6]

The 1917 policy was still a harsh contract. A survey of fire insurance policies in the Champaign-Urbana (Illinois) area showed that in the 1930's, under the "new" New York standard policy, which was essentially the same as the 1917 Wisconsin policy, 28 per cent of all policies and 55 per cent of those covering jointly owned property were void for breach of a moral hazard condition (Goble [1937]). Even if company claims policy were very generous, the result was shocking. Considerations of this sort, together with the complexity of the standard policy, led the 1931 legislature to appoint a special committee to revise the standard fire insurance policy. The committee held hearings, obtained the help of insurance company representatives, and drafted a revised policy which would have further ameliorated and simplified the 1917 contract. But the proposal was premature and received little attention. Nevertheless, throughout the country the problem was beginning to concern people. The Illinois survey illustrated academic concern for the injustice of the contract. Even company spokesmen were not unsympathetic to modification. Finally the 1945 legislature adopted a modernized contract which made all the moral hazard clauses merely suspensory. The absence of serious opposition to the revision shows the success achieved by the courts in the long contest with the companies over the interpretation of the insurance contract; hostile interpretation left the companies little advantage from harsh clauses; on the other hand amelioration of the contract offered possible improvement in the judicial attitude toward insurance companies.[7]

The Standard Provisions Law

In the field of personal insurance, greater variety was permitted to the contract draftsman. In the aftermath of the life insurance investigations of 1905 and 1906 there was some sentiment for standard life policies, and New York even had a standard policy law for a short time, but the standard policy movement got nowhere in Wisconsin. The Wisconsin committee recommended standard provisions, but not a complete standard policy. Even the less sweeping proposal was not successful.[8]

More success was achieved in standardizing the complicated disability insurance contract. The 1911 legislature initiated the development with a law providing that the policy and application with attached papers should be the whole of the contract. The statute also limited the effectiveness of the insured's representations to avoid the policy; specified the time permitted for notice of loss; provided for pro rata reduction of coverage instead of avoidance of the contract upon transfer to a more hazardous occupation; provided for return premiums on cancellation; and it also forbade certain clauses. In 1913 the legislature repealed and re-enacted the standard provisions law in more elaborate form, to conform to recommendations of the National Convention of Insurance Commissioners. Among other things, the 1913 statute required that clauses reducing the amount of the claim under any circumstances be printed in boldface type; subsequently the Supreme Court refused to give effect to such a clause when printed in ordinary type.[9]

Despite the attempt at standardization, there was great diversity. The 1911 legislature required that disability policy forms be filed with the Commissioner for his approval. Under this law over 5,000 policy provisions were submitted for approval in ten years. Out of this great diversity of policy form, and also, out of bitter competition that led companies to make rash promises, came numerous complaints to the Commissioner on rejection and reduction of claims. Litigation was no answer, for most claims were too small to litigate, and the companies usually had valid technical defenses. Simplification and standardization of forms was the answer urged by the Commissioner.[10]

After there was an abortive attempt in 1921 to get an investigation of accident and health insurance, Commissioner Smith decided in 1923 that he could require the simplification and standardization of policy forms under the 1911 form approval law. He ordered insurers to insert certain provisions in their policies. After a hearing, he reaffirmed the order; some companies then sought an injunction to restrain him from denying licenses to companies refusing to comply with the order. The Supreme Court held that the companies might use any clauses not inconsistent with the standard provisions law. A vigorous dissent pointed to the abuses in the business and the excessive expense ratio, and approved the Commissioner's effort to control the business. Despite the merits of the Commissioner's position, however, he had to acquiesce in the relatively chaotic condition of the business.[11]

There were attempts to revise the standard provisions law in 1917, 1923, and 1931, but there was no substantial change until 1951, except for the addition of provisions for group accident and health insurance in 1939. The 1951 legislature revised the law; the Insurance Commissioner proposed the bill to bring the law into conformity with the Uniform Individual Accident and Sickness Policy Provisions Law, which was recommended in 1950 by the National Association of Insurance Commissioners.[12]

Warranties, Representations, and Conditions

The uniform policy movement was the most sweeping effort to ameliorate the insurance policy. But it was not the most effective; its complexity enabled industry representatives to water down its reforms, in the process of giving needed technical assistance. The standard policy laws seldom went beyond what the companies were willing to grant. On the other hand, specific reforms were less easily diverted into innocuous channels. Successive waves of these reforms had some relation to the attitudes that underlay the rise of the Granges, of Populism, and of the Progressive movement.[13]

The inherited law of warranties and representations bore very harshly on the policyholder. Early and persistent attempts were made to assist the courts in their prolonged effort to modify the harsh doctrines. The 1869 legislature required, for all insurance, that a duplicate copy of the application for insurance be delivered to the policyholder; if it was not, the company might not use the application in evidence. This would render ineffective misrepresentations contained in any nonconforming application. The law disappeared in the 1878 revision of the statutes. An 1874 bill would have converted statements of description or value from warranties to representations, and would have made certain misrepresentations ineffective to defeat recovery unless they contributed to the loss or increased the risk. In recognition of the fact that the dogma of freedom of contract was at the root of the problem, the bill forbade "contracting out" of the statute. The 1878 legislature took the 1869 duplicate copy law a step further by requiring, for fire insurance only, that the application be attached to the policy, before the company might plead its contents.[14]

In 1897, 1899, 1901, 1903, and 1905, efforts were made to provide that failure of condition must result in substantial loss before it would defeat recovery. The 1899 bill passed, but only after it was narrowed to provide merely that vacancy of insured premises must continue till loss to constitute a defense.[15]

The 1906 investigation of life insurance led to enactment, for life insurance, of a variant of the 1869 duplicate copy law; policyholders might demand a copy of the application, and the company's failure to supply it within thirty days would bar a defense based on a representation in the application.[16]

The 1909 legislature modified the doctrines of warranty and representation for all lines of insurance. No representation nor warranty would defeat recovery unless false and made with actual intent to deceive, or unless the falseness increased the risk or contributed to the loss. This requirement of either fraud or materiality greatly softened the harshness of the warranty doctrine. It still proceeded on an "all or nothing" basis, however. If the requirements of the modified doctrine were satisfied, the policyholder got nothing; otherwise he lost nothing. But misinformation had an adverse effect on the company's operations, and a proportional reduction of recovery might be a more discriminating, if more difficult, solution. One problem clearly lent itself to this approach, and the 1919 legislature provided that if the policyholder misstated his age, recovery would be reduced to the amount the premium would have purchased at the true age. In disability insurance, too, the legislature provided for proportional reduction of recovery if the insured changed to a more hazardous employment.[17]

Nonforfeiture Laws

Early life insurance contracts provided that on lapse, the policyholder should forfeit his interest in the policy, no matter how nearly paid up it was. The injustice of this result was recognized early in American insurance development, but the Wisconsin legislature was nevertheless reluctant to interfere to restrict the freedom of contract. An attempt to get a nonforfeiture law in Wisconsin came first in 1871, when a bill would have provided for extended term insurance on lapse. Nothing more was attempted for over twenty years, during which time many companies voluntarily established nonforfeiture provisions. The issue was not wholly quiescent, however. There was much discussion, and Secretary of State Doyle even took a position in opposition to nonforfeiture laws, which would compel all companies to do what some were doing voluntarily. Doyle thought compulsion by the state in such matters was contrary to the true purposes of government, which should merely hold the company to its contract. One thing he would do; he would borrow the New York law requiring a notice before forfeiture.[18]

After an abortive and ill-conceived attempt in 1893 to forbid forfeiture in fraternal societies, the legislature began seriously to consider the problem in 1901. The move was much entangled with the growing opposition to the tontine policy, where forfeiture had consequences transcending mere injustice to the individual policyholder. Various bills would have compelled the company to include in the policy information about the reserve attributable to each policy; to render an annual accounting on participating policies; to prevent lapse, by making a policy loan; or to furnish extended term insurance, or paid up insurance or cash, exactly as in the later required nonforfeiture clause. The standard provisions bill of the 1906 investigating committee provided for automatic premium loans and forbade forfeitures; so also did the proposed standard policy law. The 1909 legislature finally enacted automatic premium loan and nonforfeiture provisions; they remained in effect in mid-century, though revised in details by the 1943 legislature.[19]

Cancellation of Policies

The standard fire insurance policy provided that the policyholder might cancel the policy without notice, the company by five days notice. If the company cancelled, it kept a pro rata portion of the premium; if the policyholder did, the company kept a larger portion measured by a "short-rate" table. An attempt was made in 1911 to require the company to return all but a pro rata portion of the premium even if the policyholder cancelled, but it was unsuccessful. However, in 1919 the legislature established a statutory short-rate table, making it applicable to all property insurance, except steam boiler, fly wheel, or elevator insurance, where the cost of inspection was so great as to make compulsory return of premiums unfair to the company. The dislike for the company's reserved right to cancel was persistent; a 1925 bill would have forbidden cancellation of a fire insurance policy by the company, except for nonpayment of premium. The 1949 legislature repealed the statutory short-rate table, but required the companies to file tables with the Commissioner.[20]

The accident and health insurance companies usually retained a right to cancel, and frequently cancellation on short notice created grave hardship for policyholders. Bills in 1955 and 1957 would have required twelve months notice to cancel any such policy which had been in effect for a year or more. An earlier bill, in 1949, dealt with a similar problem; it forbade termination of group accident and health policies in less than thirty days after the cessation of employment, and forbade it even then if premiums continued to be paid and if the cessation was a result of lockout, strike or other work stoppage. The policyholder was not the only person concerned with cancellation problems; the interest of employees and the public led to a 1923 amendment to the workmen's compensation insurance laws, forbidding cancellation without notice to the Industrial Commissioner. For similar reasons unsuccessful attempts were made in 1939, 1941, and 1943, to restrict or forbid cancellation of insurance on trucks.[21]

Extension of Coverage

It was important to twentieth-century society that substantially the entire population be covered by automobile insurance, so that innocent victims of accidents would be protected. The legislature interfered to extend the coverage of the policy to include persons the companies might prefer to exclude. Thus in 1925, the legislature required that automobile policies apply to any person, firm, or corporation legally responsible for the operation of such automobile, and to any person riding in or operating the automobile with the insured's permission. The 1931 legislature then forbade limitations excluding drivers of an age authorized by law to drive, or use of the car for unlawful purposes, or use while the driver was intoxicated, or use for transportation of liquor in violation of law, or reckless use. In *Quin v. Hoffman* (265 Wis. 636), the Supreme Court in 1954 placed a narrow construction on "permission," holding that it meant "permission legally granted" and "permission to one legally authorized to drive." The 1955 legislature quickly acted to make it clear that it sought to protect injured persons, not drivers; it amended the omnibus provision to apply even when the operation was not authorized by law. In 1957 the Supreme Court reconsidered the policy ground for the 1925 statute and explicitly overruled the *Quin* decision in *Pavelski* v. *Roginski* (1 Wis. 2d 345). However, in 1959, the court held in *Schall* v. *Company* (6 Wis. 2d 350) that the public policy applied only to automobile liability insurance, and refused to extend collision coverage by the omnibus clause contrary to other limitations of the policy.[22]

The 1931 legislature forbade, also, any contract provision excluding coverage or benefits for persons related by blood or marriage to the insured. This last provision made unquestionable what the Attorney General had already ruled to be law—that clauses excluding relatives from benefits in order to prevent collusive lawsuits violated the 1925 law.[23]

In 1927, in *Wick* v. *Wick* (192 Wis. 260), the Supreme Court of Wisconsin had held that a minor son might not sue his father in tort. The social policy effectuated by such a rule was said to be the preservation of satisfactory relations within the family unit. The doctrine was not of ancient origin; Justice Owen admitted in adopting it that no case had appeared on the question in either England or America before 1891, when the American courts began to lay down the rule. By 1927, however, the rule was already obsolete, and there was a vigorous dissent by Justice Crownhart, based on the change in the structure of the family and the use of liability insurance, which should protect the child equally with the stranger. Notwithstanding the minority view expressed in 1927, the Supreme Court held in 1937 that the 1931 statute forbidding the exclusion of blood relatives from the coverage of automobile liability policies was not intended to overrule the *Wick* case. Blood relatives might still recover from the insurance company only if there were no such rule of law barring them from bringing suit. In 1957 a bill was introduced in the legislature to give a minor an action against his parent for injuries resulting from his parent's negligent operation of an automobile. The bill passed the Assembly but not the Senate. A similar bill not limited to automobile accidents was introduced in 1959.[24]

Similar considerations of family unity, together with the ancient notion of the legal identity of husband and wife, prevented the husband and wife from suing each other. In 1944 the Supreme Court held that the husband still might not sue the wife in tort, notwithstanding the long history of emancipatory statutes for women; it followed that the husband might not recover from the wife's insurer, since direct action statutes did not create liability where there was none.[25]

Other Proposed Reforms

Though a wide variety of other reforms were proposed, few were enacted. The successful proposals responded to significant needs of modern society or to serious injustices in the existing operation of the insurance business. Whenever there was the actuality or even the possibility of unfair claims settlement, based on technical defenses arising out of policy terms, there was a possibility that a corrective bill might be introduced. Success for such proposals probably depended on the dramatic character of the injustice, or on the fact that a large number of persons were affected.

Various unsuccessful bills would have made life insurance policies incontestable on the ground of fraud after a specified number of years, required disability policies to cover partial as well as total disability, limited the effect of certain moral hazard clauses in the fire insurance policy, required exceptions in casualty insurance to be printed in boldface type, and would have forbidden the lapsing of a life policy after ten years for a period of four years.[26]

Prevailing contract dogma provided that an insurance company was under no liability to the insured until it had accepted the offer contained in the application. No matter if the company solicited the business, nor if it delayed unreasonably its acceptance or rejection of the application, it was not liable on an unaccepted application. Unreasonable delay to act on the application produced hardship, and many courts solved the problem by holding the company liable in the event of unreasonable delay, either on a contract or a tort theory. The 1935 legislature saw an attempt to provide by statute for liability for delay in processing the application, on a contract theory.[27]

Some of the miscellaneous reform measures were successful, even though they may have resulted from individual complaints and did not muster the support of large groups of interested people to put pressure on the legislature. Thus the 1929 legislature provided that the sole ownership and change of ownership clauses of the standard fire insurance policy should not invalidate policies where there was joint tenancy of husband and wife or where there was a change from sole ownership of one spouse to joint tenancy of both. The same legislature also provided that the "other insurance" clause might only reduce recovery proportionately, rather than make coverage void. The statute was enacted to overrule the court's application of the clause to invalidate an insurance policy in 1929.[28]

The 1943 legislature provided that in spite of a mortgage clause specifying that losses be paid to the mortgagee, the company should pay small fire losses under $50 to the mortgagor. The 1945 legislature extended this provision to windstorm insurance, and the 1951 legislature increased the amount to $100.[29]

§4. The Valued Policy Law

The legislature intervened in the formulation of many provisions of the insurance contract. The story of one clause deserves especially detailed treatment, however, for in this case Wisconsin was the pioneer in leading nearly half the states down a very controversial path.

Before the catastrophic fires of the early 1870's, competition reduced premiums to levels at which reserves were inadequate for disasters. A wave of insurance company failures after the fires led the companies to develop industry organizations to fix premium rates at higher levels and to tighten up loose claims adjustment, underwriting, and marketing practices. Insurance men were suspicious about the causes of the fires, and some identified the central problem as one of careless underwriting:

If there is any one cause more prominent than another, for the large and frequent fires now occurring, it *is carelessness on the part of agents in granting insurance* upon applications of parties, without a proper *knowledge or regard for values.* This is the crying evil of the hour, that agents write up almost any amount of insurance demanded in their eagerness to get their commissions. Policies are granted on country property and remote risks, and even on property in their immediate neighborhood, without its having been seen or examined by the agent. . . . (FUA, *Proc.,* 1873, p. 28).

Overinsurance, they thought, led to incendiary fires. The companies sought protection against overinsurance through an indemnity principle, which restricted the policyholder's recovery to his actual loss, no matter how much the face of the policy might be. In more serene days loss settlement was generously, even carelessly, administered. But under the impact of the big fires, loose loss settlement practices were abandoned, and the companies made "more deliberate and critical investigation of claims, origin of fires, value of property destroyed, and the performance of conditions precedent on the part of the assured. . . ." But some felt that the "instances of over-insurance on almost all kinds of property are still lamentably frequent, and call for the most earnest and persistent means for prevention" (FUA, *Proc.,* 1873, p. 46).

Insistence that the insured should receive no more than indemnity for his loss, whatever premium he may have paid, seemed to legislators to be a refusal to bear the burdens of the transaction after receiving its benefits. An insurance adjuster from Racine, writing in 1872 to the Fire Underwriters' Association of the Northwest (FUA, *Proc.,* 1872, p. 31), described the result: "Hence it has come to this, that so few comparatively get their full insurance on their buildings, even when totally destroyed, they are seeking by legislative enactments to compel payment of the sum insured, without regard to the question of value." The reference was to a bill proposed in the 1872 Wisconsin legislature, which was passed in 1874. It was Wisconsin's first important innovation in the insurance field, the "valued-policy" law. It provided that in the event of total loss of real property, without criminal fault of the insured, the face value of the policy was conclusively presumed to be the loss suffered. The basic indemnity principle of the insurance contract was thus overridden by statute in the affected situations. From this Wisconsin beginning the valued policy law spread, slowly at first, to approximately half the states.[1]

The valued policy bill was strongly contested but the results were decisive. The measure was not involved in a partisan way in the Granger revolt, then at its peak in Wisconsin; had it been, it could not have passed the Senate. Nevertheless it was undoubtedly the beneficiary of Granger unrest and hence partly the result of agrarian radicalism. Whatever the original source of the idea, the farmers rather than Milwaukee Germans were the principal moving force behind the valued policy law, though widespread resentment created by the tighter loss settlement policy of the companies in the early 1870's was an additional factor. Industry spokesmen themselves identified the law with native agrarian radicalism: "Born of the same idea that breeds populism and anarchy, i.e., a nurtured hatred for all corporative power, without understanding whether or not any reason exists for it, this symbol of oppression seems marching on" (FUA, *Proc.*, 1896, p. 100).[2]

The companies profoundly disliked the new law, and it was a generation before they learned to live with it. For decades it was the theme of constant industry discussion, often described as "the Wisconsin problem."[3] At first the severely critical comments assumed without demonstration that the statute encouraged incendiarism. Thus in 1878 a spokesman estimated that 50 per cent of fires in insured property were deliberately set:

Recent decisions from a court of last resort in a neighboring state, would seem to encourage the criminal classes in thus destroying their property and defrauding the insurers, under the really *good* plea of putting a stop to *over insurance* (FUA, *Proc.*, 1878, p. 25).

Eventually the insurers sought to support their thesis with statistics, and then the more extravagant statements ceased. Even as early as 1882 some industry spokesmen were more cautious in their pronouncements:

I am not so sure that the Wisconsin valued policy law caused the vast amount of incendiarism that was predicted, but I do know that it *made us careful not to over-insure*, and I submit that *had we exercised the same care in Wisconsin before the law made us do so*, the law might not now be on the statute book of any state.*

The insurance fraternity did more than rail at the law. Though some of them were realists enough to know the futility of attempts to repeal it, there were abortive attempts at outright repeal in 1875, 1878 and 1881. Subsequently attempts were made to repeal the law by subterfuge, or to remove its sting. Various bills would have made the face value of the policy express merely a rebuttable presumption concerning the actual value of the property; would have limited the insured's recovery to four-fifths of the value of the property and obligated the company to repay the premium with interest on the remainder of the insurance; would have made it unlawful knowingly to issue a policy

*FUA, *Proc.*, 1882, p. 29. In 1877 an urbane insurance man thought the valued policy law was "a reaction on the part of the public against the schemes and systems which we have ourselves made."—FUA, *Proc.*, 1877, p. 106. This was in a year when the threatened spread of the heresy made the meeting frenetic.

for more than 90 per cent of the value of the property and reduced recovery to 90 per cent of the total value, even in the event of total loss; would have made the law inapplicable when the fire started on the insured premises; or would have limited the face of the policy to the assessment roll valuation.[4]

In 1909 the companies were unsuccessful in another attempt at repeal, but in 1915 they succeeded. The valued policy law was repealed by a statute which substituted for it a moral disquisition against over-insurance, with the sanction of a forfeiture of from two to ten times the excessive premium. The repealer must have slipped through unawares. There was no opposition; the Senate even gave unanimous consent to a suspension of the rules in order to hasten passage. In the next session, however, the action of 1915 was decisively reversed after considerable legislative controversy.[5]

Two more efforts were made to repeal the valued policy law, in 1929 and in 1933. When overt repeal failed again, attempts were made in 1933 and 1935 to make the presumption rebuttable. There was much controversy over some of these attempts, but after so many failures, the enemies of the valued policy law must have realized finally the futility of opposition to it, and after 1935 there were no more attempts either to repeal it or to change it materially.[6]

When legislative action failed, the companies might withdraw from the state as a sanction against the law. Threat of withdrawal, and actual withdrawal by many companies, were factors in forcing repeal of the bond deposit law of 1865, and were used unsuccessfully in the fight against the actuarial bills of 1907, but success required concerted action, and the competitive nature of the insurance business made concert difficult. Withdrawal was never used effectively against the valued policy law.[7]

For a long time the Wisconsin Insurance Commissioners were generally hostile to the valued policy law; this was especially true of Fricke and Host. By the time the law was repealed in 1915, the Commissioners had become relatively unconcerned about it, though Cleary did oppose reinstatement of the law in 1917. In 1926 and 1933 Commissioners Johnson and Mortenson expressed complete agreement with the law. This change in climate paralleled a shift in the legislature from the introduction of bills to repeal or emasculate the law to the introduction of bills to extend it or make it more effective.[8]

In 1877 and 1878 the Supreme Court of Wisconsin applied the new law in a series of four cases.[9] No one could doubt the legitimacy of the objective of the act, as expressed by Justice Cole:

The manifest policy of the statute is to prevent over insurance, and to guard, as far as possible, against carelessness and every inducement to destroy property in order to procure the insurance upon it. Where property is insured above its value, a strong temptation is presented to an unscrupulous and dishonest owner, either to intentionally burn it, or not to guard and protect it as he ought. Not sharing in the risk, with the insurer, it is for his advantage that it be destroyed; and it often is destroyed with other property, when it would not have been but for the fact of such excessive insurance. And insurance companies, too, actuated by motives of gain, or incited by sharp competition in business, take risks, frequently, recklessly and for amounts in excess of the real value of the property insured; which they would be less likely to do if compelled to pay the amount of insurance written in their policies (*Reilly* v. *Co.*, 43 Wis. 449, 455 [1877]).

The act assumed that only the companies could take effective action against the basic evil of overinsurance, and it tried to force them to organize their marketing procedures to prevent the mischief. One possible change in marketing procedures would be valuation of the property in advance of the issuance of the policy. It seemed unfair for the companies to collect premiums for a coverage in excess of the maximum amount the insured could ever receive. A sense of this unfairness undoubtedly played a larger role in decisions about the valued policy law than any rational appraisal of its consequences.

Doubt whether the act was aptly framed to lessen overinsurance was suggested by proposed amendments directed not to the frustration of the measure but to its more adequate implementation. The more important of these proposals were variations on a single theme, espoused most vigorously by Commissioner Spooner, who thought the valued policy law did not reach all the parties who should share responsibility for overinsurance. It punished the company by compelling it to pay the face value of the policy, irrespective of the amount of the loss. On the other hand, the law rewarded the insured who overvalued his property, since he received a windfall in the event of fire. Moreover, the valued policy law let the agent go scot-free, though he was most likely to be the villain of the piece. Overinsurance increased his commissions, and unlike the company, he did not need to fear additional losses resulting from increased incendiarism.[10]

The theme first appeared in 1877 in an industry meeting, where a company official suggested that every policy should entail company liability for full face value, but that the insured should receive only three-fourths of the value in the event of loss, the excess to go to the school fund. It should be made a misdemeanor to procure or issue excessive insurance. The Committee on Revision of the Statutes made a similar proposal. Only three-fourths of the value of the property should go to the insured, together with the excess of premium. The rest of the face amount of the policy should go into the treasury of the county for the school fund. The agent's license should be revoked.[11]

From 1879 to 1889 almost every legislative session saw attempts to change the valued policy law in some similar way. All came to nothing. The main thrust of the bills was essentially to take the windfall away from the policyholder and also to punish the agent. The serious problem in most proposals was how to determine the permissible valuation, so that parties acting in good faith could protect themselves. The 1879 bill would have imposed a duty on the county assessor to value the building for insurance purposes. This parallel of the European practice had the merit that it would have given the policyholder opposing interests in valuation with respect to property taxation and fire insurance, and thus would have been partly self-policing. Control of the company was effective. Not only would the company have to pay the face of the policy, but the insured would have been entitled to recover three times the excess premium paid, and the company's license would be revoked for "knowingly" writing overinsurance. The agent "knowingly" writing overinsurance was subject to fine, and also to recovery by the policyholder of three times the excess premiums. Thus the insured and the Commissioner would coöperate in the control of the agent and the company, while the insured would be controlled by his disinclination to pay higher property taxes than necessary.[12]

Some contrivances were naive and gave little attention to problems of motivation and administrative mechanism. An 1885 proposal would have required the agent to report to the city clerk the amount of insurance and the value of the property; such reports were to be placed on public record. On formal complaint, the company had to appraise the property and reduce the insurance to three-fourths of the value; the city treasurer was then authorized to collect a penalty of fifty dollars for overinsurance. An 1889 proposal would have authorized district attorneys to prosecute for the misdemeanor of knowingly over-insuring. An 1880 proposal would have authorized the appointment of two deputy commissioners to enforce a law forbidding overinsurance, apparently by systematic inquiry into company books and other sources of information. The sanction would be the administrative revocation of the licenses of agent and company.[13]

The 1895 standard fire policy carefully preserved the valued policy rule, with the one modification that "It shall be optional, however, with this company . . . to repair, rebuild or replace the property lost or damaged . . . within a reasonable time" (*Laws* 1895, 387). This gave the company a right to rebuild even against the wishes of the insured and thus gave substantial protection against gross overvaluation. The 1903 legislature saw an unsuccessful attempt to reverse this decision. The right was also available as a club to enable the companies to reach a compromise settlement at actual value, and some companies were so using it in the early 1920's, but the Commissioner insisted that the companies must either rebuild in fact or else pay the face of the policy.[14]

The insurance company's best protection against the adverse effects of the valued policy law was careful underwriting to keep the face of the policy within the value of the property. This became difficult, however, if the policyholder had insurance with several companies. Before 1929 the companies might protect themselves against such an eventuality by the "other insurance" clause, voiding the policy where the insured held such additional insurance without the company's consent. Because the clause was contained in a complicated and lengthy contract, innocent policyholders might thereby unwittingly lose their protection. In 1929 the legislature made such clauses ineffective, though it provided that "in no event shall the insured be entitled to recover . . . a sum greater than his actual loss or damage" (*Laws* 1929, 456). Despite this language, the Attorney General ruled that the valued policy law applied even when there were multiple policies and whether or not the companies had knowledge of the additional insurance. The legalistic opinion failed to see that the ruling frustrated the purpose of the act, by permitting the dishonest insured to duplicate the insurance elsewhere, without full disclosure. Attempts were made in 1933 and 1935 to amend the 1929 act to make the valued policy law inapplicable where there was other insurance, but none was successful.[15]

Overinsurance and Underinsurance

The companies' solution to the problem of overinsurance was self-serving. Repeal of the valued policy law would have left them free to settle losses on a tight basis; it would also have permitted them to incorporate three-quarter clauses to limit maximum recovery either to three-fourths of the total value of the property or to three-fourths of the loss. Industry spokesmen even suggested that such clauses be required by statute, and in 1887 the Governor suggested forfeiture to the state of insurance in excess of two-thirds of the loss, on the ground that full insurance encouraged arson and carelessness. This limitation on the quantity of insurance had respectable antiquity, for there were various limitations of the sort in early charters. Such a limit was required as far back as 1838 by the bylaws of the Racine Mutual Fire Insurance Company. The 1867 charter of a horse insurance company limited the payment of loss to two-thirds of the value of the animal. An 1870 mutual charter limited recovery to three-fourths of the value of the property. Later, insurance by bicycle mutuals was limited to half the value of the bicycles. This facile solution to the problem of moral hazard from overinsurance was not without its critics even within the industry; some thought that such laws and clauses would lead to underwriting carelessness and therefore to overinsurance. Moreover, the economic role of insurance could not be fully performed if there were not the possibility of full insurance, and there was doubt whether a three-fourths value law was politically possible against the opposition of the large capital interests handling such commodities as pork and grain.[16]

In addition, growing sophistication of commercial policyholders created the problem of underinsurance. As fire prevention and control measures became ever more effective, total losses from fire became relatively infrequent, and policyholders learned to cut the cost of fire insurance by reducing coverage to the part of the property likely to be burned in a serious fire, carrying the excess risk themselves. Concern about the danger to premium revenue from underinsurance tended to overcome the fear of overinsurance. As early as 1873 an industry committee complained that merchants now know how to regulate the amount of insurance so as to get maximum protection for minimum premium. The suggested remedy was the insertion of an average or coinsurance clause, to provide that unless the insurance was at least a stated percentage of the risk, usually 80 or 90 per cent, the policyholder was a "coinsurer" and must bear a part of the loss; the company's liability was that proportion of the loss that the amount of insurance bore to the part of value required by the clause. The coinsurance clause thus compelled the policyholder to insure at or near full value, at penalty of loss of much of his protection. Councils of the business suggested as early as 1873 that rate reduction might be a *quid pro quo* for the insertion of the clause, but the companies made no such concession. They looked upon a move toward full insurance as a source of additional premium income and salvage.[17]

Though coinsurance clauses sought to require full coverage and three-quarter clauses sought to prevent full insurance, or at least full recovery, legislators tended to lump the clauses together as company efforts to keep policyholders from getting all the protection they had paid for. After an abortive effort in 1893 to outlaw coinsurance clauses, the legislature in 1895 forbade insertion in a policy of "three-quarter" clauses or any other clause requiring the policyholder to carry any part of the risk or limiting the amount to be paid him below the actual cash value of the property, if within the amount for which premium was paid. Though the statute was ambiguous, and "three-quarter clause" may have meant a 75 per cent coinsurance clause, it was apparently designed to forbid both coinsurance clauses and three-quarter clauses. The standard policy law, approved two days later, said that

any other matter necessary to clearly express all the facts and conditions of insurance . . . may be written upon or attached or appended to any policy. . . . [Such] facts or conditions shall in no case be inconsistent with or a waiver of any of the provisions or conditions of the standard policy. . . . (*Laws* 1895, 387, § 3, par. 2).

Commissioner Fricke and the Attorney General agreed that these words effected an implied repeal of the chapter enacted two days earlier, and hence permitted coinsurance clauses. Logically the argument could be applied equally well to repeal the valued policy law by implication, but the officials did not push their logic to that extent.[18]

That by this highly questionable executive interpretation the Commissioner and Attorney General had frustrated the legislature's reasonably clear intent was soon apparent; the next legislature witnessed introduction of five bills, four forbidding coinsurance clauses, and two also forbidding three-quarter clauses. The fifth bill, which became law, represented a compromise position; it forbade any provision limiting the amount to be paid for loss below the actual cash value, if within the amount for which a premium had been paid, with one significant exception. The company might use coinsurance clauses, if it gave to every applicant the choice of a policy without a coinsurance clause, and one at a lower rate with the clause.[19]

With this enactment the legislature had declared its policy to forbid both coinsurance and three-quarter clauses, with an ambiguously worded exception in the case of the coinsurance clause. Though there were Supreme Court decisions, Attorney General's opinions, and amending statutes thereafter, all having significance for the technical scope and effect of the 1897 statute, the underlying public policy was not changed thereafter.[20]

Chapter Six

INSURANCE IN THE
LARGER SOCIETY

As insurance grew to size, it came to have significant impact on the whole society, and the law was compelled to control it in the interest of the larger social goals. Insurance had effect upon the basic power structure of society. Insurance companies, on a less dramatic scale than the railroads, sometimes sought to subvert the legislative process, and in a later age to infiltrate the Commissioner's office; thus the reality, as well as the appearance, of control of the insurance enterprise in the interest of the whole society became the concern of the law. Combinations of insurers to fix the rates were quite early opposed by the law, and by the twentieth century, rate making was one of the main issues in the social control of insurance. Insurance also had effect upon society through the organized attempts that grew up around the enterprise to reduce insurable risk, whether by preventing fires, promoting safety, or controlling crime. The localistic effort to prevent sectional domination of enterprise, too, had real meaning for the insurance business, dominated as it was by large eastern corporations. As insurance became widespread, it involved the transfer, and in its more sophisticated forms the accumulation, of substantial amounts of liquid capital. In the twentieth century, assets of insurance companies and similar financial institutions became large in relation to the total wealth of the nation, and came to have a large impact on the process of capital formation and the capital structure of enterprise. In mid-twentieth century the law must either control the investment of insurance assets with careful concern for these problems, or risk serious distortion of that capital structure because of narrowly conceived investment regulations.

§1. *Insurance as Capital Mobilizer*
—Broadening the Tax Base

Legislators early saw the extensive liquid assets of insurance companies as a ready source of considerable tax revenue. From mid-nineteenth century onward, insurance taxation was no inconsequential factor in the revenues of the typical American state. It began even earlier. Soon after national independence, the new state of Massachusetts reinstituted the infamous stamp tax, and in 1785 placed an imposition of two shillings on each policy of insurance, for the express purpose of reducing the war-born public debt. In 1818 the charter of the Massachusetts Hospital Life Insurance Company provided that a third of the net profits should go to the Massachusetts General Hospital, in return for a monopoly of the life insurance business in the state. In the early 1820's the legislature began to insert in charters a clause subjecting the companies to any general tax law. The Massachusetts general acts of 1832 and 1835 also sought to preserve the taxability of insurance.[1]

In 1814, as a result of war-time hostility to British insurance interests, a New York statute forbade aliens to engage in the fire insurance business in New York. In 1824 a 10 per cent gross premium tax was placed on out-of-state fire insurers; in 1829 both statutes were extended to cover marine insurance. Such discriminatory taxation produced a heavy concentration of the New York fire insurance business in local companies, and an 1835 conflagration wiped out most of the New York companies. The 1837 legislature then reduced the tax to a realistic 2 per cent, nicely balancing the protective and revenue purposes. In 1849 the tax became a 2 per cent levy payable by out-of-state corporations on fire premiums, to the fire departments of the cities and towns where the insured property was located.[2]

The Fire Department Tax

In this form this levy became Wisconsin's first insurance tax. The Wisconsin legislature copied the New York law almost verbatim in 1851 in a local act applying only to Kenosha and in 1852 in a general act applying wherever there was a fire department. The tax was effectively sanctioned by a penal bond in favor of the fire department and by monetary forfeits to be sued for and collected by the fire department.[3]

In its New York origins and in its Wisconsin history this tax was involved in the conflict between local and foreign companies. Out-of-state companies inspired citizens' petitions to the Wisconsin legislature and bills to reduce or repeal the tax. One attempt was made in 1860, after an 1859 three per cent general premium tax on out-of-state companies had been added to the 2 per cent tax, giving local companies a 5 per cent competitive advantage. The new premium tax was payable to the general fund rather than to fire departments. To placate adversely affected local interests the bill repealing the fire department tax would have had the state treasury pay the amount of the erstwhile fire department tax to the fire departments. Political action to eliminate the differential tax was futile, and in 1862 a test case was taken to the Wisconsin Supreme Court on state constitutional grounds, but the discriminatory tax was vindicated, on the ground of the state's power either to exclude foreign corporations altogether or to admit them on such conditions as it might see fit.[4]

Opposition to the fire department tax itself, divorced from its implications for competitive position within the industry, seems never to have been strong, for the companies were themselves interested in encouraging fire prevention. After 1859, opposition was focused on the general premium tax, the proceeds of which went into the general fund, in which the insurance industry had no special interest. When the legislature extended the fire department tax to include local companies in 1869, little reason remained for opposition to it. After the Chicago and Boston fires of 1871 and 1872, fire underwriters even established fire patrols financed by a premium levy; this indicated willingness on the part of the industry to pay for loss prevention activities and explained the cessation of serious opposition to the fire department tax. In mid-twentieth century the tax remained essentially the same. The desperate twentieth-century search for sources of tax revenue led to some efforts to raise the rate, and there was also concern whether the state fire fund and uninsured property must pay it, and whether "premiums" included "assessments." But serious legislative interest was exhibited only in facilitation of collection of the tax, determination of the qualifications which made fire departments eligible to receive the proceeds, development of alternative uses for the revenue, and definition of the legitimate geographical scope of rural fire department tax collection.[5]

Statutes in 1887, 1893, 1899, and 1911 sought to improve techniques for collecting the tax, by making it the duty of the Insurance Commissioner to revoke the license of a company or agent failing to pay, by permitting actions to be brought in the name of the town, city, or village, by making the insured liable for the tax if he procured insurance from an unadmitted company or through a nonresident agent of an admitted company, and by providing for administrative control of the reporting and collecting process. Facilitation of tax collection was also a major reason for the law prohibiting sale of insurance through nonresident agents.[6]

An 1878 act made the tax applicable wherever there was an organized fire department, whether or not the parent municipal unit was incorporated; acts in 1885 and 1889 lessened the minimum qualifying requirements of equipment and personnel. The 1913 legislature provided that the newly created fire marshal inspect fire departments and certify their qualifications to the Commissioner.[7]

Alternative but derivative uses exerted some pressure against the primary use of the fund. An 1899 statute set aside two-thirds of the revenue in first-class cities for a firemen's pension fund. A proposal in 1905 would have appropriated a part of the tax to the use of the Firemen's Relief Associations. The Attorney General had to rule against use of the tax in villages for sick benefits of fire department members. In 1957 the legislature diverted some of the fund for use in training volunteer firemen.[8]

There was more persistent concern with determination of the size of the area rural fire departments might claim as tributary for the collection of fire department dues. The Attorney General ruled that agents in a town must pay the dues even on property unprotected by a fire department if there were a village with a qualified fire department within the town. He thought that this unjust result was imperatively demanded by the wording of the section. The legislature in 1913 remedied the injustice by setting at a mile the radius for the department's tributary area; in 1927 it permitted the extension of the radius to two miles if there were a contract for fire protection between the fire department and the municipality within which lay the property. Other bills would increase the limit more or remove it altogether.[9]

Establishment of the General Premium Tax

The 1859 legislature levied the first premium tax for general revenue. The initial motivation seems to have been two-fold: (1) a desire to give competitive advantage to local companies and (2) the desire for revenue. The former motivation was not publicly stated but seems apparent in the legislative history. The bill ultimately adopted imposed on out-of-state insurers a 3 per cent gross premium tax on all types of insurance, with an initial $500 fee for the first year in which the company operated in the state.[10]

There was more persistent opposition of the industry to the general premium tax than to the fire department tax, since attitudes were not moderated by interest in the use to which the money was put. At first, however, the effectiveness of opposition to it as a revenue measure was lessened by obsession with it as an aspect of the competitive conflict between foreign and local corporations. In 1861 the out-of-state companies succeeded in getting the tax reduced to 2 per cent, but in 1862 it was restored to 3 per cent. In 1864 there was an unsuccessful proposal to raise it to 5 per cent. In 1866 the Secretary of State urged liberal legislation to favor local companies, in order to keep premium money in the state.[11]

But the revenue, rather than the protective, purpose of taxation was gaining ascendancy, and the 1867 legislature imposed a 1 per cent premium tax on all local companies. In 1870 the legislature revised the tax, and instead of a "burdensome and almost prohibitory tax" (*Rept. Ins. Comm'r,* 1870, p. 6) mainly designed to favor domestic companies, the tax became one primarily for revenue. A distinction was now made between life companies on the one hand, and fire and marine on the other. On fire and marine companies the tax was reduced to 2 per cent and applied both to domestic and out-of-state companies; the domestic firms retained only slight advantage by permission to deduct officers' salaries and office expenses from gross receipts. Out-of-state life companies must pay a flat sum of $300 per year, and local companies a 1 per cent gross premium tax on Wisconsin premiums. The flat $300 levy would favor out-of-state companies with very large Wisconsin operations, but penalize small ones, since the extent of the burden imposed by the tax would depend on the size of the income over which it must be apportioned. An unsuccessful attempt was made in 1871 to return local companies to an ordinary property tax basis.[12]

In the 1870 statutes, a retaliatory provision was inserted for both fire and life insurance, which imposed reciprocally on companies of other states any additional taxes, license fees, deposit requirements, or like burdens imposed by such states on Wisconsin companies. Ostensibly this statute protected Wisconsin companies from other-state discrimination, but as events demonstrated, it give little such protection, since Wisconsin was a state of high insurance taxes. Similar retaliatory provisions were more frequently invoked elsewhere against Wisconsin companies.[13]

Non-Life Insurance Taxation after 1870

The revenue purpose substantially triumphed over the protective in the 1870 legislation, and led insurance company opposition to become better organized and more self-conscious. Nevertheless, persistent division within the industry prevented united action. There was much indifference, too, since any moderate tax burden could be passed on to the public. Industry opinion was divided on the course to be taken; some advocated vigorous action, by litigation to test constitutionality and by organized lobbying; others advocated a more temperate course to avoid antagonizing the legislature, on the theory that legislators were beginning to see the error of their ways. Disagreement on method prevented organized action.[14]

An 1874 bill would have changed the tax basis for local fire and marine companies to 1 per cent on personal property assessed at value, leaving foreign companies to be taxed at the 2 per cent gross premium rate. Local companies writing only fire insurance (most of the operating mutuals) would have been freed from any taxation. A similar bill included life companies, too; its tempestuous legislative history reflects the greater interest in life insurance taxation. The bill reflected various cross currents—a concern with revenue, a desire to give competitive advantage to Wisconsin companies, a desire to give a favored position to localized and noncommercial mutuals.[15]

The concern with revenue was now dominant, however, because insurance taxes provided an important part of the state's revenue. Thus Secretary of State Doyle complained in 1877 of the drop in insurance tax revenues, and considered ways to increase receipts. Commissioner Spooner said in 1878 that he would enforce the law against unauthorized agents and companies, because failure to enforce it deprived the state of tax revenues; to him taxation, not regulation, was the purpose of the laws concerning unauthorized agents and companies. In 1885 and 1889 the Governors noted with gratification the substantial increase in insurance tax revenue, and in 1899 the Governor criticized the inadequacy of the taxes insurance companies were paying.[16]

Pleasure at large insurance tax revenues was not unanimous. Commissioner Fricke opposed insurance taxation on principle. Property insurance minimized the adverse effect of the destruction of wealth and thus contributed to the welfare of the state; it should not be taxed. Even the fire department tax was wrong in principle. The Commissioner should not be made a tax collector—his role was regulation to protect the public.[17]

For a decade after 1897 there was extensive consideration of problems of insurance taxation. Though life insurance received most attention, other insurance was not neglected. There was an increased sophistication in dealing with a complex problem, as shown by the enactment in 1905 of a new basis for taxation of fire insurance, applicable both to domestic and foreign companies. Four per cent was levied on gross premiums, less premiums for reinsurance in authorized companies, and less losses paid. This change was proposed by Commissioner Fricke as early as 1896; it would eliminate the apparent injustice of high taxes in years when loss experience was bad, which seemed to impose the duty to pay for the privilege of losing money. But the legislature abandoned the subtler approach and returned to the 2 per cent gross premium tax in 1909, forced to that retreat by the worsening, under retaliation, of the position of Wisconsin companies in other states, because of Wisconsin's isolation in the new approach.[18]

Basically the gross premium approach to taxation of fire insurance companies was still in effect in the 1950's; most controversy in the twentieth century centered on the exemption of mutuals, with some concern manifested for the amount of taxation.[19]

The localistic bias of the nineteenth century produced tax and other discriminations in favor of local-focused mutual companies. It was not the form of organization that was the original basis and justification for the distinction, for in the nineteenth century commercial mutuals and stock companies were taxed on the same basis and controlled by the same regulatory statutes; rather, it was the localized and noncommercial character of the business which was decisive. Commissioner Fricke decried the tendency to give tax advantage to the local mutuals, but he was out of sympathy with the attitudes of his time. Manufacturers' and millers' mutuals, town insurance companies, church insurance companies, fraternals, mutual livestock companies, mutual bicycle companies, mutual plate-glass companies, were all given preferential filing fee schedules. There were no tax provisions for druggists' mutuals, inter-insurance exchanges, retail lumber dealers' mutuals, mutuals for the insurance of county asylums and almshouse property. A 1903 bill would have exempted all mutuals from premium taxation. In 1905 the legislature specifically exempted from premium tax town, church, druggists', lumber dealers', hardware dealers', and city and village mutuals; in 1909 it excluded from such taxation all the domestic mutuals writing insurance other than life, except the companies organized before 1909 under the general insurance act. Inter-insurance exchanges, however, it taxed at 2 per cent. The 1917 legislature saw an effort to limit the favorable treatment of mutuals to truly noncommercial ones, by exempting from taxation only those which paid no salary larger than $2,000 per year. By a slow process, the exemption, which was originally based on the informal and noncommercial character of the operation of the company, had become one based solely on the mutual character of the organization of the company.[20]

In 1923 an effort was made to extend the exemption from premium tax to all domestic mutuals, commercial or not, and whether or not organized before the 1909 act. Presumably the change was intended to exempt the Germantown Farmers' Mutual and the Herman Farmers Mutual, the only two Wisconsin mutuals paying such taxes. In fact, however, both companies, though existing long before 1909, had been specially chartered, not organized under the general statutes. The Herman woke up first to the situation, and paid its 1923 taxes only under protest. When the Attorney General ruled that the statutes did not require the Herman to pay the tax, but that the protested 1923 tax might not be recovered because the statute of limitations had run on the company before it began suit, the legislature appropriated funds to repay the 1923 taxes. In the following year the Germantown, too, ceased to pay taxes, and in fact, though not in terms, all Wisconsin mutuals except life mutuals were exempt from premium taxation.[21]

Toward mid-century mutual companies occupied a larger share of the insurance field, partly because of tax advantages, partly because of the competitive advantage derived from a less costly marketing system. As the mutuals ceased to have the appearance of the local-focused coöperative enterprises of the early nineteenth century, it became more difficult to justify tax exemption for them, but also more difficult to take it away, as larger proportions of the populace acquired a stake in tax exemption for their companies.

From 1920 on, repeated efforts were made to tax all except town mutuals, but the efforts were uniformly unsuccessful and in mid-century the broad exemption still remained. The effort was led by the stock companies, which disliked the competitive advantage thus given the mutuals, and which probably hoped also for some relief from the tax burden. In some years the controversy became heated, and the mutuals were accused of enjoying a "racket."[22]

In 1945 the determination of the United States Supreme Court that insurance was "commerce" led to fear that Wisconsin's discriminatory taxes would be held unlawful as a burden on interstate commerce. The Commissioner led an effort to achieve uniform taxation of companies, whether local or foreign, at 1.5 per cent of the gross premium. The proponents of the change tried to formulate the issue in terms of constitutional doctrine, but the opposition put it in other terms; in their view this was a drive of big business, spearheaded by the National Tax Equality Association, to tax the coöperative movement out of existence. The United States Supreme Court did not aid the drive for uniformity, for in the *Prudential* case about a South Carolina tax, it held some discriminatory taxation constitutional. Companies which had paid taxes under protest or made claims to the legislature got no relief.[23]

Still the effort to tax mutuals continued with no signs that the bitterness would abate. In 1955 the state administration supported an effort to tax the large mutual casualty companies, on grounds both of equality of treatment and the need for increased state revenues. Bitter personal attacks featured the controversy. Notwithstanding the organized weight of the administration political machine, the political strength of the mutuals could not be overcome, and in mid-century their preferred position appeared impregnable.[24]

The conflict between domestic and out-of-state companies continued, too, though it was now subordinated to the mutual-stock controversy. A 1947 statute reduced the rate of tax for domestic stock fire insurers, giving them a tax advantage over out-of-state companies and narrowing the advantage possessed over them by domestic mutuals. Bills in 1951 would have eliminated the advantage of the domestic stock companies. In 1957 the legislature exempted all domestic companies from payment of gross premium taxes on disability insurance.[25]

Unadmitted companies initially insured Wisconsin property without paying taxes, since tax collection procedures were keyed to the licensing process. The 1909 legislature put a clear obligation on unauthorized companies to pay premium taxes on insurance covering Wisconsin property, and under heavy monetary penalty required policyholders paying premiums to such companies to notify the Commissioner. As a result of the law some unauthorized companies complied with admission requirements. The 1913 legislature imposed a fine of up to $5,000 on unauthorized companies doing business in the state. Moreover, it declared that natural persons aiding such unauthorized business were guilty of a felony; the object was to render them subject to extradition. In addition, the statute made the policies void, punishing mainly the buyer of the insurance. Large corporate policyholders who could shop for insurance out of the state probably bought most of such insurance, and for them the sanction was quite apt.[26]

Various penalties were proposed to add force to the law. Unsuccessful bills would have increased the taxation on unauthorized companies, penalized officers of authorized companies who had anything to do with unauthorized companies doing business in the state, required adjusters to notify the Commissioner about such insurance, permitted the Commissioner to call on property owners to furnish information about insurance, and taxed property owners who insured with unauthorized companies. The 1949 legislature imposed a 3 per cent tax on unauthorized companies in lieu of all other taxes and fire department dues. The insured must pay the tax if the company did not, and must notify the Commissioner if his premium exceeded $100. There was a heavy monetary penalty.[27]

Life Insurance Taxation after 1870[28]

After the Civil War the rapidly growing assets of life insurance companies offered a readily available source of tax revenues. At the same time, Wisconsin's own Northwestern Mutual was becoming one of the leading life companies in the nation. The availability of life insurance funds for Wisconsin tax levies was limited by the retaliatory provisions of the insurance laws of states where the Northwestern Mutual sought to extend its operations. Since most such states were low insurance tax states, high taxation of life insurance in Wisconsin meant that the Northwestern Mutual not only had to pay tax on its Wisconsin business to the state of Wisconsin, but would pay the same tax on its out-of-state business to the other states where it operated, though other companies might pay none. This was true no matter how fair and nondiscriminatory might be the Wisconsin tax laws. Thus Wisconsin was in a dilemma; it could tax foreign life insurance companies only at the expense of the competitive position of the Northwestern Mutual. The story of life insurance taxation in Wisconsin thus became one of conflict between sympathy for the Northwestern Mutual in its competitive drive toward high rank in the business and Wisconsin's persistent need for additional tax revenues.[29]

In the nineteenth century the conflict was one between agrarian radicals and the business community in the mercantile centers. In 1874 a much amended bill would have levied a 2 per cent gross premium tax on foreign life companies, and on domestic companies a personal property tax of one half of one per cent or 1 per cent, plus a 2 per cent gross premium levy on their out-of-state business, less a credit for out-of-state taxation.[30] The change would have burdened the Northwestern Mutual through the operation of the retaliatory laws and because the personal property tax would have been roughly equivalent to a 10 to 20 per cent tax on investment income. An Assembly committee reported the bill unfavorably: life insurance protected widows and orphans against want and thus relieved the community of poor taxes; the reserve of a life insurance company was "a charity fund raised by self-imposed taxation," and should be encouraged, not penalized. (*Assembly J.*, 1874, pp. 541–42). The President of the Northwestern Mutual convinced the committee that such a change in the tax structure would drive foreign companies from the state and eliminate competition. The argument seems disingenuous; the Northwestern's vigorous opposition probably resulted from fear of the worsening of its competitive position by reason of the heavy personal property levy and the operation of retaliatory laws.

After modification in committee of the whole, a less drastic form of the 1874 bill passed the Granger-dominated Assembly by a vote of 60 to 25 but lost in the more conservative Senate by 15 to 11. The split was not a party matter in the Assembly but followed a significant geographical and occupational distribution. Thus farmers supplied 68 per cent of the affirmative votes, and only 32 per cent of the negative votes. Many of the remaining affirmative votes were of small town merchants and lawyers with the rural viewpoint; most of the nonfarm votes among the negative group were by persons whose occupations were likely to represent more capital investment, including several manufacturers. Geographically, too, there was a clear tendency for the negative votes to be concentrated in the lake front counties and other commercial centers. The Senate's contemporaneous consideration of tax equalization may have been a factor in its decision, but more likely determinative was the generally conservative complexion of that body in that year. Analysis once again shows an economic, and to a lesser extent geographical, orientation to the vote; in the Senate this corresponded roughly with the party division. The vote against the bill came primarily from manufacturers and the larger merchants; that for the bill from farmers and their small-town allies.[31]

The bill was a heated issue in the Senate; the pitch of temper was particularly evident when Senator Schmidt alleged that bribery had been tried by a representative of the Northwestern Mutual. After a superficial and hasty investigation, a Senate committee absolved the company of blame.[32]

Two years later essentially the same bill was again introduced, and was opposed by a campaign organized by the Northwestern Mutual, which obtained memorials from all over the state, bearing several thousand signatures. An Assembly committee recommended indefinite postponement, emphasizing the competitive disadvantages which would be imposed on the local company. The Assembly voted the bill down, 60 to 20; the affirmative votes were again predominantly rural, reflecting the persistence of agrarian radicalism.[33]

In 1878 the premium tax on the Wisconsin business of domestic life insurance companies was increased to 2 per cent. As originally introduced the bill repeated the proposals of 1874 and 1876; as in 1874 the legislature was deluged with identical, printed petitions from all portions of the state, protesting the tax increase. Despite vigorous efforts to pass the drastic original version of the bill a more moderate tax increase resulted. One may see in two Senate roll-call votes a threefold division of attitudes toward insurance taxation. A modest but conclusive majority favored some increase in the tax revenues from life insurance companies. A sizeable minority was hostile to any increase in the tax, and another sizeable minority was prepared to support drastic increases, even at the expense of harm to the domestic company. The two extreme positions show a fairly clear-cut regional and occupational division. The seven members favorable to drastic increase in taxation were overwhelmingly Republican and represented the rural center of the state. They were predominantly farmers. The eight members opposed to any increase in taxation were predominantly Democratic (in a Republican house) and represented the lake front counties and some Mississippi river counties. They were by occupation predominantly business men and manufacturers. The first group represented that portion of the population deeply influenced by the attitudes underlying the Granger movement, ready to tax and regulate public utilities, and with no especial interest in giving competitive advantage to local companies.[34]

The persistent agrarian radicals tried in 1879 to levy 1 per cent on the policy reserves of all life companies. The bill was killed in committee on the sole ground of competitive disadvantage to the Northwestern Mutual. In 1880 the proposal was a 5 per cent gross premium tax on domestic life companies. A Senate committee criticized the naive view of the proponents, which regarded such assets as a kind of surplus subject to heavy taxation, rather than as a liability to the policyholders. It criticized the use of the word "dividends" for repayment of overcharges, since the term misled people to suppose that great profits were being made. An Assembly roll-call vote once again revealed the predominance of rural representatives among the proponents of heavier taxation.[35]

Though a revenue motivation unmodified by concern for the needs of the business community was an aspect of agrarian radicalism, a more temperate revenue motivation was the prevailing attitude of the time, as shown by the success of the 1878 bill increasing insurance taxes. It was shown also by the expressed concern of most public officials to increase insurance tax revenues. Commissioner Fricke was an exception. He opposed insurance taxation in principle, as a tribute on people who benefited the state by buying insurance; life insurance prevented dependents from becoming public charges; gross premium taxes on life insurance were indefensible and should be replaced by taxation of only the surplus of fixed premium companies.[36]

But critical as he was of the taxation laws, Fricke insisted that the companies meet their legal obligations to the state. Thus he made a concerted drive to collect back taxes owing because his predecessors had misinterpreted the law and failed to collect. The 1870 law permitted out-of-state life or life and accident companies to operate in the state upon paying a license fee of $300. The 1880 legislature subjected foreign accident companies to the 2 per cent gross premium tax imposed on fire companies. The Travelers' Insurance Company entered Wisconsin before 1870, and from 1870 to 1895 it conducted a life and accident business on the payment of a single annual fee of $300, the 1880 law notwithstanding. Fricke demanded 2 per cent of all accident premiums collected from 1880 to 1895, a total of over $16,000, and threatened to revoke the license of the company for its refusal to pay. The company contended that the two acts taken together created three classes of companies: life companies, life and accident companies, and accident companies, and that the first two might operate upon payment of the $300 fee, but the third class had to pay the 2 per cent gross premium tax. The Travelers' was, of course, in the second category. The company's contention was given substantial support by a long history of administrative interpretation. Nevertheless, the Supreme Court upheld the Commissioner and denied the company an injunction against revocation of license for nonpayment of the 2 per cent tax for the current year; however, it refused to decide whether the company must pay back taxes. The following year the Commissioner raised that issue by threatening to revoke the company's license for refusal to pay back taxes for all years from 1880, together with interest, a total he now claimed was over $35,000. Once again the court upheld the Commissioner.[37]

These two cases established the Commissioner's basic position. He then proceeded to complete his program of collection. He compelled companies doing only an accident business and paying 2 per cent under the 1880 statute, but not the $300 fee under the 1870 statute, to pay up back fees of $300 per year as a condition of continuing business. Further, he insisted that companies issuing plate glass insurance were also subject to the $300 license fee imposed by the 1870 statute dealing with life and accident insurance. Thus far he had used the licensing power to compel the companies to take action against him. Finally he sued to collect the $300 fee from an assessment accident company which had departed from the jurisdiction. The Court upheld him in all these controversies. Fricke's program resulted in the collection of about $100,000 in back taxes.[38]

The companies adversely affected by this litigation sought relief in several ways. The Standard Life and Accident Company of Detroit appealed to the Michigan Commissioner to invoke the retaliatory law. This the Michigan official did by ruling that the Standard was a life, not an accident company, and hence that the Northwestern Mutual was subject to retaliation. The Fidelity and Casualty Company of New York requested the same treatment of the Northwestern Mutual by the New York Commissioner. Several of the companies sought relief from the 1901 legislature, but the Assembly Committee on Finance, Banks and Insurance recommended that the petitions be tabled, and the matter was closed with the Commissioner victorious on all fronts.[39]

Beginning with 1897, there was an extensive reconsideration of the insurance tax structure. There were three basic objectives among the bills presented in this period: (1) to increase the state's revenue by raising rates, (2) to give local companies competitive advantage, and (3) to penalize excessive accumulations and tontine or deferred dividend operation.

An 1897 bill would have taxed general surplus, beyond the legal reserve, presumably to suppress excessive accumulation. Another in 1899 would have taxed tontine policies at 2 per cent, semi-tontine at 1 per cent, and straight life not at all. Other 1899 bills would have given competitive advantage to local companies. Thus one would have charged life companies a flat $300 license fee, plus 3 per cent of gross premiums for Wisconsin companies, 4 per cent for the companies of other states, and 5 per cent for alien companies.[40]

The proposal of a tax differential unfavorable to alien companies met an insuperable obstacle. The 1850 Convention of Friendship, Commerce and Extradition, between the United States and the Swiss Confederation, provided that "No higher impost . . . shall be exacted from the citizens of one of the two countries residing or established in the other than shall be levied upon citizens of the country in which they reside . . ." (Treaty of Nov. 25, 1850, Art. II, in 11 *Stat.* 589). This provision was brought to the attention of the legislature; it was no merely academic matter, for in 1896 and 1897 two Swiss fire insurance companies were admitted to Wisconsin and were doing an increasing business. Any notion of giving a competitive advantage to local companies against alien companies thus foundered on the supremacy clause of the Federal Constitution.[41]

One of the 1899 bills, introduced by P. A. Orton, a local agent and policyholder of the Northwestern Mutual, emerged as law. This "Orton law" taxed out-of-state life companies 1 per cent of their Wisconsin premiums, local companies 1 per cent on gross income from all sources, except income from taxed real estate or tax-exempt securities, pure assessment companies a flat $300 per year, and exempted fraternals with a lodge form of organization. Although the rate was decreased, the extension of the tax on the Northwestern Mutual to its gross income in other states resulted in a large increase in its taxes, from $33,000 to $153,000 in the first year. The bill may have succeeded because of the great need of the state for revenue, coupled with superior effectiveness of the railroad lobby, which prevented an increase in railway taxation. The Northwestern fought the bill, both with petitions to the legislature and extensively in hearings before the tax commission. In addition to arguments against the principle of insurance taxation, the Northwestern exhibited in detail the bad results it suffered from the retaliatory tax system. In 1899 it paid $17,694.63 in retaliatory tax to Illinois in return for $8.52 received by Wisconsin from the one or two small Illinois companies operating in the state. If emergency needs required additional tax revenues from life insurance, the Northwestern Mutual said it would rather pay the state directly what it needed, for it was paying approximately two dollars to other states in retaliatory taxation for every one dollar Wisconsin received from out-of-state companies.[42]

This curiously inverted wish of the Northwestern Mutual for lower taxes for its competitors than for itself was rewarded by a quick reversal of state policy in 1901; the legislature reduced the tax on out-of-state companies to the flat $300 license fee and granted the company's request for taxation on Wisconsin premiums, at 3 per cent of gross income less income from taxed real estate and out-of-state premiums. There was little opposition to the change; the competitive interests of the Northwestern Mutual prevailed for the time being over the need of the state for revenue and the desire for a kind of abstract justice within the boundaries of the state.[43]

Governor LaFollette thought the state should tax fairly within its borders and ignore the retaliatory action of other states: "The legislature of this state should not be moved to the rejection of a just law when proposed, by the consideration that an unjust law might be enacted in some other state in retaliation" (Assembly J., 1905, p. 34). Local life companies were paying 84 per cent of the life insurance tax paid to the state, on but 28 per cent of the business done in the state. His recommendation was heeded in 1905, and the legislature imposed a gross premium tax of 3 per cent on out-of-state life companies, despite the competitive interests of the Northwestern Mutual and over its vigorous protest.[44]

Governor LaFollette's recommendations illustrated a more sophisticated approach to life insurance taxation; he urged that the crude gross premiums tax give way to a tax based on the cash value of policies. Such a bill was introduced and narrowly failed of passage. The Northwestern opposed it because of the retaliatory burden. Former Commissioner Fricke argued, on behalf of the Union Central Life of Cincinnati, that a tax on net values discriminated against long established policyholders in favor of younger ones and in favor of preliminary term and other extravagant plans of operation as against the conservative full reserve companies. Fricke's argument illustrated the importance in insurance taxation of the retaliatory element and a protective attitude toward the Northwestern Mutual, for though he represented a foreign company, he based much of his argument on the harmful effect the proposed tax would have on the Northwestern Mutual, through retaliation.[45]

In 1906 the Wisconsin Tax Commission held hearings on insurance taxation; Fricke urged taxation of the undivided surplus of participating policies and gross premium taxation on nonparticipating policies. This introduced new variations into the basic revenue theme. It would favor participation and discourage withholding of dividends. Commissioner Host, too, would have taxed undistributed surplus very heavily. The Northwestern Mutual was agreeable to this suggestion, and in 1907 a bill was introduced embodying those recommendations. However, the bill that passed repealed the 1905 law and thus terminated the taxation of foreign life companies except on a retaliatory basis; the domestic company must still pay on a gross income basis, less premium receipts in other states and income on taxed real estate.[46]

By this time the Northwestern Mutual was changing its position on the question of discrimination, and it now urged taxation at the same rate on both domestic and foreign companies, despite the retaliatory laws. In 1907 it suggested 2 per cent on Wisconsin premiums. Though this seemed high, the company recognized the probable reluctance of the legislature to go further in granting relief, pending more adequate investigation by the Tax Commission and the legislature. A 1909 bill would have taxed foreign and domestic companies alike 1 per cent of Wisconsin premiums; this represented the position of the Northwestern Mutual. The new strategy of the company became clear in arguments on this bill. The retaliatory law was now to be used, together with an appeal to Progressive notions of fairness, to achieve parity within Wisconsin for domestic and foreign company taxes, and to limit the rate of taxation and the form of taxation to that prevailing elsewhere, so that the retaliatory laws would not come into operation. This would greatly reduce the taxes of the company. The gross premium tax was thus favored to put the tax on the same basis as the levies of most other states, to reduce the burden of retaliation. The shift in position probably reflected a rise in the rate of taxation elsewhere. A 1905 tabulation by the Northwestern had showed that many states were now taxing at 2 or 2.5 per cent of gross premiums.[47]

In a temperate report in 1911, the Tax Commission stated its view that life insurance did not deserve tax exemption any more than other fruits of frugality, that accumulated assets should be the basis of the tax system, that the tax should be limited to such assets as equitably belonged to citizens of Wisconsin, that real estate should be taxed under the general property tax laws, that other assets should not be taxed "at the rates usually imposed upon property or capital employed in productive enterprises carried on for ... pecuniary profit ... ," but that, in view of the purpose of insurance investments and the low rate of income from them, a tax of perhaps 5 per cent of the income from such assets would be a reasonable rate.* It proposed a reciprocal provision to shield the domestic companies from retaliatory laws of other states; no foreign company would pay more than Wisconsin companies would pay in the state of its domicile. This protection from retaliation by other states would save the domestic companies far more than the state would lose, and the domestic companies should be required to make up the loss to the state from the operation of the reciprocal provision. The Northwestern Mutual adopted the position of the Tax Commission, and well it might, for its taxes under the Tax Commission bill would be but a tithe of those under existing law. The bill was much praised as "scientific," but it was not successful. In 1913 and 1915 it was equally unsuccessful. The Senate was hostile to a reduction in life insurance taxation, even in the guise of a more "scientific" method. A substitute acceptable to the Northwestern would have given domestic corporations the option of paying 3 per cent on premium income from Wisconsin business, or else a tax on investment income beginning at 9 per cent and decreasing in 1 per cent stages

*The 1911 special report of the Tax Commission relating to the taxation of life insurance companies, summarized in *Assembly J.*, 1911, pp. 202–6.

annually to 6 per cent. A second substitute would have reduced the tax on domestic companies to 3 per cent on investment income.[48]

A new factor appeared during these years. One of the 1909 bills would have exempted Wisconsin premiums, too, from the tax base of domestic companies. The exemption of Wisconsin premiums was directed to the amelioration of the tax load of five new Wisconsin companies, upon which the burden of the tax fell more heavily than the Northwestern Mutual, because of their concentration of activity in Wisconsin. In 1915 the needs of the five new companies prevailed. The legislature reduced the tax to 3 per cent of gross income after deducting all premiums and the rents on taxed real estate. In this form the levy was essentially a tax of 3 per cent on investment income, though its disadvantage to the nationally operating Northwestern Mutual was that it applied also to such income on the assets derived from operations outside the state. The legislation was widely approved as an act of simple justice.[49]

At last life insurance taxation had been put on a "scientific" basis. However, those concerned with the need for state revenues might urge that the rate was very low. Even so, in 1921 an effort was made to decrease the tax by exempting the interest necessary to maintain the reserve.[50]

Even the most radical of the "Progressives" wanted to protect the Northwestern Mutual from retaliatory tax burdens in other states; moreover, the principle of retaliatory taxation offended the sense of fairness of the Progressives. In 1915, therefore, the legislature passed without dissent a reciprocal provision that out-of-state companies need pay Wisconsin taxes only to the extent that their domiciliary states taxed Wisconsin companies. Unlike the retaliatory provision it complemented, this did not reflect localism; it was not an attempt to set up tariff barriers to interstate operation of insurance, but an attempt to relieve them even at direct cost to Wisconsin tax revenues.[51]

Not only morality but also administrative convenience urged repeal of the retaliatory law, since it involved Wisconsin officials in the difficult task of interpreting the tax laws of other states. There were efforts to repeal the retaliatory law, even without coöperation from other states. Repeal was not successful; instead the retaliatory device was extended to examination fees in 1917 and to fraternals in 1919. There was even more persistent effort to repeal the reciprocity provision of 1915, because of its adverse effect on state tax revenues. The companies, however, consistently opposed repeal since the reciprocal law protected them from retaliation elsewhere. Despite the desire to eliminate the retaliatory tax provision as a "relic of barbarism,"* and the reciprocity provision as costly to tax revenues, both remained in effect in the 1950's.[52]

The increasing level of taxation elsewhere made the retaliatory laws less significant; a 1927 revision of the tax laws ignored retaliation by taxing foreign companies at 2 per cent on premiums. The revision also narrowed the tax base for domestic companies by exempting the interest required to maintain the legal reserve. The Northwestern favored the bill, which would substantially decrease its Wisconsin taxes while resulting in a smaller increase in out-of-state retaliatory taxes. The success of the companies may have resulted partly from their retreat from the untenable high ground where they urged that life insurance should bear no tax burdens, to a position where they sought only a better balance with foreign companies. The foreign companies made some effort to repeal the 2 per cent tax on them, but their opposition was not vigorous, perhaps because the change put Wisconsin more nearly in line with other states. Opposition to the new tax basis centered mainly in the fear, groundless as it proved, that the change would greatly diminish the state's revenues.[53]

Though the Northwestern's main effort in opposition to taxation was in the legislature, it did not forget litigation. In 1912 and 1913 it paid its taxes under protest, and then made claim for recovery of nearly a million dollars in taxes for the two years, on the ground that the tax was discriminatory, in violation of the uniform tax provision of the Wisconsin Constitution and the Fourteenth Amendment to the United States Constitution. The position taken by the company was inconsistent with its half–century–old lobbying posture, and the legislature disallowed the claims. The company again made similar claims of over a million dollars in 1915; again the legislature disallowed them. After recourse to the legislature had thus failed, the company sued. But the Wisconsin Supreme Court and the Supreme Court of the United States upheld the discrimination as a lawful one based upon a reasonable classification, and the Northwestern did not succeed in recovering its taxes.[54]

Though its main contention was unsuccessful, the company con-

*Rept. Wis. Joint Committee of Senate and Assembly on the Affairs of Life Insurance Companies (1906), p. 229.

tinued to try, through the courts, to obtain relief from some of the tax load. It sought unsuccessfully in 1920 to avoid taxation of interest on policy loans, to the extent that the interest was unpaid, contending that since such interest was thereupon merely offset against the reserves on the policy, there was no receipt of "income" subject to taxation. This specious reasoning gave no difficulty to the court, which pointed out that the interest was paid by the company to itself out of the policy reserve. The amount in issue was about $20,000 each year, and thus substantial enough to justify litigation, though by no means a major factor in the economics of the Northwestern Mutual. In 1923 Attorney General Ekern ruled that interest on tax-exempt United States government bonds must be included in the computation of income for tax purposes. The Northwestern Mutual was assessed $208,000. The company was unsuccessful in the state courts in its efforts to have the interest excluded from income for tax purposes, but the company persisted and won its point in the Supreme Court of the United States; that court held such bonds immune from state taxation in any guise.[55]

§2. *Insurance in a Federal System*

Impact of Localism on the Foreign Insurance Corporation

An important theme of American legal history was the conflict between foreign and local corporations. On the whole, what happened in American law in the working out of this tension was a pragmatic expression of the strength of opposing forces in the society. The constitutional principles which tempered otherwise naked resort to political power in the solution of the conflict expressed the society's dominant interest in the essential economic unity of a great nation. One theory, or set of attitudes, treated the foreign corporation as an interloper and sought to subject it to substantial restriction. In its extreme form this view denied existence to the corporation outside the state of its charter. A more liberal view treated foreign corporations as normal business units, subject to no greater restrictions than local firms.

Of the restrictive theory, the economic substratum may be said to be the jealousy of local interests, the fear of world competition. Of the liberal theory, the material basis is the growing internationalism of business, of trade, of investment.*

The history of insurance law in Wisconsin was in no small degree a commentary on this conflict between localism and the unifying tendencies of an increasingly complex and interdependent national and even world economy. Though these problems seldom loomed large in conventional political history, there was hardly a year in the decades after statehood that the Wisconsin legislature failed to have before it some aspect of the struggle.

In this conflict, in Wisconsin as elsewhere, a powerful weapon was differential taxation. Even in the 1950's the taxing power was sometimes involved in efforts to combat sectional domination of the financial structure of the country—to impede by artificial barriers the free flow of capital from one section to another. In contrast, and often in conflict, with the use of taxation as a weapon, was its use to provide revenue. Sometimes the one purpose was dominant, sometimes the other, but seldom was either wholly absent from the objectives of the legislature.

Security Deposit Requirements.—Second only to differential taxation as a weapon in the conflict between foreign and local companies was the requirement of the deposit of securities with state officials. This subtle weapon could always be rationalized plausibly in terms of the need for policyholder security, and it could easily be cast into terms superficially appearing to impinge alike on foreign and local companies, while in fact operating as a discrimination. The United States Supreme Court upheld the constitutionality of discriminatory deposit requirements in *Paul* v. *Virginia* (1868), as against objections based on the privileges and immunities clause and the commerce clause.[1]

In 1850 the Wisconsin legislature required that companies chartered by other nations deposit with the State Treasurer stocks of the United States equal in amount to the capital required for the organization of Wisconsin insurance companies. In 1858 a hundred leading Milwaukee business men and property owners, headed by the mayor and the man who was the Milwaukee agent for the Aetna, the Hartford, the Home, and other leading eastern companies, protested a proposal to

---

*Henderson, pp. 3–9. Jackson, J. speaks of the constitutional "principle that our economic unit is the Nation," in *Hood* v. *Du Mond*, 336 U.S. 525, 537 (1948). Complete acceptance of this view came only with the unification of the economy.

require out-of-state companies to deposit $25,000 in Wisconsin. Their argument was simple; because of voluntary underwriting limitations on the maximum size of risk any company would take, local companies had inadequate insuring capacity for the needs of Milwaukee commerce; out-of-state companies must refuse to accede to any such deposit requirement, lest it be duplicated in all states, and they be driven from Wisconsin, leaving too little insuring capacity to service Wisconsin business.[2]

In 1859 the conflict between foreign and local companies came to a head, with many proposals for differential taxation and deposit of securities. An unsuccessful proposal, looking to the competitive advantage of local companies, would have required all out-of-state insurers to deposit bonds with the State Treasurer, ostensibly to provide security for Wisconsin policyholders. In its original form the bill showed its localistic bias in the requirement that foreign life insurance companies deposit the net premiums collected from Wisconsin policyholders with the United States Trust Company, a newly organized Wisconsin company. This absurd proposal was quickly replaced by a more reasonable bill requiring merely a security deposit with the State Treasurer, which nonetheless engendered more opposition than the 3 per cent premium tax bill; an organized campaign of opposition developed, and petitions came in from all parts of the state. It was argued that such a deposit requirement would be impolitic because it would drive capital from the state, that it would be unwise and immoral because it would compel citizens to evade the law (since local insurance was not adequate for the market needs of the community), that it would encourage monopoly and exorbitant rates, that it would compel business men who might feel safer insured with eastern companies to patronize local ones, that it would be unjust discrimination, and that it would replace responsible eastern companies with small irresponsible domestic ones.[3] One remonstrance stated that

such a provision is not demanded by the people at large, but is a measure originating with moonshine "Insurance Companies" so called, for the express purpose of endeavoring to drive away companies of real capital and responsibility in order to give themselves a better chance of gulling and swindling the community.[*]

In 1863 Congress enacted the National Banking Law, in a move toward centralized control of banking. At first the new system was

*Memorial 288A (1859). [In Archives, bound with ms. bill S 70.]

merely permissive, but on March 3, 1865, in an effort to drive state
bank currency out of existence and to bring state banks into the national bank system, Congress imposed a 10 per cent tax on the circu-
lation of state bank currency. Since no bank could afford any longer
to pay out state bank notes, these were presented for payment in
specie by the national banks of Milwaukee. This precipitated a financial panic in the state. The principal reserve of the state banks was in
Wisconsin state bonds; these would have to be sold in a weak market
so that the banks could buy federal bonds if they wished to become
national banks, or in order that they could obtain specie if they
simply wished to redeem their notes. When the crisis broke, a bill
was under consideration to require a $25,000 deposit of Wisconsin
bonds by all insurance companies. The need to resolve the critical
banking situation reinforced whatever interests were behind the original security deposit bill, and in short order a substitute bill was
passed which required that all insurance companies doing business
in the state of Wisconsin deposit with the state treasurer bonds to an
amount approximately half of the gross premiums received in the
state in the previous year. The insurance companies were sacrificed
to the banks.[4]

Despite the urgency of the crisis, some assemblymen and senators
tried in every way to soften the blow on insurance companies, by permitting the companies to deposit federal or New York bonds instead
of Wisconsin bonds, by exempting corporations whose charters might
forbid such deposits, by making certain exemptions for small mutuals,
by permitting the deposit to be made with the treasurer of the state
of incorporation. All such attempts were summarily defeated. Opponents even tried to amend the bill merely to state unequivocally
that its purpose was the relief of the banks, but the proponents refused to be so candid.[5]

The deposit bill, with other remedial measures, quickly resolved the
banking crisis by creating a solid market for the state's bonds. But
it drove a majority of out-of-state companies out of Wisconsin, ful-
filling the threat made by many companies before the bill was passed.
The withdrawal was less unanimous than the threat, but still it promised to create a crisis in trade, less dramatic than the financial crisis it
solved, but serious at least to the Milwaukee grain trade. Milwaukee
was important as a point of transshipment for grain gathered in the
northwest by railroad and then shipped east by water; insurance was

important to that grain trade. Each insurance company had a limit on the amount it would accept or retain on a single risk. This net retention limit averaged less than $10,000. Since only seventeen fire and marine insurance companies complied with the deposit requirements, the insuring capacity of the companies in the state was but a fraction of that needed to service the grain trade.[6]

In an editorial the Milwaukee *Sentinel* called for the repeal of the "odious and oppressive law of 1865" and pointed out that shippers of grain would have to go to Chicago for insurance and might do their banking business there. "In fact they are now obliged in many instances to insure abroad." The editorial argued that the future effect of the law would only be to build up a monopoly, to put shippers to inconvenience and additional expense, to provoke retaliatory legislation against local companies, and to induce a move by the companies to obtain congressional supervision of insurance, depriving the state of control and substantial revenue (Milwaukee *Sentinel*, Mar. 8, 1866).

Similar sentiments had already been expressed in the legislature. Early in the 1866 session the legislature permitted late depositors to qualify. A minority of the committee reporting that bill proposed complete repeal, emphasizing the loss of tax revenue to the general fund and the fire departments, the difficulties of servicing the grain trade, the thrust toward monopoly, and the fear of congressional action. As the session proceeded pressure mounted to repeal the deposit requirement. Finally the Milwaukee bankers, who had been responsible for the adoption of the system, also memorialized the legislature for repeal. Their argument was based on the needs of the grain trade, in which it was the practice to insure nearly to full value, and which found it increasingly difficult, even impossible, to find adequate insuring capacity. Though some effort was made to retain the system, the repealer was finally passed.[7]

The deposit requirement was short-lived, but much of the sentiment which made its passage possible not only antedated the financial crisis of 1865 but also survived it. There was strong feeling that policyholders should receive such protection against default by out-of-state corporations as would be provided by a reserve fund deposited with a state agency. Thirty-four assemblymen and senators (of 105 voting) opposed repeal; there were subsequent attempts to preserve the system but eliminate its role in supporting the bond market, and the repeal measure excepted from the repeal a specific out-of-state company whose securities were needed to pay off defaulted losses. The persistence of the attitude was demonstrated by efforts in 1870 and 1872 to re-enact substantially the same deposit bill. The effort was no longer designed to support the state bond market; thus the bill was broadened to include United States bonds. As late as 1879 the discriminatory bond deposit bill was advanced in narrower form, to apply only to non-American companies. The bill met an organized campaign of opposing petitions, protesting the implication that non-American companies were less safe than American companies, and objecting to the limitation on competition.[8]

It was not unusual for states to require of out-of-state companies a deposit of United States bonds with an official of the state of incorporation. An 1866 statute authorized the Wisconsin State Treasurer to receive such deposits for any Wisconsin companies required to make them by the laws of other states where they did business. Such a requirement was neither burdensome nor discriminatory. On the other hand, requirements of deposit in each of many states where business was done would bear most hardly on corporations with a widespread operation, by adding to the multiplicity of requirements to which they must conform. A desire to give competitive advantage to local companies may have played a large part in the matter, though that is a factor too elusive to demonstrate in detail.[9]

The voting on the bills to create and to repeal the deposit system suggest regional disparity of interests within the state. On both bills the Milwaukee delegation unanimously opposed the deposit system. Except for Sheboygan, this was also substantially true of all lake front counties. No direct evidence explains this peculiarity of the voting. Perhaps representatives from the lake ports understood the need for foreign insurance companies to service the grain trade. This would help to account for the unanimity of the Milwaukee delegation, otherwise surprising in 1865, when the deposit requirement saved the Milwaukee bankers.* On the other hand, the position taken on the deposit rule may have represented a measure of antagonism among the people of Milwaukee and other lake towns toward the bankers, derived from recurring crises in which the city populace was victimized. An anti-banking heritage from the Jacksonian period may thus have been reinforced by the course of recent events.[10]

*Continuance of the deposit requirement might have hastened the inevitable victory of railroads over lake shipping in the grain traffic, and hastened predominance of Chicago over Milwaukee.

By the turn of the century there were few deposit requirements in Wisconsin. Such requirements as there were, were ordinarily imposed for legitimate objectives and did not represent discrimination in favor of local companies. For example, alien fire companies had to make a deposit with the insurance department of at least one state in which they did business or with trustees for American policyholders. So also the 1913 legislature required alien members of Lloyds' groups to make a deposit with the attorney in fact. One requirement, however, could only be read as implying a large element of suspicion of non-American companies. The 1905 legislature required life insurance companies organized in foreign countries to deposit with the State Treasurer approved securities in the amount of the net value of all policies written on Wisconsin residents. That requirement remained in effect in mid-twentieth century.[11]

The reforming 1907 legislature saw an attempt to require all companies to deposit the net value of all policies with the State Treasurer, or else to make an agreement with the state for the deposit of securities on withdrawal from the state. The purpose of this proposal was to protect against small companies writing on some new plan, but it was postponed because inconvenient to the large companies. The bill would have put Wisconsin policyholders in the position of preferred creditors and the spokesman for the Connecticut Mutual thought his company would have to withdraw from the state rather than comply. There were other less drastic bills, but none of these measures was successful.[12]

The localistic bias that was always in the background of the bond deposit requirements was secondary in all twentieth-century developments; it showed most strongly in the use of the retaliatory law to punish companies chartered by states that required such deposits from Wisconsin companies.[13]

Removal of Causes.—Still another aspect of the competition between foreign and local insurance companies in Wisconsin played a role in the making of American constitutional history. In the struggle over the Fugitive Slave Law, the Wisconsin Supreme Court occupied the center of the national stage. In protracted litigation over the propriety of the federal detention of Sherman M. Booth, a Wisconsin abolitionist who had violated the Fugitive Slave Law, the Wisconsin Supreme Court espoused an extreme doctrine of nullification and refused to make return to the writ of error issued by the Supreme Court of the United

States (Winslow, pp. 67–84, 116–121; Roe, pp. 69–101). Though the Wisconsin court came out second best in that contest for judicial supremacy, the underlying attitude was not changed, as the Wisconsin judges showed when they held as late as 1861 that Congress had no power to provide for removal to a federal court of a suit begun in a state court between citizens of different states—though they thereby challenged a provision Congress had made as early as the Judiciary Act of 1789 and which had frequently been acted on ever since.[14]

The next phase of the conflict began in 1869. To an action brought in Wisconsin on a fire insurance contract, the defendant, an out-of-state company, replied with an effort to remove the cause into federal court on grounds of diversity of citizenship. Though a majority of the court allowed removal, Mr. Justice Paine dissented, justifying his position in a lengthy exposition of the doctrine of states' rights. Before his elevation to the bench Paine had been counsel for Booth and was elected by an overwhelming vote in a campaign in which states' rights was the clear-cut issue. Notwithstanding his emotional involvement, his statement is a persuasive warning of the dangers of continued centralization of power in the federal government. He decried the war-born tendency toward the strong assertion of federal power, and he instanced a growing federal control over waterways and an increasing refusal by federal courts to allow supremacy to state law in cases governed by state law.[15]

The Booth incident had produced a violent reaction in Wisconsin, and left a legacy of strong states' rights feeling, which was not quickly overcome, in spite of the strong drive toward centralism in the Reconstruction period. Because those feelings were effectively expressed in litigation, the state of Wisconsin was able to delay for two generations one aspect of the centralization of government and to retain additional local control over foreign corporations.

In 1870 Wisconsin passed a new general act for the incorporation of fire and marine insurance companies. This statute contained a clause which was indigenous to Wisconsin, the objective of which was probably to overcome the effect of the 1869 removal decision. It required foreign companies to agree, as a contractual condition of obtaining a license to do business in Wisconsin, not to remove into the federal courts any cases brought against them in Wisconsin. In *Morse* v. *Home Insurance Company*, one of the leading out-of-state companies operating in Wisconsin sought to remove a case into the federal courts, after having agreed not to do so in order to obtain its license. While this case was pending, the Wisconsin legislature passed an act which required the Secretary of State to revoke the license of any company which removed litigation to the federal courts. When the case came on for decision, the Wisconsin Supreme Court conceded that self-executing legislation forbidding removal would be unconstitutional, but decided on the authority of *Paul* v. *Virginia* that any terms, including waiver of constitutional rights, might be imposed on the company as a condition of admission to do business. The agreement itself was voluntary, in view of the state's right to impose terms, and would be given effect. The United States Supreme Court thought differently; it held that a citizen of another state (including in this context a corporation) had a right to remove cases into the federal courts and that a state statute might not abridge this right; thus such legislation and the agreement were unconstitutional and void.[16]

The opinion in the *Morse* case was so sweeping that it should have settled the question, but localism was not so easily overwhelmed by fiat of the United States Supreme Court. In 1875 the federal circuit court for Wisconsin enjoined the Secretary of State from revoking licenses as the 1872 statute required. But in 1875 when the Continental Insurance Company refused to pay a claim to a Mr. Drake, he sued the company, and the company removed the cause into the federal courts. Drake then sought to mandamus the Secretary of State to revoke the license of the company for its breach of the agreement not to remove. If the state court were to grant mandamus, the local and the federal court systems would thus be in direct conflict.[17]

In 1874, in the interval between the *Morse* case and the *Drake* litigation, Edward G. Ryan, perhaps the most brilliant of Wisconsin's judges, became Chief Justice of the Supreme Court of Wisconsin. Ryan had been a vigorous opponent of the Lincoln administration, and was widely regarded as a Copperhead. He had a deep hatred for the "new and dark power" in the "vast corporate combinations" seeking political control. These views made him attractive to Governor Taylor, who appointed him to the court. In this litigation, Ryan spoke more as advocate than as judge—as advocate for an extreme states' rights position. His vigorous opinion was the authentic voice of localism, both in the economic and in the political spheres:

We spoke with just severity of the utter *mala fides* of a foreign insurance company coming here under a voluntary and advantageous license of the state, upon condition not to harass citizens of the state dealing with it, by removing actions on its policies from the state court of the vicinage to distant and expensive federal courts (*Continental Ins. Co.* v. *Doyle*, 40 Wis. 220, 230 [1876]).

Ryan made no effort to deny, indeed he emphasized, that an issue of the political balance of power was involved; he sternly counselled moderation by the federal authority:

We abide by the letter and spirit of the constitution. Unfortunately many things in its administration are tending toward centralization, which the history and temper of the American people give grave warning might be closely followed by disintegration. The integrity of the union has been tried. The integrity of the states is on trial. Much rests upon the moderation and forbearance of the federal courts (*Drake* v. *Doyle*, 40 Wis. 175, 216 [1876]).

The comments illuminated his underlying bias, but only to this extent did the real reasons come to the surface. In a brilliant display of casuistry, in an opinion more like a lawyer's brief than a dispassionate judgment, Chief Justice Ryan argued that Wisconsin might revoke the license of a foreign insurance company for doing what the United States Supreme Court had solemnly held it entitled to do. There is no doubt, as dissenting Justice Bradley made perfectly clear in the United States Supreme Court, that to permit revocation of the license under these circumstances was in practical effect to nullify the *Morse* decision. The United States Supreme Court seemed overwhelmed by the art of Chief Justice Ryan's arguments, however, and accepting them completely without the courtesy of mentioning Ryan's opinion, distinguished the *Morse* case on the ground that it only ensured the power of the company to remove; the state might still impose upon the company the necessity of choosing between removal and remaining in the state.[18]

The courts had thus failed to protect the foreign companies against compulsory submission to the jurisdiction of local tribunals, and in 1877 a last effort was made to achieve the objective by political means. An unsuccessful bill was introduced to repeal the implementing legislation of 1872. It did not even get out of committee. The legislature confirmed the existing law, and made it the "imperative duty" of the Secretary of State to revoke the license of any foreign company removing cases to the federal courts, but a proviso did except orders for removal obtained before 1877, and permitted relicensing of the companies obtaining them. In 1885 the legislature extended the removal statutes to foreign life and accident companies.[19]

The Wisconsin court and legislature thus played a significant role in a victory of localism in constitutional doctrine, which lasted through the first decade of the twentieth century, permitting a state arbitrarily to exclude or expel a foreign corporation. Though the cases involved in this development speak in technical language, the pattern of legislation and decision shows that the underlying struggle was of localism against the national character of American society. It was a belated, partial, and temporary victory of the states' rights doctrine over triumphant centralism, and was so regarded by industry spokesmen, in whose estimate Judge Ryan showed more zeal for states' rights than even Calhoun in his most intense convictions.[20]

Though localism long remained a factor in the law, there was little doubt after the turn of the century that the United States was a single economic unit, and that inevitably those notions that stood in the way of the integration of the economy must give way. Except in the field of taxation, where reciprocity and retaliation remained aspects of the law in mid-century, after 1900 localism was a submerged factor, of relatively little influence and little apparent on the surface of the law.

Subjecting the Foreign Corporation and Agent to Wisconsin Jurisdiction

Control of Unauthorized Companies.—One of the most persistent problems of insurance regulation was how to prevent companies and agents which were not licensed by the state and which were secure in a position of freedom from Wisconsin regulation or taxation from appropriating Wisconsin business. The proscription of unauthorized companies, and the insistence that business be done through authorized agents, were related but distinct aspects of this problem of control; the legislators often did not distinguish them, since the most facile way to control unauthorized companies was through their agents.[21]

The problem of unauthorized companies was already acute in the middle 1870's. Secretary of State Doyle commented in 1877 on mail solicitation by unauthorized companies. He thought the law might be enforced if an agent could be found doing any act for the company within the state; Doyle announced his intention of enforcing the statute against any such agent found. In 1878 a Chicago broker was arrested within Wisconsin. Though there were numerous postponements of the litigation, the Supreme Court gave its approval in 1880 to Commissioner Spooner's enforcement program; it upheld a conviction on eighteen separate offenses of unlawful solicitation, based on a single transaction in which insurance was placed with eighteen companies.[22]

Control of agents was the most direct way to control unauthorized companies. The 1871 legislature forbade, under a pecuniary sanction, any officer, agent, or subagent to do business without a license for each company for which he acted. The statute did not in terms cover activities of a "broker," and the dogma of strict construction of penal statutes might make the statute ineffective against brokers, who technically represented the policyholder and not the company, and thus did not fall within the strict construction of the word "agent." On the other hand, a prior section of the statute defined "agent" to include any person soliciting insurance on behalf of any insurance corporation, or transmitting an application or policy, unless he could show that he received no compensation. To remove any doubt whether a broker was caught by the broad sweep of this definition, the 1880 legislature added "brokers" to the list of persons forbidden to transact an insurance business without a license and defined "agent" even more broadly than before. In 1905 the statute was put in even more sweeping terms by forbidding any "person," as well as any "agent" or "broker," to act without a license for an insurance company.[23]

To supplement the proscription of unauthorized agents, the legislature in 1875 provided for commencement of action against a company by service of process on any agent found within the state, within the broad meaning of "agent" under the preceding statute. In 1887 the court gave some effect to this clause in an action by the state to recover a penalty against an unadmitted company. But, in general, the court strictly construed these penal statutes to frustrate the control sought; thus it ruled that the statute did not apply to unadmitted companies. As late as 1910 the strict construction dogma frustrated control of withdrawn companies.[24]

Service of process posed problems, also, especially for admitted but relatively inactive companies. The legislature required the appointment of an attorney within the state on whom process might be served; later it required that the companies appoint the Insurance Commissioner their agent to accept service of process. Such statutes were not universally applied, and some peripheral insurance operations escaped these requirements. As late as 1931 it was deemed necessary to provide expressly that the Commissioner was attorney for service of process whenever the statute required the company to appoint him, whether the company did so or not. It is possible that service on the Commissioner would have been effective even before the statute; the Attorney General advised the Commissioner to receive service of process, on the theory that the company might be presumed to have complied, if in fact it was doing business in the state. In 1959 the Commissioner proposed to the legislature a systematic and well-drafted Unauthorized Insurers Act.[25]

Commissioner Spooner's program to end business by unauthorized companies depended on finding an agent within the jurisdiction. The problem was how to subject unauthorized companies to Wisconsin penal laws when no person representing the companies was present within the jurisdiction. The difficulty in obtaining service of process was probably what Commissioner Root had in mind when in 1892 he complained of "underground" companies and asked for stronger penal laws. Enforcement must be indirect and diverse—as varied as the ways in which the company exposed its activities to any attack in Wisconsin.[26]

For example, in 1897 the legislature provided for the prosecution and revocation of license of any company or agent soliciting insurance for, or placing insurance with, an unauthorized fire company. In 1899 it imposed on such agents liability as surety for the payment of claims by the unauthorized company; sometimes agents were compelled to pay such losses. In an attempt to close off one avenue for evasion of the unauthorized-company laws, the 1899 legislature forbade even specific reinsurance in unauthorized companies. The need for reinsurance facilities resulted in the reversal of that rule in 1903. If unauthorized companies subsequently sought admission to the state, the Commissioner might make payment of back fees and taxes a prerequisite to admission.[27]

A bill in 1927 would have revoked the license of an authorized company whose officers placed insurance with unauthorized companies. It would also have provided for recording the violation for future reference, would have prohibited later admission until after the payment of penalties, and would have made countersigning in blank or *pro forma* a criminal offense.[28]

More direct methods were sought. The Attorney General concluded in 1910 that solicitation took place where a soliciting letter was received, so that an out-of-state unauthorized company was guilty of a violation of the Wisconsin laws even on the basis of this minimum contact within the state. To obtain jurisdiction of an absent defendant, he suggested that the offense be made a felony and hence extraditable. This the 1913 legislature did for fire insurance, but the next Attorney General saw further difficulties, because the corporation was, of course, not extraditable, and its officers could not be extradited because they were not in the jurisdiction at the time of the offense. Thus the Attorney General suggested that Congress provide a remedy by forbidding the use of the mails for such solicitation.[29]

In 1915 the Commissioner again sought the Attorney General's help. The United Druggists Mutual Fire Insurance Company of Boston sold a policy by mail to the Winterburn Drug Company of Fort Atkinson and, in effect, defied the state to do anything about it. The Attorney General ruled that though there was an offense, nothing could be done without service of process in the jurisdiction. He suggested that as an "educational" measure, the Winterburn Drug Company be sued for its fire department dues. This suggested a promising solution to part of the problem; discriminating imposition of sanctions on the policyholder might encourage the policyholder to report unauthorized insurance to the Commissioner; or he might even be discouraged from purchasing unauthorized insurance by criminal responsibility for its purchase. Most violations probably occurred in the case of specialized trade insurance companies (as in the instance of the United Druggists company) or of very large insurance buyers such as chain stores, which could reduce insurance costs by buying from direct-selling companies in other jurisdictions and avoiding Wisconsin restrictive laws and taxes. Sanctions imposed on the policyholder thus might be effective to terminate most unauthorized insurance. As early as 1895, there was a bill to require the policyholder to report, or be subject to a monetary penalty. Perhaps with this in mind the 1913 legislature declared completely void all unauthorized contracts of insurance. But this promised to be an inept means of control; astute insurance buyers might nevertheless continue to purchase from unauthorized companies that enjoyed a good reputation for loss settlement, but on the unsophisticated purchaser of insurance from a law-evading company the rule would work a hardship.[30]

In 1931 the legislature invoked taxation to enforce the unauthorized-insurer laws. It empowered the Commissioner to require that property owners file a verified statement showing the insurance they had on their property, and if this insurance were with an unauthorized company, to pay the fire department tax on it. The department used the new power to discover unauthorized insurance, and uncovered a great deal written by New York and Chicago agencies, with the attendant loss to Wisconsin of taxes and local commissions. As a result of the enhanced enforcement program, several unauthorized companies doing an illicit business in Wisconsin entered the state to do business legitimately, and the practice of illegally insuring large mercantile and manufacturing risks outside of the state was perceptibly lessened, or so the Commissioner reported in 1932.[31]

World War II brought to Wisconsin a great many military trainees. In 1943 the Wisconsin Senate adopted a resolution transmitting a protest to the Secretary of War; representatives of at least one insurance company, which lacked authority to do business in Wisconsin and was alleged to be irresponsible and unsound, were soliciting business on army posts, with the alleged permission of the commanders of the posts. The protest was heeded; Secretary of War Stimson ordered all post commanders to refuse admission to life insurance solicitors unless they were authorized in the state in which the camp was located.[32]

Withdrawn companies presented problems of control as well. The withdrawal of a large number of life insurance companies after the reform legislation of 1907 showed a need for continued control after withdrawal. The Attorney General ruled that such companies could not maintain agencies for premium collection. The 1913 legislature contributed to the control of withdrawn companies. With the consent of the Governor and Attorney General, after affording the company an opportunity for a hearing before the Commissioner, Governor, and Attorney General, the Commissioner might institute a class action against such company on behalf of Wisconsin policyholders; the state bore the cost of the suit and the Attorney General acted as attorney for the state in the suit.[33]

Requirement of a Resident Agent.—The legislature sought to bring unauthorized companies within the power of the state in order to regulate and to tax them; it sought to subject agents to the control of the state not only for those reasons, but also to put a protective wall around the state and preserve for Wisconsin residents the benefit of agency commissions on Wisconsin insurance. Occasionally other motivations complicated the picture.

The 1880 legislature forbade any company to do a fire insurance business in the state except through the intervention of an agent licensed by the Commissioner. The limitation to fire insurance, and the title of an unsuccessful 1893 amendment—"A bill to better secure payment from fire insurance companies of taxes in certain cases"—suggest a basic motivation. The localism implicit in the restriction was apparent when the 1893 legislature required that the agent must be a Wisconsin resident; it was apparent in exaggerated form in unsuccessful bills in 1899 and 1903 requiring that an agent writing such insurance reside in the locality of the property. The 1899 legislature passed a law to enforce the local agent law by requiring that the resident agent countersign a fire policy. The countersigning local agent must receive the commission of fire insurance policies, thus preventing a practice of *pro forma* countersignature by local agents for a small portion of the agency commission. The localistic bias inherent in the countersignature law was mitigated by recognition of the interstate character of transportation; the provision was inapplicable to insurance covering rolling stock of railroads or property in transit or property of other common carriers.[34]

In 1901 the legislature extended to casualty and surety insurance the requirement that policies issue only through resident agents. The extension was by amendment of the 1893 statute for fire insurance, and inadvertently the words "on property herein," were retained; as a result the Attorney General ruled that nonresident agents might issue any casualty or surety insurance which was not on property, such as accident and health. Public policy was not thus to be restricted, however, and the legislature quickly broadened the statute by deleting the offending words.[35]

It was not the state's policy to impose a marketing structure on domestic companies; policies issued directly by the home office of a domestic company, without the intervention of an agent, were exempt from the local agent requirements. So also were policies issued directly by mutuals and inter-insurers, when no commissions were paid except to the home office manager or attorney in fact for such company.[36]

In the twentieth century, there was a substantial tendency to relax the prohibition against nonresident agents. A 1917 bill would have permitted nonresident agents to obtain licenses to write fire, windstorm, and sprinkler leakage insurance in authorized companies, provided they caused policies to be countersigned by a licensed resident agent. In 1935 the legislature authorized nonresident life insurance brokers. The use of the word "broker" was curious; properly speaking, insurance brokers represented the insured, rather than the company. The Attorney General construed the statute as intended to permit the activity of nonresident agents of life insurance companies. In 1947 the legislature at last adopted the policy of the 1917 bill, permitting the licensing of nonresident agents for all lines of business; such agents might not countersign policies, however, but commissions might be divided between the licensed nonresident agent and the countersigning local agent.[37]

The Supreme Court of the United States upheld the state's program of control. The Chrysler Corporation worked out a sales program which included the sale of cheap automobile insurance to all purchasers of automobiles, as a part of the original price. Chrysler Sales Corporation, the marketing subsidiary, and the Palmetto Fire Insurance Corporation of South Carolina, which was not admitted to Wisconsin, made a master contract in Michigan, to avoid the laws of various states requiring the intervention of local agents. The threat to the local agency system was one of the chief reasons for opposition to the Palmetto-Chrysler system. When Commissioner Smith threatened to prosecute under the Wisconsin penal statutes, the Chrysler Sales Corporation sought an injunction against him in the federal courts. In the United States Supreme Court, the control of the Wisconsin Commissioner was completely vindicated. Since the insurance did not go into effect until the retail sale of the car, it was apparent that the insurance transaction took place in Wisconsin and was completely subject to the Wisconsin laws.[38]

Surplus Lines.—The policy of the state did not forbid resort to unauthorized companies when the needs of the Wisconsin insurance market required. The lack of adequate insuring capacity among local companies constantly compelled modification of the localistic restrictions. Both by statutory limitation and by sound underwriting practice there were limits on the amount of risk any company might undertake on a single unit of exposure. Less severe limits also existed on the amount of risk to be undertaken in any single concentrated area, such as the heart of a great city. We have seen how the principle requiring an adequate dispersion of risk operated to help overthrow the bond deposit requirement of 1865. The limited insuring capacity of the relatively few local companies, especially compared with the large commercial insurance needs of Milwaukee, was a persistent factor weakening the forces of protectionism. Around the turn of the century the inadequate insuring capacity, not only of local companies but for some purposes also of all admitted companies, compelled some relaxation of the restriction of business to authorized companies. As early as 1895 a Milwaukee representative introduced a bill to authorize the appointment of up to 200 "surplus line" brokers empowered to place insurance with unadmitted companies, on the execution of an affidavit that it was not possible to place the insurance with admitted companies. At that time, however, sentiment against unauthorized companies was too strong.[39]

But by 1901 the strict provisions of the 1899 act against reinsurance in unauthorized companies were apparently beginning to pinch a little. A bill was introduced which would have relaxed that prohibition to permit reinsurance in companies authorized in Massachusetts or New York, even if not authorized in Wisconsin. In view of the thorough regulation of insurance in those states, such a relaxation could certainly not be opposed on the ground of security of the insured. In the following session, an even stronger bill did pass, permitting authorized companies to reinsure in "any other responsible company." The enactment of this law made it unnecessary for reinsurance companies to be authorized in Wisconsin. It resulted in the withdrawal of a number of them from the state, owing $15,000 in taxes for which the Attorney General had to sue.[40]

Most insurance needs could undoubtedly be handled under this statute, by finding an admitted company which was willing to underwrite the risk initially, even if it immediately reinsured substantially all of it. Occasionally it would not be possible to provide required insurance in that way, however, for familiar contract principles provided that delegation by the initial carrier of its duties to the reinsuring company would not relieve the initial carrier of direct obligation to the policyholder for the full amount of the policy. Unless the carrier intended to retain a fairly substantial portion of the insurance, it would normally be reluctant to write the policy at all. This problem must have been felt most often in the more complicated commercial and industrial life of Milwaukee, and again, in 1905, a Milwaukee representative introduced a bill to authorize "surplus line brokers" to place insurance in unauthorized companies, on a showing by affidavit that it was not possible to place it in admitted companies. The bill passed both houses, but Governor LaFollette vetoed it on grounds superficially plausible, but betraying a consistency to principle that disregarded practical needs. He thought that if it were necessary to permit unauthorized companies to transact business in order to handle the insurance needs of the state, "it would be far better . . . to provide that licenses be required of none. . . ." The need was not yet urgent enough to become a regional issue; Milwaukee representatives divided on the vote to repass in about the same proportion as the rest of the state.[41]*

A "surplus lines" broker statute for fire insurance passed in 1911 and was approved by the Governor. An effort was made in 1923 and again in 1925 to extend the statute to all insurance except life, but on both occasions the Governor vetoed the attempt; he could see no real need for the law. On neither occasion was any real effort made to pass the bill over his veto; the fact suggests that he may have been right on the question of present need.[42]

§3. *The Prevention and Mitigation of Loss*

Throughout the American story, the insurance industry played a significant social role as an active participant in efforts to decrease insurable losses of all kinds. The preventive role grew quite naturally out of the concern of the companies to decrease the loss ratio. Some preventive activities were tried and abandoned; some continued from nineteenth-century beginnings into the mid-twentieth century. In some classes of insurance, indeed, only a small part of the premium went to pay losses, and the insured actually bought primarily loss prevention services. The 1919 legislature emphasized this fact by exempting steam boiler, flywheel, and elevator coverage from the required short-rate

---

Assembly J., 1905, p. 1578 (veto); *Assembly J.*, 1905, p. 1610. In this veto message, LaFollette betrayed his inflexibility when faced with ideas he did not originate. This was his greatest weakness. See, e.g., Nils P. Haugen, "Pioneer and Political Reminiscences" (undated), p. 151. [Reprinted from *Wisconsin Magazine of History*, Vols. 11, 12, and 13 (1927-28, 1928-29, and 1929-30). [In Hist. Soc. Library.]

cancellation tables. To set return premium requirements for the companies in those lines would do serious injustice, because of the initial expense involved in inspection of the risk.[1]

The distribution of health literature, provision of visiting nurse service, financial contributions to voluntary health agencies, and the support of the Life Insurance Medical Research Fund, which invested several million dollars in medical research, especially on the circulatory system, illustrate the preventive activities of life insurance companies in mid-twentieth century.[2]

The National Board of Fire Underwriters, organized in 1866 to control rates, soon ceased to be a rating body and became in large part a loss prevention organization. From the Board's work came a National Electrical Code in 1892, a Model Building Law in 1896, and Underwriters' Laboratories, Inc. in 1901. Its Committee on Fire Prevention and Engineering Standards performed significant service in mid-twentieth century in finding and reducing conflagration hazards in large cities. Its Committee on Public Relations led in fire prevention education.[3]

The lack of fluid capital forced colonial society to delegate many public jobs to private associations, in order that meager tax revenues might be saved for more urgent needs.* Fire fighting thus tended to fall to voluntary associations of interested persons. These groups were fiercely competitive; membership often represented a mark of status in the community. The fire insurance companies, as they came into being, adopted the practice of making contributions to the volunteer companies for the purchase of equipment. It was late before fire companies received any public funds—not until 1811 in Philadelphia, for example.[4]

The era of private fire companies was not entirely over when Wisconsin was settled. The persons who organized the Milwaukee Mutual Fire Insurance Company in 1837 also organized a hook and ladder company to fight fires. The private fire company was rapidly becoming outdated, however, and was soon replaced by publicly sponsored firefighting organizations, related to municipal government. Initially the fire departments organized in Wisconsin were hybrids; though they had many of the earmarks of the modern municipal department they

*Handlin (1947), p. 65, points out the resistance in Massachusetts to any increase in the absolute amount of taxation, despite increase in population and increasing complexity of society. Ends had to be achieved by indirection, not by direct expenditure.

yet retained much of the older independence of status. Thus the charter of the fire department of Oshkosh gave wide powers of self-government to its members, including even provision for mutual benefit activities on behalf of indigent and disabled firemen and their families.[5]

Relative independence of public control was not the only feature exhibiting the earlier heritage of the fire departments. The propensity of a capital-starved society to get the public business done by private agencies was evident in more sophisticated form in the 2 per cent tax on fire insurance premiums, payable to the publicly sponsored but semi-independent fire departments of mid-nineteenth century. It was easier to obtain tax revenues for purposes in which the taxed class had a real interest. Though there might be legitimate complaint that policyholders were paying for services rendered to all citizens alike, insurance company opposition to the fire department tax was never very vigorous. The activity which it financed was little more than the companies had already been supporting voluntarily for a long time.[6]

When the big fires of 1871 and 1872 showed the inadequacy of existing techniques of fire prevention and control, the insurance companies gave thoughtful attention to prevention of fire loss; lobbying for wise fire prevention laws and helping to finance preventive activity were scarcely less important to the organized industry of the 1870's than the development of rate-making combinations.[7]

The companies assumed additional burdens voluntarily. The first was the creation of fire patrols to supplement the work of the fire departments.* Though there were fire patrols in the late 1860's, notably in New York City, it was after the Chicago and Boston fires that the formation of fire patrols became central among the objectives of the industry. In the 1870's there were papers and discussion on this matter at all association meetings. For several years a demonstration by the Chicago patrol was a standard part of the convention program. In 1876 the Wisconsin legislature authorized local boards of fire underwriters

---

*The horse protective association had a role rather like the fire insurance company's role in fire prevention, especially the company's role in operating fire patrols. E.g., *Laws (P. & L.)* 1869, 199, said it was "to guard against the loss by theft of all horses that are . . . insured therein, and . . . to be the better enabled to institute a search for the horse or horses stolen, and to remunerate the owner therefore." Such associations were known much earlier in New York. See, e.g., Samuel H. Adams, *Grandfather Stories* (Random House, N. Y., 1955), pp. 9, 101. The Farmers' Alliance, which played an important part in the history of Populism, began in such an organization in Texas.—S. Buck (1920), p. 112. *Laws* 1861, 222, was a general act authorizing such companies.

to establish fire patrols to discover and prevent fires and to save and preserve life and property after fires. To defray expenses, the board of underwriters might make an assessment of not more than 2 per cent per annum on fire insurance premiums on property within the municipality. The tough resistance to change, which often opposed public assumption of clear public responsibilities even when the increasing availability of fluid capital for revenue made that assumption possible, tended to keep the job of fire prevention and control in private hands, even when to do so necessitated a limited delegation of the taxing and police powers of the state to private hands.[8]

The 1876 statute provided that all insurers writing insurance in the area of the board had a right to attend the meetings and vote on the proposed expenditures of the patrol and the assessment to support it. The Milwaukee Board of Fire Underwriters established a patrol in 1885 and assessed the cost against the companies doing business in the city. In 1939 the Supreme Court refused recovery to the board when it brought suit for assessments to support the fire patrol against a nonmember insurer, to whom it had denied membership. The court ruled that the attempted application of the statute would be unconstitutional as depriving nonmember insurers of equal rights in the control of the patrol to which they contributed. The board must open its doors before it might assess nonmembers.[9]

The willingness of insurance companies to assume additional burdens of fire prevention delayed public assumption of functions that a later generation would think indubitably public. Thus in the forty years after 1873 a committee of the National Board of Fire Underwriters offered nearly $2,000,000 in rewards, and paid out $83,719 for 277 convictions for arson. On the other hand, Commissioner Ekern, fir example, thought it the task of the state to provide a systematic fire prevention program. There was no justification for a fire marshal tax; since the service was public, the cost should be borne by all property, insured or not. In 1931, in a period of severe suspicion of the motives of businessmen, the Wisconsin Legislative Interim Committee on Fire Insurance took a suspicious view of the purposes of the Underwriters' Laboratories in determining what equipment was approved for fire rating purposes. The committee thought that this might be a device to favor the equipment produced by manufacturers who supported the laboratories. Again the implication was plain; such testing was a public responsibility, not one for a private agency. Nevertheless, no change had been effected up to mid-twentieth century.[10]

In mid-twentieth century several bills (to permit fire trucks of town mutual insurance companies to be licensed for a nominal fee of one dollar, to permit such companies to buy fire fighting equipment or to pay fire departments furnishing service in their areas, and to permit private associations to collect fire department dues) although unsuccessful, nonetheless indicated that in the more remote areas there were still conditions conducive to continuation of the informal society of an earlier era. In 1945, however, the insurance department forbade town mutuals to continue an established practice of purchasing fire trucks or equipment, since they were organized for "mutual protection against loss by fire and lightning only." A 1947 bill to permit such companies to buy such equipment was opposed by the commercial mutuals and by the insurance department. Opposition was rationalized by appeal to the public nature of the fire fighting task, though on the part of the commercial mutuals the opposition was undoubtedly motivated by other considerations.[11]

In the 1870's petroleum came into common use as an illuminant. Its dangerous propensities were recognized as early as 1868 in a Wisconsin statute forbidding the use of kerosene oil to illuminate passenger trains. The fire insurance companies early joined the effort at control. In 1873 an industry spokesman reported that through the influence of two state boards in the Northwest, general laws had been enacted to control the sale of petroleum oils. He urged enactment of uniform legislation and of local ordinances to implement it. Though he did not identify the states in question, it is possible that Wisconsin was one of those whose legislation resulted, at least in part, from insurance company pressure. There was no apparent opposition when in 1873 the Wisconsin legislature made it unlawful to sell for illuminating purposes any petroleum oil or derivative unless it first met a volatility test to show that it did not emit combustible vapors below 110° Fahrenheit. In the following year a specified test was prescribed. The law proved inadequate to the needs of the state, as the continuance of destructive and fatal fires showed. In 1880 a bill provided much more elaborate machinery for inspection of petroleum-derived illuminating oils, under the management of a state supervisor of inspectors of illuminating oils, to be appointed by the Governor. The inspectors were to stamp as "approved" or "rejected" each container of illuminating oil offered for sale in the state; the law imposed severe sanctions, including the penalty for manslaughter if death resulted from the explosion of oil sold in violation of the act. The bill became law, apparently without opposition, but it was by no means perfunctorily adopted, for it was carefully considered by a committee and reasoned choice made among various possible means of implementing the public policy of the state.[12]

This basic law was still on the books in mid-twentieth century, though much amended. An 1897 revision took account of the development of gas lighting and heating by permitting the use of uninspected gas or vapor for illumination when the reservoir containing the oil from which the gas was generated was outside the building. There was also extensive modification in 1901, when the legislature acknowledged the entrance of gasoline into the market by requiring that gasoline containers be marked in a certain way. Gasoline was more adequately treated in the 1909 amendments. These also brought within the scope of the statute petroleum products used for power purposes; theretofore the act had dealt only with oils used for illuminating and heating. The advent of the filling-station civilization was marked by an amendment in 1927 requiring deliveries to motor vehicles to be made by hose from an underground container. In 1941 the act was completely revised. Among other changes the legislature repealed the harsh manslaughter penalty for violation resulting in death. The change symbolized society's acceptance of the new physical conditions of existence in the gasoline age.[13]

In the generation of the development of the petroleum industry, the insurance fraternity manifested a lively interest in the problems surrounding the use of petroleum. Numerous papers presented to the annual meetings dealt with the use of oils—often on a technical basis. After the initial period, the oil inspection process developed a dynamic of its own, and there is little evidence that the insurance industry played more than a minor role in the subsequent period.[14]

In 1878 insurance men claimed a similar success in reducing the number of Fourth-of-July fires caused by firecrackers, by a campaign to obtain prohibitory city ordinances. In 1889 a Wisconsin act providing for the government of cities authorized the enactment of such ordinances. In 1913 the Legislative Fire Insurance Investigating Committee recommended a model act prepared by the National Fire Protection Association, with an added provision forbidding the sale of matches other than safety matches.[15]

In the 1880's the companies expressed similar interest in the problems arising out of the common use of electricity, and the 1901 legislature made a beginning in the regulation of the size and installation of wiring. It is probable that the insurance companies had at least something to do with the passage of the law.[16]

Less success attended the early efforts of the companies to obtain adequate building codes. As early as 1873 it was realized that preferences in fire rating would constitute the best lever for obtaining adequate codes, as they were in obtaining more adequate fire fighting facilities. One significant fact worked against the insurance companies in this crusade, however. The accessibility of the Wisconsin pineries made wood a universal building material. Recognizing the problem, an industry committee on building laws recommended the study of means for making incombustible laths and shingles, and suggested that the National Board provide financial incentives for the requisite research. But until the exhaustion of the Wisconsin pineries, which did not occur until after the turn of the century, there was little likelihood of substantial success in efforts to achieve real reform in building practices.[17]

There was some gain, even so. In 1872 a revision of the law governing incorporation of villages gave to the village board of trustees rather extensive authority regarding fire fighting, and the power to establish village fire limits within which wooden buildings might not be erected. The Supreme Court was not sufficiently impressed with the fire hazard to extend to a village the aid of injunctive relief to enforce its regulations; the only remedy was collection of the small fine imposed by the ordinance. In 1889 the legislature even gave cities general power to regulate the construction of buildings and to declare them nuisances if unsafe. It also gave power to exclude lumber yards from the fire limits of the city. An insurance spokesman claimed in 1887 that the fire limit law and the building code were forced in Chicago by the underwriters and it is possible the insurance people played some part in getting the legislation in Wisconsin as well.[18]

But progress was not great; the Legislative Fire Insurance Investigating Committee said in 1913 that nothing showed more clearly "public indifference to fire waste and conflagration hazard than the absence of comprehensive building codes." What ordinances existed were ineffectively enforced. Too often they were merely *ad hoc* reforms, lacking in comprehensiveness. The committee unsuccessfully recommended additional investigation of the problem and proposed an inquiry into the subject of a building code and a law relating to city planning. It made the specific suggestion that the legislature outlaw the shingle roof for new construction. Though this suggestion was not embodied in a bill and hence was not made law, another committee recommendation, to forbid the sale of any but safety matches, was noted and the sale of matches carefully regulated.[19]

Commissioner Ekern was obsessed with the value of fire prevention; among other things he urged overhead sprinklers for whole districts in Milwaukee and for charitable and penal institutions, and he stressed the importance of lightning rods in preventing fires in rural districts. Commissioner Whitman followed his lead in advocating lightning rods, and as good roads, motor transportation, and chemical fire-fighting equipment became common, also urged extension of fire fighting equipment to rural areas, to be centered in the town mutuals.[20]

The 1907 legislature created the office of the State Fire Marshal. Though his role was primarily to investigate and prosecute, he had a subordinate function in fire prevention. Thus he was empowered to order the repair or removal of hazardous buildings or of combustible material which endangered other property. In 1913 the Legislative Fire Insurance Investigating Committee made recommendations for improvement of the Fire Marshal law. Although the legislature failed to make the Fire Marshal also chief inspector of illuminating oils, as the committee urged from considerations of economy, it made each fire department chief a deputy fire marshal and for the purpose of fire prevention, required him, in person or by deputy, to make an inspection quarterly in congested districts and semi-annually elsewhere of all buildings, premises, and public thoroughfares except the interiors of private dwellings. Commissioner Ekern asserted that this was the first such law in the United States, that fire chiefs were already utilizing it to eliminate transient causes of fire, and that "Wisconsin leads in fire prevention work."[21]

Legal implementation of the growing interest of society in fire prevention proceeded on a broad front. In 1866 the Wisconsin State Firemen's Association was incorporated as a trade association for volunteer fire companies in the state. Members of the constituent companies were given exemption from jury service and military duty and from some taxes. As the sentiment for fire prevention measures greatly increased near the close of the century, the legislature regularly appropriated various sums of money for the support of the state association and later of various district associations. In 1909 the appropriation was regularized and its purpose clarified by statute: it was to provide prizes and premiums for competitions among firemen, notably in firemen's tournaments. By 1931 the appropriation was 80 per cent of the amount disbursed for prizes, up to $4,000 annually for the state association or $300 to any district association. In 1933 the statute was repealed. Similarly, from 1913 to 1919, $1,000 yearly was appropriated to the Wisconsin State Fire Prevention Association, a voluntary association mainly concerned with inspection of congested districts in the cities.[22]

The legislature was consistently friendly toward fire prevention. A 1907 Assembly resolution directed an inquiry into ways to prevent fire losses. In 1929 the Senate resolved to appoint a select committee to study, with the Conservation Commissioner, the general problems of conservation and fire prevention. In 1917 the legislature made fire drills compulsory in all educational institutions. In 1921 it empowered the Industrial Commission to provide a course of study in fire prevention, teaching of which it made compulsory in the public schools for a half hour per month. The 1949 legislature permitted the owner of a proposed public building to get advice from the Insurance Commissioner on the cost of fire insurance. In 1949 there was an effort to create a state fire-training institute under the Fire Marshal.[23]

The remarkable efficiency of the factory mutuals in the inspection and reduction of risks was noteworthy among preventive activities of insurance companies. In 1887 the Wisconsin Fire Underwriters Union urged inspection as the solution to many problems, and as more important than rating. Company spokesmen also urged more careful underwriting, deliberate delay in payment of losses to permit investigation of arson, that adjusters be relieved from interference by local agents, whose loyalties were equivocal, and that commissions be made contingent upon loss experience, in order to induce more careful underwriting selection by the agents at the threshold of the transaction. This activity neither sought nor needed legal implementation, and hence lies primarily in the field of entrepreneurial history. However, the Commissioner threw the weight of his office behind the inclination of insurance management to extend the range of inspections. Moreover, as manager of the state fire fund, he adopted inspection practices after the Attorney General ruled that he had the implied power to appoint inspectors in order to run the fund according to sound business methods. In Commissioner Ekern's administration, the Independent Inspection Bureau of Philadelphia inspected the charitable and penal institutions of Wisconsin and recommended the installation of sprinklers. The 1915 legislature provided $25,000 for that purpose. Inspection early became important in the operations of the state fire fund. State property was inspected twice annually, that of other insureds once annually. In 1922 Commissioner Whitman reported the installation and use of a hose-testing machine by the state fund inspectors.[24]

When we move from the elimination of physical hazard to the lessening of moral hazard, we come to an area of prime importance to the legal historian. Much legislation and case law concerned moral hazard, and the industry reacted sharply to regulation of this kind. This book tells elsewhere of the legal regulation of moral hazard clauses, and of the valued policy law, which the companies consistently regarded as productive of great loss through incendiarism. In those fields weighty considerations overcame the concern of the law to minimize temptation to the policyholder. The companies repeatedly advised the legislature on questions of moral hazard, suggesting more stringent punishment for arson, compulsory coinsurance clauses or limitations of recovery to a specified percentage of value, elimination of the valued policy law, and the vigorous suppression of tramps. So also, to minimize carelessness, the 1913 Fire Insurance Investigating Committee recommended that the starting of a fire on certain premises be deemed prima facie evidence of negligence of those in control of the premises.[25]

In 1915 the legislature permitted the insertion of a deductible clause in any insurance policy, permitting the insurance company, in return for a reduced rate, to cast upon the policyholders small losses to an amount not exceeding 5 per cent of the amount of insurance. The purpose of such a clause was to lessen the moral hazard and thus prevent losses. In 1943 the 5 per cent limitation in the deductible clause was removed, and the insured was permitted to bear any clearly defined portion of the loss.[26]

By establishing a system of fire inquests, an attempt was made to bring the criminal law to bear in a direct effort to lessen the incidence of incendiary fires. The pressure for this development seems to have come from the insurance companies.

The system of fire inquests began in the east. The procedure and basic idea was to extend to the investigation of the burning of property the techniques used in the coroner's inquest upon suspicious deaths. New York had a statute in 1857, and Massachusetts in 1867. The New York statute provided that when it appeared by the affidavit of a credible witness that there was ground to suspect incendiarism, a coroner or sheriff, when properly requested, should investigate the matter. These early acts proved ineffective. At least as early as 1877, the compulsory fire inquest was recommended at meetings of the Fire Underwriters' Association. One speaker even thought a statute should be passed forbidding payment of claims till after an inquest on the fire. In 1891 C. C. Hine, editor of an important insurance paper, frequent speaker at association meetings, and a man with one of the most incisive minds and articulate voices among industry spokesmen, reported that since 1888 he had been engaged in a one-man campaign to achieve adoption of the system of fire inquests. He wrote the Governor and legislature of every state, to urge that coroners investigate every fire. In 1889, as a result of a request by Boston insurance men that a part of the premium taxes be allocated to fire inquests, Massachusetts made the inquest compulsory.[27]

In 1895, as a subordinate part of a bill to limit fire insurance to 90 per cent of value, there was a proposal to appoint a fire inspector in each city and village, to investigate all fires. Two years later the committee to revise the insurance statutes proposed that the Commissioner be ex officio Fire Marshal and investigate all suspicious fires, reduce fire hazards, and compile reports from fire departments. Even after the revision was abandoned, the proposal that the Commissioner investigate suspicious fires was again made separately. In 1897 sentiment for the bill was weak, but by 1905 it had greatly increased, and a bill to give coroners the duty of investigating suspicious fires passed the Senate without resistance, only to fail in the Assembly by a vote of 50 to 13. Commissioner Host, who was a moving spirit behind the drive for fire inquests, as of other preventive laws, complained that the defeat was on a technical and misleading point and that he was caught unawares because no opposition was expected. Finally in 1907, half a century after the New York law was first on the books and two decades after an effective law was passed in Massachusetts, the legislature of Wisconsin created the office of the State Fire Marshal. The insurance companies strongly supported the proposal. What opposition there was centered on arguments from economy and the adequacy of existing powers in the district attorneys. The Fire Marshal was to be appointed by the Governor. It was his primary duty to investigate fires, especially those of suspicious origin, and in proper cases to initiate a prosecution for arson. He also had minor duties in the reduction of physical hazard. The expenses of the office were to be paid from a tax on fire insurance premiums of one-fourth of one per cent. In 1909 bills to repeal the Fire Marshal law were introduced in both houses of the legislature, but instead of repeal the tax was raised to three-eighths of one per cent.[28]

The Insurance Commissioner was made ex officio Fire Marshal in 1915, pursuant to the recommendations of an investigating committee which sought to combine all insurance matters in one office. The report emphasized the educative role. The 1917 legislature transferred his preventive role to the Industrial Commission, leaving only his investigatory and prosecutory functions. By the early 1930's there was a complete merger of the Fire Marshal's department with the insurance department, and there resulted considerable agitation for the re-creation of a separate fire marshal's department, or at least of a separate division within the insurance department. The Wisconsin State Fire Chiefs Association was the instigator of at least one such bill. In the late 1940's, Commissioner Duel was anxious to get rid of the fire marshal role. As a result, a proposal was made in 1949 to transfer the Fire Marshal's duties to a State Crime Commission. Another bill would have created a Safety Commission which would take over his work, as well as have other duties. But in 1959 the task was still one of the burdens of the Commissioner's office.[29]

A 1913 statute compelled the companies to give assistance to the fire inspectors, by requiring every adjuster's report to be filed with the chief of the fire department as deputy fire marshal. In 1937 the legislature required that copies be filed both with the state Fire Marshal and with the chief of the fire department. The 1913 legislature also required the owner of premises to give notice of any fire to the local fire chief or the state Fire Marshal, before making any proof of loss. Companies were required to attach a form for such notice to each fire insurance policy issued in Wisconsin. It was contended that failure to give such notice should deprive an insured of his rights under the policy, but the Supreme Court held in 1919 that the statute was passed for public-policy reasons, not to furnish insurance companies with a defense, and further, that there was no clear indication of the legislature's intention to deprive the policyholder of his rights, and upon compliance with other policy requirements he might recover from the insurance company.[30]

Financing another large-scale preventive program by taxes on insurance premiums was urged again in 1939 and 1941 when a proposal was made to create a department of radio intelligence with a state-wide short-wave broadcasting station. To support it, a tax similar to the fire department tax and the fire marshal tax would be levied on premiums paid for insurance against loss by various crimes. In 1949 it was proposed to create a program of highway safety education under the motor vehicle department, to be financed by a tax of one-half of one per cent on automobile insurance premiums. Neither proposal was adopted.[31]

In 1955 Governor Kohler urged that the legislature give attention to the safety aspects of workmen's compensation, recommending that additional personnel be provided for safety inspections. In so doing he illustrated continued concern in mid-twentieth century for reducing, as well as spreading, risks. To the development of that attitude the insurance industry had made significant contributions; in its implementation insurance services were primary tools.[32]

Chapter Seven

CONCLUSIONS

In the half-century from 1906 to 1959, the Wisconsin legislature passed about 800 statutes dealing with insurance and considered a comparable number of other bills which it did not enact, at least on first introduction. In the same period the Wisconsin Supreme Court decided nearly 1,000 insurance cases and the Attorney General announced more than 200 opinions on insurance questions. Thus in the first half of the twentieth century, the complex process of insurance-law making continued to show as much vigor as it had in the nineteenth. Some problems had been solved and no longer perplexed the lawmakers, but new issues appeared to take the place of each one that was solved. Continued lawmaking at a high level of activity indicated the extent to which the insurance principle and the insurance enterprise had moved from a position near the periphery of nineteenth-century life to a place close to the focus of latter-day society. Whereas in the nineteenth century insurance ministered primarily to the needs of economic man, in the twentieth it became one of the main instruments by which law created a welfare-minded society. Most human activity in mid-twentieth century had insurance implications.

In its growth through the life of Wisconsin, the insurance enterprise reflected the concerns of the larger community. Despite the complexity of the insurance business, and its technicality, the law that nurtured it mirrored attitudes, hopes, and fears that pervaded society far outside the insurance office. Insurance law also reflected the growth of a market economy out of the near-subsistence economy of pioneer days, and in its own way contributed to that growth. Again, though insurance was seldom at the focal point of controversy regarding the power structure of American society, it was sometimes involved in such conflicts and made its own modest contribution to the development of the American polity. Insurance reflected developments in techniques of legal decision making, and the law's concern with insurance helped give birth to the modern administrative process. Finally, the growth of insurance law had some impact upon the development of other branches of the law.

Insurance Law and Changing Attitudes

Prevailing social attitudes broke through the artificial barriers which the technical jargon of actuary and underwriter built around the insurance industry, and had great impact on the way in which insurance law developed.

The overpowering needs of the burgeoning market economy ensured that Jacksonian anticharter policy would not stop the proliferation of corporations. The policy, nevertheless, did help channel and control the process by which the insurance business became corporate. The attitude was reflected in the high capital requirements set by the general act of 1850, which fostered continuation of special chartering for two more decades. Popular distrust of large aggregates of capital may have produced those provisions of special charters which forbade trading activities or imposed a mortmain policy on the insurance business or imposed special liabilities on directors or officers of insurance companies. Some remnant of Jacksonian policy may account for the ban on corporate insurance agents. This anticharter policy, which was so significant an aspect of Jacksonian democracy, remained part of the American heritage, to become, in altered form, a component of Granger, Populist, and Progressive credos. Granger hostility to large capital aggregations contributed much to the growth of the town mutual in fire insurance and to life insurance issued on an assessment, rather than on an advance premium, basis. It was in the Granger era that state insurance funds and social insurance were first suggested and in the Progressive period that they first achieved reality. Moreover, agrarian radicalism contributed to important decisions relating to the level and method of insurance taxation. Another aspect of Jacksonian democracy, the readiness of Americans to associate in a great variety of ways, produced the rich abundance of forms within which the insurance enterprise developed.

In the late nineteenth century, the attitudes which prevailed were largely those sympathetic to the triumph of industrial and finance capitalism in America—usually, though perhaps erroneously, identified with the maxim, laissez faire. In the field of insurance, and of commercial law generally, the most important component of this complex of attitudes was the notion that the free will of contracting parties should be given complete effect—that freedom to make contracts included freedom to make oppressive contracts. This attitude was embodied in articulated legal doctrine, and thus remained effective as a conservative factor in the judge-made law of insurance long after the extreme nineteenth-century forms of the philosophy that produced it had ceased to control community opinion. Attitudes related to this concept brought reluctance to interfere in the internal management of insurance corporations. Though the need to control some key aspects of the business overcame this reluctance to a large extent, there were areas of insurance management into which legal agencies intruded very little. There tended to be more interference with local mutuals, where professional management and the profit-seeking motive were lacking as protection against incompetence.

Attitudes stemming from practices of political democracy in America tended to affect insurance law as well. Thus there were persistent efforts to convert the town mutuals from a voting regime based on the quantity of insurance purchased to the principle of one vote for each policyholder. Similar attitudes underlay the 1907 effort to provide for controlled and democratic processes in the election of directors of the big life insurance mutuals. This attitude was limited by reluctance to interfere in internal management, however, and had no effect on the law pertaining to stock companies.

Moral attitudes, too, had their effect on insurance law. In the Gilded Age, a tacit acceptance of predatory conduct may have helped the successful raid on the Madison Mutual surplus; "Progressive" insistence on a higher level of public morality may have contributed to the frustration of the similar raid on the Germantown surplus. The moral attitudes of Progressivism resulted in tighter control of the conversion of mutuals to the stock form. There is little doubt that the gambling aspects of the tontine, together with the possibility for corruption inherent in the possession of large sums of money for which there was limited accountability, shocked the moral sensibilities of the Progressive era and were at least partly responsible for the elimination of the tontine in the state, despite the absence of demonstrable corruption in Wisconsin. Like sensitiveness to moral questions resulted in the strong demand to eliminate the Commissioner's fees for valuation of policies and examination of companies. But related attitudes demanding strict economy and opposing high salaries for public officials prevented adequate financing of the Insurance Commissioner's regulatory activity and limited its effectiveness. A persistent egalitarian motif in the "liberal" political tradition in America led, in the Progressive period, to legal limitation of executive salaries.

The attitude most closely connected with the growth of insurance law, however, was the twentieth century's insistence upon an ordered and secure existence. Of course, security was not a new human hope. But now it took on special intensity—perhaps because it seemed closer to realization. The insurance industry exists to sell security. It could scarcely fail to be a key institution in an era that held security to be a prime value. As the security-focused attitude became central, the insurance idea became one of the main organizing principles of social life. Insurance was the mechanism by which social costs were forced into the private cost accounting of entrepreneurs. Insurance was thus a key instrument in changing the laissez faire society into a society which, as an organized whole, assumed many of the risks that the unregulated market economy cast on individuals. The individual search for security was largely instrumental in producing the market-oriented insurance institutions of the nineteenth century; intensified and supplemented by the development of humanitarianism—by a sense of responsibility for the welfare of those less fortunately situated—it produced in the twentieth century the social insurance institutions of a state charged with an increasing number of positive responsibilities.

Insurance law did not respond automatically to changes in public attitude, however. Inertia was a significant factor in the course of its development. The failure, despite several serious attempts, ever to produce a complete revision of the complicated and conflicting insurance laws, testified to the hurdles in the path of legal reform. Growth in the law was the result of necessity and pressure. Needed reforms came most easily after dramatic revelations of wrongdoing, such as those presented by the Armstrong committee, or after a change in company practices produced serious hardship on policyholders, as when the companies tightened their loss settlement methods in the early 1870's. Indeed, changes could sometimes take place despite prevailing opposing attitudes, if there was a ready channel through which pressures could be focused on the law-making agencies. Thus the legislature seldom refused the industry's requests for adjustments of law, unless these seriously conflicted with attitudes strongly felt by the legislators.

The Concept of Insurance as Public Utility

From a surprisingly early date insurance was regarded, even by insurance men, as a business affected with a public interest. Eventually there were indications that the law might treat insurance as a full-fledged public utility, even in the sense that an insurer must supply its product to all who demanded it. One indication of this evolving attitude was a 1931 statute which forbade automobile insurers to refuse to sell or to rate up insurance on the basis of race or color. So also, when the workmen's compensation laws required employers to insure, and when financial responsibility laws made automobile insurance almost compulsory, the legislature created assigned risk plans. The courts contributed to this development, too. For instance, the development of a technique for holding a company liable when it merely delayed action on an application removed insurance from the area of freedom of contract and tended to make it a public utility.[1]

These developments, taken together with the regulatory regime under which the industry operated in mid-twentieth century, gave an indication of how little difference remained between insurance and the classic public utilities. This process of development was slow, however, and was not yet complete in mid-twentieth century. Perhaps it began with the nineteenth-century special charter provisions that made directors or officers personally liable to policyholders if dividends were paid out of capital, or if policies were issued knowingly after the capital was impaired.[2]

Insurance men shared the attitude that insurance was affected with a public interest. Though they tended to oppose each new form of regulation as it developed, that was seldom because of a feeling that regulation was not justified in principle. As early as 1877, the President of the Fire Underwriters' Association of the Northwest said that

Insurance companies, being semi-public institutions, should, as National Banks are, be required to publish such a statement of their financial condition as will show what their assets consist of, what their liabilities of all kinds, including capital, are; and the *net* surplus, or deficiency, as the case may be (FUA, *Proc.*, 1877, p. 20).

Insurance men repeatedly claimed that underwriting was a profession. Their insistence implicitly recognized that there was a public interest in the business, for by tradition professions exist first to serve the public, and only secondarily to produce a profit. This attitude, first expressed by industry men, was encouraged by the Commissioner. Moreover, though the main motivation for more restrictive licensing of agents may have been to restrict competition, the rationalization was in terms of the public responsibilities of the insurance agent.[3]

The Development of the Economy

The changing patterns of insurance law reflected the growth of the economy. Early Wisconsin combined a near-subsistence economy and a brash young mercantile society. Quickly the market became the dominant fact in the life of the community. However, in the early twentieth century the pressing needs of an industrial age made serious inroads into the purity of the classic stage of capitalism. Insurance was a product of the market, and moved from the periphery of society to the center as the market dominated life. However, insurance became even more meaningful in the regulated market society than it had been earlier. Now, besides the service it rendered to business in the market place, it contributed to building a more tightly structured society which assumed responsibility for the welfare of its members.

The premium note technique of the earliest mutuals reflected the primitive economy of the 1830's and 1840's. It served well a society poor in fluid capital. At the same time, the very existence of insurance in this relatively sophisticated form demonstrated the attraction of the market way of life. The use of property liens to secure the premium notes, and the use of borrowing and anticipatory assessment to minimize the expense of assessment operation, adapted the technique for the needs of the community. The assessment operation, conducted by local associations largely outside the market economy, soon gave way to mutuals using an advance premium technique. But, the mutual insurance company continued to exhibit a noncommercial side of Wisconsin life, and preserved into the twentieth century the trace of a simpler economy.

From the beginning of Wisconsin's life, the profit-seeking corporation dominated the insurance industry, despite the essential mutuality of insurance. Stock notes provided an effective, relatively painless way to mobilize capital for the entrepreneurial side of the business in days of capital scarcity. As capital became more plentiful, there was less need for this method of capital mobilization, and it disappeared with the end of special chartering. The capital requirements in the general acts remained constant during most of Wisconsin's history, despite the increasing activity in the business world. It may be questioned whether the legal agencies ever really came to grips with the problem of regulating capital supply in the insurance business to meet social needs. The hesitating steps taken in the provision of contingency reserve requirements illustrates the failure to cope with this basic problem of the industry.

Growth of the economy was also reflected in the history of the fraternal associations, which began in the late nineteenth century as a reaction to the high cost of legal reserve life insurance. Fraternal organization was greatly stimulated by agrarian radicalism in the evil days of the 1870's and 1890's. But as the economy grew, the fraternals upgraded their operations and eventually became but another kind of legal reserve life insurance company. So, too, the conversion of mutuals to the stock form, with or without misappropriation of their assets to private benefit, reflected the increasing predominance of the market patterns.

As the expanding American society created new wants, new fears, new economic and psychological needs for protection against risk, new lines of insurance developed. Marine insurance on the inland waterways, insurance on land transportation, bicycle insurance, and finally automobile insurance, followed the changing patterns of transportation. The growth of corporate suretyship illustrated the increasing scope and interdependence of business activity, with concomitant demands for spreading risk and for guaranteeing confidence. Group insurance exhibited new patterns of economic organization. In all these developments, save only the last, the law quite freely implemented the new needs, especially by grinding out charters for the optimistic projections of nineteenth-century entrepreneurs. In the case of group insurance, the problem was complicated by involvement in the pull and haul for power between capital and labor.

The legal agencies were ready to implement the needs of the insurance business by modifying existing legal doctrine, too. Thus the development of more complex forms of merchandising led to judicial modification of the insurable interest doctrine, to validate "open" contracts of fire insurance. The prevailing patterns of marketing in the fire and casualty insurance business led to the general validation of oral contracts of insurance.

Insurance law also reacted to the change from local or regional economies to the single national market. In the process, insistence on local autonomy dwindled and ceased to play a major role in insurance law. Persistence of retaliatory tax provisions and reluctance to provide adequately for the issuance of surplus lines were almost the only remnants of a force that was once vital and pervasive.

The same force, driving toward the elimination of local markets, created a continuous pressure on the town mutuals to grow—to become multitown mutuals, or county mutuals, or even four-county mutuals.

This was accompanied by a tendency to extend the scope of their operations and to operate on an advance premium basis, just as the maturation of society had resulted in the upgrading of fraternals to modified legal reserve companies. So the town mutual took on a more commercial character as rural Wisconsin became an integral part of the market society.

In mid-twentieth century, the law faced new problems arising out of the growth of the business. There was vast increase in insurance company assets. How to regulate the investment of such assets without distorting the financial structure of American business was a new problem for the law. Pressure of such assets encouraged a relaxation of the investment regime from strict limitation to fixed-dollar investments toward greater freedom to invest in equities. It appeared, too, that the law might have to come to grips with the problems of an uneconomic marketing system. Antirebating laws and resident agent laws sought to bolster up the sagging agency system, but there was some question of how long it could be preserved in competition with salaried agents and direct writing. Perhaps legal control of agents' commissions might help force the agency system back to a sound basis, and thus preserve it.

In some part, the shape of Wisconsin insurance law was a result of the development in the state of the sixth largest American life insurance company, the Northwestern Mutual. A desire to encourage the home-grown company played a significant part in fashioning the insurance tax structure of the state, and may have had considerable, though unmeasurable, effect on other parts of insurance law.

Insurance in the American Polity

Unlike the banks or the railroads or the automobile manufacturers, insurance never occupied the center of the stage in the drama of American political life. Nevertheless, no broad discussion of insurance in American society should neglect the place of the insurance business in the distribution of power.

By its very nature, insurance grew to be an interstate business. Much of the problem of subjecting out-of-state corporations to the control of local courts was worked out in insurance litigation. So too, the insurance business played the crucial role in the drama of the removal statutes, which for a generation defined significant aspects of the balance between states' rights and central power.

Around the turn of the century, insurance institutions were becoming deeply involved in the intricate network of interlocking directorates by which large financial institutions exercised control over much of American economic life. The control of enormous aggregates of assets facilitated participation by insurance executives in financial power politics. This involvement was in sharp conflict with the industry's need for sound and conservative management of what were essentially trust funds. The struggle for public control of this aspect of the insurance business, with its concomitant problems of subversion of the legislative process and corruption of other legal agencies, was fought out largely in the New York arena. There were only faint echoes of the problem in Wisconsin. Governor LaFollette saw enough evil to utter ringing calls to action, despite the fact that the Wisconsin insurance law already forbade investment in equity shares. The Wisconsin Commissioner and legislature coöperated to end the tontine, which had helped to create the problem by accumulating assets for which there was but limited accountability.

There seemed to be little danger of an undue concentration of business in the insurance field, for entry into the field was easy enough to make monopoly very difficult to achieve. Indeed, at first excessive competition threatened to make the business unsound. Then the industry organized to facilitate concerted rate making, and this created problems of social control of the rate-making process. Not unnaturally rate regulation became involved in partisan political controversy; it also was involved in the bitter struggle between the mutual and the stock insurers. In mid-century, Wisconsin was the scene of a bitter fight over the proper rate formula; the Commissioner contended for a 2.5 per cent figure for underwriting profit in fire insurance, as compared with the 5 per cent accepted elsewhere. The insurance department long lacked adequate staff to carry out a very effective program of rate regulation, but in mid-century its regulation was in process of becoming more effective.

In a multitude of other ways, insurance was involved in the minor struggles for power within the framework of American democracy. The frequent reluctance to suppress actuarially unsound life insurance demonstrated the political power of fraternals in matters affecting their interests. Numerous attempts to prohibit tax assessors from becoming insurance agents and the law forbidding public employees to write insurance on public property, were two ways in which the law sought to prevent favoritism to an official caste. The entire structure of control over unfair marketing practices, discrimination among policyholders and agents, and prohibition of controlled business was an artificial support for the agency system in competition with more efficient marketing methods.

The extent to which an activity is subject to taxation always reflects relative power in a democratic society. The industry long contended that it should be free of taxation. This position was supported by some of the more articulate Commissioners. Nevertheless, insurance income paid its share of the state tax bill, and the Commissioner most vocal in opposition to insurance taxation was also most vigorous in tax collection. In the persistent struggle within the legislature over the formula and the rates of insurance taxation, the competitive position of the Northwestern Mutual played a significant role, for protective and revenue motives continually interacted, by virtue of the retaliatory tax laws of most states. The long continued controversy also reflected the rural-urban division in the state, the struggle between mutuals and stock companies, and problems of subjecting unadmitted companies to Wisconsin taxation. The formula in effect at any given time reflected a temporary balance of motives and forces, and the formula was consequently in constant flux.

With the accumulation of large surplus assets in the state fire insurance fund, problems of political balance of power began to affect them, for they offered a source of funds for various state purposes, such as the construction of the state office building, or even, at the behest of a conservative Republican Governor, the rescue of the general fund from deficit.

The basic conflicts in our society between those who would preserve a laissez faire policy and those who would increasingly subject business to legal control were repeatedly reflected in evolving insurance law. An accommodation between the two forces resulted in an unevenness of regulation of different aspects of the business. Thus there was continued reluctance to interfere in underwriting and other management decisions, except for very cogent reasons. On the other hand, investment was very tightly controlled by the law.

There was early and continued use of insurance companies to accomplish much of the preventive work that in the twentieth century would be regarded as a public function. Fire fighting, which began in close connection with the insurance business, eventually became purely a public activity; even in mid-twentieth century, however, it was partly financed by special insurance taxes reminiscent of the early nineteenth-century practice of delegating public business to private agencies. Activities such as those of the Underwriters' Laboratories continued to be carried on privately, by the insurance companies.

Insurance was deeply involved in shaping the more tightly organized society that was emerging in the twentieth century. Caught up in the drive toward more and more administration, the insurance enterprise contributed to the most significant twentieth-century change in the over-all power structure of a society in which public policy showed a lively and increasing concern for social income and costs. The insurance industry sought to convince the American public of the virtues of the insurance idea, and in so doing, insurance leaders quite unintentionally subverted their own most cherished wish—a free enterprise, private profit economy. Insurance was inherently mutual, and the dynamic of an insurance-oriented society was toward greater social direction and administration. It was one of the striking anachronisms of the twentieth century that the individualistic insurance man was, in fact, one of the chief apostles of the socialization of risk.

Insurance and the Techniques of Decision Making

From the beginning, it was the legislature that dominated the process of insurance-law making. At first it acted through special charters and then through general acts. The pace of development in the nineteenth century was such that insurance law had to be made quickly. A corporate structure must be developed to meet the needs of nonpolitical corporations, and only the legislature was equipped to make the necessary policy judgments and provide the new instruments and procedures to implement policy. Moreover, techniques must be devised to control a complicated business in the public interest. In its earlier activity, the Wisconsin legislature copied the work of other legislatures, borrowing at first mainly from New York and then more widely. Ultimately the Wisconsin legislature made its own novel contributions to the growth of insurance law. Of these, the valued policy law was perhaps the most original. On the whole, however, Wisconsin development was merely a part of the mainstream of evolving American insurance law.[4]

It is difficult to judge the adequacy of the legislature's performance, for the efficient operation of the business was not the only value it sought. It had also the public interest to protect, and sometimes the controls that public policy demanded created difficulties for the companies. This does not necessarily condemn the controls. If one uses modest standards of judgment, he must concede that the Wisconsin legislature did a good job. On the whole it proved more flexible and creative than did the courts. It was willing to undertake any necessary job, no matter how complicated, and to a surprising degree, it was able to deal with the insurance business as a problem in social engineering, without involving insurance issues too deeply in political maneuvering.

The court was the traditional agent of legal development in the common law system. However, in but one area of insurance law, that of claims administration, was the court's contribution significant. In that one area there was a substantial continuous flow of litigious controversies sufficient for the judges to make law. The court began with Lord Mansfield's law of marine insurance, and modified it through the development of techniques of waiver and estoppel, through the modification of the law of representations and warranties, and especially by an imaginative use of techniques for the interpretation of contracts. Though the dogma of freedom of contract was a strait jacket which tended to confine the court, the judges did succeed in subjecting the will of the insurance company to the control of society for the protection of the expectations of the insured.[5]

Outside of claims administration doctrine, the court's role was very limited. The fact that it must passively await the accidents of litigation made it incapable of the systematic development of policy in areas that had no law. Moreover, the dogma of freedom of contract restricted the court's range of maneuver and made it incapable of creative formulation of new doctrine to serve new social needs. Its traditionally limited role as law finder and administrator rather than law creator, denied it the title to make the sweeping policy judgments needed to help create a new industry in an age of change. There was no time for insurance law to evolve in the slow, step-by-step way in which judge-made law must evolve. Hence the court played a relatively minor part in the creation of Wisconsin insurance law.

The Insurance Commissioner, in contrast, played an important part in the creation of Wisconsin insurance law and even more in its administration. As time passed his contribution to administration became greater, though his role as law creator may have become less important. This study does not provide a definitive examination of the activities of the Commissioner's office, but it provides enough to indicate the far-reaching significance of administrative regulation.

In developing the insurance department, the legislature contributed significantly to the growth of techniques of administrative regulation. Insurance was one of the earliest businesses so to be regulated, and thus much of American administrative law was born in the insurance department. Techniques of control through reports, examinations, publicity, licensing, liquidation, were all tried and utilized in the insurance field. But the history of Wisconsin insurance regulation shows that provision of administrative machinery in itself was not the answer to any problem. The regulation of insurance was no better than the people in the office, and that in turn depended on finding ways in which to get competent and dedicated men as Commissioners, and to give them adequate staff with which to work. It depended also on finding techniques to keep the Commissioner from being unduly involved in political controversy. On several occasions in Wisconsin's history the work of the insurance department was prejudiced by the Commissioner's involvement in unseemly political strife. It can not be said that Wisconsin ever solved all the problems implicit in the administrative surveillance of a complicated industry. On the other hand, if one does not set unreasonably high standards of performance, he must concede that the Wisconsin Commissioners, on the whole, did satisfactory work. It is striking that even the incumbents of the office who were most sympathetic to the insurance companies, sought to achieve control over them. The defined functions and the momentum of the office seemed to instill a sense of responsibility and some pride in accomplishment which led Commissioners to a better performance than their original motivation would have forecast. On the other hand, there were always serious weaknesses in regulation, caused by incompetence, inadequate financing, or inadequate legal powers.

There is considerable evidence that, within limits, the companies were not averse to regulation. They recognized that the business was affected with a public interest. They saw also that certain kinds of reserve requirements might be a protection against rate cutting or even against the incursion of new companies into the industry. The standard policy law met with some objection from some quarters in the industry, but more perceptive insurance men saw it as a method of changing the judicial rule of contract interpretation to one more favorable to the companies. Then, too, if they were coöperative, it was easy to insist that they be consulted on the formulation of insurance laws. Sometimes a coöperative attitude might divert drastic reform into innocuous channels. Such coöperation was the only effective method of resistance, for in any overt war between the companies and the state, the latter must win. Aside from political maneuver, the only weapon the companies had for fighting the state was withdrawal; the state, on the other hand, could go into the insurance business successfully, thus frustrating the effect of withdrawal.

Effect of Insurance on other Branches of the Law

In the field of insurance law, dogma rarely inhibited growth, for in the long run the persistent pressure of society's needs generally overcame the toughest doctrine. Insurance as an easily available way of socializing the risks of enterprise or of the ordinary activities of daily life, led to significant change in established doctrine, even in other areas of the law. Much of the impetus for the developing law of negligence, especially in the field of automobile accidents, came from the probability that an insurance company stood behind the defendant. In Wisconsin, this effect was enhanced by the direct action statute. So, too, Wisconsin's development of the comparative negligence idea, and the partial elimination of the sovereign immunity of the state, resulted from the growth of the insurance enterprise. In the future, the high probability that any insurable risk is, in fact, insured will certainly encourage the legal agencies to ascertain the incidence of risk in accordance with the balance of convenience for insurance of the risk, rather than in accordance with deeper notions of moral responsibility or fault. Fault becomes less and less relevant in an age of insurance.[6]

The law of administrative regulation, and the law of the corporate device, owed much to insurance. So also did the general law of contracts. Insurance had provided long experience in the use of commercial arbitration procedures. In many other ways the insurance business had contributed to the development of American law. But in mid-twentieth century, the impact of insurance on the legal system was yet in its infancy. It seemed likely that the influence of insurance on American law, as on American society, would be more significant as the century moved on toward its close.

SELECTED BIBLIOGRAPHY OF
FREQUENTLY CITED WRITINGS

Although this book is published in two editions, one with fuller documentation than the other, the same bibliography appears in both editions and includes all the writings to which there is repeated reference whether in the text, the footnotes, or the notes of the fully documented edition. Materials listed here are cited throughout by surname of the author, a volume number if necessary, and a page number. For authors with multiple entries a date is used to distinguish the works.

In addition to citation of material in the bibliography, there is extensive reference to various official compilations, annuals, reports, and other documents, which are cited throughout by abbreviated title. Those that are not standard abbreviations and easily recognizable can be identified in the list of abbreviations printed on page ix.

AF of L, Committee on Insurance. 1925. *Union Insurance.* [A report in LRef. Library.]

Andersen, Theodore A. 1954. *A Century of Banking in Wisconsin.* State Historical Society of Wisconsin, Madison.

Anderson, Lewis Albert. 1911. *Valuation of Assessment and Stipulated Premium Policies.* [A publication of the Wisconsin Insurance Department. In Hist. Soc. Library.]

———. 1912. "Valuation of Fraternal Societies," address presented at the National Convention of Insurance Commissioners of the U.S., Spokane, Washington, July 1912. 1912 Association of Insurance Commissioners. *Proceedings* 197.

Association of Casualty and Surety Companies, Dept. of Research. 1950. *Government Insurance in the United States; A Special Study.* New York.

Ballantine, Arthur A. 1916. "A Compensation Plan for Railway Accident Claims." 29 *Harvard Law Review* 705.

Bashford, R. M. 1905a. *Argument on Behalf of the Northwestern Mutual Life Insurance Company (Bill No. 304, S, 1905).* [In LRef. Library.]

———. 1905b. *No. 434 A—The Dahl Bill, Taxing Life Insurance Companies.* [A circular in LRef. Library.]

Basye, Walter. 1919. *History and Operation of Fraternal Insurance.* The Fraternal Monitor, Rochester, N. Y.

Bolles, Albert Sidney. 1879. *Industrial History of the United States . . . .* The H. Bell Publishing Co., Norwich, Conn.

Brandeis, Elizabeth. 1936. "The Employer Reserve Type of Unemployment Compensation Law." 3 *Law & Contemporary Problems* 54.

Brearley, Harry Chase. 1916. *The History of the National Board of Fire Underwriters . . . .* F. A. Stokes Co., New York.

Buck, James Smith. 1876–86. *Pioneer History of Milwaukee . . . .* Milwaukee News Co., Milwaukee, Wis. 4 v.

Buck, Solon Justus. 1913. *The Granger Movement . . . .* Harvard University Press, Cambridge.

———. 1920. *The Agrarian Crusade . . . .* Yale University Press, New Haven.

Buehler, Alfred Grether. 1940. *Public Finance.* Ed. 2. McGraw-Hill, New York.

Buley, Roscoe Carlyle. 1953. *The American Life Convention, 1906–1952; A Study in the History of Life Insurance.* Appleton-Century-Crofts, New York. 2 v.

Bushnell, A. R. 1907a. *The Contested Life Insurance Bills—Reasons Against Them.* [In LRef. Library.]

———. 1907b. *The Legislative Life Insurance Investigation Committee's Report.* [A pamphlet in LRef. Library.]

Butler, James D. 1880. "Alexander Mitchell, The Financier." 11 State Historical Society of Wisconsin. *Collections* 435–50.

Carman, Ernest C. 1919. "Is a Motor Vehicle Accident Compensation Act Advisable?" 4 *Minnesota Law Review* 1.

Clough, Shepard Bancroft. 1946. *A Century of Life Insurance; A History of the Mutual Life Insurance Company of New York, 1843–1943.* Columbia University Press, New York.

Committee to Study Compensation for Automobile Accidents. 1932. *Report by the Committee . . . , to the Columbia University Council for Research in the Social Sciences . . . .* Press of the International Printing Co., Philadelphia.

Commons, John R. 1921. "Unemployment Compensation and Prevention." *The Survey,* Oct. 1, 1921.

"Compensation for Automobile Accidents: A Symposium." 1932. 32 *Columbia Law Review* 785.

Cullen, Robert K. 1934. "Some Problems Arising Under Automobile Liability Insurance in Wisconsin." [Unpublished S.J.D. thesis in University of Wisconsin Law Library.]

Davis, Joseph Stancliffe. 1917. *Essays in the Earlier History of American Corporations.* Harvard University Press, Cambridge. 2 v.

Dawson, Miles M. 1907a. *Argument Before Joint Committee on Banks and Insurance,* May 14, 1907. [In LRef. Library.]

———. 1907b. *Opinion on [Specified Bills],* submitted to Joint Committee on Insurance, May 27, 1907. [In LRef. Library.]

Ehrenzweig, Albert Armin. 1950. "Assurance Oblige—A Comparative Study." 15 *Law & Contemporary Problems* 445.

———. 1951. *Negligence Without Fault . . . .* University of California Press, Berkeley.

———. 1955. "'Full Aid' Insurance for the Traffic Victim—A Voluntary Compensation Plan." 43 *California Law Review* 1. [Also published as a pamphlet.]

Evans, George Heberton. 1948. *Business Incorporation In the United States, 1800–1943.* National Bureau of Economic Research, [New York].

Farren, George. 1823. *A Treatise on Life Assurance . . . .* Butterworth & Son, London.

Feinsinger, N. P. 1935. "Financial Responsibility Laws and Compulsory Insurance: The Problem in Wisconsin." 10 *Wisconsin Law Review* 192–222.

'Financial Protection for the Motor Accident Victim." 1936. [A symposium.] 3 *Law & Contemporary Problems* 465–608.

Freund, Ernst. 1921. "The Use of Indefinite Terms in Statutes." 30 *Yale Law Journal* 437.

——. 1928. *Administrative Powers over Persons and Property* . . . . University of Chicago Press, Chicago.

Fricke, William A. 1902. *The Law and Distribution of Surplus of Life Insurance Companies.* [no publisher], New York.

——. 1905. *Remarks Before the Assembly Committee on Insurance, on Bill 434, A,* March 2, 1905. [In LRef. Library.]

——. 1906. *Statement to Tax Commission,* Dec. 3, 1906. [In LRef. Library.]

——. 1907. *Brief on Behalf of the Northwestern Mutual Life Insurance Co. of Milwaukee on Bills Introduced in Legislature of Wisconsin in the Year 1907.* [In LRef. Library.]

Friedmann, W. G. 1948. "Social Insurance and the Principles of Tort Liability." 63 *Harvard Law Review* 241.

Galbraith, John Kenneth. 1958. *The Affluent Society.* Houghton-Mifflin Co., Boston.

Goble, George Washington. 1937. "Moral Hazard Clauses of the Standard Fire Insurance Policy." 37 *Columbia Law Review* 410.

——. 1949. *Cases and Other Materials on the Law of Insurance.* Ed 2. Bobbs-Merrill Co., Indianapolis.

"Governmental Tort Liability." 1942. [A symposium.] 9 *Law & Contemporary Problems* 179–367.

Green, Leon. 1958. *Traffic Victims: Tort Law and Insurance.* Northwestern University Press, Evanston, Ill.

Handlin, Oscar. 1951. *The Uprooted* . . . . Little, Brown & Co., Boston.

Handlin, Oscar, and Mary F. 1947. *Commonwealth . . . Massachusetts 1774–1861.* New York University Press, New York.

Haney, Lewis Henry. 1949. *History of Economic Thought* . . . . Ed. 4. Macmillan Co., New York.

Hanson, George S. 1953. *State and Municipal Self-Insurance.* National Ass'n of Insurance Agents, New York. [In LRef. Library.]

Harper, Fowler Vincent, and Fleming James, Jr., 1956. *The Law of Torts.* Little, Brown & Co., Boston. 3 v.

Hartz, Louis. 1948. *Economic Policy and Democratic Thought: Pennsylvania, 1776–1860.* Harvard University Press, Cambridge.

Heins, Richard M. 1957. "Multiple Line Underwriting and Wisconsin Insurance Laws." 1957 *Wisconsin Law Review* 563.

Henderson, Gerard Carl. 1918. *The Position of Foreign Corporations in American Constitutional Law* . . . . Harvard University Press, Cambridge.

History of Milwaukee, Wisconsin . . . . 1881. The Western Historical Co., Chicago. [Frank Abial Flower, supposed author.]

Hoar, Roger Sherman. 1932. *Unemployment Insurance in Wisconsin.* The Stuart Press, South Milwaukee, Wis.

Huebner, Solomon Stephen. 1931. "Fire Insurance." 6 *Encyclopedia of the Social Sciences* 255.

——. 1950. *Life Insurance.* Ed. 4. Appleton-Century-Crofts, New York.

Hunt, Freeman, ed. 1858. *Lives of American Merchants.* Derby and Jackson, New York. 2 v.

"Institutional Investments." 1952. [A symposium.] 17 *Law & Contemporary Problems* 1–252.

James, Fleming, Jr., and John V. Thornton. 1950. "The Impact of Insurance on the Law of Torts." 15 *Law & Contemporary Problems* 431.

James, Marquis. 1942. *Biography of a Business* . . . . Bobbs-Merrill Co., New York.

——. 1947. *The Metropolitan Life* . . . . Viking Press, New York.

Johnson, Olaf H. 1926a. *Agency and Department Problems*, address to Wisconsin Association of Insurance Agents, Aug. 18, 1926. [A publication of the Wisconsin Insurance Department. Mimeographed copy in Hist. Soc. Library.]

——. 1926b. *Address* . . . *Before the Insurance Federation of Wisconsin*, June 28, 1926. [A publication of the Wisconsin Insurance Department. In Hist. Soc. Library.]

——. 1926c. *Conversion of the Fraternal Society into an Old Line Company* . . . , an address . . . before the National Convention of Insurance Commissioners, Los Angeles, Nov. 18, 1926. [A publication of the Wisconsin Insurance Department. In Hist. Soc. Library.]

Kapp, Karl William. 1950. *The Social Costs of Private Enterprise*. Harvard University Press, Cambridge.

Kent, James. 1826–30. *Commentaries on American Law*. O. Halsted, New York. 4 v.

Keynes, John Maynard. 1936. *General Theory of Employment, Interest, and Money*. Macmillan & Co., Ltd., London.

Kimball, Spencer L. 1955. "Warranties, Representations and Concealments in Utah Insurance Law." 4 *Utah Law Review* 456.

——. 1957. "The Role of the Court in the Development of Insurance Law." 1957 *Wisconsin Law Review* 520. [This article is a separate part of the study from which this book was prepared. It seeks to evaluate the importance of the courts in the development of various parts of insurance law.]

——. 1958. "The Development of Insurance Law." [The original manuscript of the present book, submitted for the S.J.D. degree, and on file in the University of Wisconsin Law Library. The documentation is more extensive, and at some points the textual treatment is more detailed, than in the present book.]

Kimball, Spencer L., and Ronald N. Boyce. 1958. "The Adequacy of State Insurance Rate Regulation: The McCarran-Ferguson Act in Historical Perspective." 56 *Michigan Law Review* 545.

Kip, Richard. 1953. *Fraternal Life Insurance in America*. [no publisher], Philadelphia.

Knight, Charles Kelly. 1926. *Advanced Life Insurance*. J. Wiley & Sons, New York.

Koss, Rudolph A. 1871. *Milwaukee*. Schnellpressendruck des "Harold," Milwaukee, Wis. [Typewritten translation by Hans Ibsen, in Hist. Soc. Library.]

Krier, Urban. 1951. *An Analysis of the Wisconsin State Fire Insurance Fund*. [Published by the Wisconsin Association of Insurance Agents. In LRef. Library.]

Krueger, Leonard Bayliss. 1933. *History of Commercial Banking in Wisconsin* . . . . *(University of Wisconsin Studies in the Social Sciences and History,* No. 18.) University of Wisconsin, Madison.

Kuehnl, George J. 1953. "The Wisconsin Business Corporation." [Unpublished S.J.D. thesis in University of Wisconsin Law Library. This thesis has now been rewritten and published as *The Wisconsin Business Corporation* (University of Wisconsin Press, Madison, 1959).]

Livermore, Shaw. 1939. *Early American Land Companies* . . . . The Commonwealth Fund, New York.

McCahan, David. 1929. *State Insurance in the United States* . . . . University of Pennsylvania Press, Philadelphia.

McCormick, Charles T. 1954. *Handbook of the Law of Evidence.* West Publishing Co., St. Paul, Minn.

Marx, Robert S. 1925. "Compulsory Compensation Insurance." 25 *Columbia Law Review* 164.

Mehr, Robert Irwin, and Emerson Cammack. 1952. *Principles of Insurance.* R. D. Irwin, Chicago.

Merk, Frederick. 1916. *Economic History of Wisconsin During the Civil War Decade.* The [State Historical] Society, Madison, Wis.

Merrill, Horace Samuel. 1954. *William Freeman Vilas* . . . . State Historical Society of Wisconsin, Madison.

Merrill, Willard. 1900. *Taxation of Life Insurance Companies,* argument before Wisconsin Tax Commission, Oct. 2, 1900 [In LRef. Library.]

National Industrial Conference Board. 1931. *Unemployment Benefits and Insurance.* National Industrial Conference Board, Inc., New York.

Noyes, G. H. 1906. *The Committee of Fifteen on Uniform Legislation,* brief, Nov. 12, 1906. [A pamphlet in LRef. Library.]

———. 1907. *Argument to Joint Committee on Banks and Insurance.* [In LRef. Library.]

———. 1909. *Taxation on Life Insurance Companies,* brief on S.B. 5, 1909. [In LRef. Library.]

———. 1911. *Life Insurance Taxation.* [In LRef. Library.]

Olin, John M. 1907a. *Taxation of Life Insurance Companies,* argument to Joint Committee on Banks and Insurance and on Taxation. [In LRef. Library.]

———. 1907b. *Shall Justice Be Done on Life Insurance Taxation?,* argument as to Substitute Amendment No. 1, S to No. 454, S and Substitute Amendment No. 1, A to No. 626, A, 1907, submitted in behalf of the Northwestern Mutual Life Insurance Co. [In LRef. Library.]

———. 1909. *Election of Directors of Mutual Life Insurance Companies,* hearing before Joint Committees on Banks and Insurance. [In LRef. Library.]

Orr, George W. 1954. "Fault as the Basis of Liability." 21 *Journal of Air Law and Commerce* 399.

Orton, P. A. 1915. *Life Insurance Company Taxation.* [A pamphlet in LRef. Library.]

Outerbridge, Eugenius H. 1918. *Group Insurance as an Influence in Promoting Stability in Labor Groups,* address to Association of Life Insurance Presidents, Dec. 6, 1918. [In LRef. Library.]

Patrons Benevolent Aid Society of Wisconsin. 1878. *Second Annual Circular with Articles of Incorporation and By-Laws.* Madison, Wis. [In Hist. Soc. Library.]

Patterson, Edwin Wilhite. 1924. "The Apportionment of Business Risks Through Legal Devices." 24 *Columbia Law Review* 335.

———. 1927. *The Insurance Commissioner in the United States . . . .* Harvard University Press, Cambridge.

———. 1955. *Cases and Materials on the Law of Insurance.* Ed. 3. Foundation Press, Brooklyn.

———. 1957. *Essentials of Insurance Law . . . .* Ed. 2. McGraw-Hill, New York.

Pigou, Arthur Cecil. 1924. *The Economics of Welfare.* Ed. 2. Macmillan & Co., Ltd., London.

Pound, Roscoe. 1938. *The Formative Era of American Law.* Little, Brown & Co., Boston.

Primm, James Neil. 1954. *Economic Policy in the Development of a Western State, Missouri, 1820–1860.* Harvard University Press, Cambridge.

Raney, William Francis. 1940. *Wisconsin, A Story of Progress.* Prentice-Hall, Inc., New York.

Reynolds, Dexter. 1853. *A Treatise on the Law of Life Assurance.* Banks, Gould & Co., New York.

Richards, George. 1909. *A Treatise on the Law of Insurance . . . .* Ed. 3. The Banks Law Publishing Co., New York.

Roe, Gilbert E., ed. 1907. *Selected Opinions of Luther S. Dixon and Edward G. Ryan . . . .* Callaghan & Co., Chicago.

Rollins, Weld A. 1919. "A Proposal to Extend the Compensation Principle to Accidents in the Streets." 4 *Massachusetts Law Quarterly* 392.

Schlesinger, Arthur Meier, Jr. 1945. *Age of Jackson.* Little, Brown & Co., Boston.

Smalley, Orange A. 1953. "The Northwestern Mutual Life, 1857–1950: An Historical Case Study of Investment Policy and Practice." [Unpublished study for Northwestern University. Copy in University of Wisconsin Law Library. This study was the basis, in part, for Williamson and Smalley, *infra.* The unpublished study has some information not contained in the published work.]

Stalson, J. Owen. 1942. *Marketing Life Insurance; Its History in America.* Harvard University Press, Cambridge.

Statement of Actuaries Regarding Certain Bill Recommendations by the Wisconsin Insurance Investigating Committee, submitted to the Joint Committee on Banks and Insurance, April 9, 1907. [In LRef. Library.]

Still, Bayrd. 1948. *Milwaukee . . . .* State Historical Society of Wisconsin, Madison.

Sullivan, Mark. 1928–35. *Our Times.* C. Scribner's Sons, New York. 6 v.

Sumner, William Graham, and Albert G. Keller. 1927–33. *The Science of Society.* Yale University Press, New Haven. 4 v.

Tocqueville, Alexis C. Henri M. C. de. 1954. *Democracy in America.* Vintage Books, New York. 2 v. [The Henry Reeve text as rev. by Francis Bowen, now further corr. and edited . . . by Phillips Bradley, c 1945.]

Trenerry, Charles Farley. 1926. *The Origin and Early History of Insurance . . . .* P. S. King & Son, Ltd., London.

U. S. Temporary National Economic Committee. 1946. *Investigation of Concentration of Economic Power . . . . Monograph No. 28; Study of Legal Reserve Life Insurance Companies.* U. S. Government Printing Office, Washington.

Ussing, Henry. 1952. "The Scandinavian Law of Torts—Impact of Insurance on Tort Law." 1 *American Journal of Comparative Law* 359.

Valgren, Victor Nelson. 1924. *Farmers' Mutual Fire Insurance in the United States.* University of Chicago Press, Chicago.

Vance, William Reynolds. 1951. *Handbook on the Law of Insurance.* Ed. 3. West Publishing Co., St. Paul, Minn.

Van Metre, Thurman William. 1921. *Economic History of the United States.* H. Holt & Co., New York.

Whyte, William Hollingsworth. 1956. *The Organization Man.* Simon & Schuster, New York.

Williams, Ellis T. 1938. *The Proposed Revision of the Standard Policy of Fire Insurance. (The Howe Readings in Insurance,* No. 20.) Published by the Insurance Society of New York. [In LRef. Library.]

Williamson, Harold Francis, and Orange A. Smalley. 1957. *Northwestern Mutual Life; A Century of Trusteeship.* Northwestern University Press, Evanston, Ill.

Wiltsey, Glenn G. 1944. "Administrative Regulation in Wisconsin." [Unpublished Ph.D. Thesis, University of Chicago. Copy in LRef. Library.]

Winslow, John Bradley. 1912. *Story of a Great Court . . . .* T. H. Flood & Co., Chicago.

Witte, Edwin E. 1928. Part I. *Legal Status of the Issuance of Group Life Insurance Policies to Labor Unions.* [Memorandum based mainly upon replies to a questionnaire by the Insurance Commissioners of the several states. In LRef. Library.]

———. 1928. Part II. *Legal Status of the Issuance of Group Life Insurance Policies to Labor Unions: Replies to Questionnaire by the Insurance Commissioners of the Several States, 1927.* [Bound with Part I. In LRef. Library.]

Woll, Matthew, and Carville D. Benson. 1927. *Birth and Development of the Union Labor Life Insurance Company,* address to shareholders, March 14, 1927. [A pamphlet in LRef. Library.]

Wright, Charles, and C. Ernest Fayle. 1928. *History of Lloyd's . . . .* Macmillan & Co., Ltd., London.

Zartman, Lester W., ed., and William H. Price, reviser. 1914. *. . . Property Insurance . . . .* Rev. ed. *(Yale Readings in Insurance.)* Yale University Press, New Haven.

INDEX

Accident benefits: are insurance, 192–93

Accident insurance: appears in Wisconsin, 11; rate regulation first proposed in, 97; Commissioner polices claims in, 207; taxation of, 262–63. *See also* Health insurance

Accounting methods: Commissioner may prescribe, 184

Accumulation basis: upgrading fraternals, 159

Actuarial science: origins of, 10; pension funds, 19; makes gambling difficult, 32; commercial assessment companies, 51; not understood, 57n; legal reserve, 153–62

Actuaries: oppose maximum premium, 110; criticize reserve regulation, 155; create reserve plans, 169; oppose expense regulation, 170; valuation of life policies, 178; bill to increase salary of, in department, 179

Adjusters: agent interference, 216; report to Fire Marshal, 299

Administrative law: development of Wisconsin insurance department, 174–208; techniques of regulation, 245, 301, 313; influenced by insurance, 314

Advertising, unfair: control of, 121–22

Advisory board contract, 124

Aetna Life Insurance Company: remains in state, 171

Agents: distributing public business among, 55; oppose state funds, 55, 56, 59; and rate regulation, 98, 100; withholding premiums, 115; embezzlement by, 116; corporate, 119; licensing of, 120–21; control of unfair practices, 121–26, 127; commissions, 124, 127; part-time, 127; tax assessor as, 127, 309; interference with adjusters, 216; conflict of duty and interest 223; powers, 223–29; control by companies, 224–25; unauthorized companies controlled through, 280–82; brokers as, 281, 286; surety for unauthorized companies, 282; system bolstered by law, 308

Agrarian radicalism. *See* Granger movement; Populism

Alien companies: security deposit, 78, 271, 275, 276; treaty protection, 264. *See also* Out-of-state companies; Localism

Aliens: deposit requirements for Lloyds' underwriters, 276

Allen, Thomas S.: suggests revision of insurance laws, 183, 187

All-industry bills, 105, 109

Amendment of mutual articles, 69

American Experience Table, **110–111,** 154, 168

Amortization basis, 162–63

Anderson, L. A.: replaces Ekern, 202

Annual apportionment: to suppress tontine, 165–66

Annual statement: town mutuals, 72

Annuity and Investment Board: may insure securities, 30; to invest state funds, 142

Anticharter doctrine: in Wisconsin, 65–67, 302; multiple lines problems, 117

Anticompact laws, 96–97

Antitrading clause, 68, 302

Antitrust laws: concerted rate making, 97; Southeastern Underwriters case, 105. *See also* Competition; Monopoly powers

Apparent authority doctrine, 224

Application: to be attached to policy, 233; copy to be delivered to policyholder, 234, 235

Approval of insurance: advertising copy, 8; banks disguised as, 8; new lines, 9–16; mid-20th century, 30

Armstrong investigation: Equitable Life, 56; control of mutuals, 72; control of management practices, 164, 173; tontine, 166; control of expenses, 168, 169

Arson: and technical defenses, 215; valued policy law, 242; rewards, 291; fire inquests, 298; Fire Marshal, 299

Assessment companies: local fire mutuals, 42; mutual benefit, 49; life and casualty regulated, 51; reinsurance reserves, 153; actuarial requirements, 157; benevolent societies, 161; Breese criticizes, 197

Assessments: equivalent of capital, 83; Madison Mutual, 85; Commissioner's consent, 88; creates surplus for raiding, 88; fraternal life, 112; collection problem, 113–15; premium notes, 115; weakness in life insurance, 156–57; horizontal, 191; give way to advance premiums, 306

NOTES

to the Fully Documented
Special Edition

ABBREVIATIONS USED
IN THE NOTES

References and the abbreviations for official compilations, annuals, reports, and other documents pertain to the state of Wisconsin unless otherwise specified in the citation.

A	Assembly bill
advt.	advertisement
AG	Opinions of the Attorney General
AJ	Assembly (or House) Journal
AJR	Assembly Joint Resolution
AL	Acts and Laws
amdt.	amendment
ann.	annual
ans.	answer
AR	Acts and Resolves
Archives	Archives Division of the State Historical Society of Wisconsin, Madison
ass'n	association
Ass'y	Assembly
bd.	board
ben.	benefit
BFU	Board of Fire Underwriters
C	Report of the Insurance Commissioner
comm.	commission
comm'r	commissioner
CR	Wisconsin Legislative Committee Report

I Wis. Joint Committee of Senate and Assembly on the Affairs of Life Insurance Companies (1906)

II Wis. Senate Committee on the Practicability of Government and State Insurance (1907)

III Wis. Joint Legislative Interim Committee on Pension and Retirement Plans, SJ 102–200 (1947)

IV Wis. Special Committee on Social Insurance (1919)

V Wis. Legislative Interim Committee on Unemployment (1931)

VI Wis. Legislative Fire Insurance Investigating Committee (1913)

VII Wis. Legislative Interim Committee on Fire Insurance (1931)

VIII	Wis. Joint Investigating Committee on State Fire Marshal and Insurance Commissioner (1913)
CT	Capital Times (Madison, Wisconsin)
cty.	county
frat.	fraternal
FUA	Proceedings of the Fire Underwriters' Association of the Northwest
GBPG	Green Bay Press-Gazette (Wisconsin)
Gov.	Governor's Message and Accompanying Documents
Hist. Soc. Library	Library of the State Historical Society of Wisconsin, Madison
hrg.	hearing
ins.	insurance
inv.	investigating
JR	Joint Resolution
jt.	joint
Laws	General Laws
Laws (P. & L.)	Private and Local Laws
legis.	legislative
LRef. Library	Wisconsin Legislative Reference Library, Madison
MDN	Milwaukee Daily News (Wisconsin)
MFP	Milwaukee Free Press (Wisconsin)
MJ	Milwaukee Journal (Wisconsin)
ML	Milwaukee Leader (Wisconsin)
ms.	manuscript
MS	Milwaukee Sentinel (Wisconsin)
mut.	mutual
NAIC	Proceedings of the National Association (or Convention) of Insurance Commissioners
NBFU	National Board of Fire Underwriters
pet.	petition
proc.	proceedings
ref.	reference
Res.	Resolution
S	Senate (or Council) bill
Sec'y	Report of the Secretary of State
sess.	session
SJ	Senate (or Council) Journal
SJR	Senate Joint Resolution
soc.	society
SS	Special Session
ST	Compiled Statutes
Stat.	U.S. Statutes at Large
subst.	substitute
supp.	supplementary
Treas.	Report of the State Treasurer
Wis., in case citations	Wisconsin Reports
WBB	Wisconsin Blue Book (or Legislative Manual)
WSJ	Wisconsin State Journal (Madison)

NOTES

The numbered documentation that follows is in addition to the unnumbered footnotes and citations that appear throughout the text. It is cited in an abbreviated form keyed to both the bibliography and the list of abbreviations used in the documentation. In the text the note numbers usually occur at the end of a paragraph, and the several statements in a note support individual statements in the text paragraph. To help correlate the material in each note with the material in the text a system of slashes has been employed in the notes. The slashes correspond as closely as possible with separate sentences in the text. Supplementary material, relating generally to a whole paragraph follows the last slash in the note and is separated by periods. References supporting supplementary material in the documentation are connected to that material with a dash.

CHAPTER I

1 For data on assets and premiums see <u>Life</u> <u>Ins</u>. <u>Fact</u> <u>Book</u> (Institute of Life Insurance, N.Y.,1957), pp. 51, 61 and <u>Statistical</u> <u>Abstract</u> (U.S. Bureau of the Census), various years./ For Wis. premiums see <u>A</u> <u>Plan</u> <u>Submitted</u> <u>to</u> <u>the</u> <u>Emergency</u> <u>Bd</u>., June 14, 1956. [A publication of the Wis. Ins. Dep't, on file in Dep't of Budgets and Accounts.]

CHAPTER II

1 E.g., see Milwaukee <u>Courier</u> (Wis.) advt. of Dr. McNaughton's Vegetable Cathartic Pills, 4-16-1845./ For the original sources on the bank, see Laws 1838-39, 36; AJ 97, 128, 135, 137 (2d Legis. Ass'y, 2d Sess. 1839); AJ 77, 100-02 (2d Legis. Ass'y, 3d Sess. 1839); SJ 61, 66, Appendix 542-45 (1841); SJ 360-61 (1842); AJ 83-84, 318-19, Appendix 14-25, 49-52, 105-34 (1844); SJ 106-08 (1845); AJ 40, 97, 169, 321-24 (1846). For a similar but abortive incident with the Mississippi Marine and Fire Ins. Co., see AJ 33, 37, 238, Appendix 417-43 (1845); Kuehnl 137-42. It happened in Missouri, too.—Primm 41-42, 49. See id. passim for the Missouri attitude toward banks in the Jacksonian period./ S. Buck (1913) 53 tells of the Granger attitude./ AG 1910, 478 thought the word "bankers" did not mislead insurance buyers.

2 Kent 3:203-306 dealt with marine insurance, with one page (at 241) devoted to life, and no space to any other line./ Zartman & Price 14-

38 gives a brief history of American marine insurance./ M. James (1942) 132 tells of one company's reluctance to insure steamboats on the inland waterways; MS advt. 12-18-1838 of Joshua Hathaway as agent of Hudson Fire Ins. Co.; Milwaukee <u>Advertiser</u> (Wis.), advt. 1-28-1837 of L. J. Higby Co. as agent for the "Insured Transportation Line on the Erie Canal...," reproduced in Still 62./ E.g., Laws (P. & L.) 1856, 121.

3   Laws (P. & L.) 1857, 118; Laws (P. & L.) 1866, 129.

4   Huebner (1931)./ James (1942) 95-109 tells of the development of fire insurance in a company originally chartered for a marine business.

5   Laws 1838-39, 36 (early Wis. charter)./ For premiums cf. Sec'y 1862, Appendix 945-56 with 1869, Appendix 102-200.

6   For Wis. societies see, e.g., Koss 197-98. Cf. Mich. Laws 1838, p. 242, for charter of Detroit House Carpenters' and Joiners' Mut. Ben. Soc./ The Wisconsin legislature chartered almost 60 societies in the 1860's.

7   Laws (P. & L.) 1853, 260; Laws (P. & L.) 1853, 22, 107; Laws (P. & L.) 1865, 57, 446; Laws (P. & L.) 1866, 399; Laws (P. & L.) 1869, 359./ Sec'y 1867, 33; 1868, 35; 1869, 25; 1869, 199.

8   Laws 1876, 196; 1885, 443; 1887, 352; 1891, 299./ Laws 1905, 55; S 309 (1895)./ Laws 1897, 277; Sullivan 1:240-43./ Laws 1899, 65.

9   C 1896, 1:921; 2:838.

10 Laws 1909, 460, § 1897./ Laws 1911, 275./ Laws 1911, 50 (workmen's comp.)./ Laws 1917, 444./ Laws 1919, 655./ Laws 1921, 469./ Laws 1947, 189 (extended to town mutuals by 1955, 605)./ AG 1956, 250./ Laws 1957, 417./ <u>Business</u> <u>Week</u> 11-9-57; C 1958, 19-20. See also Laws 1959, 353.

11 S 105 (1931)./ SJ 1774, 1817 (1931). Not everyone agreed; Comm'r Johnson (1926a) 6-7 thought new forms should be specifically authorized if there were a need for them.

12 Laws 1885, 443./ Laws 1885, 449./ Laws 1895, 219./ Laws 1897, 335; 349; 1905, 180; 1911, 190; 1913, 442; 1915, 104, 442; 1919, 655, § 1966-33j; 1939, 317; and see AG 1920, 581./ Laws 1905, 425 (premium on bond for Commr).

13 C 1919, <u>liv</u>; NAIC 1918, 27-30; Letter to Prof. John R. Commons from Chief of L Ref. Library./ Two bills to authorize group life for single employer groups, and one to forbid it, were unsuccessfully introduced in 1917.—A 136, 141, S 569 (1917).

14 WSJ 9-4-1925. MJ 9-27-1926.

15 AF of L, Committee on Insurance (1925); Woll & Benson./ In LRef. Library see Robbins, A Memo. to Comm'r to support request that union group life insurance be permitted, Nov. 25, 1927. See also MS, editorial 10-28-1929; and see MS 10-26-1929, where Milwaukee County supervisors frankly urged group health and life insurance as a cheaper substitute for a pension plan. That this was a real motivation of management, see Outerbridge.

16 Witte, Part II./ Witte, Part I.

17 Laws 1929, 317./ N.Y. Laws 1929, 292./ Laws 1931, 151 and CT 3-19-1931; Laws 1937, 41, 217; 1939, 246./ Laws 1939, 44; 1943, 119; 1945, 346 (ordinary group accident and health might be written only for groups of twenty-five or more)./ S 542 (1949).

18 Laws 1949, 458./ S 793 (1951).

19 S 353 (1945); A 687 (1949); the 1945 bill passed by a large majority

but only after reluctance shown by six roll-call votes, some close.—
SJ 1013, 1086-88 (1945); SJ 1359-60, 1378 (1945)./ S 431 (1955).

20 For support see MJ 6-2-1955; Letter to Assemblyman Nestinger
from Richard Rice, a lobbyist, in LRef. Library; Sheboygan Press
(Wis.), 6-2-1955. For opposition see ibid.; Memorandum in opposition to 431S, in LRef. Library; Letter from Comm'r Lange to
Actuary Wolberg, instructing him to appear against the bill, May 26,
1955, in LRef. Library.

21 SJ 1127, AJ 1671 (1955)./ AG 1958, 16./ AG 1958, 184; MJ 7-30-58./
See also AG 1958, 271, 317, 326 for three additional rulings on the
scope of group insurance.

22 A 673 (1889). Laws 1889, 202 created a pension for widows, children,
and dependent widowed mothers of firemen and policemen killed on
duty; its purpose was more akin to workmen's compensation. Laws
1891, 287 (fire and police); Laws 1911, 323 (teachers)./ S 51 (1913);
S 37 (1915).

23 S 105, 570, A 335 (1919) were vetoed on actuarial grounds.—AJ 1944-
45, SJ 1466-69 (1919). AJ 189-241, 1159-79 (1921) was the report of an
investigating committee on actuarial soundness; it may have produced Laws 1921, 459. SJ 741 (1929) gives a brief history of the
teachers' pension fund. For pension laws commissions, see, e.g.,
Laws 1919, 514; 1921, 506. See also CR III./ Laws 1947, 376 created
the survey committee.

24 AJR 5 (1905); AJ 149 (1905)./ AJR 19 (1905) (Memorial to Congress).

25 S 189, S 486, AJR 52, (1909)./ Laws 1911, 50./ Laws 1913, 599./ In AJ
38-39 (1921) and AJ 37 (1923) the Governor urged more adequate
sanctions against nonconforming employers.

26 Laws 1923, 328./ Laws 1919, 680. N.Y. Laws 1916, 622 created the
first state disabled employees fund.—Ass'n of Casualty & Surety
Companies,...., p. 114.

27 A 669, S 279 (1913)./ S 503 (1913) and Laws 1913, JR 31./ SJ 1285-87
(1913).

28 Laws 1917, JR 24./ The health insurance bills were A 610, S 464,
(1917); S 307 (1919); S 456 (1921). See Legislative Journals for intro-
ducers, and WBB for their politics.

29 CR IV./ AG 1918, 502.

30 AJ 251 (1919)./ SJR 67 (1919), SJ 1205, AJ 1648 (1919).

31 S 134, A 533 (1933)./ AJ 1127, SJ 1489 (1933). WBB gives political
affiliation./ A 807, AJ 1793 (1939); A 586 (1941); A 327, AJ 1106 (1943);
S 412 (1945). But see Laws 1935, 350; 1945, 494.

32 An unemployment insurance law was passed in Austria in 1920.—
National ... Board, p. 61. A bill was introduced in Massachusetts in
1916, but was not pushed.—Hoar 1. S 122 (1921)./ SJ 980, 1021 (1921)./
S 53, SJ 1388 (1923)./ S 103, SJ 1147 (1925); A 296; AJ 752 (1927); A
276, AJ 1519 (1929)./ A 225, 259, 940 (1931); Laws 1931, JR 113; CR V;
AJ 63 (1931-32SS). See also Hoar 3.

33 CR V, 33-44, 54; Commons.

34 CR V, 64-69.

35 Laws 1931-32SS, 20./ AJ 205-06(1931-32SS)./ Laws 1931-32SS, JR 6./
AJ 27-28 (1933); Laws 1933, 186./ The flexible formula was preferred to fixed periods, as in S 13 (1933) (two years); S 204 (1933)
(four years). See Brandeis for explanation of the Wisconsin-type
law.

36 A 754 (1915)./ Laws 1915, 546./ AG 1921, 528, 545, 753 ruled that any
possibility of defeasance violated the jitney law, thus converting the
contract from one indemnifying the policyholder against loss to one
insuring him against liability./ Laws 1927, 395./ Laws 1929, 239,
328; 1937, 290; 1939, 290./ A 748 (1939); A 828 (1941)./ Laws 1945,
299./ For increases see Laws 1949, 311; 1955, 316.

37 Rollins; Carman. Cf. Ballantine./ S 185 (1927); S 67 (1929); S 31
(1931)./ MJ 8-1-1926; WSJ 7-27-1930; Wisconsin News (Milwaukee)
12-10-1930./ SJ 1579 (1929)./ For discussion of automobile compensation insurance by its leading advocate, see Marx. See also "Compensation...Symposium" (1932).

38 William Mearkle, "Compulsory Automobile Insurance," a radio address, Nov. 20, 1924, in LRef. Library./ Mass. Acts 1925, 346, as
amended by 1926, 368; N. Y. Laws 1956, 655.

39 A 274, S 225 (1921)./ A 206, S 256 (1923); A 289, S 82, 182 (1925); A
121, 136, 623, S 112 (1927); A 456 (1929); A 169, 275, S 171 (1931); S 212
(1933); A 383, S 176 (1935); A 246 (1937); A 43 (1939); A 322, 423, 723
(1941); A 216; S 271 (1943); A 55 (1945); A 400, S 328, 343 (1951); A 435,
596 (1955). See also Laws 1929, JR 63 (memorial to Congress urging compulsory insurance on cars crossing state lines into states
having compulsory insurance); AJR 26, SJR 78 (1931) (calling for
popular referendum on compulsory insurance); "Around the Statehouse," in WSJ 7-3-1931./ Laws 1933, JR 97 created the committee./
SJ 211, 1830-36 (1935); and see Hrgs. of Committee, in LRef. Library./ N. Y. Laws 1956, 655./ MJ 10-21-56; GBPG 11-1-56./ A 4
(1959); MJ 2-11-59; MJ, editorial 2-16-59; AJ (Mar. 25, 1959).

40 S 282 (1935); S 402 (1937)./ A 489 (1939).

41 S 344 (1927); Laws 1931, 478./ Laws, 1935, 489 required suspension
of license for a judgment unsatisfied up to the limits of the act. For
discussion of responsibility acts, see Feinsinger./ Laws 1945, 375./
CT 10-11-1945; 10-12-1945./ Laws 1953, 339 raised the required
policy limits.

42 A 729 (1931)./ Laws 1951, 697./ Laws 1953, 332./ SJR 113 (1955)./
GBPG 3-2-1951; Coöperative Builder (Superior, Wis.), editorial 12-
13-1951. For general treatment, see "Financial Protection...;" symposium (1936) and Committee to Study Compensation...(1932). For
provocative suggested solutions of the automobile problem see
Ehrenzweig (1955) and Green.

43 AG 1924, 387, 415; see also 1927, 345 and 1929, 559./ Laws 1925, 319./
Laws 1929, 77, restrictively interpreted by Pohland v. City, 251 Wis.
20 (1947). The 1929 statute was extended by Laws 1955, 493, among
others./ A 655, 757 (1931); A 740 (1935); Laws 1935, 124; 1937, 207;
1943, 80; 1953, 267; and see AG 1946, 265./ AG 1932, 982./ Laws 1937,
290; 1939, 290.

44 Laws 1949, 311./ A 272 (1953)./ See also Laws 1951, 459 (passengers
on aviation education flights); 1953, 33 (state-owned aircraft). On
sovereign immunity see also "Governmental Tort...," symposium
(1942).

45 Laws 1931, 242; CT, editorial 4-29-1935.

46 Laws 1919, JR 41; S 165 (1919)./ SJR 13 (1931). See also Laws 1943,
248.

47 Laws 1925, 382; 1955, 170 (AG 1952, 225 had informed the State Athletic Comm. it could not require insurance); Laws 1929, 252./ A 520

(1937); S 516 (1939).

48 Laws 1913, 188; 1935, 159; 1943, 144; and see AG 1925, 99.

49 Laws 1929, 307 (passed to overcome AG 1929, 157); Laws 1947,603./ Laws 1933, 231./ Laws 1949, 287; SJ 387 (1949); Laws 1951, 406; <u>Wis.</u> <u>Medical</u> <u>Journal</u>, Oct. 1941; Laws 1955, 407; 1929, 372; 1949, 120; but see AG 1941, 222; 1947, 28./ SJ 29 (1957); Laws 1957 , 512; A 276 (1959); WSJ 10–4–58./ Laws 1959, 211./Laws 1947, 580; and Laws 1959, 536./ Laws 1957, 574./ See, e.g., AG 1925, 593; 1931, 494; 1942, 215; 1953, 225.

50 Laws 1862, 182, § 1./ Laws 1870, 59, § 19./ ST 1878, § 2347./ Laws 1931, 425./ Laws 1933, 320./ See also Kimball (1957) 528.

51 Laws 1862, 182, broadened by 1931, 425./ Laws 1895, 175, § 11; con-solidated with other exemptions in ST 1898, § 2982; Laws 1891, 287 , § 15, extended by 1907, 671, § 925–52s./ Laws 1933, 299./ Governor LaFollette vetoed S 230 (1935), an extension of the poor relief ex-emption, on the ground that it would benefit insurance companies rather than persons on relief.—SJ 1466–67 (1935).

52 Laws 1911, 658, § 1087 m–4(j) (income); Laws 1939, 168, 405 (inheri-tance). Will of Allis, 174 Wis. 527 (1921) and Estate of Siljan, 233 Wis. 54 (1939) frustrated attempts to use insurance to evade inheri-tance taxation./ 39 Geo. III, c. 13 (1798) (the English statute)./ See also Olin (1907a) 4; A 442 (1957) and A 11 (1959) sought to increase the life insurance exemption for inheritance tax.

53 19 Geo. II, c. 37 (1746)./ 14 Geo. III, c. 48 (1774)./ Refusal of aid to assignees did not prevent sale of policies to persons without insura-ble interest.—Farren 25.

54 See, e.g., Hurd v. Doty, 86 Wis. 1, 9 (1893); see, e.g., Reynolds 40.

55 Sadlers v. Badcock, 2 Atk. 554 (1743).

56 Albert v. Spencer, 275 Wis. 127 (1957); 3 Wis. 2d 273 (1958).

57 See "Child Insurance in the United States," in 22 <u>Public</u> <u>Opinion</u> (June 20, 1897), reporting a strong prejudice against juvenile insur-ance./ S 294 (1901); S 246 (1903); S 49 (1905); A 483 (1909); but cf. C 1904, 2:25–26, where Comm'r Host approved industrial insurance for children, for it ensured decent burial and taught thrift; and see article by Host in MFP 3–5–1905; Laws 1917, 365; 1925, 73; 1931, 176.

58 E.g., Laws 1887, 1, § 12./ Patterson v. Co., 100 Wis. 118 (1898); Ritter v. Co., 169 U.S. 139 (1898)./ A 101 (1903) would have forbidden exclusion of insane suicide. S 356 (1913) would have invalidated in-surance on property used for prostitution for over thirty days; and see Laws 1913, 637, § 3, concerning validity in the event of war with the foreign insurer's country.

59 AG 1929, 124./ Gelo v. Co., 132 Wis. 575 (1907); and see Wendlandt v. Co., 222 Wis. 204 (1936) (surety bond invalid because of illegality of guaranteed contract).

CHAPTER III, Section 1

1 Hunt 1:140; Davis 95; Livermore 253; Kent 3:206.

2 Wright & Fayle 35–42, 64–65.

3 Laws 1895, 325. But see AG 1908, 486, ruling that Dowell Brothers of Springfield, Illinois, doing business as livestock insurers in partnership form, were subject to the insurance laws.

4 Laws 1901, 249; S 459 (1907); S 396 (1909)./ Laws 1911, 277./ AJ 20 (1912SS); Laws 1912SS, 3, amended by 1913, 210.

5 ST 1955, § 201.33./ C 1955, 8.

6 Laws 1909, 63, and 460, § 1(4) gave perpetual life to insurance companies lacking it./ See also Farren 29, 59—60 for additional disadvantages of unincorporated associations.

7 Davis 2:27. Evans 21. Handlin (1947) 137./ Kuehnl 348, 352, 558—831 for the Wisconsin incorporations.

8 Failure of the banking activities of the Ohio Life Insurance and Trust Company is said to have started the panic of 1857.—Van Metre 353./ Laws 1838—39, 36.

9 E.g.Laws (P. &L.) 1856, 121; Laws (P. &L.) 1854, 252.

10 AG 1921, 432; S 430 (1923), vetoed at SJ 1529—32 (1923); (restrictions) AG 1932, 294, 999; 1937, 463, 603; A 533 (1935), vetoed at AJ 3107—08 (1935); but see Laws 1953, 56./ Laws 1955, 433 (title insurance and abstracting)./ See also AG 1912, 484 (travel agency doing an insurance business); MJ 7-7-1953 (automobile insurance firm set up own repair shop).

11 Laws 1901, 232./ Laws 1909, 130 authorized town mutual reinsurance companies.

12 At least one such agency was operating in Wisconsin in the 1870's — Northrup v. Co., 48 Wis. 420, 422 (1880)./ Laws 1891, 195, § 4, par. 5; 1895, 387, § 3, par. 5; FUA 1897, 135./ Laws 1927, 125.

13 E.g., Laws 1837-38, 13./ E.g., N.Y. Laws 1836, 41./ Cf. incorporators of Milwaukee Mutual, Laws 1837-38, 13,with founders of the Milwaukee hook and ladder company, History of Milwaukee, Wis.,., p. 347./ E.g., Laws 1851, 395 authorized the Milwaukee Mutual to issue nonassessable policies and Laws (P.&L.) 1858, 142 authorized the Merchants' Mutual to convert to the stock form./ Sometimes stock company charters contemplated organization as mutuals if not enough investors could be found.—See, e.g., Laws (P.&L.) 1865, 381.

14 Laws 1836-38, p. 152./ J. Buck 2:246; Racine Advocate (Wis.), advt. 8-26-1845./ Laws 1851, 395; 1868, 402./ SJ 361 (1851).

15 E.g., Laws 1853, 107; 1853, 111; 1854, 278./ Laws 1868, 363./ Laws 1878, 255; 1889, 524; 1895, 64; 1903, 128; 1903, 247; 1905, 373; 1909, 4; 1909, 52. These acts resembled the town mutual law. In New England, factory mutuals date from 1835 and were among the most successful of companies, emphasizing fire prevention.—Mehr & Cammack 39./ Unsuccessful bills were A 294, S 211 (1899); A 594, S 333 (1905); A 461, S 312 (1907); S 268 (1909)./ Laws 1889, 346./ Church Co. v. Cheek, 77 Wis. 284 (1890); Laws 1891, 268./ Laws 1895, 184; 1903, 205./ S 26 (1881) was an earlier attempt to create a church insurance company.

16 Laws 1897, 316; 1899, 167./ Laws 1899, 65./ Laws 1909, 460, § 1897a (1); 1911, 275, § 2.

17 Valgren 11—22 gives a brief history of farmers' mutuals./ Laws 1859, 46, patterned after N.Y. Laws 1857, 739./ See, e.g.,Memorials 11, 17, 81, 379, AJ Index 70—79 (1872)./ Laws 1872, 103./ Laws 1870, 2; ST 1871, LXXII, §§ 37-53.

18 Scarcity of liquid capital was a pervasive influence in the life of the Grange.—See,e.g., S. Buck (1913) 276./ S. Buck (1913) 53.

19 C 1882, 57-60./ C 1884, 58-61; 1886, 54-57; 1888, 66-70./ C 1955, 8.

20 Laws 1859, 46, § 10./ Laws 1860, 67; 1875, 240; 1875, 304./ Laws
    1876, 344, § 1; ST 1878, § 1927./ E.g., A 193 (1874); A 38, 384 (1875).
21 Laws 1881, 260./ Laws 1885, 421; 1889, 38; 1907, 439./ Laws 1927,
    281./ Laws 1939, 340; 1943, 214./ Laws 1945, 288./ A 382 (1959)./
    There were many unsuccessful bills, too. E.g., see S 463 (1935)
    (to raise the limit to sixty towns).
22 Laws 1947, 346; S 401 (1949)./ CT 4-1-1949; and see AG 1935, 255./
    See also Laws 1929, 440 (registered town mutuals).
23 ST 1898, § 1931; Laws 1913, 242. The town mutuals were actually
    insuring automobiles.—C 1919, xi./ Laws 1929, 418./ Laws 1957, 335;
    Letter to Assemblyman Toepel from President of LaCross Scandi-
    nevian Mutual Ins. Co., dated 4-29-57, opposing the bill, in LRef.
    Library./ The commercial mutuals did not always oppose extension
    of town mutual authority.—Cf. CT 6-1-1951 with GBPG 6-25-1953.
24 C 1914, 3:xi-xvi./ Laws 1909, 130; Wisconsin Town Reinsurance Co.
    v. Calumet Co., 224 Wis. 109, 115 (1937); and see Appellant's Brief
    5.
25 Laws 1887, 305. A 655 (1907) would have created wind companies
    on a similar basis./ A 95 (1889); A 334, 655 (1891)./ Laws 1895, 12./
    S 112 (1901); Laws 1901, 69; 1903, 93.
26 C 1896, 2:xiii; 1898, 3:vi-xxviii (Fricke); 1904, 3:vii (Host)./ Laws
    1909, 460; C 1916, xvi./ Ins. Post Pub. Co., Wis. Mut. Fire Failures
    (1909), a propaganda sheet in LRef. Library.
27 C 1913, 2:65-72, esp. at 66; Wilhelm, "The Story of Reciprocal Fire
    Ins.," in World's Work (N.Y.) June 1931./ Laws 1893, 230 (miscalled
    "Lloyd's"). S 133 (1895) sought to repeal the 1893 law./ Laws 1913,
    210; ST 1955, § 201.39. S 103 (1931) was an effort to repeal the 1913
    law. A 392 (1937); S 105 (1941); S 353 (1943) were all efforts to sub-
    ject inter-insurers to all insurance laws.
28 E.g., Laws (P. &L.) 1866, 65./ E.g., the Madison Relief Ass'n ex-
    isted prior to incorporation by Laws (P. &L.) 1869, 315.—Dietrich
    v. Ass'n, 45 Wis. 79, 80n (1878)./ Laws 1872, 166 made members of
    paid fire departments into firemen's relief associations, for aid to
    sick and disabled members and their families. Laws 1889, 168 ex-
    tended the 1872 act to police forces.
29 Laws 1879, 204 was the initial exemption statute; subsequent laws
    merely extended the list./ Laws 1882, 281/ ST 1898, § 1771 was the
    general incorporation provision./ There were many subtle prob-
    lems related to the exemption of benefit societies from legal con-
    trol. For some of them, see Kimball (1958) 79-80. See also Laws
    1959, 462.
30 S 104 (1872) (proposal contained only in title); S 324 (1899)./ Cf.
    Laws (P. &L.) 1869, 343 with Laws (P. &L.) 1869, 43, as amended
    by, e.g., Laws 1887, 1, for contrast in complexity.
31 Callahan v. Order, 169 Wis. 43 (1919); and see AG 1915, 992./
    Dietrich v. Ass'n, 45 Wis. 79 (1878) (policy loans). Chief Justice
    Ryan, dissenting vigorously, would recognize the investment
    function of such policies.—Id., 84. But see Laws 1887, 1, § 14 and
    1895, 175, § 3.
32 Laws 1945, 517.
33 C 1873, 218-222; 1874, 89-90. See also C 1871, 146-48; 1870, 65.
34 C 1906, 2:40./ C 1878, 92./ A 231 (1887); S 92, 298 (1889); Laws
    1891, 418./ See C 1895, 2: xiv-xvi and 1897, 2:xii for Comm'r

Fricke's criticism of assessment companies. Laws 1907, 447./ C 1915, 2:xi.

35 Laws 1899, 270; Laws 1907, 121.

36 As early as 1829, New York had a short-lived bank guaranty plan.— N.Y. Laws 1829, 94. This was a kind of government insurance.— Ass'n of Casualty & Surety Companies,..., p.69, n.1.

37 Laws 1872, 122./ AJ 234 (1874)./ On the Grange, see S. Buck (1913). For some industry views about the ultimate result of regulation see FUA 1877, 125; 1891, 151.

38 A 105 (1881)./ S 75 (1893); A 486 (1895).

39 SJR 16 (1907).—This was a German system./ Laws 1911, JR 56; 1913, JR 12. Laws 1913, JR 35 would have permitted the state to issue annuities, too./Laws 1913, 770 provided for submission to the people; for results see Laws 1915, pp. 1027–28. Accompanying reform amendments for iniative, referendum, and home rule also failed.— Ibid./ For opposition to the amendment, see MDN 10-10-1914; MS 10-16-1914; Madison Democrat (Wis.) 10-18-1914; MFP, editorial 10-23-1914; ML 10-27-1914; Madison Democrat (Wis.) 11-3-1914./ The Att'y Gen. was not excited about the Constitutional issue raised by state insurance.—AG 1915, 287, 291; 1917, 188; 1915, 1010, 1013; 1927, 264.

40 AJR 39 (1913)./ AJ 926, SJ 768 (1913).

41 ST 1849, ch. 10, § 27(4). ST 1878, ch. 40, § 892(8); ST 1898, ch. 27, § 441(a). Laws 1893, 292, § 35 required Wisconsin Nat'l Guard commanders to insure state property.

42 AJ 27 (1899)./ S 68 (1901)./ Laws 1903, 68. The bill passed the Assembly unanimously and suffered but a single dissent in the Senate. —AJ 632, SJ 471 (1903). S. Carolina Laws 1900, 222 preceded Wisconsin with a sinking fund on insurance principles.—Ass'n of Casualty & Surety Companies,..., p. 72.

43 AJ 27–29 (1915); AJ 32–34 (1917)./ AG 1908, 469./ A 672, AJ 1482, SJ 1192 (1915); A 65, AJ 460, SJ 981 (1917); A 160, AJ 872 (1917).

44 Laws 1911, 603./ For premium rates, see Laws 1903, 68; 1917, 482; 1929, 117; 1947, 524; C 1958, 59./ CT 9-23-1924./ See Sheboygan Press (Wis.) 7-24-1958; 8-5-1958 for the story of a bitter fight in a city Common Council over the question whether to insure in the state fund.

45 A 677 (1923); A 24, 389, S 109, 142 (1927); A 852 (1939); A 505 (1941)./ Laws 1937, 158./ A 669 (1933); A 68 (1939); A 376 (1953); A 464 (1959); GBPG 12-9-1952./ A 877, AJ 2880 (1935)./ Laws 1947, 524 (revision)./ Kimball (1958) 93, n. 46 gives journal references for voting on all the above bills. See also AG 1957, 107.

46 Laws 1905SS, JR 1; Laws 1905SS, 9.

47 CR II.

48 CR II, Minority Rep.

49 S 258, A 538, AJR 10 (1907)./ C 1911, 2:26; Laws 1911, 577./ Evening Wisconsin (Milwaukee) 5-22-1911.

50 The lack of solicitation is suggested by Comm'r Ekern in C 1911, 2: 24, 27.

51 A 186 (1913); A 152, (1919); A 43 (1921); A 358 (1927); A 856 (1939); A 244, AJ 893 (1949); A 355, AJ 584 (1951)./ A 152, AJ 1146, SJ 1077, AJ 1832-33 (veto), 1869 (1919)./ AJ 78–79 (1919) (Governor recommends repeal); A 110 (1919) (repealer)./ AJ 524 (1919); CT 3-13-1919./

For some vigorous expressions in favor of the fund, see CT 11-20-1945; ML 12-15-1926; CT, editorial 5-5-1949. See also Laws 1957, 172.

52 A 623, S 112, 185 (1927)./ S 67 (1929); S 31 (1931); A 246 (1937); S 566 (1949)./ S 321, SJ 1428 (1935); S 114, SJ 672 (1937); and cf. A 322, 423 (1941) where compulsory insurance was proposed without a state fund./ SJR 37, AJR 43 (1947); AJ 716, 791 (1947); A 604, AJ 930 (1949).

53 McCahan 8-16, and passim./ S 189 (1909); A 669 (1913); A 199, S 121 (1927); A 675 (1937)./ ST 1955, §§ 102.49, 102.59.

54 Business Week 11-9-1957 (mortgage insurance)./ A 203, AJ 1366 (1927); A 214, AJ 915 (1929)./ A 28, AJ 2720 (1931)./ Four states created such funds between 1915 and 1935, including the Dakotas, which were the pioneers.—Ass'n of Casualty & Surety Companies, ...,p.81.

55 A 538, S 258, AJR 10 (1907)./ V. Wrabetz, "A Bill to Create Sections 1973 to 1973-35 Inclusive of the Statutes Relating to State Insurance ...," May 3, 1911, in LRef. Library; S 503, SJ 1110, 1285-87 (veto), AJ 1549, 1631 (1913); Laws 1913, JR 31./ A 610, S 464 (1917)./ S 307 (1919); S 456 (1921); A 533, S 134 (1933)./ A 807 (1939); A 586 (1941); A 327 (1943); S 412 (1945).

56 Laws 1935, 350./ Laws 1939, 118, amended by Laws 1945, 553./ E.g., A 245 (1941); A 333 (1943).

57 See, e.g., Laws 1907, 671; S 62 (1925). The Wisconsin development paralleled that in other states.—Ass'n of Casualty & Surety Companies, ...,p.83./ Laws 1931-32SS, JR 6.

58 McCahan 196. N.Y. Laws 1829, 94 created a short-lived deposit guaranty fund.—Ass'n of Casualty & Surety Companies, ...,p. 69,n.1./ Id., p. 78; S 470 (1909). Laws 1911, 275 authorized deposit insurance by private companies./ Laws 1925, 449; Laws 1931-32SS, 1.

59 48 Stat. 162, 168 (1933); Laws 1933, 484; AJ 2726-28 (1933).

60 S 414 (1858), ms. bill in Archives. The ms. originally designated Plattsburgh as the company's location; this was corrected to "Janesville."/ S 129 (1856), ms. bill in Archives.

61 Bolles 828./ See, e.g., N.Y. Laws 1836,131./ Mass. Laws 1826, 141./ Laws 1837-38, 13./ Cf. Laws 1837-38,29 with N.Y. Laws 1816, 52./ Laws 1838-39, 36 (Wis. Marine & Fire Ins. Co.).

62 Cf. Laws 1847, 139 with N.Y. Laws 1841, 252.

63 Laws 1851, 394 (Madison); 1852, 43; 1852, 416; Laws (P.&L.) 1868, 363./ Laws (P.&L.) 1867, 309 (Vernon); for the nature of the operations, see various reports of the Sec'y of State and the Ins. Comm'r.

64 Cf. Laws (P.&L.)1857, 129 with N.Y. Laws 1842, 246; Williamson & Smalley 8./ Laws (P.&L.) 1859, 240; Laws (P.&L.) 1869, 122; Laws (P.&L.) 1869, 398.

65 Cf. Laws 1850, 232 with N.Y. Laws 1849, 308./ Cf. Laws 1852, 257 with N.Y Laws 1846,178./ Cf. Laws 1859, 46 with N.Y. Laws 1857, 739.

66 Cf. S 129 (1856) and Laws 1870, 56 with N.Y. Laws 1853, 466./ N.Y. Laws 1853, 466, as amended by N.Y. Laws 1854, 369; 1861, 92; 1863,242; 1865, 199; 1867, 91, and cf. ms. of A 399 (1870), esp. §§ 21, 24, in Archives, with Ill. Laws 1869, p. 127. Careful textual comparison makes it almost certain that Illinois was the immediate source of Laws 1870, 56./ Ms. of A 426 (1870)(life ins.), in Archives, was a much modified version of Ill. Laws 1869, p. 142; the printed Illinois act was the basis of the ms. This became Laws 1870, 59; cf. with N.Y. Laws 1853, 463.

67 Catalogue of Wis. State Library (1852)./ Raney 138 (population)./

E.g., cf. Laws 1925, 372 with N.Y. Laws 1917, 524, as amended by N.Y. Laws 1919, 182; 1920, 563, § 10; 1923, 434; 1924, 639./ E.g., Laws 1951, 614 was a Commissioners' act.

CHAPTER III, Section 2

1 See, e.g., AJ 11–12 (1839) (Governor's message)./ Laws 1838–39, 36.
2 S 14, 19 (1846); AJ 260 (1846).
3 Laws 1850, 232./ Kuehnl 348, 352, 558–831.
4 A 116, S 52 (1850); S 234 (1851)./ AJ 829 (1858) (veto of A 18); sustained at AJ 1092./ A 103, 165, 276, 281, 374, 574, 589, S 219, 225, 414 (1858)./ Laws 1859, 240; Laws 1860, 90, 92.
5 Nine special charters were passed in 1865, eight in 1866, six in 1867, three in 1868, eight in 1869, seven in 1870, and two in 1871.—Kuehnl 558–831; the unsuccessful bill was S 105 (1867); A 220 (1870); A 668, 677, and S 185 (1871) were the unsuccessful bills just prior to the end of special chartering.
6 Laws 1893, 230; 1895, 325.
7 Early charters prohibiting trading were Mass. Acts. & Laws Jan. 1799, 16; N.Y. Laws 1798, 41. Laws 1854, 327 was a Wisconsin charter forbidding trade; cf. Laws 1850, 271. For general acts forbidding trading, see Laws 1870, 56, § 5; 1897, 277, § 18./ ST 1955, § 201.24(1)./ Some charters forbade specified activities such as stock and bond dealings./ See, e.g., N.Y. Laws 1798, 41. An antibanking provision was frequent and persistent, reflecting the special violence of the policy as applied to banks.—E.g., Laws 1850, 271, § 11.
8 Laws 1837–38, 13 and Laws 1840–41, p. 126 suggest logrolling, in the combination in each of charters for different parts of the state./ Laws 1838–39, 36, § 10 (added during passage); AJ 135, 137 (2d Legis. Ass'y, 2d Sess. 1839).
9 A 17, SJ 77, 107, 152 (1857)./ Cf. Laws (P. & L.) 1854, 289 with Laws 1851, 394.
10 Laws 1915, 30; AJ 424, SJ 358 (1915)./ Laws 1945, 101/ Laws 1947, 470.
11 Luthe v. Co., 55 Wis. 543 (1882), followed by Batzel v. Co., 220 Wis. 581 (1936); Bank v. Co., 216 Wis. 513 (1934) (mortgage case)./ Gilman v. Druse, 111 Wis. 400 (1901) (hail co.).
12 N.Y. Laws 1798, 41./ Mass. Acts, May 1803, 41./ See, e.g., Mass. Laws Jan. 1804, 1./ E.g., Pa. Laws 1808, 55; Va. Laws 1834–35, 149.
13 E.g., Laws 1883, 304 increased Laws (P. & L.) 1869, 467 from $25,000 to $50,000./ See, e.g., Laws (P. & L.) 1857, 129 § 3 (Northwestern Mutual charter —N.Y. pattern)./ Laws 1850, 232, §§ 8,9; 1870, 56, §9./ Laws 1837–38, 13, § 8. See also Laws (P. & L.) 1855, 261, § 8 (escheat provision, 10 years).
14 Smalley 4–51; Laws 1885, 199. But cf. A 222 (1885).
15 Laws 1859, 46, § 11./ See, e.g., A 77 (1883); A 92 (1899); A 494 (1909)./ Pet. A 44 (1885)./ Laws 1911, 165./ Laws 1929, 440.
16 AG 1934, 126.
17 Laws 1917, 201./ Laws 1921, 170.
18 Laws 1887, 305, § 2; A 709 (1887)./ S 58 (1889); Laws 1891, 296, § 2./ E.g., Laws 1895, 64, § 6 (retail lumber dealers', one vote per $1,000 of insurance); Laws 1905, 373, § 7 (school district, same)./

Laws 1909, 460, § 1897c.
19 Laws 1878, 277, § 4./ See, e.g., A 46 (1887); Laws 1895, 275; 1901,
    81./ Proposed changes were A 599, S 451 (1907); A 494, S 33 (1909);
    A 213 (1915)./ Laws 1959, 128./ For other mutuals, see Laws 1929,
    440; 1887, 305, § 2; 1909, 459; 1905, 55, § 4.
20 Laws 1859, 46, § 12./ Laws 1883, 168.
21 E.g., C 1903, 2:xvii urged elimination of proxy voting. Comm'r Host
    said in 1906 that it had been urged even as early as 1897.—C 1906,
    2:60, 67.
22 Laws 1907, 389.
23 Laws 1907, 667; this was Bill No. 2 of the 1906 life ins. investigating
    committee./ CR I, 238. Cf. S 161, 1907, the bill of the Committee of
    Fifteen. The latter was an interstate committee resulting from a
    conference of Governors, Attorneys General, and Insurance Com-
    misioners, called at the instance of President Roosevelt as a result
    of the Armstrong investigation disclosures.—Buley 1:264-68./ Laws
    1925, 326./ Laws 1957, 95 increased the number of policyholders re-
    quired for nominations to 500 for big companies. It was requested
    by the Northwestern Mutual, SJ 273 (1957).
24 Laws 1907, 667./ Bushnell (1907a). The provisions for contested
    elections were not much used, but by their very existence might
    curb the worst excesses of management./ See AG 1941, 120 (election
    invalid for failure to comply precisely with filing requirement).
25 Williamson & Smalley 57-63./ MDN 7-18-1906.
26 Laws 1943, 121.
27 Laws 1917, 599; revised by 1955, 537.

CHAPTER III, Section 3

1   Vance 1-2, Richards 2.
2   N. Y. Laws 1798, 41./ And see Livermore 215, 236; Davis 2:317.
3   E.g., Laws (P. &L.) 1866, 524 ($20,000); Laws (P. &L.) 1866, 129 ($1
    million to $2 million); Laws (P. &L.) 1853, 111 ($500,000); Laws (P. &
    L.) 1871, 429 ($100,000); Laws (P. &L.) 1868, 507 ($100,000—$500,000)./
    Laws 1850, 232./ For special charter paid-in capital requirements,
    see, e.g., Laws 1850, 271 ($5,000); Laws 1852, 286 ($2,500); Laws (P.
    &L.) 1853, 22 ($10,000); Laws (P. &L.) 1853, 260 ($400); Laws (P. &
    L.) 1853, 111 ($200)./ On nature of security see, e.g., Laws (P.&L.)
    1856, 167 § 5; Laws (P.&L.) 1853, 111, § 2./ On the illusion of a capi-
    tal fund, see Farren 14-18.
4   Laws 1933, 120./ Laws 1899, 270./ See also Kimball (1958) 130.
5   C 1896, 1:xi reported that the Badger State Fire and Marine Ins. Co.,
    chartered a year earlier, had not yet received enough subscriptions
    to begin operations./ S 388, SJ 1219-20, 1243 (1903).
6   Laws 1899, 166./ Laws 1909, 39, 460. Laws 1919, 655 required a 50%
    surplus for surety companies./ A 355 (1927); S 104 (1931); Laws 1933,
    120; C 1934, 11-12./ Laws 1935, 54. See also Kimball (1958) 131-132.
7   Laws 1850, 232, § 7. Laws 1870, 56, § 22./ Laws 1877, 233.
8   A 197 (1879), and see letter accompanying ms. bill, in Archives. The
    letter was from the Superintendent of the Western Department of an
    English company to its Mineral Point agent, asking him to get signa-
    tures to an enclosed petition opposing the discriminatory require-
    ment. AJ 233 (1879) is an unfavorable report on the bill, arguing

that new trust deeds and New York laws gave adequate protection. Comm'r Ekern pointed out in C 1915, 1:v the possibility of war as a reason to treat American branches of foreign companies virtually as independent companies./ Laws 1895, 325.

9   Laws 1895, 325./ Laws 1901, 249./ Laws 1912SS, 3./ Laws 1913, 210./ A 763 (1935), A 256, 443 (1937) proposed deposits of $1,000,000 or $500,000 for foreign Lloyds' underwriters.

10   E.g., Laws 1837–38, 13, § 10; 1847, p. 139, § 8; 1857, 129, § 16./ Laws 1850, 232, § 5.

11   But see Fitzpatrick v. Co., Fed. Cas. #4844 (1857), where the Federal court saw more clearly the real problem behind the conceptual facade. See also Kimball (1957) 532.

12   Bolles 831. The state comptroller of New York thought 33 of 42 companies formed under N.Y. Laws 1849, 308 (Laws 1850, 232) were outright swindles. N.Y. Laws 1853, 466 closed the loophole./ Laws 1870, 56, § 6.

13   Laws 1909, 460./ Laws 1935, 216. AG 1930, 321 ruled that applicants need not pay the premiums themselves. Laws 1933, 148 required personal payment. AG 1939, 541 thereupon ruled that applicants might borrow the money to pay the premiums.

14   Laws 1913, 210, § 4./ Laws 1949, 109.

15   Laws 1937, 203./ Laws 1941, 127; id., § 2; CT 2–20–1941; MJ 2–20–1941.

16   Laws 1878, 255./ Laws 1887, 94. Modest requirements were set for peripheral lines, like plate glass (Laws 1905, 55), but more substantial ones for the major lines./ See also Kimball (1958) 139.

17   E.g., Laws 1851, 394; 1852, 416./ Laws (P.&L.) 1867, 309 (Vernon)./ C 1873, 61. Laws 1880, 82 authorized the newly formed Hanbury town mutual to reinsure the Vernon.

18   Laws 1850, 232, § 6; 1870, 59, § 1./ Bushnell (1907b) 5–6 (Wisconsin Life)./ Laws 1907, 640./ See also Kimball (1958) 141, n. 19.

19   Laws 1891, 418, §§ 1, 2, 11./ Laws 1895, 175, §§ 1, 4; 1911, 175; 1945, 517, § 5./ See also Kimball (1958) 141–43.

20   In 1823, Farren 6 expressed the view that capital was unnecessary./ C 1904, 2:36; 1905, 2:20; 1906, 2:37 (Host)./ A 112 (1905); A 238, (1927)./ Laws 1955, 190.

21   CR VI, 15 distinguished between ordinary and catastrophe losses and remarked the need of a surplus for the latter. Id., 23 found capital and surplus in Wisconsin to be about equal to unearned premium reserve, thus approximately doubling security./ Laws 1919, 101. See also Kimball (1958) 144–45.

22   Laws 1875, 314./ C 1877, 30.

23   C 1904, 1:2; 1906, 1:5./ C 1907, 1:4.

24   C 1912, 1:xxxii./ CR VI, 18, 63, 92; Laws 1913, 464; and see AG 1921, 84./ In re Liquidation of Co., 247 Wis. 485, 490 (1945) (other than fire insurance).

25   S 66 (1947)./ New York Times 8–2–1950 (atomic catastrophe).

26   Laws 1851, 394./ C 1870, 11./ C 1871, 8–10 warned of the danger of the practice of taking notes./ Laws (P.&L.) 1859, 213 authorized the company to issue nonassessable policies.

27   Laws 1877, 147./ See also Laws 1878, 8 (deletion of "mutual" from company's name).

28   A 364 (1879)./ SJ 479–80 (1879).

29 C 1879, 10–15./ AJR 12, AJ 69–70, 577, 597 (1881).
30 <u>Home Dairy</u>, Vols. IV and V. Welch stated in Vol. V, No. 50 that Vilas was sent a copy of every issue for more than forty years. A good file of <u>Home Dairy</u> may be found in Hist. Soc. Library.
31 Two decades earlier Nazro v. Co., 14 Wis. 295 (1861) showed that the Supreme Court had legal power to protect dissenting policyholders in such a situation by ordering distribution to them of their shares of assets.
32 Laws 1883, 245, § 5./ Id., § 3; and cf. Laws 1879, 83.
33 Laws 1897, 314.
34 Laws 1903, 229./ Defendant's Answer, at 7–26 of Case on Appeal, Huber v. Co., Huber v. Martin, 127 Wis. 412 (1906). The decision put the old Germantown back in business. While the case was pending the legislature amended the 1903 statute to require return of shares of surplus to nonsubscribing policyholders, even without request.—Laws 1905, 107.
35 Zinn v. Co., 132 Wis. 86 (1907).
36 Laws 1907, 555./ AG 1910, 438, 470; 1908, 485. But see C 1896, 1: 1915.
37 A 288 (1909); and see A 43 (1909), forbidding cancellation except for underwriting reasons./ A 288 (1909), Subst. Amdt. 1A.
38 Laws 1911, 158. Comm'r Ekern thought this act the solution to the raid problem.—C 1911, 1:xxix./ For Germantown surpluses, see various Commissioner's reports./ Ins. Dep't Actuary Anderson told of a raid on an $84,000 surplus by putting up $100,000 of capital. Only 19 out of 23,000 members participated. He does not identify the case; it may have been in another state.—Anderson (1911) 1.
39 C 1905, 2:23–24./ Laws 1905, 170./ Laws 1937, 203./ Laws 1947, 174.
40 AG 1906, 255, 351 (National)./ AG 1910, 480 (Old Line).
41 C 1910, 2:13; and see C 1909, 2:10./ Laws 1911, 280, 287; 1915, 173./ Insurance securities issues at first were not within the blue sky laws.—AG 1920, 238. Laws 1920, 442 brought them under control.—AG 1921, 906.
42 AG 1910, 441./ Jacobs v. Co., 162 Wis. 318 (1916).
43 Laws 1850, 232, § 19./ E.g., Laws 1850, 271, § 10./ Laws 1870, 56, §§ 12, 23./ The provision about making up deficiencies of assets was still in effect in mid–20th century.—ST 1955, § 200.06. Laws 1913, 155 repealed the other provisions.

CHAPTER III, Section 4

1 CR VI, 38.
2 FUA 1875, 130–31 points out the profit illusion.
3 The Salamander Society was organized in New York in 1819.—Zartman & Price 85./ Brearley (NBFU)./ FUA 1874, 6–8; see also FUA 1880, 236. The Ass'n President said the Boston fire put the "cement" in the board structure.—FUA 1873, 6.
4 See President's address, NBFU, in FUA, Supp. Proceedings, 3d Ann. Mtg. 1872, 17./ The Fire Underwriters' Association of the Northwest was effective and for decades was the sounding board for midwest industry sentiment. Its fully reported proceedings supply much information about the thinking of insurance men in the last third of the 19th century.

5 See, e.g., FUA 1873, 8; 1877, 59, 207; 1880, 111, 140; 1891, 118.
6 FUA 1890, 87; 1873, 32, 67, 69; 1875, 17, 40./ There was a classic
   rate war in Wisconsin in 1892 between board and non-board companies.—WSJ 3–31–1932; 1–2–38.
7 CR VI, 38; FUA 1883, 49; 1887, 144; but cf. 1897, 109./ An unsuccessful anticompact bill was introduced in Michigan in 1883, and bills became law in New Hampshire and Ohio in 1885, in Michigan in 1887,
   and in other states thereafter.—N. H. Laws 1885, 93; Ohio Laws
   1885, p. 231; Mich. Laws 1887, 285. Lumber and woodworking interests were said to be behind the Michigan law.—FUA 1887, 150./ See
   also Brearley 289.
8 See, e.g., C 1898, 1:vi-viii./ A 844, AJ 329, 1887 (original text not
   preserved; subject changed in printed bill). For projected state
   company, see back of ms. bill A 684 (1887), in Archives .
9 A 695 (1889)./ A 694 (1889).
10 A 537 (1893); S 233, A 394 (1895); A 416, 459, 473 (1897); S 235 (1899);
   S 56 (1901); S 176, 184, A 430 (1903); S 92 (1905)./ Laws 1897, 356.
   Local boards were organized under ST 1878, § 1922./ S 235 (1899); S
   56 (1901); S 176, 184, A 430 (1903); S 92 (1905); A 616 (1909)./ Pets. S
   90, A 89, 99 (1903).
11 A 376, § 6 (1899)./ A 99 (1901).
12 AJ 41–88 (1905)./ AJ 44–50 (1905SS); AJ 45–47 (1907) (life insurance)./ See, e.g., Kansas Laws 1909, 152; letter to Gov. from H. B.
   Seely of Chicago, Jan. 25, 1911, in LRef. Library.— The writer had
   been acting as an expert in Kansas, a pioneer in the field./ Laws
   1911, JR 40; 1911, 512.
13 CR VI, 12, 38–44, and see the transcript of the Committee hearing./
   The Dean schedule, in force in Wisconsin from 1907, provided a
   basis charge for each city, depending on size, fire protection, and
   other conditions. It then added percentage charges for hazards and
   defects, and deducted for advantages. A valid system of this kind
   took decades to develop. In the 1870's and 1880's industry meetings
   were filled with discussions of rating.—See, e.g., FUA 1873, 29;
   1874, 17; 1882, 110.
14 CR VI, 45–49, 62–65.
15 A 901–15 (1913); Laws 1913, 257, 282, 316, 317, 366, 464, 465, 489./
   AJ 1112, 1114 (1913); C. E. Sheldon, western manager of the American
   Insurance Company, and founder of the Western Bureau, urged most
   of the committee system. See his testimony in transcript of hearing
   of CR VI./ Some Milwaukee Socialists voted against the bill; apparently they looked on compulsory bureau membership as tending
   to monopoly.—AJ 1212 (1913); WBB 1913, 670–77.
16 WSJ 10–3–1914; MDN 12–15–1914; MFP 12–30–1914; C 1914, 1:xxviii-
   xxx; NAIC adjourned meeting of Apr. 15, 1915, 11; NAIC adjourned
   meeting of Dec. 8, 1914, 16–25./ German Alliance v. Lewis, 233 U.S.
   389 (1914) held rate regulation constitutional.
17 S 88 (1915); and see A 315, 316, 326 (1915)./ The bill also provided for
   a classification plan adopted by NBFU and NAIC, an indication of increasing industry–commissioner coöperation./ On the 1915 legislative fight, see Subst. Amdt. 1S, 1A, 2A to S 88 (1915); roll call votes
   at AJ 1090–91, 1150–51, 1373–74 (1915); MJ 5–26–1915; Madison Democrat (Wis.) 7–16–1915; WSJ 7–16–1915.
18 Sometimes industry representatives urged Ekern's continuance in

office, even while opposing his bills.—E.g., see WSJ 5–26–1915./
On the polemics, see MFP 3–25–1916; Madison Democrat (Wis.) 3–
28–1916; 3–29–1916; WSJ 6–21–1916 (a timely reduction of rates by
the Wisconsin Inspection Bureau); WSJ 8–22–1916.

19 WSJ 1–11–1917; S 8; AJ 31–32 (1917). A Progressive critic proposed
S 38 and Subst. Amdt. 1S to S 8 (1917)./ MFP 1–25–1917 (monopoly)./
WSJ 3–20–1917 (compromise). SJ 361, AJ 639 (1917).

20 Laws 1917, 61./ S 407 (1917) to regulate plate glass insurance, was unsuccessful.—Such elaborate control made little sense for peripheral
insurance.

21 Bureau v. Whitman, 196 Wis. 472 (1928), Case on Appeal 2; CT 2–19
–1918; Hobbins v. Hannan, 186 Wis. 284 (1925), Case on Appeal 38,
stating an order of Nov. 28, 1922; MS 5–24–1926; CT 12–9–1926.

22 Hobbins v. Hannan, 186 Wis. 284 (1925); and see Case on Appeal 65–65.

23 See Case on Appeal 279–84 for judgment of Circut Ct. Cf. Dowling
v. Co., 92 Wis. 63 (1896).

24 Letter from Deputy-Comm'r Timbers to Author, Nov. 21, 1957./ A
298 (1929); CT 2–3–1929; 4–10–1929./ For steamroller, see AJ
1450–52, 1533–34, 1708–10 (1929); CT 6–20–1929./ Circular in opposition to Bill No. 298 A, June 1929, in LRef. Library.

25 Laws 1929, JR 82./ Sheboygan Press (Wis.) 6–27–1929; Racine
Times-Call (Wis.) 6–27–1929./ CR VII, passim./ Pending the
investigation, the bureau made another timely rate cut in 1930, of
which many people were suspicious.—MJ 2–18–1930; 2–21–1930;
Sheboygan Press (Wis.) 3–3–1930.

26 CR VII, 84–93.

27 The original bill was A 943 (1931); the law was Laws 1931, 437; WSJ,
editorial 3–16–1930 (industry opposition)./ MS 7–9–1931 (real power)./
See also A 469 (1931) (voluntary bureau membership); A 936 (1931)
($10,000 for expert fire rater and supporting statistical services).
Laws 1941, 115 permitted five or more insurers to form an actuarial
bureau. Laws 1931, 437, § 203.45 authorized the Comm'r to set up
risk classifications; he adopted a classification at variance with the
rest of the country. See also C 1934, 15; U.S. Daily 12–11–1931: 7–14–
1932, in LRef. Library ; WSJ 2–28–1932; Sheboygan Press (Wis.)
7–12–1932.

28 S 392 (1935)./ Northwestern v. Mortensen, 230 Wis. 377, 379 (1939).
CT 12–30–1937; WSJ 1–2–1938; WSJ 9–25–1938.

29 WSJ 1–2–1938./ AJR 56 (1943)./ AJ 1241 (1943); id., 3–7 for party
affiliation; Sheboygan Press (Wis.) 4–29–1943./ S 364 (1945).

30 CT 11–24–1942; New York Times 1–11–1944 (background of litigation).

31 Laws 1947, 487./ See also Kimball & Boyce. The Comm'r opposed
the All-Industry bill for fire insurance, contending that existing
statutes were better. Letter from Deputy-Comm'r Timbers to
Author, Nov. 21, 1957.

32 CT 5–19–1948.

33 For newspaper accounts of the rate regulation controversy see MJ
2–2–1950, 6–2–1950, 7–18–1950; 2–8–1951; 10–28–1955; 5–27–1956;
CT 3–2–1950; 7–19–1950; 7–20–1950 editorial; 8–2–1950 editorial;
8–15–1950; 8–30–1950; 9–14–1955; 10–31–1955 editorial; 11–2–1955;
11–4–1955; 11–10–1955; 1–11–1956; WSJ 10–5–1950; 10–6–1950 (Under
the Dome); 3–20–1951; 11–11–1952; 12–8–1953; 12–9–1953; 1–15–1954;
11–4–1955; 1–14–1956; 3–29–1956; GBPG 10–19–1950; 10–31–1950; MS

6–23–1956. Other details on rate regulation were supplied in a letter from Deputy-Comm'r Timbers to Author, Nov. 21, 1957. The companies agreed to an 11% reduction in interim rates; an additional 6% was involved in the outcome of an appeal to the Courts.— MJ 7–9–1956. FIRB v. Rogan, 91 N.W. 2d 372 (1958) decided the issue equivocally in 1958; the Court upheld the Comm'r in his disapproval of the filed rates, but refused to settle the basic issue of permissible underwriting profit. The court partly rested its decision on the refusal of the 1947 legislature to enact S 69 (1947) to provide a 2.5% underwriting profit./ On the interest of the League, see, e.g., The Municipality (the League organ) 221–26, Oct. 1950; CT 2–22–1951; WSJ 3–20–1951./ See also C 1957, 10–22; 1958, 23–29.

34   Laws 1917, 61, § 1946–18; 1919, 425, § 17; 1925, 378; 1931, 437, § 203. 49; 1935, 126; Laws 1941, 115, § 2.

35   Laws 1913, 599, § 2394–27(4)./ Laws 1917, 637./ AJ 29–30 (1917) was the Governor's recommendation./ Laws 1933, 353 abolished the Board and transferred its functions to the Comm'r. C 1923, 154 said that compensation insurance rate regulation was far ahead of that for other casualty.

36   A 538, S 203, AJ 1671–72, SJ 1273, AJ 1843–44 (veto) (1921)./ Laws 1925, 399./ Bureau v. Mortensen, 227 Wis. 335 (1938) involved control of experience rating by the Comm'r. The provisions were essentially the same in mid-century, except for the power given the Comm'r by Laws 1941, 196 and 1951, 514 to approve special rates or rating plans on emergency national defense projects.

37   Laws 1919, 136./ Laws 1923, 281.

38   S 82 (1925); cf. Subst. Amdt. 1S; letter from Att'y Gen. Ekern to Sen. Titus, Feb. 9, 1925, in LRef. Library./ E.g., A 87, 921 (1935)./ CT 2–9–1938; MS 2–15–1938; MJ 2–15–1938./ SJR 37, AJR 43, AJ 791–92 (1947); Laws 1947, 521./ CT 4–15–1948; 4–16–1948; 4–20–1948 editorial; 10–8–1951/ MJ 9–7–1957./ See Kimball & Boyce. The Comm'r claimed that a 1956 department reorganization made rate regulation more effective in all lines.—C 1957, 9.

39   Laws 1919, 655, § 1966–33g./ ST 1919, § 1966–38 (bond premiums)./ S 289, SJ 1255–56, 1265 (1921)./ AJR 39, AJ 1217–19, SJ 1287 (1945); Laws 1947, 521.

40   CR I, 178, 188./ Dawson (1907b) 11./ Laws 1907, 668.

41   Dawson (1907a), esp. at 13./ Laws 1947, 42./ ST 1955, § 206.26./ In 1957 over strenuous opposition of the affected companies, the Comm'r sought and obtained power to regulate premium rates for credit life, a rapidly growing field.—CT 5–8–1957; CT 5–29–1957; MJ 6–11–1957; Laws 1957, 321, § 4. He then demanded a 25% cut in rates.—CT 8–14–1957. In this development Wisconsin was the pioneering state.

42   The deficiency reserve was enacted by Laws 1907, 209, § 1950, amended by Laws 1909, 209, § 2.

43   See MS 6–22–1905, "Fraternal Insurance", a statement for laymen on the methods of fraternal operation. Laws 1895, 175, § 1.

44   Buley 1:129; Knight 376, 379; Minneapolis Journal (Minn.) 2–23–1905./ A 339 (1901); S 332, § 19, A 412, § 19 (1905); dozens of petitions favored and opposed the 1905 bills; Laws 1907, 511. § 23a of the "Force Bill" required the reduction of deficiencies in solvency in existing societies by 5 per cent each three years; it was not passed

in Wisconsin. — C 1912, 2:xxxviii. Laws 1899, 270, § 5 provided a
minimum premium for stipulated premium life companies.

45 Laws 1837-38, 13, § 4./ See also Kimball (1958), 204.
46 Sec'y 1870, 9-11; 1871, 8-11.
47 Laws 1909, 521, § 2.
48 Laws 1929, 440, § 211.04 (registered town mutuals)./ For provisions
    "voiding" the policy, see, e.g., Laws 1878, 255, § 14; 306, § 13; 1887,
    305, § 10.
49 E.g., Laws 1837-38, 13, § 5 (registrable lien); 1849, 145, § 1 (auto-
    matic lien)./ E.g., Laws (P.&L.) 1854, 278 (omitted lien); Laws 1855,
    69 (repealed liens). Exceptional charters after 1855 granted a lien.
    —E.g., Laws (P.&L.) 1860, 90./ This change was in policy and not
    in habit; the draft of S 260 (1857) contained an automatic lien pro-
    vision, but the enacted law, Laws 1857, 268, omitted it. Laws 1872,
    95 gave a lien for premium charges for fire or marine insurance
    on ships; this was stil in effect in mid-20th century. —ST 1955, § 290.
    01(1)./ E.g., A 350 (1889); S 239, 240, 262, 263 (1925) (attempts to re-
    vive or extend liens).
50 Laws 1877, 281./ A 11 (1883).
51 For borrowing see Laws 1877, 263, § 2; 1909, 459; 1933, 142./ For
    advance assessment, see Laws 1879, 251; 1881, 42; 1887, 305, § 10;
    1911, 156, 167. Laws 1909, 274 reflected technical difficulty in as-
    sessment procedure by validating defective assessments through
    subsequent notice.
52 E.g., see C 1912, 3:xxxvii; 1913, 3:xxi; 1914, 3:xix./ CT 3-1-1956.
53 A 905 (1913); A 467 (1915); S 223 (1917); A 611 (1933)./ Aetna v.
    Mabbett, 18 Wis. 667 (1864); and see C 1912, 1:xxxi.

CHAPTER III, Section 5

1 Stalson, passim; Kimball (1957) 554.
2 Laws 1870, 56, § 28./ Statutes imposed many duties on agents, but
   these had nothing to do with marketing; to act on the agent was
   merely the easiest way to control the company. —See, e.g., Laws
   1870, 56, § 34 (agent must execute bond for payment of fire department taxes).
3 At least 15 Wis. Supreme Court cases held oral insurance contracts
   valid.— See, e.g., Stehlich v. Co., 87 Wis. 322 (1894)./ Davis v.
   Union, 94 Wis. 472 (1896) held the evidence insufficient to establish
   an oral contract.
4 A 78 (1897); A 391 (1905) (fire); A 577 (1909) (fire).
5 Schilbrch v. Co. 180 Wis. 120 (1923), interpreting Laws 1911, 84; 1913,
   601./ Kiviniemi v. Co., 201 Wis. 619 (1930); Neuberger v. Ass'n,
   207 Wis. 133 (1932).
6 On multiple lines coverage, see Heins. For early charters see
   Laws 1838-39, 36, 58.
7 Cf. Heins 567-70.
8 For extensions see Laws 1883, 44; 1887, 308; 1903, 104; C 1896, 2:
   834-36. Fire and marine were regarded as a single line, as were·
   life and accident. See also Kimball (1958) 215-16.
9 Laws 1909, 460./ Northwestern v. Freedy, 201 Wis. 51 (1930).
10 Laws 1915, 73./ S 551, 631 (1915)./ Laws 1919, 70.
11 Laws 1947, 365./ Laws 1951, 269./ MJ 10-13-1957. See also Laws

1957, 188.
12 AG 1904, 236, 397./ Laws 1907, 599./ Laws 1911, 27. AG 1916, 282./
    AG 1917, 244, 832./ S 389 (1919)./ AG 1925, 461./ Cf. AG 1927, 825
    with 1928, 512 and 1927, 26.
13 AG 1908, 497./ Laws 1911, 311. But if the coporation was a coöpera-
    tive, the coöperative law superseded the anti-rebating law.— AG
    1937, 261./ See also Laws 1919, 177. AG 1958, 317 made it clear that
    banks could receive commissions on the sale of credit life insurance
    from the employees of the bank who were the licensed agents.
14 Laws 1870, 56, § 28./ Laws 1909, 116 (and see 1947, 75); C 1909,
    1:ix./ Laws 1917, 107; S 180 (1919); A 433 (1927)./ Laws 1951, 574./
    Laws 1939, 468 provided for licensing of solicitors for insurance
    other than life; control was minimal.
15 Comm'r Ekern thought the role of the agent required a test of qual-
    ifications.—C 1912, 1:xxxi; 1914, 1:xxvi; 1915, 1:viii./ A 905 (1913)./
    Lerdahl, Raising Agency Standards, address to Wis. Ass'n of Mut.
    Ins. Cos., Dec. 16, 1927, in LRef. Library, urged qualifications tests
    to eliminate parasites from the business, in order to lessen criti-
    cism and demand for state insurance.
16 A 855, AJ 2207, SJ 1658 (1931); S 289 (1935); A 901 (1939); A 255
    (1943)./ CT 5–21–1946./ A 230 (1947)./ Sheboygan Press (Wis.) 3–6
    –1947./ GBPG 10–31–1947 ("Government and Politics")./ AJ 1566–
    68 (1947).
17 Sheboygan Press (Wis.) 4–22–1949./ Laws 1949, 399./ Laws 1957,
    624 excepted credit life insurance companies. The power of the
    Comm'r to make rules about examinations did not authorize waiver
    for completion of a company training course.—AG 1951, 20. S 253
    (1957) would have required a life insurance agent to have two years
    of college education.
18 MJ 1–8–1950./ GBPG 12–18–1950 (farm organizations); and see CT
    1–23–1953./ A 672 (1951)./ A 375, AJ 952, SJ 1367 (1953)./ GBPG
    8–29–1955; CT 8–30–1955; Laws 1955, 600./ Laws 1957, 74 excepted
    agents for certain domestic mutuals on the assessment plan.
19 AJ 407 (1878); Laws 1878, 90./ Laws 1882, 166./ ST 1898, § 1946(a),
    (b), (c)./ The Att'y Gen. ruled that the Comm'r might revoke the
    license of the New Amsterdam Cas. Co. for misleading advertising.
    —AG 1904, 350.
20 Laws 1907, 126./ Laws 1913, 517. The Comm'r ruled that this
    statute precluded the use of "average" dividends in sales talk.— C
    1918, xliv.
21 Laws 1915, 86. Laws 1941, 241 extended this provision to under-
    writers' agencies.
22 S 629 (1919)./ SJ 1475–76, 1492 (1919)./ Laws 1919, 512./ A 338 (1923)./
    Laws 1931, 459.
23 A 526 (1923).
24 Laws 1895, 175, §§ 17, 18./ Laws 1901, 202./ Laws 1935, 463 applied
    the provisions about misrepresentations in life insurance to mutual
    benefit societies.
25 Stalson 486–87. AG 1904, 85 ruled that a ton of coal given as a
    bonus was an illegal rebate.
26 Stalson 535./ Laws 1891, 267, introduced earlier as A 700 (1889)./
    Laws 1909, 159 forbade rebating in other lines of insurance. This
    was proposed earlier by A 280 (1899) and A 391 (1905). Large

insurers defeated the latter.— SJ 829, 942, 969 (1905); C 1906, 1:23.
See also Laws 1913, 599, § 2394–27 (workmen's comp.); 1933, 429
(reciprocals); 1945, 494 (medical society plans for indigents). Discrimination was not limited to rebating. It was discriminatory for
a savings and loan corporation to buy term life for each borrower
with uniform premiums not graded to underwriting characteristics
of the borrower.— AG 1924, 229. But compensation policyholders
might participate in profits in relation to loss experience.—AG
1929, 58.

27 E.g., Laws 1917, 61, § 1946–8 (fire)./ C 1916, xxviii; AG 1920, 71.
28 AG 1940, 374./ Id., 430.
29 AG 1904, 368; but see id., 295, where a local advisor contract was
    upheld./ AG 1906, 618./ Urwan v. Co., 125 Wis. 349 (1905)./ Laun v.
    Co., 131 Wis. 555 (1907) (to recover payments)./ Richmond v. Co.,
    166 Wis. 334 (1917)./ Laws 1907, 504 made public policy clear by
    making advisory board contracts void.
30 AG 1908, 463. See also Richmond v. Co., 166 Wis. 334 (1917).
31 Laws 1907, 504./ Laws 1911, 270./ A 498 (1901) would have required
    a stamped statement on each policy that it was void if there were
    rebating. A 382 (1915) would have required both applicant and agent
    in life and disability to sign a statement in the application about re-
    bates. AG 1910, 457 permitted agents to get commissions on their
    own insurance. Id., 454 ruled that agents might share commissions
    only with other agents of the same company. Attempts to forbid
    commission splitting with non-residents showed localistic sentiment.
    —See, e.g., A 237 (1915)./ Laws 1911, 310 gave the Comm'r discretion
    as to the time of suspension./ Laws 1913, 455 permitted limited
    credit on the premium; longer credit was a rebate.
32 C 1896, 2:xi. Fricke would discourage twisting by forcing com-
    missions down through enforced publication of expenses in the poli-
    cy. See also C 1912, 2:xxi./ Laws 1907, 126./ Laws 1915, 323./ Laws
    1929, 296.
33 A 555 (1937)./ AJ 2060 (1937)./ A 237 (1939); Laws 1939, 392./ A 326
    (1951); A 492 (1953)./ Lange v. Rancher, 262 Wis. 625 (1952).
34 S 409, SJ 690, AJ 902 (1909)./ A 236, AJ 996, 1022 (1915)./ A 350
    (1891); A 418 (1897); A 456 (1905); A 689, 690 (1913)./ S 75 (1915)./ SJ
    904, AJ 1395 (1915).
35 S 327, A 300, AJ 1268 (1941); A 445, AJ 1793 (1945).
36 Laws 1945, 360.
37 Laws 1947, 520./ 59 Stat. 33 (1945), 15 U.S.C. §§1011–15(1952)./ Laws
    1957, 448./ GBPG 8–30–1957./ See also Laws 1959, 55.
38 AG 1908, 472; 1912, 847 (library cases)./ AG 1922, 68; 1913, 1:488;
    1:546; 2:732./ AG 1922, 127 (stockholder)./ See also AG 1923, 27,
    237, 279, 429.
39 Laws 1915, 612; AG 1915, 1004./ AG 1922, 127; and see 1923, 279./ AG
    1938, 841./ Laws 1937, 270 increased the exemption to $300.
40 AG 1924, 114. Cf. Menasha v. Winter, 159 Wis. 437, 452 (1915) with
    Laun v. Co., 131 Wis. 555, 570–71 (1907).

CHAPTER IV, Section 1

1 E.g., Hazelton v. Co., 148 Wis. 19 (1912) (company as trustee).
2 E.g., Laws (P.&L.) 1868, 507; Laws (P.&L.) 1869, 122, 172, 398./

Laws 1870, 56, 59.

3   Mass. AR 1795, 22./ For Massachusetts charters, see Mass. AR
1797, 67; Mass. Laws 1823, 112; Mass. Laws 1818, 180; Mass. Laws
1825, 69; Mass. Laws 1828, 51; Mass. AR 1797, 67, § 3./ The general
act was Mass. Laws 1818, 120.

4   See, e.g., Laws 1850, 232, §§ 8, 9./ Laws (P.&L.) 1857, 129, § 10
(100% margin)./ Laws 1860, 90, § 18 (one year limit).

5   Laws 1837–38, 29, § 2./ Laws 1850, 232, §§ 6, 8./ Laws 1857, 89./
A limitation of the permissible interest rate probably sought prevention of usury, not preservation of assets.—The limit was usually
from 7 to 10%; often it was the "lawful rate".— E.g., Laws (P.&L.)
1865, 57 (7%); Laws (P.&L.) 1853, 107 (10%); Laws (P.&L.) 1853, 260
(lawful rate).

6   Laws (P.&L.) 1857, 129, §§ 3, 10, 11./ See Smalley for history of the
Northwestern's investment policy.

7   See, e.g., Laws (P.&L.) 1867, 405; Laws (P.&L.) 1868, 507; Laws
(P.&L.) 1869, 398.

8   Cf. Laws 1870, 56 with Laws 1870, 59.

9   Laws 1870, 59, §§ 1, 11, 12./ The safety margin might lower the
yield.—See Smalley 7–46./ C 1895, 2:483./ See, e.g., AG 1921, 647;
AG 1939, 49; AG 1934, 71.

10 Laws 1882, 204; Laws 1893, 115./ Laws 1901, 22; Laws 1903, 6./ Laws
1905, 263./ Smalley 3–52.

11 AJ 44–48 (1905SS)./ C 1903, 2:xxii; C 1904, 2:32; C 1905, 2:26./ E.g.,
C 1905, 2:15; C 1906, 2:29.

12 C 1905, 2:15; CR I, 62–70.

13 Laws 1911, 502.

14 Laws 1917, 270.

15 Laws 1921, 310./ Laws 1925, 255./ Laws 1931, 34.

16 Laws 1933, 107./ Laws 1933, 162.

17 Laws 1935, 260./ Laws 1937, 221./ Laws 1939, 141./ Laws 1941, 50.

18 Laws 1945, 277./ Laws 1947, 11./ Laws 1947, 324. S 66 (1921) was an
attempt to get housing project authority after World War I; this was
repeated as S 422, A 453 (1923); and A 337 (1927)./ Laws 1953, 64./
Williamson & Smalley 302./ Laws 1955, 94; AJ 538 (1957); Laws 1957,
358./ Laws 1957, 69./ See also Laws 1959, 235. Investment control
for stipulated premium companies and fraternals was much like
that for legal reserve life companies. However, fraternals had
authority to invest up to 20% of assets in a home office building.—
See Laws 1899, 270; 1901, 221; 1911, 216, § 1957; 1945, 517, § 3;
Knights v. Levy, 261 Wis. 284 (1951).

19 Laws 1959, 23; A 139 (1959)./ C 1895, 2:483./ New York Times 1–26
–1947; Business Week 10–28–1950; U.S. Temporary Nat'l Economic
Committee, p. 378./ S 192 (1927); but see S 529, SJ 1184, AJ 1945
(1955). Strout, "Investment Snowball," in Christian Science Monitor
4–23–1949, reported SEC Comm'r Sumner T. Pike as stating in
1941 that life insurance companies were "experiencing great difficulties in investing their funds," and urging permission for them to
invest in common stocks. See also 57 Yale Law Journal 1256 (1948).
For a more general treatment of these economic and legal problems,
see "Institutional Investments," symposium, p. 15./ For variable
annuities in retirement systems, see Laws 1957, 381, 423.

20 Laws 1870, 56, § 8./ The capital-surplus distinction is found as

late as Laws 1953, 355.
21 Laws 1887, 352./ Laws 1927, 534, § 92; ST 1955, § 212.01./ Laws
   1897, 277; 1897, 56; 1909, 460.
22 Laws 1909, 267.
23 Laws 1911, 157./ Laws 1913, 553./ Laws 1921, 465; 1931, 30; 1933, 321;
   1939, 522./ Laws 1943, 341./ Laws 1945, 436./ Laws 1947, 325./
   Laws 1953, 312./ Laws 1955, 90; 1955, 89, 93./ Laws 1957, 373; AJ
   538 (1957)./ Laws 1957, 169.
24 Laws 1915, 444.
25 S 528 (1921); A 257 (1923)./ Laws 1935, 45; 1939, 383.
26 Laws 1907, 671./ Laws 1903, 68./ Laws 1917, 482, § 2./ Laws 1911,
   577, § 2./ Laws 1913, 291.
27 Laws 1911, 323./ Laws 1921, 459.
28 AJ 33 (1927)./ Laws 1927, JR 58 (committee appointed)./ SJ 733–63
   (1929)(findings of committee)./ Laws 1929, 491./ Laws 1955, 441.
29 Laws 1929, 486./ Laws 1929, 490./ Laws 1931, 385./ Laws 1935,256./
   Laws 1935, 268./ Laws 1937, 120. MJ, editorial 7–12–1938 criticized
   this financing. It is true that the assets were not liquid, especially
   when the legislature kept repealing its obligation to repay./ Laws
   1951, 399./ AJ 30 (1945); S 179, 180 (1945); C 1955, 80./ See also Laws
   1939, 54; 1945, 357; 1957, 519.
30 AJ 1211–15 (1955)./ Laws 1955, 285; AJ 1551, SJ 1267 (1955); AJ 3–8
   and SJ 4–5 for party affiliation.
31 Laws 1933, 126; see also A 240 (1933) for stronger proposal.

CHAPTER IV, Section 2

1 FUA 1873, 8 urged companies to be prepared to lose in a single fire
  the entire risk written in any compact city or town./ C 1920, 1:x;
  1922, 1:viii./ Laws 1951, 588; and see also Laws 1959, 340.
2 Laws (P.&L.) 1853, 260, § 2./ Laws 1859, 46, § 4./ Laws 1870, 2./
  Laws 1876, 344, § 11./ E.g., Laws 1883, 189 ($2,500); 1907, 442
  ($3,500); 1923, 33 ($10,000); 1953, 416./ E.g., Laws 1878, 255, § 9
  (manufacturers' and millers' mutuals, $10,000); 1889, 524, § 3 (drug-
  gists' mutuals, $5,000); 1897, 316, § 8 (livestock, $250)./ Laws 1909,
  460./ See also C 1907, 3:16 (city and village mutuals).
3 Laws 1917, 482./ AJR 115 (1927)./ Laws 1951, 237./ AJ 32–34 (1917);
  A 160 (1917); AJ 78–79 (1919); A 110 (1919)./ S 29 (1917).
4 A 329 (1891); S 339, A 698 (1907) proposed in CR I, 276; A 16 (1923)./
  Laws 1937, 41; 1943, 120; 1947, 90./ Laws 1949, 458.
5 Mass. Acts & Laws 1803, 85, § 12 (10%); 1805, 47, § 1 (7.5%); Mass.
  Laws 1819, 78, § 7 (7%); 1832, 99, § 7 (5%); 1835, 8, § 4 (8%)./ Mass.
  Laws 1818, 120, § 7./ Laws 1850, 232, § 5; 1870, 56, § 6./ Laws 1897,
  277, § 17 applied the 10% limit to casualty;1909,460 made it general./
  Laws 1909, 118; 1912SS, 3; 1913, 210./ S 508 (1913); MDN 8–9–1913; SJ
  1203–04, 1228 (1913)./ Laws 1913, 277./ See also Laws 1955, 433.
6 C 1898, 1:966–67./ S 687 (1917)./ Laws 1919, 655, § 1966–33i. Surety
  companies might execute transportation or warehousing bonds for
  internal revenue taxes up to 50% of capital and surplus, ibid.
7 Laws 1903, 56./ Laws 1905, 373, § 6; 1909, 459./ Laws 1909,460, increased to .25%by 1913, 196./ E.g., A 310 (1921) proposed an increase
  to six times the average policy, or .5% of risks in force.
8 Laws 1911, 577./ Laws 1925, 168.
9 Laws 1859, 46, § 4./ See, e.g., Laws 1878, 255, §9 (manufacturers'

and millers'); 1889, 524, § 3 (druggists'); 1895, 64, § 5 (lumber dealers'); 1897, 316, § 8 (livestock);1899, 167, § 7 (bicycle)./ Laws 1909, 459, § 1941–5; 1909, 460, § 190ln./ A 283 (1923); A 356 (1925); S 438 (1941); Laws 1943, 357.

10 Laws 1876, 344, § 11./ Laws 1881, 48; 1887, 217; 1905, 36; 1929, 403; 1935, 126; 1939, 366; 1943, 111./ Laws 1949, 507./ Laws 1953, 416./ Laws 1878, 277, § 3./ Laws 1880, 134; S 175, 235 (1881); A 253 (1889)./ Laws 1903, 352./ A 576 (1905); A 26 (1907).

11 Laws 1895, 175, § 1; 1911, 216, § 1957./ Laws 1917, 365; AG 1927, 617, 739 (juvenile)./ A 383 (1915); A 141, S 562, Subst. Amdt. 1S (1917) but but see S 264 (1929)./ Laws 1895, 175, § 4, amended by 1911, 216.

12 See, e.g., Johnson (1926c)./ Laws 1929, 317./ Laws 1949, 458./ See also Laws 1957, 122.

13 Laws (P.&L.) 1867, 483. Laws 1897, 316, § 8 limited livestock insurance to horses, mules, and cattle./ Lange v. Rancher, 262 Wis. 625 (1952).

CHAPTER IV, Section 3

1 E.g., Laws (P.&L.) 1856, 49, § 16; Laws 1850, 232, § 19./ E.g., Laws 1850, 232, § 13; cf. 1870, 56, § 23.

2 Laws 1870, 56, § 12./ FUA 1875, 131 (illusion of prosperity).

3 Laws 1862, 66./ C 1870, 15–17. The Comm'r remarked that 1869 N.Y. reinsurance estimates varied from $2.47 to $10 per thousand dollars of risk.

4 Comm'r Fricke thought the percentage basis "unscientific." —1898, 1:ix./ FUA 1880, 13 (protection to industry)./ C 1898, 1:966 announced Fricke's intention of calculating reserves on the old rates, during a rate war; this implicitly recognized the inadequacy of a percentage basis.

5 E.g., Laws 1880, 105 (accident); 1919, 655, § 1966–33k (suretyship)./ ST 1898, § 1966–47; Laws 1919, 655, § 1966–33k./ Laws 1911, 235./ Laws 1929, 246./ Laws 1949, 366./ Since title insurance premiums went largely to pay for title examination costs, Laws 1955, 433, § 4 required an initial reserve of only 5% of the premium, of which 5% could be charged off annually.

6 A 365 (1923)./ MJ 1–26–1950; WSJ 1–30–1950.

7 WSJ 3–13–1932. Many prominent progressives were associated with the firm.— See, e.g., MS 3–15–1932./ A 912 (1939)./ AJ 2316 (1939)./ WSJ 8–16–1939; CT 8–16–1939.

8 S 427 (1941); WSJ 1–22–1941./ CT 5–23–1941./ WSJ 6–12–1941; MJ 6–12–1941.

9 Duel v. Co., 240 Wis. 161 (1942).

10 CT 5–24–1948./ State Farm Mutual v. Duel, 244 Wis. 429 (1944); 324 U.S. 154 (1945). Laws 1957, 72; SJ 228 (1957). The original bill, S 167 (1957) was somewhat different.

11 Laws 1945, 488 exempted town mutuals.

12 The occasional reserve funds for life companies not operating on a legal reserve basis provided a cushion for unexpected losses, but did not purport to put the company on a theoretically sound basis.— See, e.g., Laws 1887, 1, § 13.

13 C 1871, 171.

14 Laws 1870, 59, § 10./ C 1870, 59. Breese pointed out that the lower

premiums under the New York standard favored the transient policyholder, while the higher protected the long term policyholder.—
C 1870, 61/ Interest earnings in early days were higher in the capital-scarce west, and the Northwestern Mutual used its strategic
geographical position to earn better interest than many eastern
companies.—Smalley 1–25, 26; but see Williamson & Smalley 48.
Nevertheless it adopted a 4% reserve system in 1870, on recommendation of Elizur Wright, the pioneer in America of insurance regulation.—C 1870, 59; Williamson & Smalley 60.

15   C 1895, xvi–xvii./ S 393 (1897); S 73, 183 (1903)./ For most of the
history of life insurance, the rate earned on investments steadily
declined, to a low of under 3% in 1947.—See a tabulation in Life Ins.
Ass'n of America, Ann. Proc., 1947, 46.

16   CR I, 126, 181./ Dawson (1907b) 8–9./ Committee Bill No. 7 became
S 319, A 684 (1907). Cf. Subst. Amdt. 2A to A 684. See AJ 1215, SJ
1208 (1907)./ Laws 1907, 132, 150; Laws 1909, 209./ Dawson (1907a)
13–15.

17   Laws 1941, 329; 1943, 143; 1943, 166./ Laws 1943, 166, § 206.201(6)./
Laws 1959, 76./ Laws 1909, 536 set valuation standards for industrial life, annuities, and disability. Laws 1911, 577, § 1989m(4), (5) set
the state life fund assumptions, and Laws 1917, 106, § 4 those for
total and permanent disability.

18   Knight 373 says a third of the voters belonged. See also id. 374./
Laws 1895, 175, § 4 (required fund)./ Laws 1891, 418, §§ 4, 11 (voluntary reserve)./ Laws 1899, 270, § 6 set reserve requirements for
stipulated premium companies.

19   Knight 371.

20   S 203 (1895).

21   C 1898, 2:xi–xv; 1897, 2:ix–xvi; 1896, 2:xv–xix.

22   See C 1905, 2:23–24 for case history of a society several times reorganized, each time at a higher level. Morse v. Modern Woodmen,
166 Wis. 194 (1917) was a libel suit illustrating the bitterness such
problems might engender; MFP 8–13–1905; 9–2–1906. Madison
Democrat (Wis.) 9–29–1906 tells of revocation of licenses of two
fraternals for using funds contributed by new members to keep up
dividends on old policies.

23   Wuerflur v. Trustees, 116 Wis. 19 (1902); Smith v. Co., 123 Wis. 586
(1905)./ Voss v. Co., 137 Wis. 492 (1909) (estoppel).

24   C 1904, 2:30–32; C 1912, 2:xxxviii–xlii./ C 1906, 2:48. Comm'r Host
sought to educate the fraternals; he asked them to report assessments and losses by age groups. At his suggestion, Laws 1905, 357
was passed to compel recalcitrants.—C 1905, 2:22. Zeno M. Host,
What is Needed to Preserve the Future of Frat. Ben. Societies, address to Legis. Inv. Committee, June 29, 1906, in LRef. Library.

25   Laws 1907, 511./ Laws 1911, 32, 175./ Laws 1913, 167./ See also AG
1915, 434, which seems clearly wrong. See ST 1915, § 1958(3). Laws
1943, 147 permitted fraternals to use the 1941 C.S.O. table. Laws
1907, 447 provided that stipulated premium companies must value
policies as yearly renewable term.

26   Anderson (Wis. Ins. Dep't actuary) (1912) 197. Anderson says he
made some contributions to the retrospective formula.—Anderson
(1911) 7. The method made raids on assets of fraternals more difficult.—Anderson tells of one shocking raid, id. at 3./ Laws 1913, 251.

Laws 1911, 265 applied the method to stipulated premium companies./ Laws 1915, 311./ Laws 1917, 365 required the new juvenile divisions of fraternals to be actuarially sound on the prospective basis.

27 A 335 (1913); A 526 (1915); C 1915, 2:xi–xii./ C 1910, 2:18–19 and
annual statements of valuation results by Comm'r as of Dec. 31,
1918 and Dec. 31, 1925, in Hist. Soc. Library.

28 Order v. Miller, 178 Wis. 299 (1922)./ Hall v. Co., 185 Wis. 507
(1925) (this company started as an assessment company, was then
upgraded to be a stipulated premium company, and ultimately became a legal reserve company).

29 A 376 (1915)./ Laws 1917, 369 and see C 1918, liii–liv./ S 577 (1919);
S 247 and A 638 (1927) were similar bills in general terms, probably
intended to meet the needs of particular fraternals.

30 WSJ 3–24–1929; AG 1929, 142; but see id., 144. AG 1931, 607 (reversal)./ MJ 4–3–1932 (Comm'r's request)./ Amdt. 1S to S 206 (1931);
A 515 (1945)./ SJ 1927–28 (1931); AJ 1865–66, 1870–71 (1945)./ Amdt.
1S to S 513 (1945); SJ 1390 (1945); Laws 1945, 586, § 22b (omnibus)./
A 242 (1947)./ Martin v. Ass'n, 247 Wis. 220 (1945) (charter annul-
ment)./ AJ 516–17, 1652–53, 1722, SJ 1218 (1947)./ The Governor
noted a decrease of such companies from about a hundred in 1931 to
one or two in 1947.

31 S 335, A 597 (1903)./ Laws 1917, 160./ Laws 1919, 655, § 1966–33k.

32 Smalley 4–68, 69; Laws 1903, 237./ AG 1908, 506.

33 Smalley 6–52, 7–32./ Stalson 556./ Laws 1915, 81, extended to all
companies by 1933, 20. See C 1934, 12 for department's adverse attitude. Comm'r Host suggested the law in C 1904, 2:20–22; after a
slow start it was widely adopted.—Smalley 7–33./ See S 550 (1951),
proposing support of a valuation committee of NAIC.

34 Sauerhering v. Rueping, 137 Wis. 407 (1908)./ C 1906, 2:38–39.

35 A 574 (1885).

36 Laws 1905SS, 9./ CR I. The committee took 1,800 printed pages of
testimony in 60 public sessions. Laws 1907, JR 38 authorized a
second printing of 5,000 copies, suggesting wide interest. Former
Comm'r Fricke thought the proposals unfortunate.—MS, editorial
6–30–1907.—But he was now a spokesman for the Northwestern
Mutual. Besides N.Y. and Wis., there were about five other American investigations, and English and Canadian Royal Commissions.—
C 1907, 2:18.

37 Clough 19./ Vance 64./ Stalson 326. A tontine aided the construction
of the first Tammany Hall.—Davis 2:285./ If the principal sum were
forfeited on lapse, it was full tontine; if only dividends were forfeited, it was semi-tontine.—CR I, 198. See id., 22 for a forfeiture of
$17,000 deferred dividends by death 6 days before expiration of the
tontine period.

38 James (1947) 55–56./ Equitable v. Host, 124 Wis. 657 (1905), Case on
Appeal 146–61 tells of the Northwestern's practices./ Laws (P.&L.)
1857, 129, § 13; Laws (P.&L.) 1863, 323, § 5; Laws 1887, 328, § 2./
The unsophisticated Semi-Centennial History of the Northwestern
Mutual...(Pub. by authority of its executive committee, 1908) pp. 199–
200 thought the tontine significant in providing agents with incentive.

39 Tourtellotte v. Co., 155 Wis. 455 (1914) held the policyholder entitled
only to guaranteed dividends, not to those predicted by agents or
circulars. The Equitable's own Frick Committee condemned the

tontine.—C 1905, 2:930-93 has the report in full. See also Kimball (1958) 298, n. 38.

40   S 245 (1899)./ S 104, A 519 (1901); S 141, A 541 (1903)./ S 183 (1903)./ S 189 (1903)./ S 322 (1903), repeated in S 114 (1905)./ S 50 (1905).

41   C 1904 2:60-98; Equitable v. Host, 124 Wis. 657 (1905).

42   Laws 1905, 448./ C 1905, 2:27-45. See also Kimball (1958) 300-01, n. 40, 41, 42.

43   C 1906, 2:60, 64./ Laws 1907, 658, 636, amended by 1915, 312, § 11 and 1927, 148; C 1915, 2:vii. Laws 1911, 210 forbade deferred dividend policies for fraternals./ A 331 (1917) sought to repeal the 1911 law.

44   Acc't book in Rountree papers, in Hist. Soc. Library./ FUA 1871, 14./ FUA 1887, 181-82; and see FUA 1897, 134./ C 1911, 1:xix; and see C 1912, 1:xxvii and 1914, 1:xxv./ High commissions did not necessarily mean high incomes for agents; it might mean only more severe competition.—C 1915, 1:viii; FUA 1897, 134.

45   CR I,185. C 1905, 2:15. Knight 181.

46   S 383 (1897); S 103,A 578 (1901); S 173, 174, 323 (1903). Comm'r Host thought elimination of the tontine would halve commission rates, but he also urged legal limitation.—C 1905, 2:14-15; C 1906, 2:60, 62, 66.

47   MDN 4-27-1906; Laws 1907, 657.—These restrictions did not apply to nonparticipating stock companies nor to industrial policies./ Statement of Actuaries..., p. 3-5. Miles M. Dawson, the committee's renowned consulting actuary, also opposed the bill as impractical.—Dawson (1907b) 12./ S 320, A 686 (1907). The permitted loading was increased from a fourth to a third under pressure from the companies.—CR I, 161, 259; C 1907, 2:25./ Laws 1907, 668; SJ 1209 (1907); ST 1955, § 206.26(1)(b)./ See also Kimball (1958) 304, n. 46.

48   CR I, 260. Dawson (1907a) 28. Knight 181.

49   Knight 171./ Dawson (1907a) 12, 16-20.

50   S 319, A 684 (1907)./ Statement of Actuaries..., p.3-5./ SJ 1208 (1907); Laws 1909, 209.

51   Statement of Actuaries...,pp. 3,4. CR I, 143-44; C 1908, 2:14./ Dawson (1907a) 3, 5, 6, 24./ S 375, A 685, § 1948d (1907); AJ 1215, SJ 1208 (1907).

52   MS 3-13-1907; 6-29-1907; MDN 6-7-1907; MDN 6-9-1907.

53   MFP 7-14-1907. MS 7-14-1907. Eastern Underwriter (N.Y.; Boston) 11-14-1907. MS 11-30-1907. C 1908, 2:15. Of the 23 companies, 4 gave no notices, 4 no reasons, 11 blamed the new laws generally, while 3 blamed the limit on commissions.—Id. 8./ C 1910, 2:14.

54   MFP 12-1-1907; 12-7-1907; MS 12-1-1907; 12-2-1907. 12-21-1907.

55   MJ 11-24-1908. MFP 8-10-1908. MDN 3-23-1909.

56   Laws 1915, 312./ WSJ 6-30-1915./ Cf. C 1918, lxxxii with 1909, 2:86; Union Mutual Life of Maine, C 1948, 224./ See also Kimball (1958) 311, n. 55.

57   AJ 48-49 (1905SS)./ S 191 (1907). Ex-Pres. Cleveland submitted a brief against the bill.—MS 4-8-1907./ Laws 1907, 621./ Laws 1915, 31./ A 639 (1927); A 475 (1929); A 699 (1931)./ ST 1955, § 206.15.

58   Laws 1933, JR 87./ Res. 13A (1933); AJ 107, 459 (1933)./ See Galbraith for very provocative observations on the liberal demand for equality.

59   A 894 (1939)./ A 659 (1953)./ Res. 62A in AJ 1477 (1943) called for an investigation of management contracts, which some regarded as a

way of "siphoning" money out of mutuals.—CT 6-11-1943.
60 For a speech commenting on corruption and high salaries, see <u>Wis.</u>
    State <u>Bd. of Agriculture</u> Rept., 1906, 416. S 166 (1907)./ Laws 1907,
    146./ Laws 1907, 391./ A 121 (1909)./ Laws 1937, 178./ AJ 44 (1905SS).

CHAPTER IV, Section 4

1   Laws 1850, 232./ See generally Samuel Becker "Administrative
    Control of Ins. in Wis.," 4 <u>Wis.</u> <u>Law</u> <u>Review</u> 129–69 (1927); Wiltsey,
    esp. at 58–64.
2   Laws 1850, 232, §§ 7, 11./ Laws 1858, 103.
3   Gov. 1866, <u>vii</u>; Sec'y 1866, 36–37.
4   A 492 (1868)./ Laws 1870, 56, 59. The Att'y Gen. long retained
    some administrative duties; thus there was uncertainty whether he
    had a duty to prosecute for violations.—See, e.g., Laws 1870, 56,
    §§ 10, 23; 1885, 395; AJ 25 (1887); Laws 1887, 517.
5   A 113 (1872); A 10 (1872)./ C 1877, 8; AJ 23 (1878)./ SJ 266–67 (1878);
    S 211 (1878) (Committee's bill)./ SJ 413–14 (1878)./ Laws 1878, 214;
    AJ 26 (1879).
6   A 401 (1891)./ A 649 (1915); AJ 888 (1915).
7   Laws 1878, 214, § 2./ Laws 1881, 300, § 1; 1891, 84.
8   AJ 130–61, 1156–59; SJ 179, 1084–88 (1909)./ Laws 1911, 484./ Ekern
    v. McGovern, 154 Wis. 157 (1913)./ S 482 (1913)./ST 1955, § 200.01.
9   Laws 1878, 214, § 2; 1881, 300, § 6; 1883, 43./ AJ 200, 211, 215 (1883)./
    E.g., A 297, 856 (1887)./ Laws 1895, 31; 1897, 355./ Laws 1885, 395,
    § 2 made special provision for prosecutions, and Laws 1889, 520
    for attendance of the Comm'r at NAIC. In 1911 the Governor vetoed
    a regular appropriation for travel expenses.—S 344 (1911); SJ 1301–
    02 (1911). Laws 1915, 361 was a special appropriation for particular
    litigation.
10 C 1895, 2:<u>xvii–xviii</u>.
11 Laws 1870, 59, § 17.
12 To actuaries in Chicago, says C 1904, 2:40./ AJ 848–51 (1897); SJ
    1251–57 (1903).
13 AJ 61, 848 (1897); C 1895, 2:<u>ix</u>; S 10, § 1896t (1897)./ A 166 (1903)./
    SJ 1251–57; AJ 1379 (1903). Comm'r Host pointed out, in C 1905, 2:
    67 that Laws 1903, 44, § 15 (2) required him to value future interests
    for probate courts.
14 A 113 (1905) which became Laws 1905, 519 (bill signed by LaFollette)./
    AJ 2140–41 (1905). Comm'r Host supplied a detailed financial state-
    ment at request.—Res. 30A; AJ 582, 605–11 (1905). Laws 1909, 296
    extended the new policy of having fees paid to the state, not the
    Comm'r. See also AJ 57 (1909).
15 A 449 (1905)./ AJ 2133 (1905); MS 5-17-1905./ A 447 (1905); AJ 2134–
    35 (1905)./ A 446 (1905), which became Laws 1905, 503; amended SJ
    1497 (1905).
16 Laws 1907, 643./ Laws 1911, 609; 1913, 556./ Laws 1959, 136.
17 E.g., C 1909, 1:<u>xix–xxi</u>; 1910, 1:22; <u>A</u> <u>Plan</u> <u>Submitted</u> <u>to</u> <u>the</u> <u>Emergen-</u>
    <u>cy</u> <u>Bd.</u>, June 14, 1956. [A publication of the Wis. Ins. Dep't on file in
    Dep't of Budgets & Accounts.]/ SJ 444 (1941); Griffenhagen Rept. No.
    5, at 2 (1946), in LRef. Library./ See C 1908, 1:4 for tax collection.
    See C 1958, 52 for 1955, 1956, and 1957 expenditures. On the issue
    of federal vs. state regulation, and on rate regulation see Kimball
    & Boyce.

18 As early as 1878, a special deputy went to Connecticut for an examination.—C 1879, 96./ For Fricke's views, see FUA 1898, 92–93; C 1896, 2:x. C 1904, 2:38 expresses Comm'r Host's similar views.
19 S 322 (1899)./ A 253 (1905).
20 Cf. C 1895, 1:440 with AG 1904, 340./ AJ 130–61 (1909). MFP 1–26–1909. MS 1–28–1909. SJ 386–96 (1909). AG 1910, 437.
21 AJ 1156–60 (1909)./ Laws 1909, JR 51./ AG 1910, 17; Laws 1911, JR 49./ AG 1916, xxxiv./ AG 1919, xxxvi./ State v. Giljohann, State v. Fricke, dismissed for want of prosecution, Dec. 31, 1925.—Drawer 533, Microfilm Roll 174–B–101, Dane Cty Circuit Court records. State v. Host—Drawer 524, Microfilm Roll 174–B–48 -nothing in file about disposition. State v. Beedle–Drawer 474, Microfilm Roll 174–A–195, tried.
22 Laws 1909, 126, 438./ S 592 (1909)./ SJ 1140 (1909)./ AG 1910, 451–54./ C 1909, 1:xiii–xxvii./ C 1910, 1:19–22./ Laws 1911, 648.
23 AG 1948, 318 analyzed the situation before the 1949 law. A 180 (1927). For a depression budget cut, see SJ 189 (1933)./ MJ 12–14–1940; MS 12–7–1946./ WSJ 8–11–1948./ Laws 1949, 615./ Comm'r Lange refused to extend the examination program.—CT 9–20–1949.
24 Laws 1850, 232, §§ 7, 13./ Laws 1858, 103; 1859, 190./ Laws 1867, 158, 179.
25 Sec'y 1869, 27./ Laws 1870, 56, §§ 21, 22; 1870, 59, §§ 7, 8./ C 1872, 17–18; 1873, 10–12./ Laws 1899, 270, § 15 gave the Comm'r wide discretion to specify forms for stipulated premium companies.
26 C 1903, 2:xxxii–xxxiii./ C 1905, 2:16; 1906, 2:32, 67; 1907, 2:30; Laws 1907, 584./ CR I, 279 proposed a detailed form of gain and loss exhibit. Laws 1907, 584 gave the Comm'r some discretion in prescribing the form.
27 Laws 1907, 131, 391, 657, 658; 1917, 599./ See also Laws 1909, 459 (city and village mutuals). A 529 (1935) would have empowered the Comm'r to prescribe the form of accounting records. Of course, he could do so indirectly through prescription of report forms.
28 Laws 1859, 46, §§ 3, 12./ Cf. ST 1878, § 1938 with Laws 1905, 356./ Laws 1937, 226, § 202.19./ Despite their general exemption from insurance laws, Laws 1889, 334 subjected mutual benefit societies to reporting and publicity requirements.
29 Sec'y 1852, 20. C 1877, 123./ Certificates did not impress insurance men. E.g., FUA 1876, 124. However, they often urged fuller reports instead of the 1907 legislation; but as the Comm'r pointed out, all students of insurance knew about the tontine long before—more information was not the whole answer.—C 1908, 2:20.
30 Laws 1858, 103.
31 Laws 1858, 103./ Laws 1870, 56, §§ 21, 23.
32 C 1918, xxii; Smalley 6–42 to 6–45./ C 1905, 2:26 reported an examination of the Northwestern Mutual for the first time in 9 years. The mere cost of examination was a screening device; occasionally a company withdrew rather than pay it.—C 1877, 118.
33 C 1895, 2:ix./ S 222 (1907)./ Laws 1919, 655, § 1966–33g(2).
34 Laws 1915, 69; 1943, 234.
35 Laws 1850, 232./ Laws 1858, 103./ Laws 1859, 190.
36 Sec'y 1866, 36–37.
37 Laws 1870, 56, § 23./ Laws 1882, 281 gave broad discretion to exempt mutual benefit societies from the insurance laws.

38   Laws 1879, 171./ Cf. C 1878, 16; 1879, 10–15; 1881, 7 with C 1898, 2:
     vii./ Comm'r Fricke reported that 32 companies that were refused
     admission had since failed; most of them probably had a legal right
     to a license, he thought.—C 1898, 2:vii.
39   Laws 1887, 503; 1891, 267, § 2./ Laws 1891, 418, § 3; 1895, 175, § 6./
     Comm'r Root excluded a majority of such societies.—C 1892, iv.
     Laws 1897, 277, §§ 22, 30.
40   AG 1904, 128./ Laws 1911, 235; 1919, 655, § 1966–33k; 1911, 310; 1917,
     13; 1917, 19./ Laws 1919, 425, § 9./ See C 1904, 2:32–37, 1306–09;
     1905, 2:26, 1064–1137 for exercise of discretion with respect to the
     Prudential Ins. Co. See C 1919, xxiii for requirement that policies
     and records be in English.
41   A 688 (1927)./ Laws 1933, 31. Comm'r Ekern foresaw such need in
     C 1912, 2:xx./ C 1934, 15 (use of law)./ Many states had similar laws.
     They might pose constitutional questions, but this was crisis legis-
     lation and was not challenged during its brief life.
42   AG 1927, 459, 476, 529. AG 1946, 459 talks a more modern language
     about separation and delegation of powers and due process./ Wiltsey
     469./ Id. 139–51; Freund (1928) 71–74; Freund (1921).
43   Laws 1911, 83./ Laws 1911, 581./ Laws 1943, 375.
44   C 1896, 1:xi./ Laws 1911, 152, following N.Y. Laws 1909, 300./ Laws
     1909, 300./ Laws 1907, 150 permitted suspension for mere technical
     insolvency. See Laws 1893, 293; Wyman v. Kimberly-Clark, 93 Wis.
     554 (1896) for Wisconsin aspects of out-of-state dissolutions.
45   Boesel & Fieldman, "Liquidation of Mut . Ins. Cos. in Wis.," 1951
     Wis. Law. Review 493, esp. at 516–17. In re Wisconsin Mut., 241
     Wis. 394 (1942). See Davis v. Shearer, 90 Wis. 250 (1895) for excess
     assessment.
46   CT 4–9–1943; WSJ 5–13–1943 (opposition)./ AJ 1022 (1943)./ Davis
     v. Parcher, 82 Wis. 488, 498 (1892) held horizontal assessment vio-
     lated basic mutuality of mutual insurance, but see In re Builders'
     Mut., 229 Wis. 365, 380–81 (1938) (court satisfied with practical so-
     lution, even if not theoretically accurate).
47   CT 6–4–1948. E.g., Duel v. Ramar, 246 Wis. 604 (1944)./ CT 1–22–
     1947; 5–5–1948.
48   Laws 1911, 216; 1917, 55; 1927, 170. For interpretations, see AG 1927,
     259; 1935, 232.
49   Laws 1903, 130; 1909, 234./ Laws 1931, 256.
50   AG 1904, 347./ AG 1908, 533. Title guaranty companies were in-
     surance companies or not depending on whether they were organized
     under the insurance laws or the general incorporation statutes.—AG
     1921, 1095.
51   AG 1906, 398./ AG 1908, 492./ AG 1912, 492.
52   AG 1915, 778./ AG 1926, 368./ AG 1926, 354./ AG 1912, 1:317, 320
     (Woodland Farms)./ For some recent sales warranty problems, see
     AG 1958, 260, 271.
53   AG 1906, 716; 1908, 437; but see 1924, 369./ AG 1908, 508.
54   AG 1921, 178, 183.
55   AG 1950, 509; AG 1958, 242./ Laws 1949, 287; 1951, 406 (athletic
     plans); AJ 34–35 (1955); Laws 1945, 494.
56   Laws 1895, 280. A 660 (1895) even proposed codification of the
     common law of insurance./ S 10 (1897)./ AJ 61, 1282–84, SJ 27, 707–
     08, 724–26 (1897).

57 S 175 (1925); AJ 657–59 (1925). See Edwin E. Witte, Memo. on the Hist. of Ins. Revision Bill, 175S, Feb. 6, 1925, in LRef. Library./ Amdt. 1S incorporated changes at the suggestion of insurance interests./ For reports on the struggle see WSJ 3–16–1925; 5–8–1925; SJ 1364 (1925); CT 4–29–1925./ SJ 1309 (1925) (defeat of bill).

58 MJ 10–10–1925./ SJR 48, AJR 62 (1927)./ S 50 (1931); SJ 1925–27 (1931)./ Laws 1933, 344, 487, 489./ AJR 87 (1943); AJ 1638 (1943)./ MS 4–11–1957.

59 Laws 1937, 197 authorized destruction of obsolete records; it was amended by Laws 1947, 41. In the 1956 reorganization, 176 file drawers of records were disposed of.—C 1957, 8.

60 See generally, Reports of the Secretaries of State in 1850's and 1860's.

61 Breese had experience in farming, small town business, and local public office. He soon left politics and became a prosperous manufacturer.—James E. Jones, ed., A History of Columbia County, Wis. (Lewis Pub. Co., Chicago, 1914), 2:447–49.

62 C 1870–73, inclusive.

63 C 1874–77, inclusive.

64 C 1878–82, inclusive.

65 C 1883–98, inclusive.

66 C 1895–98, inclusive. Since there was no effective national regulation, to urge it was mainly to urge freedom from state control, and was a laissez faire position. Thus, see FUA 1873, 9; 1874, 19; 1879, 170; 1895, 33. See FUA 1895, 29; 1898, 90 for speeches by Fricke. His tax views were ignored by legislators seeking new sources of revenue.

67 C 1895–98, inclusive.

68 C 1899–1902, inclusive.

69 C 1903–06, inclusive. Host was chairman of the Committee on Ann. Acct'g & Distribution of Surplus of Life Ins. Cos. for the Conference of Govs., Att'ys Gen. and Ins. Comm'rs.

70 WSJ 11–9–1908.

71 AJ 130–61, 1156–59, SJ 179, 1084–88 (1909). E.g., AG 1908, 435–537; 1910, 423–89.

72 Ekern lost in 1908 by a vote of 2,162 to 2,010.—WBB 1909, 543./ See C 1910, 2:7./ WBB 1911, 733; 1913, 529.

73 Ekern v. McGovern, 154 Wis. 157 (1913). See also Case and Supp. Case on Appeal. ST 1911, § 970 (removal power).

74 SJ 142–44, 168–73, Appendix I (1913).

75 WSJ 7–1–1915. WSJ 10–3–1914. MFP 12–30–1914. MJ 1–26–1950. WBB 1925, 641.

76 WSJ 8–11–1915./ C 1916, vii (denial).

77 WSJ 8–6–1923.

78 For the first stages of the Smith–Ekern fight, see AJ 1210–14, 1249, 1261, 1277–81, 1303–07, 1327 (1925); SJ 1366 (1925); Res. 59A (1925); Res. 62A (1925); CT 5–14–1925; 6–6–1925.

79 For the second stage of the fight, see SJ 920–22, 923–25, 940–41 (1925); WSJ 5–15–1925; WSJ 6–12–1925.

80 For the concluding round, see WSJ 5–18–1925. SJ 1364–75 (1925). Wisconsin News (Milwaukee) 5–15–1925; MJ 5–17–1925; 5–30–1925.

81 C 1856–1959 inclusive./ Laws 1957, 321 (credit life); the credit life story is told in MJ 5–3–57; CT 5–29–57; MJ 6–11–57; WSJ

6-11-57; Executive Office Release, 5 P.M. 7-5-1957; MJ 8-14-57; CT 8-14-57; WSJ 12-31-57; MJ 1-3-58; CT 3-31-58; MJ 4-7-58./ Laws 1957, 552; see also 1959, 2 (welfare funds)./ CT 7-25-56 (advertising code)./ MJ 4-7-58; 5-23-59; WSJ 4-4-58 (investigations)./ MJ 9-15-57; WSJ 12-26-57 (automobile damage claims)./ For editorial comment favorable to Rogan, see WSJ 6-18-59; MJ 6-6-59; and see news story on his testimonial dinner in MJ 6-30-59./ MJ 7-8-59 tells of the Senate debate.

82   AG 1908, 457./ E.g., AG 1916, 488; 1924, 622.

83   C 1921, 243; 1924, 150-56, 173-74; 1925, 162; 1926, 12./ Time Ins. Co. v. Smith, 184 Wis. 455 (1924). Once the Assembly directed the Att'y Gen. to aid tobacco farmers who claimed a company defrauded them on hail insurance policies./ Res. 51A, AJ 1095-96 (1925).

84   AJR 61, 1939./ Res. 62A, 1943; AJ 1477, 1638 (1943).

CHAPTER V, Introduction

1   Kimball (1957).
2   See also Kimball (1957) 545-48.
3   E.g., Troy v. Carpenter, 4 Wis. 20 (1855).
4   See, e.g., Joliffe v. Co., 39 Wis. 111, 119 (1875).
5   For examples of interpretative problems, see Kimball (1958) 379-80 and n. 6. For industry thinking, see FUA 1875, 13, 43, 121, 155; 1876, 90.
6   See Kimball (1955). Kimball (1958) 381, n. 7.

CHAPTER V, Section 1

1   Kimball (1957) 548-49.
2   Comstock v. Ass'n, 116 Wis. 382 (1903)./ Graves v. Order, 165 Wis. 427 (1917); but see Sheafor v. Co., 166 Wis. 498 (1918); 170 Wis. 307 (1919).
3   A 760 (1893)./ Laws 1901, 235, expressly extended to automobile insurance by Laws 1931, 393; but see Corwin v. Salter, 194 Wis. 333 (1927) on the need for the extension./ Immediate notice requirements were in Laws 1876, 344, § 6; 1878, 255, § 11; 1887, 305, § 9; 1891, 268, § 7; 1895, 387./ Laws 1911, 84. Laws 1913, 601./ Laws 1911, 84 (accident and health); 1925, 372 (liability).
4   Laws 1911, 84./ Laws 1911, 154./ S 272 (1913)./ SJ 651, 776 (1913).
5   FUA 1872, 42; 1873, 46; 1875, 56; 1876, 31; 1877, 117 indicate industry policy./ Laws 1931, 244./ Laws 1915, 98.
6   E.g., FUA 1873, 81./ A 201 (1931), which became Laws 1931, 330; AJ 442, 488, 1070, SJ 1372, 1448, 1532, 1597 (1931).
7   Laws 1870, 56, § 37; 1870, 59, § 26./ Laws 1889, 480; 1891, 418, § 8./ A 295 (1881)./ A 760 (1893); S 444 (1911)./ A 260 (1895); A 376 (1899); A 49, 99 (1901); A 902 (1913)./ A 49 (1901)./ A 706 (1949)./ S 385, 389 (1897).
8   A 198 (1869)./ S 25, § 2 (1874)./ S 146, A 299, (1943)./ SJ 203 (1943).
9   Laws 1895, 387./ AG 1908, 470./ AG 1912, 475. C 1919, xxv./ See also AG 1914, 432.
10 Laws 1849, 145./ E.g., see Laws (P.&L.) 1857, 331.
11 Laws 1859, 46, § 6. A 395 (1881) would have given this committee of reference subpoena powers./ Laws 1878, 255, § 11./ Laws 1880, 111./ Laws 1878, 306, § 11./ Laws 1895, 387.

12 AJ 33 (1927)./ Laws 1927, 162.
13 Laws 1913, 316./ S 265 (1945)./ Laws 1915, 29 exempted town mutuals from the 1913 law; 1919, 425, § 15 extended it to marine, plate glass, sprinkler leakage, and livestock.
14 Cullen treats exhaustively the cases and statutes on the direct action problem, as they stood in 1934./ Glatz v. Co., 175 Wis. 42 (1921). Dissenting judges thought defense of the suit subjected the company to direct liability.—Id. 48, 53./ Laws 1915, 546./ A 334 (1907) proposed that the employers' liability policy be a liability rather than an indemnity policy.
15 Remmel v. Czaja, 183 Wis. 503 (1924); Lozon v. Leamon, 186 Wis. 84 (1925)./ But see A 617 (1941).
16 Laws 1925, 341./ Laws 1925, 372./ S 454, SJ 1265, A 588, AJ 1578 (1927).
17 Stone v. Exchange, 200 Wis. 585 (1930)./ Fanslau v. Co., 194 Wis. 8 (1927); Bro v. Co., 194 Wis. 293 (1927) (no enlargement of coverage)./ Morgan v. Hunt, 196 Wis. 298 (1928) (new kind of clause)./ Ducommun v. Exchange, 193 Wis. 179 (1927).
18 Laws 1929, 467.
19 S 35 (1931); SJ 866 (1931); AJ 2457 (1931); Laws 1931, 375. See also S 54 (1931), which prohibited insertion of no-action clauses.— It passed the Senate but lost in the Assembly.—SJ 1721, AJ 2731 (1931)./ E.g., Polzin v. Wachtl, 209 Wis. 289 (1932) (adherence to position); Lang v. Baumann, 213 Wis. 258 (1933) (statute given effect)./ The court adhered to its old position for general liability, where the statute did not apply.—Sweitzer   v. Fox, 226 Wis. 26 (1937).
20 Wiechmann v. Huber, 211 Wis. 333 (1933); but see Suschnick v. Co., 211 Wis. 474 (1933)./ Ritterbusch v. Sexmith, 256 Wis. 507 (1950) (court hesitant); Perlick v. Co., 274 Wis. 558 (1957); Pinkerton v. United Services Auto Ass'n, 5 Wis. 2d. 54 (1958); Schultz v. Hastings, 5 Wis. 2d. 265 (1958) (waiver by filing SR-21)./ Laws 1959, 380.
21 Laws 1893, 235./ S 183, SJ 1204 (1937); S 361 (1939).
22 AG 1928, 570 approved such a fraternal bylaw./ Laws 1941, 81./ Laws 1943, 394./ A 411, AJ 1228, SJ 1174 (1945).
23 Wisconsin Zinc v. Co., 162 Wis. 39 (1916); Hilker v. Co., 204 Wis. 1, 15 (1931)./ A 439, AJ 1379 (1951); S 443 (1953).

CHAPTER V, Section 2

1 See Kimball (1957) 552-58.
2 Farren 63 showed early appreciation of the conflict.
3 E.g., Kelly v. Co., 3 Wis. 254, 266 (1854) (Wisconsin's first in-surance case).
4 Kimball (1958) 406, n. 4.
5 For a modern case to same effect as May case, see, e.g., Fish v. Co., 241 Wis. 166 (1942). Schomer v. Co., 50 Wis. 575, 580 (1880) recognizes the parol evidence rule as a difficulty./ For modifica-tion see Winans v. Co., 38 Wis. 342 (1875); Hotchkiss v. Co., 76 Wis. 269 (1890)./ E.g., McDonald v. Ass'n, 93 Wis. 348 (1896) (informa-tion obtained in other capacity).
6 For industry concern see FUA 1874, 21; 1876, 134; 1886, 212. For efforts at reform, see FUA 1874, 83; 1876, 134; 1882, 57; 1888, 91; 1897, 127.

7 ST 1878, § 1977./ Laws 1870, 59, § 22; 1871, 13, § 1./ ST 1878, § 1977./ S 14, A 11 (1905) were efforts to extend the law to uncompensated agents. Laws 1905, 353 excluded fraternals and noncommercial mutuals. The conflict there was between one policyholder and the aggregate of policyholders rather than between one policyholder and the soulless and distant corporation. Laws 1911, 577, § 13(b) made persons transmitting applications or premiums to the state life fund agents of the policyholders, not of the fund. Laws 1911, 507, extended to fraternals by Laws 1917, 67, estopped a life or disability company to defend on ground that insured was not in the condition of health the policy required, if its medical examiner issued a certificate of health. A 290 (1915) sought to repeal this statute.

8 S 148 (1885).

9 Knox v. Co., 50 Wis. 671 (1881) (geographical limits)./ Stehlick v. Co., 87 Wis. 322 (1894) (oral contract).

10 E.g., Palmer v. Co., 44 Wis. 201 (1878) (clauses ineffective)./ Renier v. Co., 74 Wis. 89, 98 (1889)./ Zell v. Co., 75 Wis. 521 (1890); but see Goldberg v. Co., 170 Wis. 116 (1919) (a town mutual).

11 Laws 1891, 195, § 4 (2d)./ For the suggestion on motivation, see Welch v. Ass'n 120 Wis. 456, 464 (1904)./ Dowling v. Co., 92 Wis. 63 (1896) (declaring unconstitutionality); Bourgeois v. Co., 86 Wis. 606 (1893).

12 Laws 1895, 387.

13 Chamberlain v. Co., 109 Wis. 4 (1901), in effect overruling Mathers v. Ass'n, 78 Wis. 588 (1891), supra, n. 9./ Tomsecek v. Co., 113 Wis. 114 (1902)./ Bostwick v. Co., 116 Wis. 392 (1903)./ Id., at 423–24.

14 DeGroot v. Co., 179 Wis. 202 (1923)./ Spohn v. Co., 190 Wis. 446 (1926); accord, Klingler v. Co., 193 Wis. 72 (1927); but see Stillman v. Co., 192 Wis. 204 (1927)./ Sachs v. Co., 201 Wis. 537 (1930).

15 Company complaint of mistreatment did not seem fully justified; indeed an occasional decision seemed unrealistically to circumscribe the agent's power. Thus Mattice v. Society, 270 Wis. 504 (1955) would not require company to repay money borrowed by agent when it appeared to lender that transaction was purchase of single premium annuity. Jeske v. General Accident Fire & Life Assur. Corp., 1 Wis. 2d. 70 (1957) was a recent case dealing at length with a problem of agents' powers.

CHAPTER V, Section 3

1 A 492 (1868).

2 Massachusetts adopted a standard fire policy by Acts 1873, 331; New York by Laws 1886, 488. The latter was the first extensively adopted./ S 7 (1881)./ C 1881, 6./ FUA 1876, 90–113. FUA 1881, 40 suggested elimination of excessive competition as an objective of the uniform policy movement.

3 AJ 19 (1883)./ S 106, A 272 (1883)./ A 192 (1883)./ A 632 (1885)./ S 130, 168, A 750 (1889)./ Laws 1891, 195./ Laws 1895, 289.

4 SJ 313 (1895)./ Laws 1895, 387./ Dowling v. Co., 92 Wis. 63 (1896). Despite the Dowling case, A 376 (1899), and A 99 (1901) would have directed the Comm'r to prepare a standard accident policy.

5 FUA 1877, 116./ FUA 1895, 21, 32 (criticism of Comm'r)./Williams 3 said the N.Y. standard policy was drafted by a committee of the

BFU of N.Y.

6 Laws 1895, 387./ Laws 1917, 127./ In 1914 NAIC approved a revised policy; as amended it was adopted in Wis. in 1917, and in N.Y. in 1918.—This was known as the "new" N.Y. Standard Policy.—NAIC 1917, 113. Cf. Laws 1917, 127 with 1918 N.Y. Standard Fire Policy, in Goble (1949) 894.

7 SJ 902–09 (1933); S 355 (1933)./ For favorable company attitudes, see Williams. He was a company man, with Ins. Co. of North America. He favored revision to forestall demand for more legislative control of insurance./ Laws 1945, 474; and see also S 207 (1957); Laws 1959, 41. Cf. N.Y. Standard Policy of 1943 in Goble (1949) 898./ AG 1945, 304 ruled the standard policy law did not apply to the state fire fund. See also S 370 (1945) (standard multiple perils policy); S 65 (1947) (standard provisions for multiple perils policy); Laws 1929, 440 (registered town mutuals); A 528 (1935) and A 546 (1937) (all town mutuals). Laws 1939, 394 was a standard fire policy for town mutuals, revised by 1951, 730. See also S 561 (1919) (casualty); A 735 (1931) (automobile).

8 N.Y. Legis. Ins. Inv. Committee Rept., Vol. X, Bill 1030; N.Y. Laws 1907, 714, replaced by standard provisions law in N.Y. Laws 1909, 33, § 101./ CR I, 253–59./ A 685 (1907); AJ 1215, SJ 1208 (1907).

9 Laws 1911, 84./ Laws 1913, 601; Time Ins. Co. v. Smith, 184 Wis. 455, 457 (1924) (recommendation of NAIC)./ Williams v. Co., 168 Wis. 456 (1918)./ See also Kimball (1958) 423, n. 9.

10 Laws 1911, 208. Time Ins. Co. v. Smith, 184 Wis. 455, 483 (1924) (5,000 provisions; problem of standardization, in general)./ C 1924, 152; 1921, 244.

11 SJ 803 (1921); SJR 68 (1921); Time Ins. Co. v. Smith, 184 Wis. 455 (1924)./ See also C 1924, 150; 1926, 12–13. But see U.S.F. & G. v. Smith, 184 Wis. 309 (1924).

12 S 85, 358 (1917); A 253 (1923); S 390 (1931); SJ 1721, 1662, 1718 (1931); A 815 (1931); AJ 2715 (1931); Laws 1939, 44./ Laws 1951, 614; published as a pamphlet by NAIC in 1950./ See also Laws 1949, 458 (standard provisions for group life).

13 See, e.g, FUA 1895, 32.

14 See Kimball (1955) 460–65./ Laws 1869, 93./ A 336 (1874)./ Laws 1878, 304./ S 627 (1915) would have applied this doctrine to all insurance. Laws 1905, 51 exempted domestic mutuals from attachment of the application.

15 S 256 (1897); S 80, A 94 (1899); S 141 (1901); S 181 (1903); S 81 (1905)./ Laws 1899, 316.

16 Laws 1907, 127./ S 268 (1907) would have required the life policy to contain the "entire contract." Laws 1911, 84 applied the "entire contract" law to disability, Laws 1939, 44 to family expense accident and health.

17 Laws 1909, 288, extended to fraternals by 1917, 67. Spray v. Order, 221 Wis. 329 (1936) illustrates how the statute overturned the common law of warranties. A 539 (1935) and A 400 (1937) would further soften warranty law./ Laws 1919, 652./ Laws 1911, 84./ See also Kimball (1958) 428, n. 17.

18 A 405 (1871)./ C 1877, 120–23. Doyle did not often take a position on insurance.

19 A 343 (1893)./ S 330 (1901); S 172 (1903); S 45 (1905); S 322 (1903);

S 188 (1903); S 327, A 685 (1907). CR I, 255; S 438 (1907)./ Laws 1909, 108; 1943, 166./ Laws 1911, 175 extended the principle to fraternals.

20 Laws 1895, 387./ S 443 (1911); SJ 600, AJ 1022 (1911)./ Laws 1919, 361./ S 78 (1925)./ Laws 1949, 483.

21 A 616 (1955); A 482 (1957); and see AJR 101 (1957)./ A 221 (1949)./ Laws 1923, 437./ A 166 (1939); A 552 (1941); A 210 (1943). See also A 908 (1959).

22 Laws 1925, 372, § 2./ Laws 1931, 393, 477./ Laws 1955, 349. See also S 119 (1959) and A 920 (1959).

23 Laws 1931, 477./ AG 1927, 225.

24 Segall v. Co., 224 Wis. 379 (1937)./ The Wick case was followed by Schwenkhoff v. Farmers Mut. Auto Ins. Co., 6 Wis. 2d. 44 (1959)./ A 689 (1957)./ AJ 1447; SJ 1794 (1957)./ A 250 (1959).

25 Fehr v. Co., 246 Wis. 228 (1944)./ Haumschild v. Company, 7 Wis. 2d. 130 (1959), the most recent of a series of cases dealing with the choice of law problem as to interspousal immunity, decided that the law of the domicile should govern.

26 A 640 (1871); S 210 (1876); S 235 (1893); S 161 (1895); A 403 (1899); S 235 (1903); S 28 (1901); S 175 (1903); S 177 (1903); S 156 (1913); A 216 (1933); A 535 (1935); A 199 (1937); A 219 (1929); A 750 (1929).

27 A 754 (1935).

28 Laws 1929, 320./ Laws 1929, 456, overruling Struebing v. Co., 197 Wis. 487 (1929). Filipkowski v. Co., 206 Wis. 39 (1931) held the statute did not apply retroactively to existing policies. A 607 (1933) sought to repeal the "other insurance" act of 1929. Laws 1933, 487, § 92 confirmed it. A 187 (1957) would have permitted the "other insurance" clause to be added by endorsement.

29 Laws 1943, 192./ Laws 1945, 90; 1951, 452. But see A 232 (1935); AJ 1506, SJ 1616 (1935).

CHAPTER V, Section 4

1 A 41 (1872); Laws 1874, 347. This analysis of the origin of the valued policy law essentially agrees with that in FUA 1875, 151. The valued policy existed earlier in marine insurance, but there it was contractual. See, e.g., Kent 3:220. The source of the idea is obscure. One thoughtful London insurance man thought it had European origins.—FUA 1880, 26. It was, he thought, an attempt to force valuation before issuance of the policy. In Europe, valuation was made simultaneously for insurance and for taxation. The supposition is plausible, though European derivation was probably remote, for the law was introduced by Ass'yman Felt of Rock cty. in 1874.— AJ 5, 51 (1872); SJ 71 (1874); WBB 1874, 450.

2 For crucial votes, see SJ 499, 538, AJ 722 (1874). Raney 247 (on Grangers in legislature). WBB 1874, 448–71 for political affiliation. See also FUA 1879, 51–52 and 1896, 102 for connection of law with agrarian radicalism. See infra, Chapt. 6., Sect. 1, "Life Insurance Taxation After 1870," for voting on life insurance tax bill. There was close correlation in the voting on these two measures.

3 E.g., FUA 1897, 49. Cf. FUA 1886, 87 with 1897, 106.

4 FUA 1879, 52; A 147 (1875); A 218 (1878); A 168 (1881)./ A 82 (1887); S 111 (1887); A 381 (1895); A 433 (1905); S 148 (1909). The 1905 bill

would have exempted town, church, and city and village mutuals from the law, for the Att'y Gen. ruled that town mutuals were caught by the statute.—C 1898, 3:xx. The 1909 bill would have included personal property, too.

5 A 568 (1909); Laws 1915, 265./ SJ 763 (1915) (vote on A 377)./ Laws 1917, 461; for controversy over the repeal of the repeal law, see AJ 566, 594, SJ 957 (1917); and Subst. Amdt.1S to A 200 (1917).

6 S 382 (1929); A 605 (1933)./ S 377, A 918 (1933); A 336 (1935). For legislative controversy, see SJ 788 (1929); AJ 1264, 1494, 2591 (1933); SJ 2168 (1935), and journal indices.

7 FUA 1880, 131. C 1896, 1:viii said that the valued policy law and taxation were the main reasons for company withdrawal from the state.

8 See, e.g., C 1895, 1:vii; 1896, 1:viii; 1897, 1:v; 1905, 1:14; 1906, 1:4./ C 1915, 1:xviii; 1917, ix; Madison Democrat (Wis.) 7-15-1917./ Johnson (1926b) 6; SJ 902, 908-09 (1933)./ A 292 (1919); A 55 (1931); S 19 (1935).

9 Reilly v. Co., 43 Wis. 449, 455 (1877); Thompson v.Co., 43 Wis. 459 (1877); Bammessel v. Co., 43 Wis. 463 (1877); Thompson v. Co., 45 Wis. 388 (1878).

10 For Spooner's views, C 1878, 16; 1879, 16; 1880, 10. The Governor adopted Spooner's report and recommendations.—AJ 33 (1881).

11 FUA 1877, 124./ C 1878, 18.

12 A 257 (1879); A 232 (1880); S 246, A 168 (as amended) (1881); A 272 (1883); A 140, 244 (1885); A 684 (1887); A 571 (1889).

13 A 140 (1885)./ A 571 (1889)./ A 232 (1880).

14 Temple v. Co., 109 Wis. 372 (1901); Bank v. Co., 214 Wis. 6 (1934). A 211 (1903)./ Winfield V. Alexander, "The Wis. 'Valued Policy' Law," 10 Wis. Law Review 248, 253, n. 21a (1935).

15 AG 1932, 634./ A 565, 918, and Subst. Amdt. 2A (1933); AJ 2076 (1933); S 221 (1935).

16 For distinction between the kinds of three-quarter clauses, see FUA 1877, 130./ FUA 1876, 13; 1877, 96; AJ 24-25 (1877)./ Racine Argus (Wis.), 3-31-1838 (Racine bylaws)./ Laws 1867, 483, § 6./ Laws 1870, 374, § 28./ Laws 1899, 167, § 7 (bicycle mutuals)./ FUA 1877, 106, 108./ FUA 1877, 130; id., 112.

17 FUA 1877, 114, 120 (concern about under-insurance)./ FUA 1873, 94, 95; NBFU, Exec. Committee, Proc., 1873, 81./ FUA 1886, 65 (additional income).

18 A 537 (1893), Laws 1895, 256./ C 1895, 1:ix, This reversed an earlier opinion of an Ass't Att'y Gen.— C 1895, 1:444-45./ Id., 447.

19 S 322, 326, A 417, 597 (1897)./ S 384 (1897); Laws 1897, 343./ See also C 1913, 17.

20 See Newton v. Co., 125 Wis. 289 (1905); Bloch v. Co., 132 Wis. 150 (1907); AG 1908, 439; 1912, 1:321; 1913, 2:431, 434; 1917, 491; 1920, 274; Laws 1913, 208; 1933, 149; 1943, 327.

CHAPTER VI, Section 1

1 Wisconsin insurance tax revenues were over $7,000,000 in 1955.— C 1956, 8-9./ Mass. Laws May 1785, 18./ Mass. Laws Jan. 1818, 180,/ E.g., Mass. Laws Jan. 1823, 80./ Mass. Laws 1832, 95; 1835, 147.

2 N.Y. Laws 1814, 49./ N.Y. ST 1829, I:714 (1824 law); N.Y. Laws 1829, 336./ Zartman & Price 80./ N.Y. Laws 1837, 30./ N.Y. Laws 1849,

178.
3   Laws 1851, 177; 1852, 257, § 5.
4   E.g., AJ 150 (1853); Pets. A 123 (1853) and S 343 (1858) (to reduce
    tax to 1%)./ A 48 (1860) (to eliminate tax); Laws 1859, 190, §§ 4,5./
    Fire Dep't v. Helfenstein, 16 Wis. 136 (1862).
5   Laws 1869, 105. S 251 (1871) would have excluded premiums on
    buildings too far from water to get real protection. FUA 1878, 120;
    1896, 33 illustrate occasional later criticism./ ST 1955, § 201.59./
    E.g., A 227 (1925); A 415 (1937) (to increase tax). AG 1914, 437 ruled
    the state fund could not pay the tax; Laws 1927, 113 required it to do
    so on municipal property, though not on state property. Laws 1933,
    168 required self-insured property owners to pay. AG 1945, 372
    ruled that premiums included assessments.
6   Laws 1887, 486; 1893, 147; 1899, 32; 1911, 578./ Town mutuals had to
    pay on protected risks.—AG 1904, 104. They did not pay very well.—
    C 1920, 1:ix.
7   Laws 1878, 303; 1885, 308; 1889, 242./ Laws 1913, 465.
8   Laws 1899, 264./ A 266 (1905)./ AG 1902, 134./ Laws 1957. 453; and
    see also S 205 (1957)./ But see AG 1928, 298.
9   AG 1904, 469./ Laws 1913, 465; 1927, 215, 512./ E.g., A 181 (1927)(ten
    miles); S 152 (1927) (remove limit).
10 Laws 1859, 190./ Competitive advantage was probably the purpose of
    A 349 (1859); it would have imposed a $2,000 license fee on out-of-
    state companies. Wisconsin premiums varied from $400 to $57,000;
    such a fee would drive the smaller companies from the state.
11 Laws 1861, 201; 1862, 166./ A 439 (1864)./ Sec'y 1866, 37.
12 Laws 1867, 158, § 5./ Laws 1870, 56, § 33; 59, § 27./ A 689 (1871)./
    C 1872, 51 urged elimination of the initial $500 fee for fire and ma-
    rine firms. Laws 1876, 300 did eliminate it. Laws 1877, 182 closed
    up a loophole causing the state to lose money. It designated proper-
    ty in the state rather than premiums paid in the state as the tax
    basis.—See C 1877, 27. As new forms of insurance became common,
    they were usually assimilated to fire insurance for tax purposes.—
    E.g., Laws 1880, 105 (accident); 1880, 281 (hail). But see Laws 1897,
    277, § 24 (domestic casualty and surety). Modern multiple line un-
    derwriting created administrative problems because of different tax
    treatment for different lines.—See John R. Lange, The Problems of
    Multiple Line Taxation (1952), memo, in LRef. Library.
13 Laws 1870, 56, § 29; 59, § 20.
14 Industry views on taxation may be found in FUA 1872, Supp. Proc.
    19; 1873, 71–80; 1874, 59–65 (putting the constitutional case against
    discriminatory taxation); 1876, 115; 1877, 20 (denouncing gross
    premium taxation as a "political crime"); 1878, 13; 1879, 107 (criti-
    cizing retaliatory laws as Chinese walls); 1884, 20.
15 A 200 (1874)./ A 401 (1874); AJ 541–42, 616–17, SJ 585, 600 (1874).
16 Sec'y 1877, 77–78./ C 1878, 12./ AJ 17 (1885); AJ 15 (1889); AJ 21
    (1899)./ In 1913 insurance taxes provided about 6% of the state's
    revenue.—AJ 62 (1913).
17 C 1895, 1:v–vii; 1897, 2:xxii–xxiii; 1898, 3:xxiii–xxiv.
18 E.g., A 13 (1899); A 408 (1903); S 453 (1905). Laws 1905, 325./ C 1896,
    1:v; 1904, 1:2; 1906, 1:26./ Laws 1909, 290; C 1909, ix.
19 ST 1955, § 76.30.
20 FUA 1898, 93 (Fricke)./ Laws 1878, 255, § 18; 1879, 162; 1889, 346,

§ 11 and 1891, 268, § 11 (both church companies); 1895, 175; 1897, 316; 1899, 167; 1905, 55./ Laws 1889, 524 (druggists') 1893, 230; 1895, 64; 1903, 128./ A 408 (1903)./ Laws 1905, 325; 1909, 290./ Laws 1913, 210./ S 30 (1917).

21 A 497 (1923)./ AJ 325–27 (1925)./ AG 1924, 260; Laws 1925, 414./ Cf. C 1926, 20 with 1925, 15.

22 E.g., A 391 (1921); A 893 (1931); A 762 (1939); A 660 (1951); ST 1957, § 76.30./ MJ 4–9–1943; CT 4–8–1943.

23 CT 2–22–1945; 3–23–1945; Public Adm'n Clearing House, Release No. 5, 4–6–1945, in LRef. Library./ S 273 (1945) (effort by Comm'r)./ WSJ 3–23–1945; MJ 3–23–1945; CT, editorial 3–27–1945./ Prudential v. Benjamin, 328 U.S. 408 (1946)./ CT 5–10–1945; WSJ 7–31–1945; Claims 2S, 3S, 4S (1945); SJ 1337–44, 1456 (1945).

24 CT 4–12–1951; A 660 (1951); A 101, Subst. Amdt. 1A, 2A (1953); GBPG 4–27–1953. CT 2–24–1955; A 118 (1955); AJ 115 (1955). MJ 6–18–1955; CT 10–21–1955./ See also A 583 (1957); A 484 (1959). A 567 (1941) reflected the need for more money; it would have made agents' licensing fees real revenue producers.

25 Laws 1947, 276./ S 433, A 660 (1951).

26 Laws 1909, 259./ C 1909, 1:ix; 1910, 1:16; 1911, 1:xx./ Laws 1913, 366, following a suggestion in AG 1912, 467, 472./ Laws 1925, 375 extended the 1913 law to all insurance. AG 1956, 186; MJ 6–3–56; 12–13–56 all deal with the problem of a national union welfare plan, insured by an unadmitted insurer.

27 S 293 (1927); A 944 (1931)./ Laws 1949, 436.

28 Stipulated premium companies, assessment companies, fraternals and mutual benefit societies were treated differently. The first two were taxed more lightly; the latter two were exempt. See Laws 1899, 326; 1901, 21; 1899, 326; ST 1955, § 76.34.

29 N.Y. Laws 1865, 694 seems to have been the first retaliatory law.

30 A 401 (1874).

31 AJ 617 (1874); SJ 600 (1874)./ WBB 1874, 448–71./ Raney 247 (party division).

32 SJ 600, 630–35 (1874); Res. 34S (1874).

33 A 106 (1876); Williamson & Smalley 82. For memorials, see AJ Index 87–89. AJ 340 (1876)./ AJ 366 (1876); WBB 1876, 451–81.

34 Laws 1878, 256./ S 163, A 508 (1878), SJ 246 (1878). There were at least 230 petitions in the two houses. For list, see Gen'l Index to SJ 113–18 (1878)(originals in Archives)./ SJ 454–56 (1878); WBB 1878, 455–86. A similar split occurred in the Assembly.—AJ 707–09 (1878); WBB 1878, 455–86.

35 S 156 (1879)./ SJ 374–76 (1879)./ S 253, A 241 (1880)./ SJ 399–402 (1880)./ AJ 558 (1880); WBB 1880, 498–528. The Northwestern Mutual's vigorous opposition was important in 1880.—See W. Merrill 9.

36 Fricke's opposition to taxation, in C 1895, 1:v–vii; 1897, 2:xxii–xxiii expressed the industry point of view.—FUA 1896, 136. Cf. Comm'r Beedle's attitude in C 1908, 2:29–32. Fricke's willingness to tax surplus was based upon his dislike of the tontine.—Fricke (1902) 67.

37 Laws 1870, 59, § 27./ Laws 1880, 105./ Travelers' v. Fricke, 94 Wis. 258 (1896); and see Case and Briefs on Appeal./ Travelers' v. Fricke, 99 Wis. 367 (1898). C. J. Cassoday dissented on collection of back taxes, id. at 376, essentially on an estoppel ground.

38 Fidelity v. Fricke, 102 Wis. 107 (1899)./ Metropolitan Plate Glass

Co. v. Fricke, 102 Wis. 117 (1899)./ State v. Society, 103 Wis. 208 (1899) (C. J. Cassoday dissenting again for the reasons he expressed in the Travelers' case)./ Cf. C 1898, 2:<u>xxxiv</u> with 1899, 2:<u>x</u>.

39 C 1898, 2:<u>xxxvii</u>–<u>xxxviii</u>.

40 S 403, A 664 (1897)./ S 245 (1899)./ A 117, 14 (1899); S 55 (1899).

41 SJ 391–92 (1899) (attention of legis.)./ C 1898, 1:<u>lix</u>; 1899, 1:<u>xlvii</u>.

· U.S. Const. art. VI, para. 2.

42 Laws 1899, 326; Orton 14./ Id., 10. Olin (1907a) 10. W. Merrill 1, 31–32./ Illinois even retaliated against states where no Illinois companies operated, if they would meet taxation if they were admitted.— Charles E. Dyer, <u>Taxation of Life Ins. Cos.</u>, argument to Tax Comm., Oct. 23, 1900, p. 17, in LRef. Library.

43 Laws 1901, 21./ AJ 292, SJ 304 (1901)./ The quick reversal of policy necessitated Laws 1903, 208 to repay fees paid in advance by foreign companies.

44 Laws 1905, 455. By 1905 the Northwestern was protesting more against the tax rate than against equal treatment in Wisconsin.— Bashford (1905a).

45 For policy considerations, see Buehler 630. AJ 33–36 (1905)./ A 434 (1905); AJ 1876 (1905)./ Bashford (1905b) alleged that net value taxation would cost the Northwestern an added $1,500,000, for a gain to the state of $150,000./ Fricke (1905).

46 The Northwestern Mutual urged these hearings, to obtain tax relief. —Olin (1907a) 3./ Fricke (1906). Host, in C 1906, 2:64–65./ A 626 (1907)./ Laws 1907, 656.

47 The change in attitude was already evident in 1905, in Bashford (1905a) 14./ Olin (1907b) 10./ MDN 5-24-1907 (probable reluctance)./ S 5 (1909)./ Noyes (1909)./ Bashford (1905a) 11 gives the table.

48 Noyes (1911)./ S 338, A 836 (1911); MDN 2-18-1911./ S 55 (1913); S 63, A 277 (1915)./ Subst. 1S to S 55 (1913); MS 4-14-1915; SJ 1033 (1913) (lost 13 to 12)./ Subst. 2S was adopted 14 to 11.—SJ 1033 (1913). But the bill lost 17 to 7.—SJ 1108 (1913).

49 A 614 (1909)./ MS 3-23-1909./ Laws 1915, 434. Eight former Commissioners supported the law by petition, in LRef. Library. See also C 1915, 2:<u>viii</u>–<u>ix</u>. See Plea and Pet. for Passage of Bill No. 55S, in LRef. Library, for the companies' own statement. The Stalwart Governor approved the new law.—Madison <u>Democrat</u> (Wis.) 7-23-1915.

50 The Northwestern's tax dropped from $559,000 in 1915 to $484,000 in 1916.—<u>Rept. State Treasurer</u>, 1915–16, 31./ A 337 (1921)./ P. A. Orton, an agent of the Northwestern and author of the 1899 law, urged life insurance taxation on a scale more nearly comparable to railways.—See Orton.

51 Laws 1915, 132; AJ 682, SJ 563 (1915).

52 C 1905, 2:66. For administrative difficulty, see SJ 630, 1203–06 (1907); Laws 1907, 639; AJ 327–44, 632–41, 954–69, 1615–18 (1925); New York Life v. State, 192 Wis. 404 (1927); Mutual Life v. State, 192 Wis. 413 (1927)./ Repeal bills were A 253 (1905); A 696 (1907)./ Laws 1917, 13; 1919, 425./ C 1916, <u>xiii</u>; MJ 4-8-1923; e.g., S 152 (1921); S 59 (1923); S 157, (1927); S 8 (1931); A 18 (1937) (repeal bills). But see S 575 (1921)./ For opposition see in LRef. Library, Jacobs, <u>Statement in Opposition to Bill 59S</u> (1923); <u>Three Wis. Cos., Memo. on Bill 8S</u> (1931); NBFU, <u>Memo. to Committee on 8S</u> (1931)./ The

Governor espoused repeal in 1931.—AJ 37(1931)./ ST 1955, §§ 76.35, 76.36.

53 Laws 1927, 411. Letter from George Lines, General Counsel of Northwestern Mut. to Chairman Heck of Interim Committee on Administration & Taxation, AJ 1119, 1547–51 (1927)./ A 715 (1929) (repeal bill); WSJ 3–29–1928 (no opposition)./ CT 8–9–1927 (fear for revenue)./ The total life insurance tax was $1,374,000 in 1927, $1,555,000 in 1930; meanwhile the Northwestern tax dropped about half.—Rept. State Treasurer, 1927–28, 37; id., 1929–30, 35. See also Williamson & Smalley 296–97 for some later changes in tax laws.

54 MFP 1–29–1914./ Laws 1913, 411 required the company to pay taxes under protest and then sue to recover./ AJ 326–30 (1913); A 684 (1913). On the traditional position and its persistence even in 1907, see C 1908, 2:30–31. SJ 821 (1913); Laws 1913, JR 32 (disallowed)./ AJ 558–64 (1915); Laws 1915, JR 20./ Northwestern v. State, 163 Wis. 484 (1916); Northwestern v. Wisconsin, 247 U.S. 132 (1918).

55 Northwestern v. State, 173 Wis. 119 (1920); id., 173 Wis. 126 (1920)./ AG 1923, 493; Wisconsin News (Milwaukee) 10–24–1923./ Northwestern v. State, 189 Wis. 103 (1926); id., 189 Wis. 114 (1926); Northwestern v. Wisconsin, 275 U.S. 136 (1927); see also Northwestern v. State, 195 Wis. 190 (1928); id., 195 Wis. 192 (1928).

CHAPTER VI, Section 2

1 75 U.S. (8 Wall.) 168 (1868).
2 Laws 1850, 232, § 7./ SJ 1166 (1858); see also Remonstrance A 324, by Oshkosh citizens, against compelling foreign companies to make deposits.—AJ 1485 (1858).
3 S 70 (1859), and Subst. for S 70./ See, e.g., Memorials A 232, 234, 235, 236, 258, 259, 260, 273, 288, 290, 317, 321, 330, 335 (1859), in Archives.
4 13 Stat. 99 (1863)./ 13 Stat. 484 (1865). Merk 212–18. The Northwestern Mutual bought Wisconsin state bonds in 1864 and early 1865 at prices from par down to 95; in Apr. 1865, it paid 84.25 to 84.5.—Smalley 2–24, n. 40./ A 270 (1865)./ Subst. for A 270 (1865); Laws 1865, 320.
5 AJ 614–17, SJ 623–25 (1865).
6 AJ 626 (1865). The agents who actually made the veiled threat offered to negotiate with their companies for loans or voluntary purchase.—Ibid./ Seventeen companies made the required deposit. —SJ 119 (1866). Memorial A 270, in AJ 491–92 (1866) explains the economics. One Milwaukee elevator had a capacity of over a million bushels.—Ibid.
7 Laws 1866, 2./ SJ 119–23 (1866)./ Memorial A 270, in AJ 491 (1866)/ AJ 702, 721, SJ 734–36 (1866); Laws 1866, 34.
8 AJ 745, SJ 736–37 (1866) (vote against repeal); for later efforts see A 717 (1870) and A 10, § 2 (1872); Laws 1866, 34, § 2 (exception)./ A 717 (1870); A 10, § 2 (1872)./ A 197 (1879), to amend Laws 1870, 56, § 22./ See, e.g., Pet. A98 (1879); Milwaukee banks signed in their corporate capacity. New trust deeds and new regulations in New York helped protect Wisconsin policyholders, and helped defeat the bill.—AJ 277 (1879).

9   Laws 1866, 100./ See also Laws 1870, 59, § 16. Laws 1933, 487, § 247
    limited the provision to life insurance, perhaps inadvertently, for
    1939, 362 extended it to all companies again. Laws 1947, 100, § 6
    revised the provision.
10 AJ 631, SJ 633 (1865); AJ 745, SJ 736-37 (1866); WBB 1866, 136-48./
    Raney 167-70 and Merk ch. 7 tell of banking crises.
11 ST 1898, § 1915./ Laws 1913, 210./ Laws 1905, 519. ST 1955, § 206.22.
12 S 333, A 681 (1907)./ C 1907, 2:22./ MS 3-31-1907./ S 223, 319, A
    684 (1907).
13 ST 1955, § 76.35. AG 1946, 387 ruled that the Ins. Comm'r had
    primary authority over the deposits; the Treasurer was merely a
    depository.
14 Moseley v. Chamberlain, 18 Wis. 700, 705 (1861); 1 Stat. 79, § 12
    (1789). C. J. Dixon took a broader view of the national power and
    dissented, as he had done in Ableman v. Booth, 11 Wis. 498 (1859).
15 Knorr v. Co., 25 Wis. 143, 150 (1869).
16 Laws 1870, 56, § 22./ C 1906, 1:21./ Morse v. Co., 30 Wis. 496
    (1872)./ Laws 1872, 64./ Paul v. Virginia, 75 U.S. (8 Wall.) 168
    (1868)./ Morse v. Co., 87 U.S. (20 Wall.) 445 (1874).
17 Hartford v. Doyle, Fed. Cas. 6160 (1875)./ Drake v. Doyle, 40 Wis.
    175 (1876)./ Continental v. Doyle, 40 Wis. 220 (1876) was the same
    company's effort to mandamus the Secretary to cancel the revoca-
    tion and reinstate the license.
18 A. J. Beitzinger, "Chief Justice Ryan of the Wisconsin Supreme
    Court" (Unpub. Ph.D. thesis, 1954, in Univ. of Wis. Lib.) is an ex-
    cellent collection of documented facts. Beitzinger has published
    some of his material in 1955 Wis. Law Review 592-608 and 1956 id.
    248-82./ Drake v. Doyle, 94 U.S. 535, 543 (1876).
19 A 284 (1877)./ Laws 1877, 16./ Laws 1885, 101.
20 Henderson, ch. 6. FUA 1876, 121.
21 The prohibition applied only to the business of insurance; companies
    might invest in Wisconsin without admission under the insurance
    laws. AG 1949, 316; 1922, 490.
22 C 1877, 22-23./ State v. Farmer, 49 Wis. 459 (1880)./ The court also
    refused to aid collection of assessments by unauthorized companies.
    —Rose v. Kimberley, 89 Wis. 545 (1895). Comm'r Johnson thought
    the unauthorized company problem still serious in 1926.—Johnson
    (1926b) 10.
23 Laws 1871, 13, § 3./ Id., § 1./ Laws 1880, 240, §§ 4, 5. This was un-
    necessary; State v. Farmer, 49 Wis. 459 (1880) applied the 1871 law
    to a Chicago broker./ Laws 1905, 38./ AG 1916, 442 ruled that a
    doctor was not an agent; 1927, 705 ruled that a newspaper publishing
    an advertisement was. Laws 1939, 38 forbade conditional vendors to
    charge as part of the purchase price any premium for insurance in
    unauthorized companies.
24 Laws 1875, 205./ State v. U.S. Mutual, 67 Wis. 624 (1887). State v. U.S.
    Mutual, 69 Wis. 76 (1887)./ State v. Columbian, 141 Wis. 557 (1910).
25 Laws 1870, 56, § 22; ST 1889, § 1915 (2)./ AG 1906, 129, 140./ Laws
    1931, 122./ AG 1915, 745./ A 431 (1959).
26 C 1892, v. Admitted companies supported the Comm'r; unauthorized
    companies were tough competition, since they were neither regula-
    ted nor taxed.—FUA 1889, 71.
27 Laws 1897, 311./ Laws 1899, 190, § 6 (added during passage, SJ 419);

see, e.g., Cordy v. Co., 177 Wis. 68 (1922)./ Laws 1899, 190, § 2./ Laws 1903, 394./ The Comm'r made payment of back fees and taxes a condition of admission to Traders Fire Ins. Co. of N.Y., a reorganization of a company previously doing an unauthorized business in the state.—C 1898, 1:968–69.

28 S 222 (1927).

29 AG 1910, 485./ AG 1912, 467./ Laws 1913, 366, extended to all insurance by 1925, 375; AG 1914, 445./ AG 1932, 1123 advised the Comm'r he could use injunctions and quo warranto. Reciprocity offered an unused possibility. A 573 (1929) would have authorized revocation of the license of any Wisconsin company soliciting elsewhere without admission.

30 AG 1915, 1024./ S 133 (1895)./ Laws 1913, 366.

31 Laws 1931, 309./ C 1932, 15.

32 Res. 31S, in SJ 1231, 1415 (1943)./ SJ 37 (1944 Adjourned Sess.).

33 AG 1908, 504, 505./ Laws 1913, 154./ See also A 410 (1927).

34 Laws 1880, 240, § 3./ A 382 (1893)./ Laws 1893, 200; S 52, A 48 (1899); S 234 (1903)./ Laws 1899, 190, § 1. This last law was perhaps unnecessary, for the Att'y Gen. had already ruled that Laws 1893, 200 required countersignature by a resident agent.—C 1897, 1:x./ See C 1915, 1:vi for the problem of pro forma countersignature for a fraction of the commission, perhaps created by Laws 1911, 270, permitting commission splitting, sometimes with nonresidents./ AG 1906, 499 construed the transportation exception to permit a nonresident agent to write a policy on a steamboat located in Wisconsin.

35 Laws 1901, 227./ AG 1906, 721./ Laws 1907, 432.

36 Laws 1911, 436.

37 A 145 (1917); but see S 180 (1919)./ Laws 1935, 130./ AG 1948, 50./ Laws 1947, 501. But cf. S 107 (1941).

38 Chrysler v. Smith, 272 U.S. 295 (1926)./ Comm'r Johnson praised Att'y Gen. Ekern for his successful fight.—Johnson (1926b) 7.

39 S 363 (1895), introduced by Sen. Austin of Milwaukee.

40 Laws 1899, 190, § 2./ A 402 (1901)./ Laws 1903, 394./ C 1905, 1:21.

41 A 545 (1905), introduced by Mr. Crowley of Milwaukee. The original bill would have repealed the 1903 reinsurance law, supra, n. 40 compelling reinsurance companies to re-enter the state. That provision was deleted.—AJ 975 (1905). Comm'r Host favored the original bill. —C 1905, 1:21.

42 Laws 1911, 87./ A 704 (1923); S 406 (1925); AJ 1895–96 (1923); SJ 1400–01 (1925).

CHAPTER VI, Section 3

1 Laws 1919, 361; C 1913, 1:8–9./ Hartford Steam Boiler v. Pabst, 201 Fed. 617 (7th Cir. 1912) held that failure to inspect as the policy required might subject the company to liability beyond the policy limits.

2 James (1947) 185–89; Dublin, "Life Ins. Business Aids Health of the Nation," in Eastern Underwriter (N.Y.; Boston) 10-7-1949.

3 NBFU, That They May be Free (1940), 16–17, pamphlet in LRef. Library. Brearley gives half his space to fire prevention. See also Pioneers of Progress (1941), a book put out by the NBFU and dealing with its fire prevention role.

4   James (1942) 98-100./ J. Thomas Scharf & Thompson Westcott, History of Philadelphia (1884), 1:551.
5   Cf. Laws 1837, 13 with History at Milwaukee..., p. 347./ Laws (P.& L.) 1861, 3.
6   Laws 1852, 257 (fire dept. tax)./ Mass. Laws Jan. 1818, 180, giving a third of net profits of the Massachusetts Hospital Life to the Massachusetts General Hospital, was much like the fire department tax. The wide use of earmarked funds in mid-20th century suggests how much easier it is to tax for purposes in which the taxed class is interested.
7   See, e.g., FUA 1875, 16. FUA 1874, 42 reports correspondence with 597 towns (52 in Wisconsin) about fire fighting facilities. Twentieth-century rate making involved grading of fire departments. See FUA 1876, 81 for an early stage in that development.
8   E.g., FUA 1875, 117./ Laws 1876, 73./ CR VI, 70 notes the effective work of the Milwaukee patrol.
9   Milwaukee BFU v. Co., 230 Wis. 60 (1939). AG 1904, 417 ruled that the board might have a closed membership. Sutter v. Milwaukee BFU, 164 Wis. 532 (1917) held the patrol function public enough to validate an ordinance giving patrol wagons the right of way on the streets.
10 C. F. Carter, "Why Fire Insurance Rates are High," American Review of Reviews, May, 1911, thought detection of arsonists and testing of equipment to be public duties./ C 1912, 1:xx; 1914, xl./ CR VII, 27.
11 A 287 (1945); A 326 (1945); A 21 (1947); A 171 (1947); S 549 (1949)./CT 2-18-1945./ CT 5-9-1947.
12 Laws 1868, 44, § 1./ FUA 1873, 13./ Laws 1873, 285./ Laws 1874, 333./ Laws 1880, 269./ SJ 341 (1880).
13 ST 1955, ch. 168 (Oil Inspection Act)./ Laws 1897, 114./ Laws 1901, 466, § 9./ Laws 1909, 363./ Laws 1927, 438./Laws 1941, 265, 305.
14 E.g., FUA 1877, 158.
15 FUA 1878, 152; NBFU, Committee on Statistics, Losses by Fire Caused by Fireworks and Firecrackers (1876) 14-20, pamphlet in Univ. of Wis. Library lists 19 Wisconsin cities and towns with such an ordinance./ Laws 1889, 326, § 52(11)./ CR VI, 75, 107.
16 See, e.g., FUA 1886, 120-30; 1883, 79; Laws 1901, 431. See also A 378 (1893) and Laws 1921, 262 (steam boilers and machinery inspections).
17 FUA 1873, 92-93; 1875, 13, 87. FUA 1874, 77 (laths and shingles). See also FUA 1895, 99, 102, where the Mass. Fire Marshal reported a new code of building laws in Boston in 1886, and for Massachusetts in 1894.
18 Laws 1872, 188, § 51(4)./ Waupun v. Moore, 34 Wis. 450 (1874)./ Laws 1889, 326, § 52(63)./ Laws 1889, 326, § 52(48)./ FUA 1887,123.
19 CR VI, 72-75./ Laws 1913, 317.
20 C 1914, 1:xxxviii; 1915, 1:xix-xlii; 1914, 3:vi-ix./ C 1920, x.
21 Laws 1907, 228./ CR VI, 71-72; A 912 (1913)./ Laws 1913, 489./ C 1913, 1:7; 1914, 1:xxxii, xli.
22 Laws 1866, 484./ E.g., see Laws 1895, 4 ($1,400); 1899, 11 ($1,000)./ Laws 1909, 308./ ST 1931, § 213.14./ Laws 1933, 140, § 2./ Laws 1913, 446, repealed by 1919, 389, § 1; CR VI, 70.
23 Res. 25A, AJ 447, 455 (1907)./ Res. 35S, SJ 1142 (1929)./ Laws 1917,

63./ Laws 1921, 225./ Laws 1949, 152./ S 595 (1949). Cf. Laws 1913, 218, which required a monthly half-hour of instruction in accident prevention.

24 C 1914, 1:xxiii-xxiv; CR VI, 69./ FUA 1887, 110./ For urging of company men, see FUA, 1872, 42, 44; 1876, 134./ C 1911, xviii and 1914, xxiv for Comm'r urging./ For adoption of inspection by Comm'r see AG 1914, 774; C 1915, 1:xliv./ Independent Inspection Bureau of Phila., Rept. on Fire Dangers at the Charitable and Penal Institutions of the State of Wis. (1914-15), in Hist. Soc. Library./ Laws 1915, 538./ C 1921, xxix./ C 1922, lii.

25 FUA 1877, 21, 96; 1896, 22./ CR VI, 66-67./ Laws 1893, 233 made it a felony to abscond so a beneficiary could collect on a life insurance policy under the presumption of death from protracted absence.

26 Laws 1915, 256./ Comm'r Ekern, addressing NAIC, said the purpose of the clause was lessening of moral hazard.—WSJ 9-22-1915./ Laws 1943, 396.

27 N.Y. Laws 1857, 504; Mass. Acts 1867, 303./ FUA 1877, 21, 117; 1886, 94./ FUA 1891, 74./ Mass. Laws 1889, 451.

28 A 381 (1895)./ S 10, § 1896n, o (1897)./ S 382 (1897)./ SJ 802, 818 (1897); S 512 (1905); AJ 1850 (1905)./ C 1906, 1:24./ Laws 1907, 228./ S 483, A 199 (1909); Laws 1909, 211./ Laws 1909, 145 returned some of the tax money collected in 1909, even though the same session raised the rate. Laws 1915, 563 also made refunds.

29 CR VIII; Laws 1915, 504./ Laws 1917, 501. A private firm of management consultants recommended in 1946 that the Marshal's assignment be transferred to the office of the Att'y Gen.—Griffenhagen Rept. No. 5, at 2 (1946), in LRef. Library./ C 1934, 11; S 198 (1933); S 291 (1935); A 507 (1939). The Fire Chiefs proposed A 309 (1937)./ Appleton Post-Crescent (Wis.) 1-19-1948./ S 98 (1949)./ S 497 (1949)./ ST 1959, §§ 200.03 (11), 200.20, 200.21.

30 Laws 1913, 316, as recommended by CR VI, 68./ Laws 1937, 235; but see A 431 (1957)./ Laws 1913, 489./ Menting v. Co., 169 Wis. 246 (1919).

31 A 336 (1939); S 281, A 794 (1941)./ S 565 (1949).

32 AJ 34 (1955).

CHAPTER VII

1 Laws 1931, 21./ Laws 1931, 327; 1949, 351./ See also A 216 (1943); A 55 (1945); A 168 (1947); A 400 (1951).

2 See Laws 1878, 322; 1878, 255. § 15; 1897, 314.

3 See, e.g., C 1910, 1:19.

4 See Kimball (1957) (general).

5 Kimball (1957).

6 On departure from fault basis for liability, see, among numerous writings, the chapter on "The Principle of Social Insurance", in Harper & James 3:759-84; James & Thornton; Ehrenzweig (1950); Ussing; Ehrenzweig (1951); Friedman; Green. For an insurance man's attack on the trend toward liability without fault where insurance is involved, as "socialism pure and simple," see Orr.